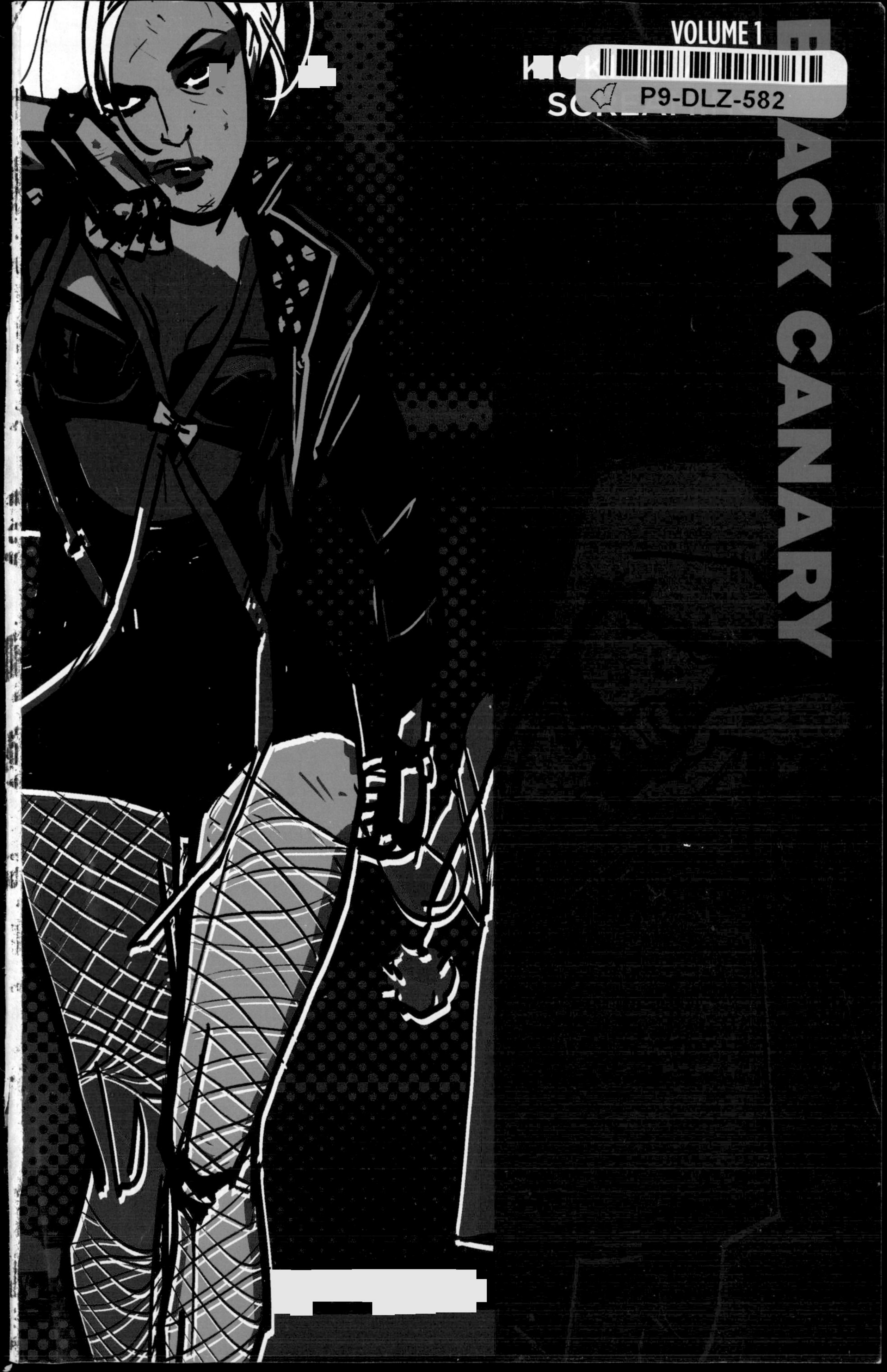
VOLUME 1
ACK CANARY

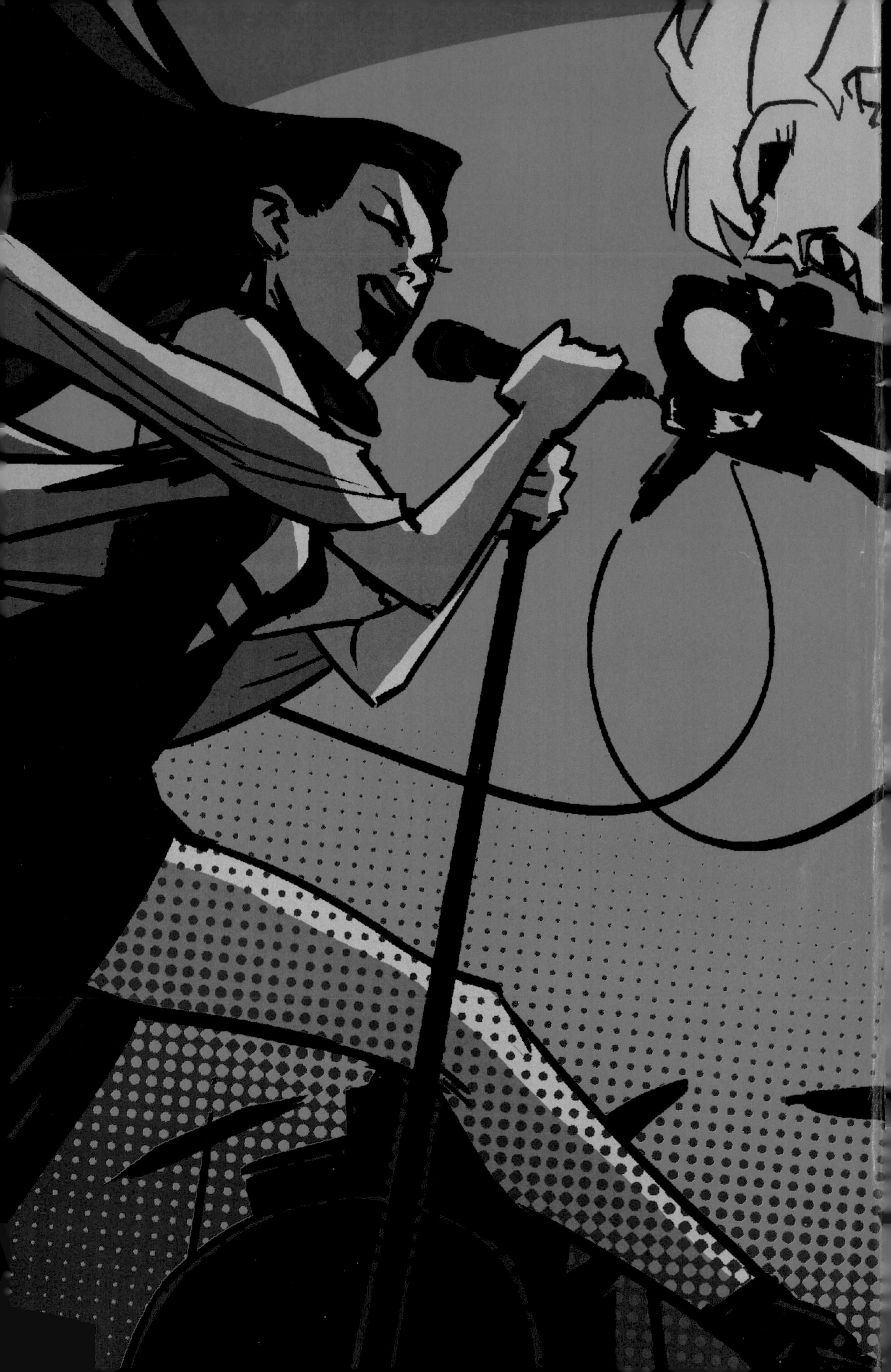

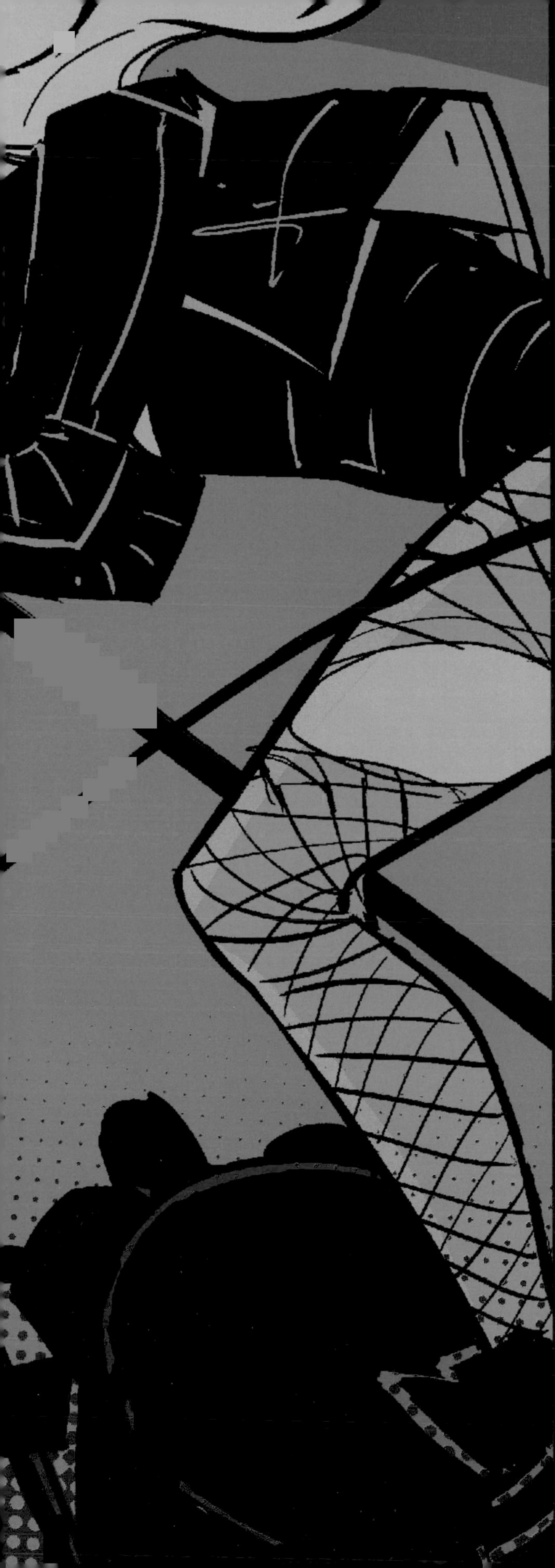

BLACK CANARY

VOLUME 1
KICKING AND SCREAMING

WRITTEN BY
BRENDEN FLETCHER

ART BY
ANNIE WU
PIA GUERRA
SANDY JARRELL

COLOR BY
LEE LOUGHRIDGE

LETTERS BY
STEVE WANDS

COVERS BY
ANNIE WU

CHRIS CONROY Editor – Original Series
DAVE WIELGOSZ Assistant Editor – Original Series
JEB WOODARD Group Editor – Collected Editions
ROBIN WILDMAN Editor – Collected Edition
STEVE COOK Design Director – Books
DAMIAN RYLAND Publication Design

BOB HARRAS Senior VP – Editor-in-Chief, DC Comics

DIANE NELSON President
DAN DIDIO and JIM LEE Co-Publishers
GEOFF JOHNS Chief Creative Officer
AMIT DESAI Senior VP – Marketing & Global Franchise Management
NAIRI GARDINER Senior VP – Finance
SAM ADES VP – Digital Marketing
BOBBIE CHASE VP – Talent Development
MARK CHIARELLO Senior VP – Art, Design & Collected Editions
JOHN CUNNINGHAM VP – Content Strategy
ANNE DEPIES VP – Strategy Planning & Reporting
DON FALLETTI VP – Manufacturing Operations
LAWRENCE GANEM VP – Editorial Administration & Talent Relations
ALISON GILL Senior VP – Manufacturing & Operations
HANK KANALZ Senior VP – Editorial Strategy & Administration
JAY KOGAN VP – Legal Affairs
DEREK MADDALENA Senior VP – Sales & Business Development
JACK MAHAN VP – Business Affairs
DAN MIRON VP – Sales Planning & Trade Development
NICK NAPOLITANO VP – Manufacturing Administration
CAROL ROEDER VP – Marketing
EDDIE SCANNELL VP – Mass Account & Digital Sales
COURTNEY SIMMONS Senior VP – Publicity & Communications
JIM (SKI) SOKOLOWSKI VP – Comic Book Specialty & Newsstand Sales
SANDY YI Senior VP – Global Franchise Management

BLACK CANARY VOLUME 1: KICKING AND SCREAMING

DC Comics, 2900 West Alameda Avenue, Burbank, CA 91505
Printed by RR Donnelley, Salem, VA, USA. 1/29/16. First Printing.
ISBN: 978-1-4012-6117-7

Library of Congress Cataloging-in-Publication Data is available.

PEFC Certified

Printed on paper from
sustainably managed
forests and controlled
sources

PEFC

PEFC/29-31-75   www.pefc.org

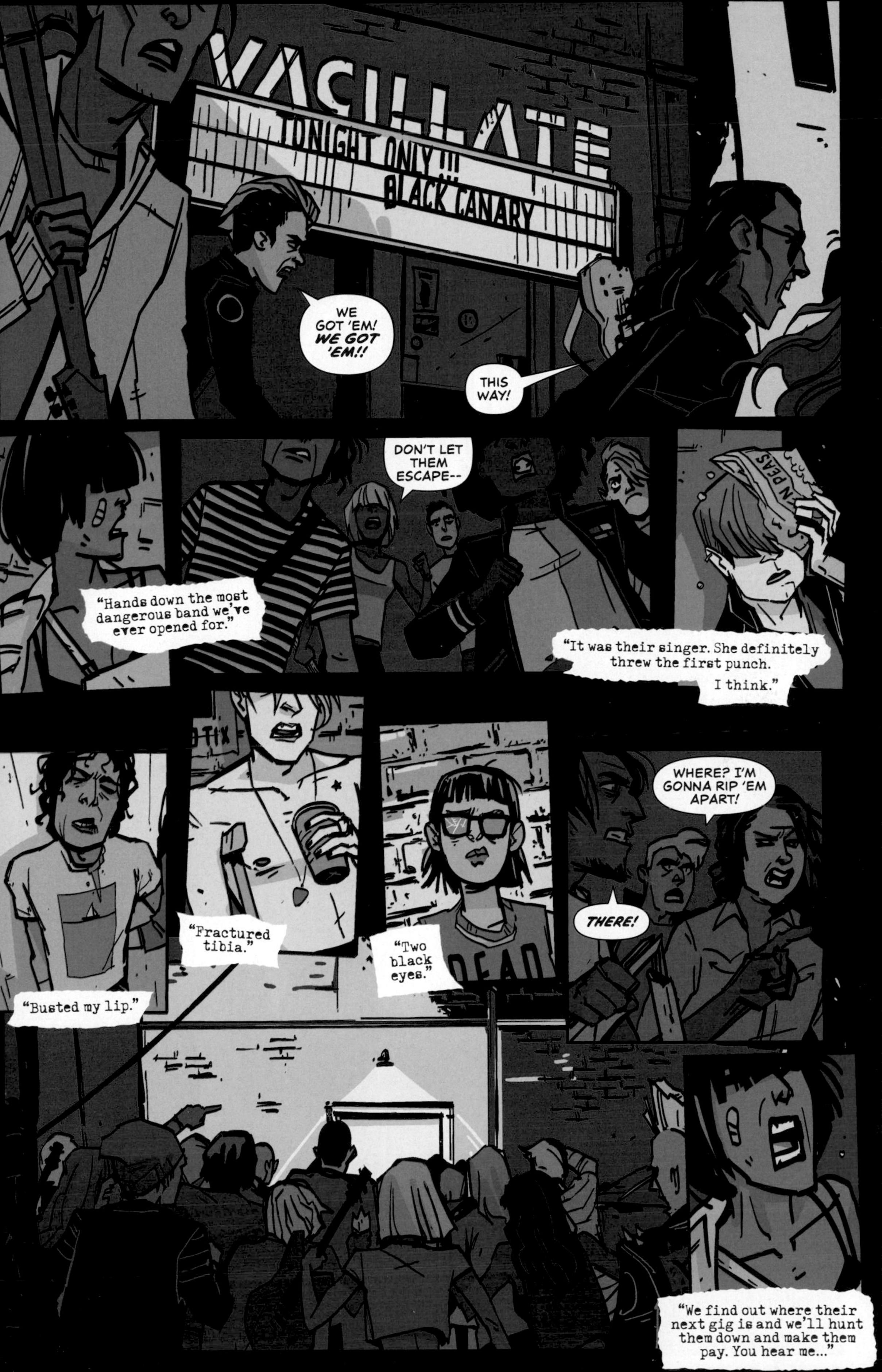
VACILLATE
TONIGHT ONLY!!!
BLACK CANARY
WE GOT 'EM! WE GOT 'EM!!
THIS WAY!
DON'T LET THEM ESCAPE--
"Hands down the most dangerous band we've ever opened for."
"It was their singer. She definitely threw the first punch.
I think."
"Busted my lip."
"Fractured tibia."
"Two black eyes."
WHERE? I'M GONNA RIP 'EM APART!
THERE!
"We find out where their next gig is and we'll hunt them down and make them pay. You hear me..."

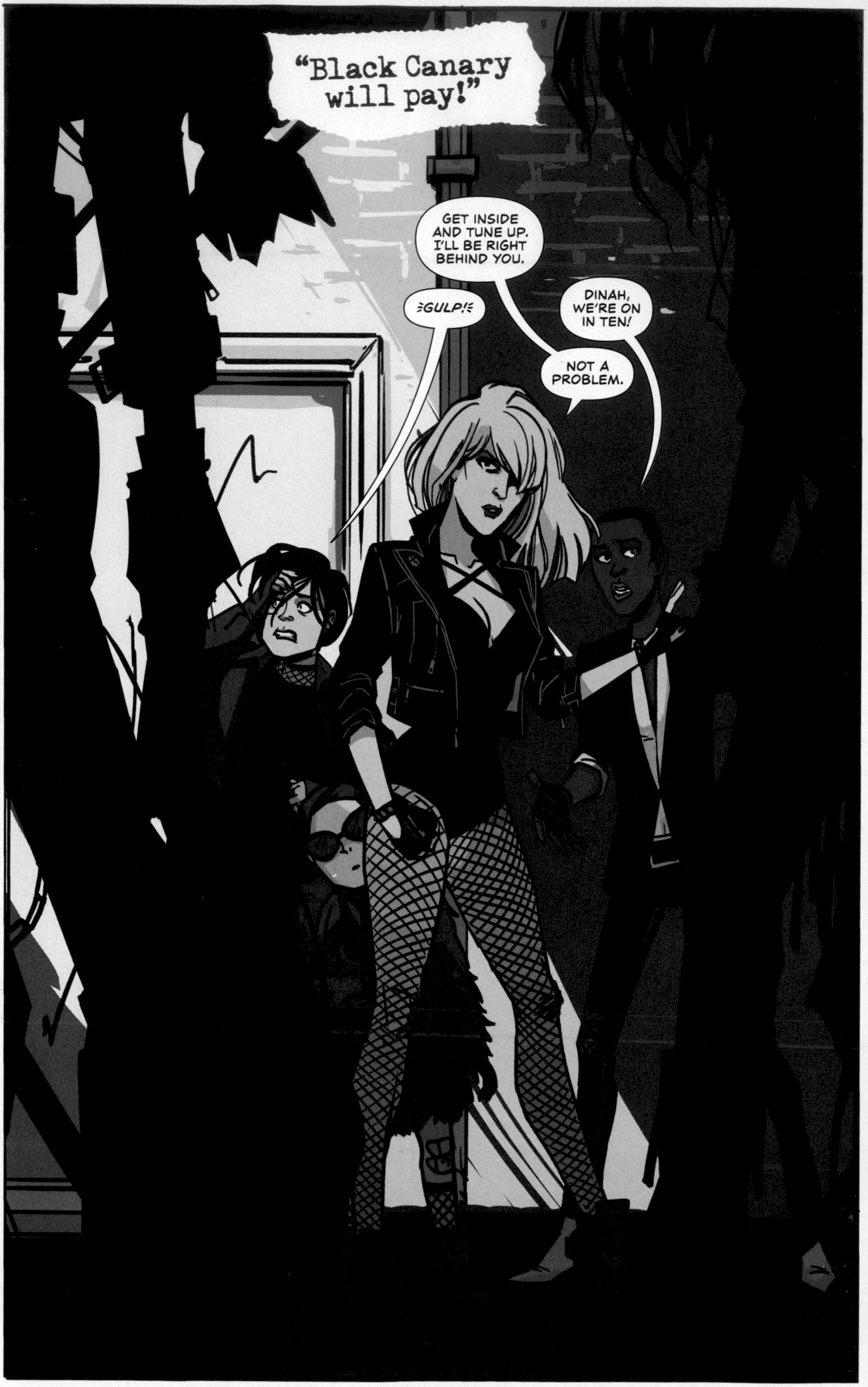
"Black Canary will pay!"
GET INSIDE AND TUNE UP. I'LL BE RIGHT BEHIND YOU.
DINAH, WE'RE ON IN TEN!
GULP!
NOT A PROBLEM.

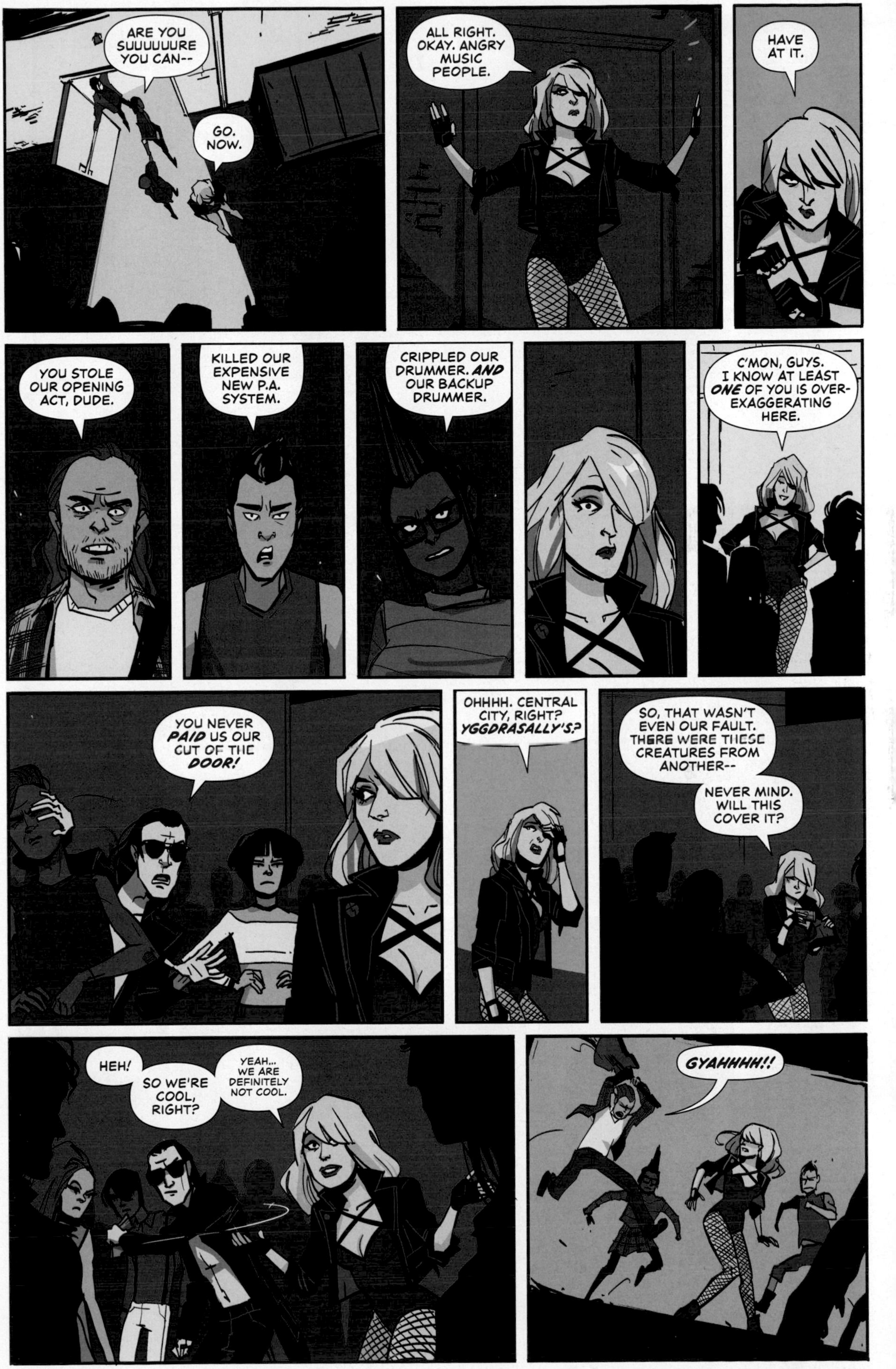
ARE YOU SUUUUUURE YOU CAN--
GO. NOW.
ALL RIGHT. OKAY. ANGRY MUSIC PEOPLE.
HAVE AT IT.
YOU STOLE OUR OPENING ACT, DUDE.
KILLED OUR EXPENSIVE NEW P.A. SYSTEM.
CRIPPLED OUR DRUMMER. AND OUR BACKUP DRUMMER.
C'MON, GUYS. I KNOW AT LEAST ONE OF YOU IS OVER-EXAGGERATING HERE.
YOU NEVER PAID US OUR CUT OF THE DOOR!
OHHHH. CENTRAL CITY, RIGHT? YGGDRASALLY'S?
SO, THAT WASN'T EVEN OUR FAULT. THERE WERE THESE CREATURES FROM ANOTHER--
NEVER MIND. WILL THIS COVER IT?
HEH!
SO WE'RE COOL, RIGHT?
YEAH... WE ARE DEFINITELY NOT COOL.
GYAHHHH!!

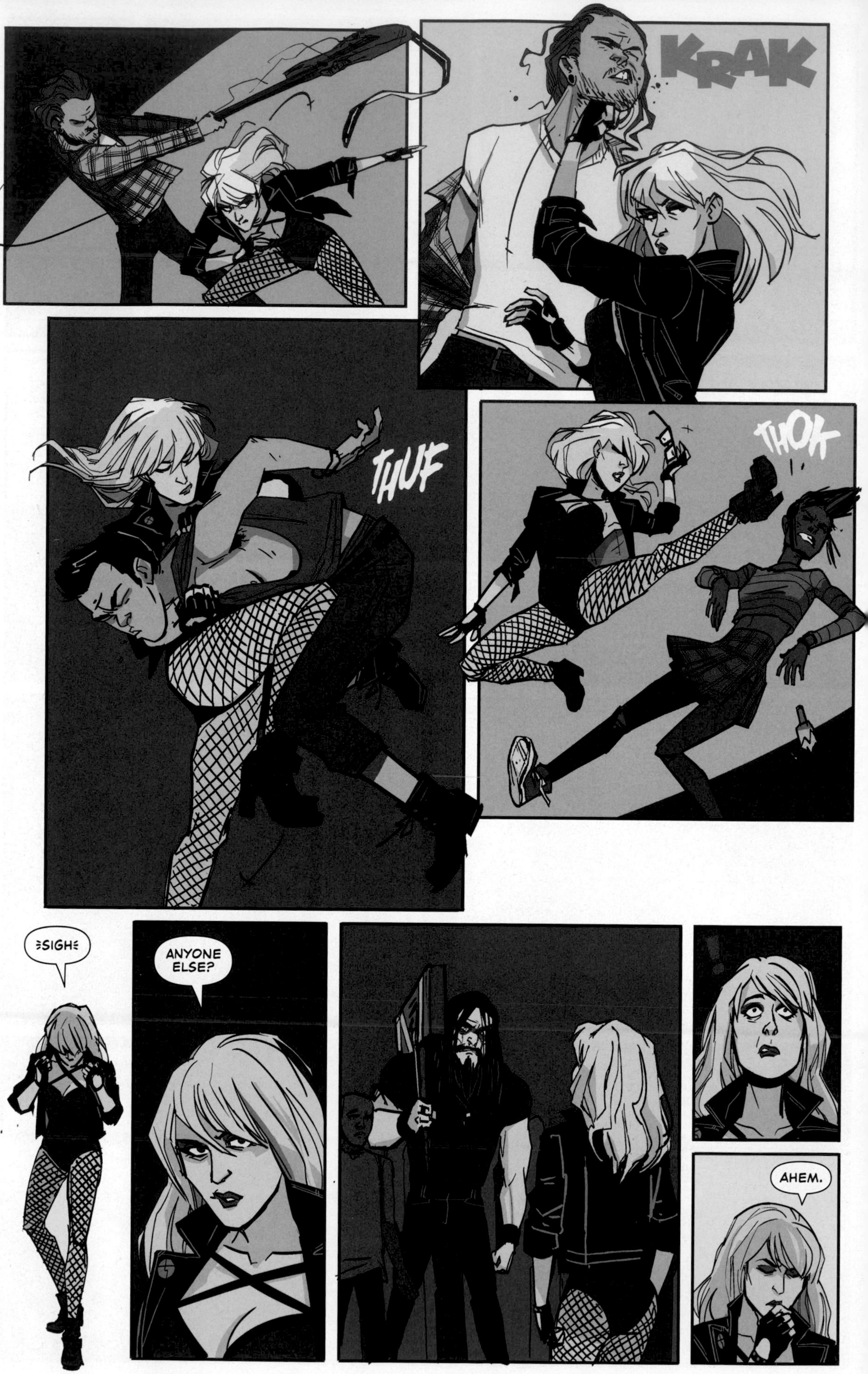
KRAK
THUF
THOK
SIGH
ANYONE ELSE?
AHEM.

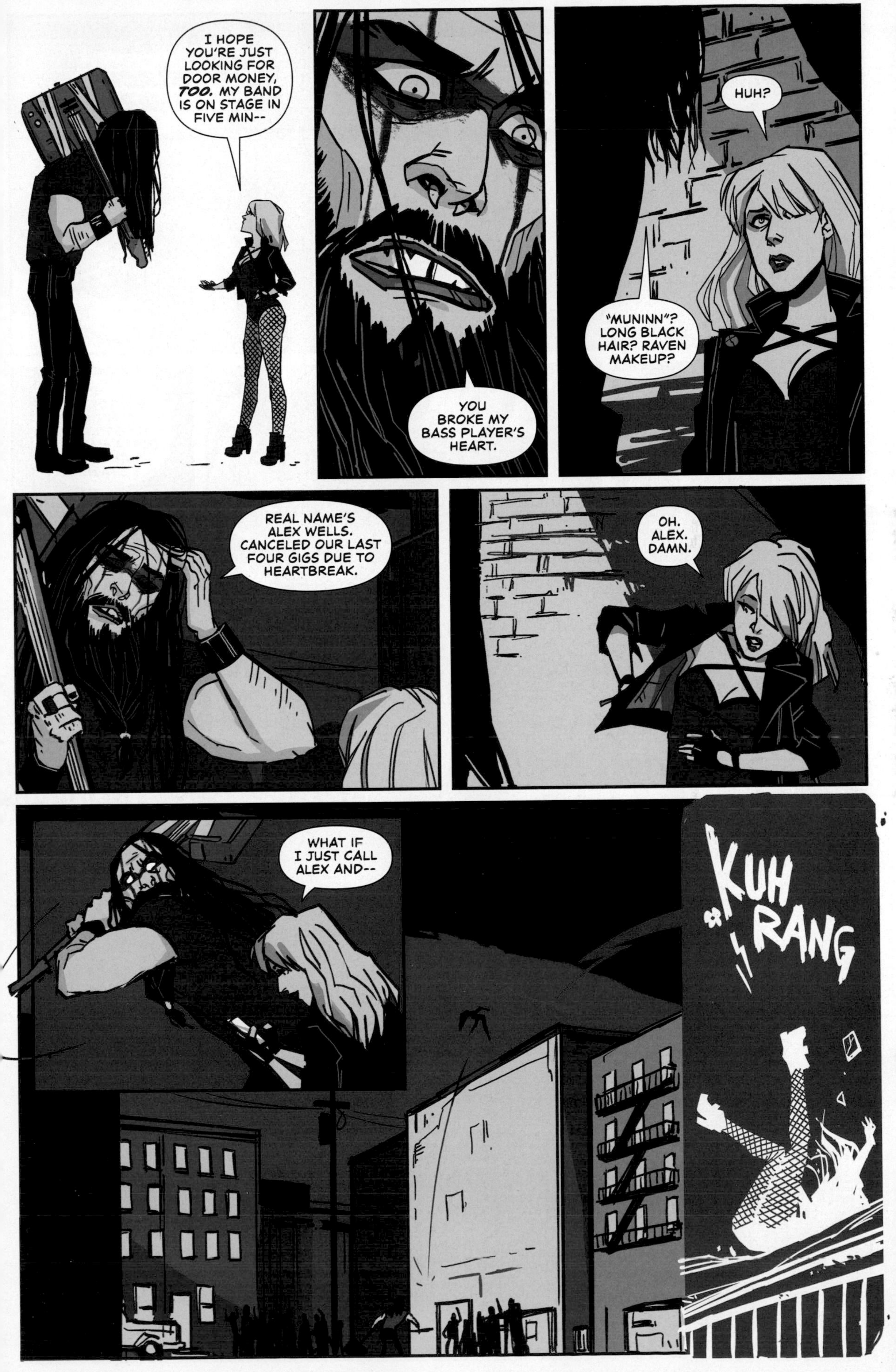
I HOPE YOU'RE JUST LOOKING FOR DOOR MONEY, TOO. MY BAND IS ON STAGE IN FIVE MIN--
YOU BROKE MY BASS PLAYER'S HEART.
HUH?
"MUNINN"? LONG BLACK HAIR? RAVEN MAKEUP?
REAL NAME'S ALEX WELLS. CANCELED OUR LAST FOUR GIGS DUE TO HEARTBREAK.
OH. ALEX. DAMN.
WHAT IF I JUST CALL ALEX AND--
KUH RANG

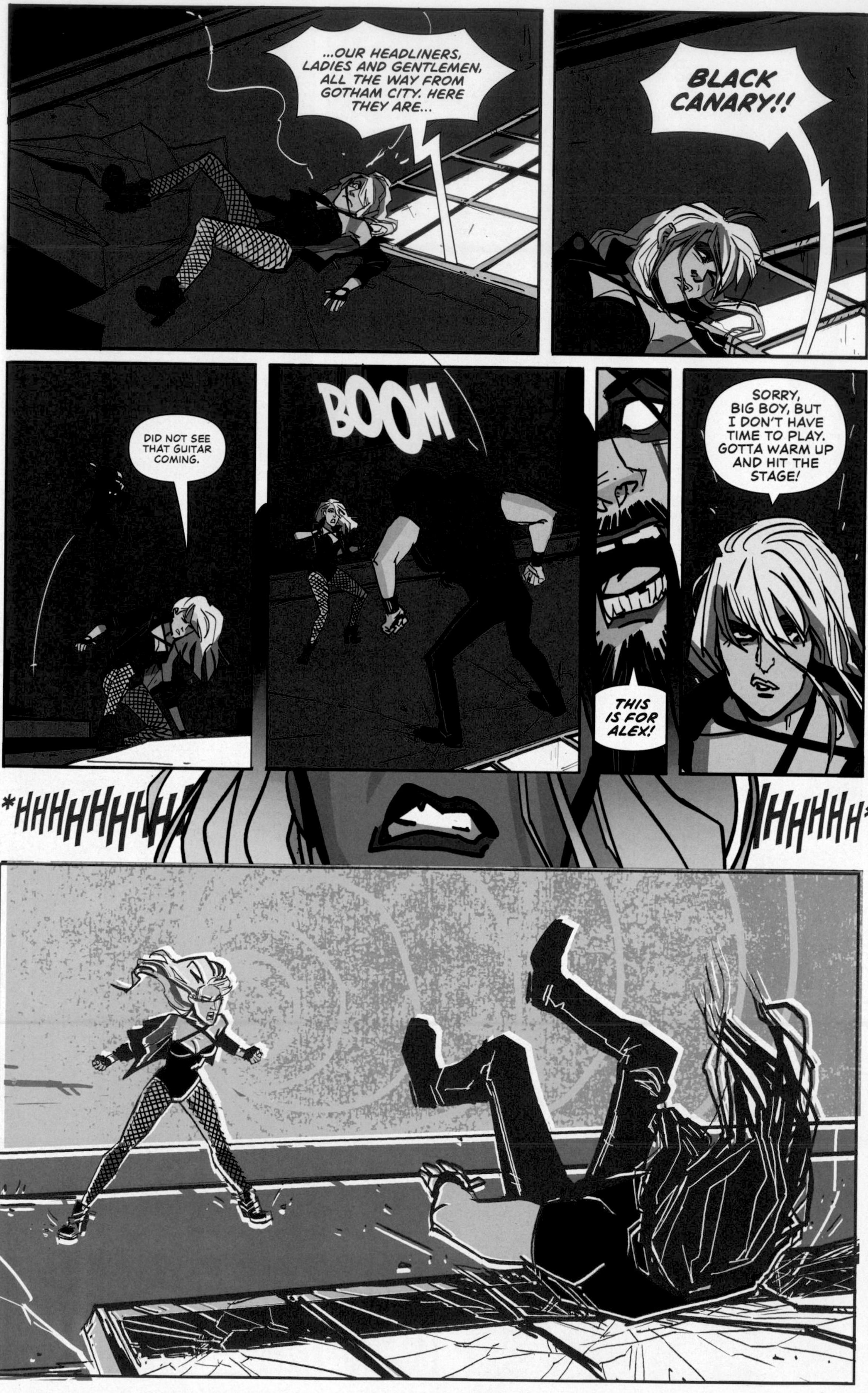
...OUR HEADLINERS, LADIES AND GENTLEMEN, ALL THE WAY FROM GOTHAM CITY. HERE THEY ARE...
BLACK CANARY!!
DID NOT SEE THAT GUITAR COMING.
BOOM
THIS IS FOR ALEX!
SORRY, BIG BOY, BUT I DON'T HAVE TIME TO PLAY. GOTTA WARM UP AND HIT THE STAGE!
HHHHHHHHHHHHHHHH

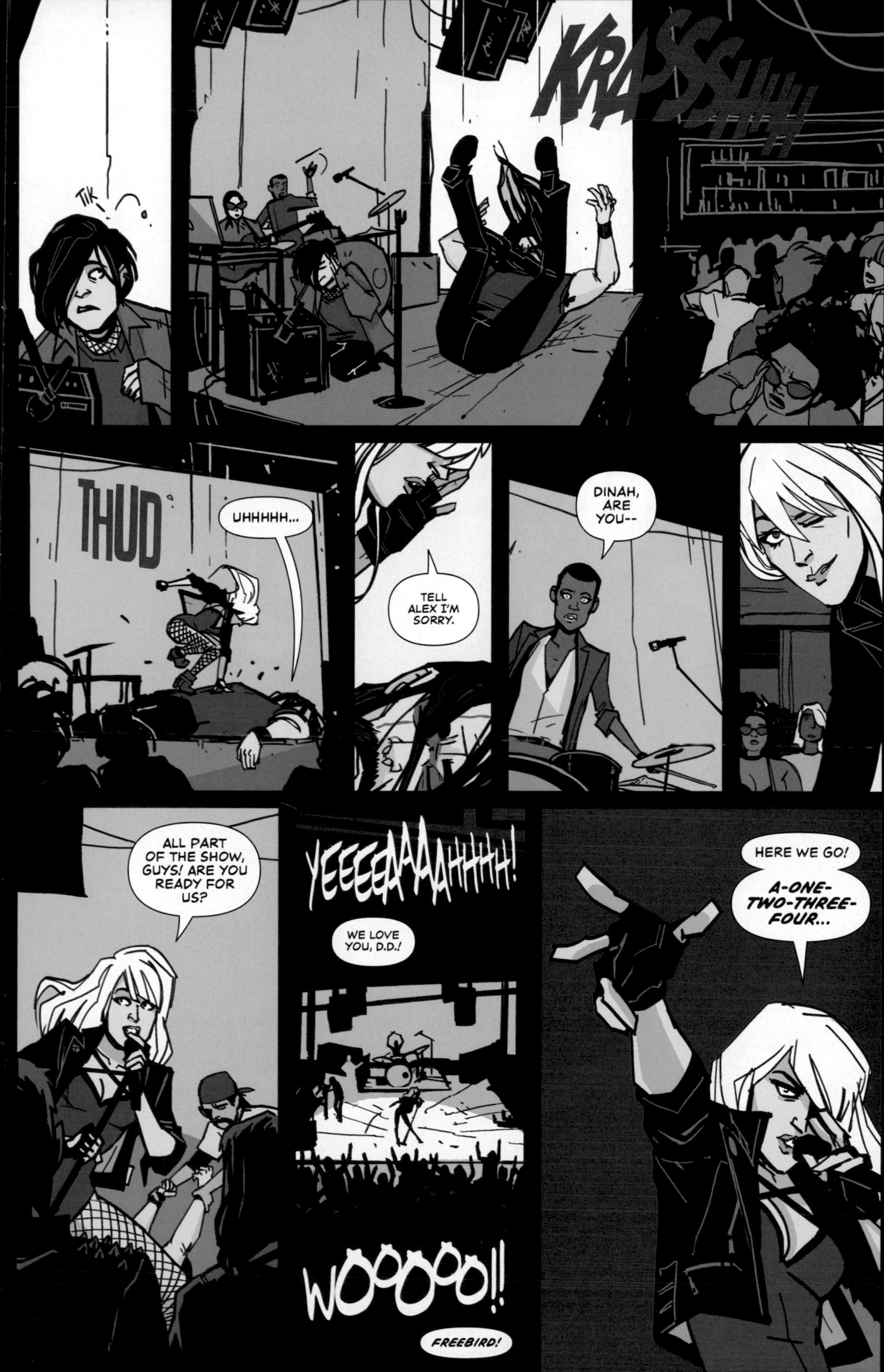
TIK
KRASSHHH
THUD
UHHHHH...
TELL ALEX I'M SORRY.
DINAH, ARE YOU--
ALL PART OF THE SHOW, GUYS! ARE YOU READY FOR US?
YEEEEAAAAHHHH!
WE LOVE YOU, D.D.!
WOOOOO!!
FREEBIRD!
HERE WE GO!
A-ONE-TWO-THREE-FOUR...

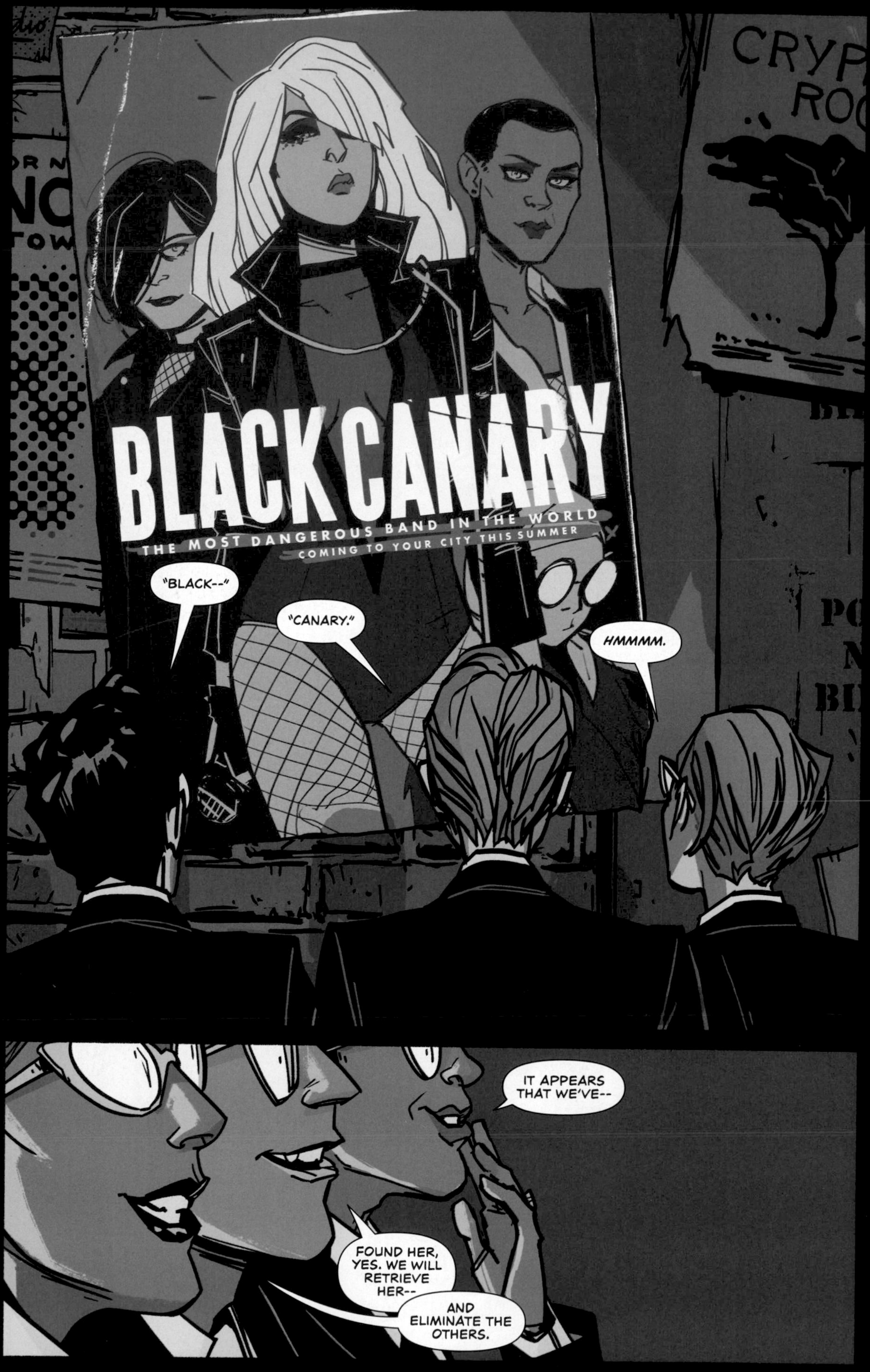
CRYP
ROC
BLACK CANARY
THE MOST DANGEROUS BAND IN THE WORLD
COMING TO YOUR CITY THIS SUMMER
"BLACK--"
"CANARY."
HMMMM.
IT APPEARS THAT WE'VE--
FOUND HER, YES. WE WILL RETRIEVE HER--
AND ELIMINATE THE OTHERS.

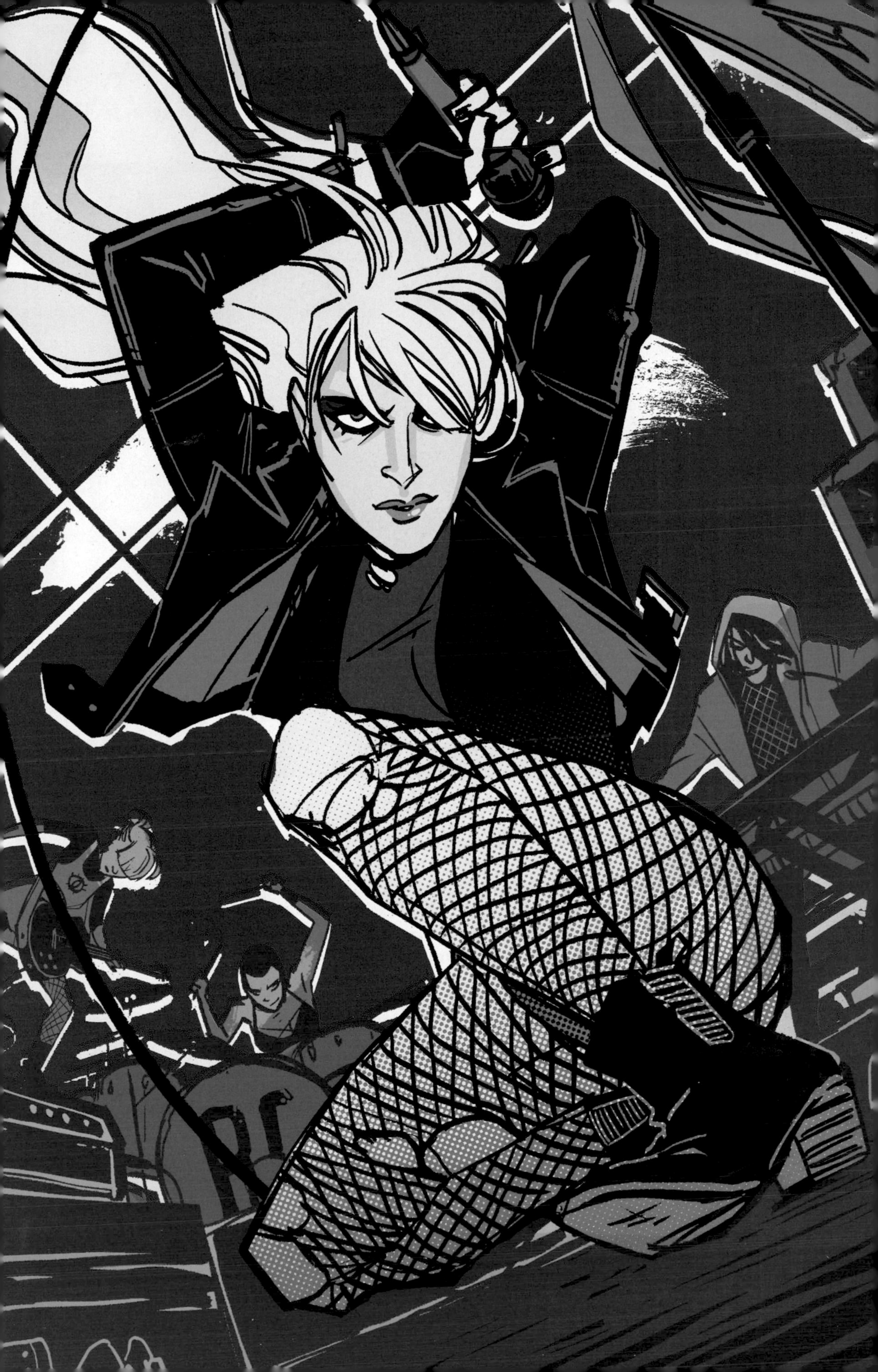

WHERE BLACK CANARY GOES, TROUBLE FOLLOWS

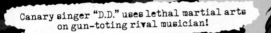

Canary singer "D.D." uses lethal martial arts on gun-toting rival musician!

A BURNSIDE TOFU EXCLUSIVE BY TANTOO LA BICHE

Gotham City-based four-piece band Black Canary have been tearing up the road on tour--literally! Five of their last seven shows have reportedly ended in violence, with witnesses at last month's EXE Festival outside Central City describing mysterious frontwoman "D.D." as "more of a UFC fighter than a singer," after she single-handedly stopped a group of armed gunmen.

Full story on page 2

BURNSIDE TOFU
The zine for people with the right kind of taste

Editor in Chief
TANTOO LA BICHE

Photo Editor
TANTOO LA BICHE

Staff Writer
TANTOO LA BICHE

Social Media Director
TANTOO LA BICHE

Audience member Sasha S. shows off souvenirs.

This guy sucked.

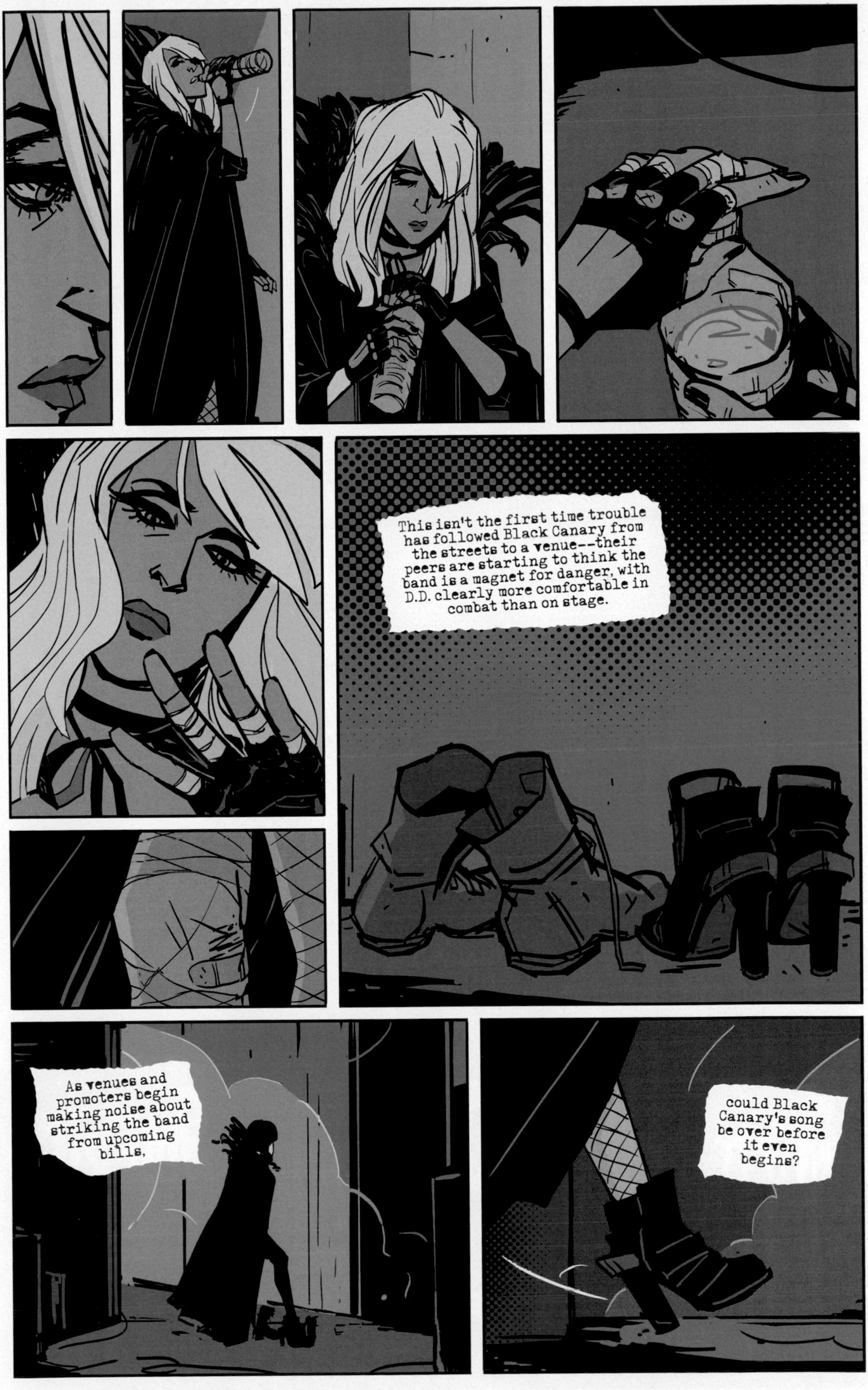
This isn't the first time trouble has followed Black Canary from the streets to a venue--their peers are starting to think the band is a magnet for danger, with D.D. clearly more comfortable in combat than on stage.
As venues and promoters begin making noise about striking the band from upcoming bills,
could Black Canary's song be over before it even begins?

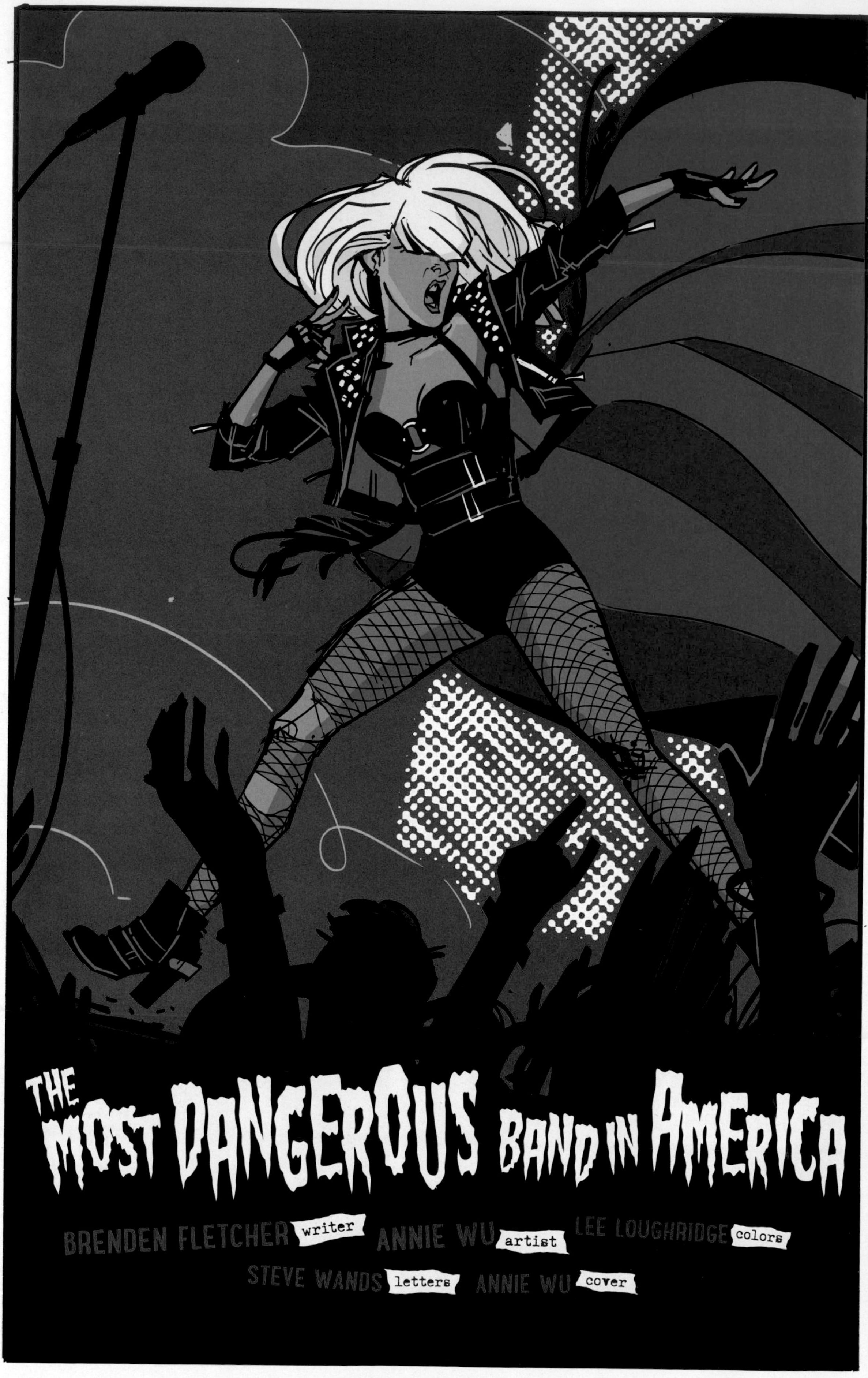
THE MOST DANGEROUS BAND IN AMERICA
BRENDEN FLETCHER writer ANNIE WU artist LEE LOUGHRIDGE colors
STEVE WANDS letters ANNIE WU cover

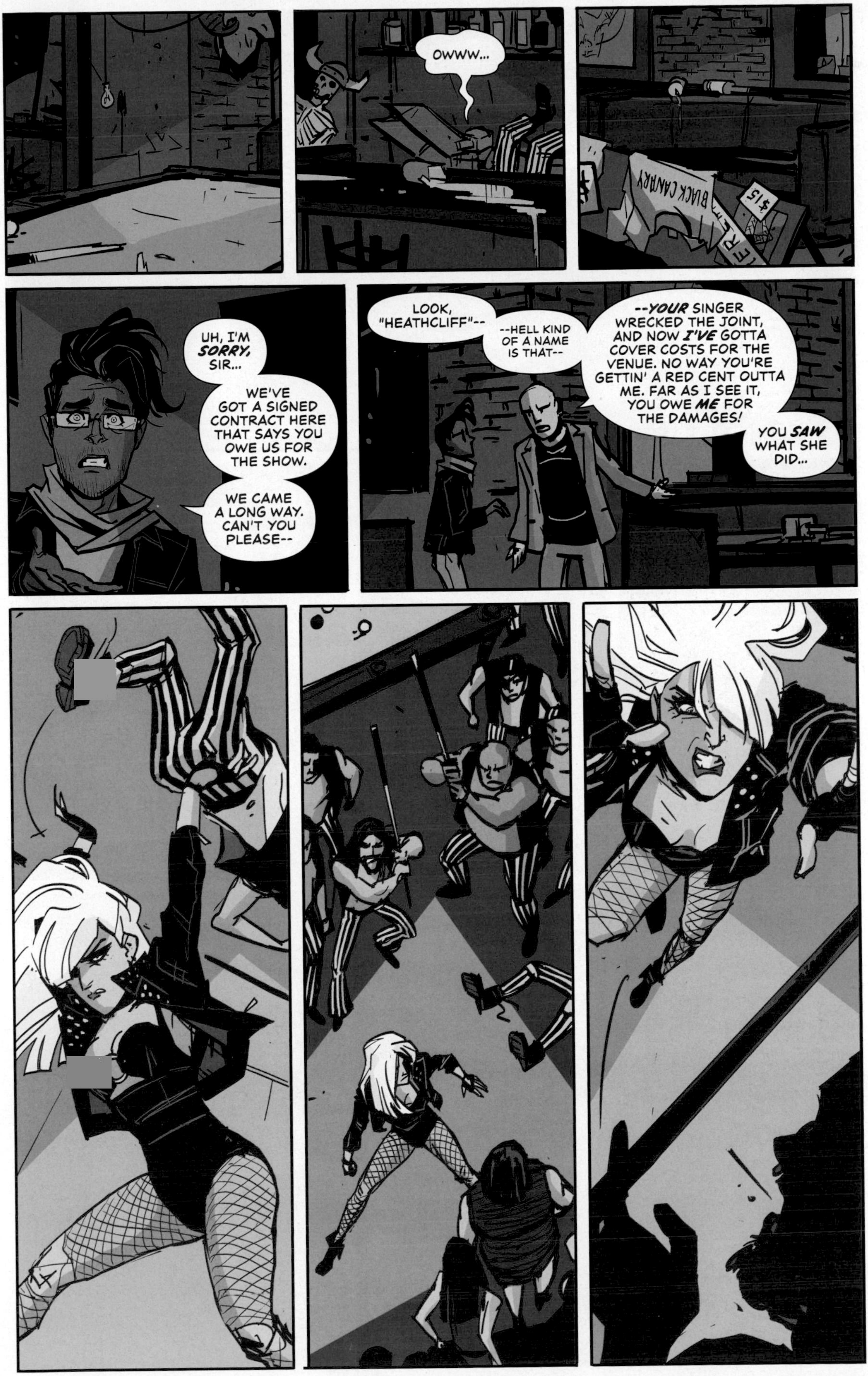
OWWW...
BLACK CANARY
$15
UH, I'M ***SORRY,*** SIR...
WE'VE GOT A SIGNED CONTRACT HERE THAT SAYS YOU OWE US FOR THE SHOW.
WE CAME A LONG WAY. CAN'T YOU PLEASE--
LOOK, "HEATHCLIFF"--
--HELL KIND OF A NAME IS THAT--
--***YOUR*** SINGER WRECKED THE JOINT, AND NOW ***I'VE*** GOTTA COVER COSTS FOR THE VENUE. NO WAY YOU'RE GETTIN' A RED CENT OUTTA ME. FAR AS I SEE IT, YOU OWE ***ME*** FOR THE DAMAGES!
YOU ***SAW*** WHAT SHE DID...

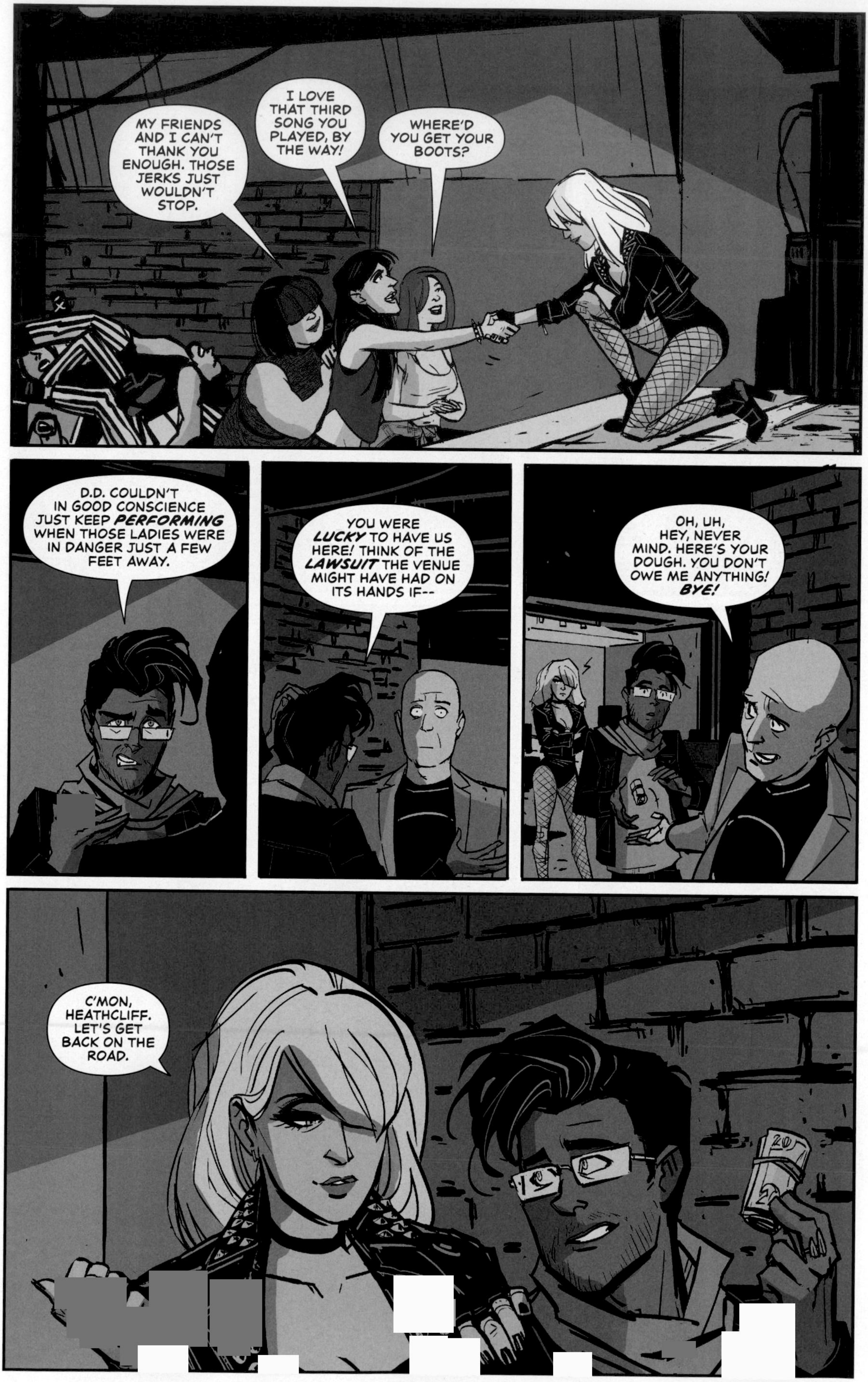
MY FRIENDS AND I CAN'T THANK YOU ENOUGH. THOSE JERKS JUST WOULDN'T STOP.
I LOVE THAT THIRD SONG YOU PLAYED, BY THE WAY!
WHERE'D YOU GET YOUR BOOTS?
D.D. COULDN'T IN GOOD CONSCIENCE JUST KEEP *PERFORMING* WHEN THOSE LADIES WERE IN DANGER JUST A FEW FEET AWAY.
YOU WERE *LUCKY* TO HAVE US HERE! THINK OF THE *LAWSUIT* THE VENUE MIGHT HAVE HAD ON ITS HANDS IF--
OH, UH, HEY, NEVER MIND. HERE'S YOUR DOUGH. YOU DON'T OWE ME ANYTHING! *BYE!*
C'MON, HEATHCLIFF. LET'S GET BACK ON THE ROAD.

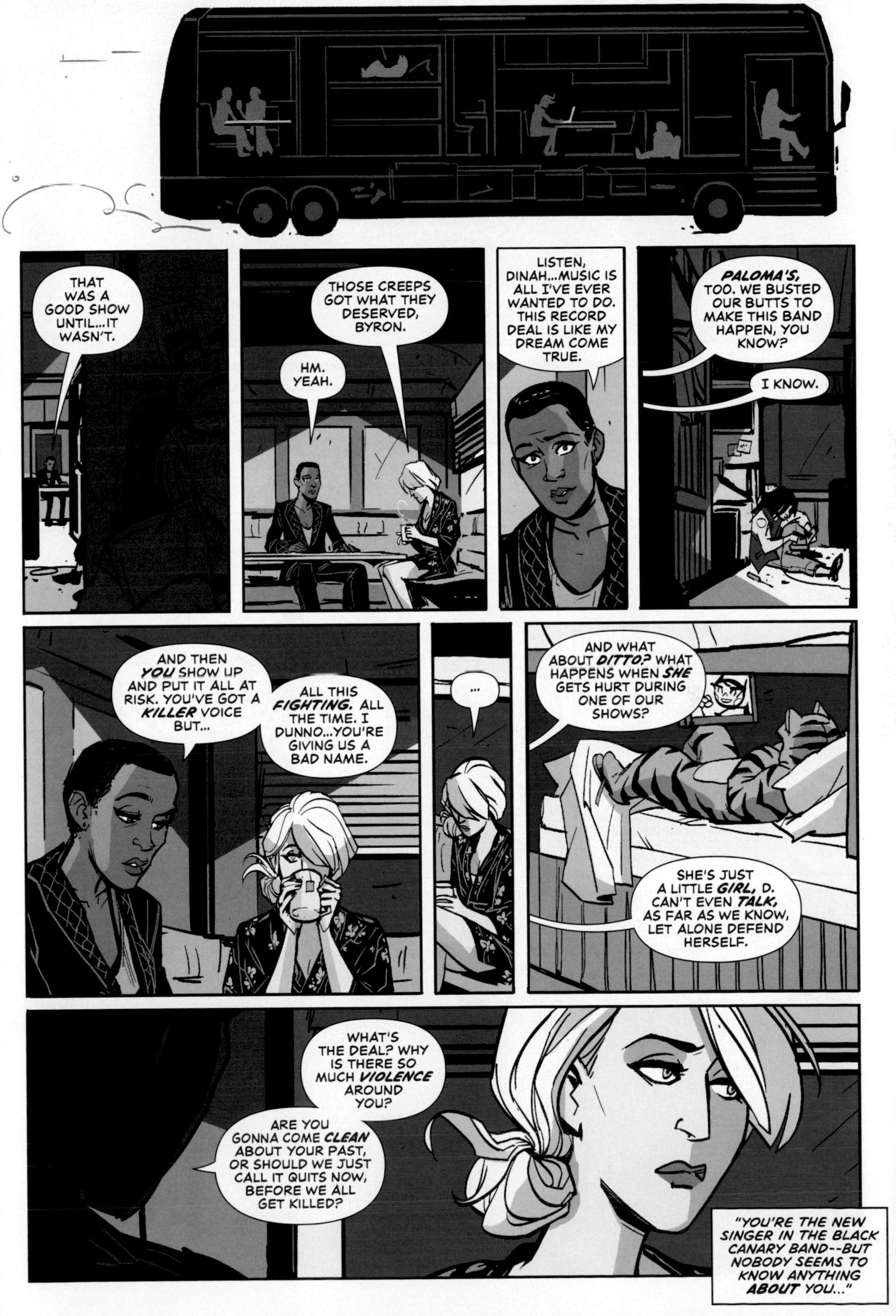
THAT WAS A GOOD SHOW UNTIL...IT WASN'T.
THOSE CREEPS GOT WHAT THEY DESERVED, BYRON.
HM. YEAH.
LISTEN, DINAH...MUSIC IS ALL I'VE EVER WANTED TO DO. THIS RECORD DEAL IS LIKE MY DREAM COME TRUE.
PALOMA'S, TOO. WE BUSTED OUR BUTTS TO MAKE THIS BAND HAPPEN, YOU KNOW?
I KNOW.
AND THEN YOU SHOW UP AND PUT IT ALL AT RISK. YOU'VE GOT A KILLER VOICE BUT...
ALL THIS FIGHTING. ALL THE TIME. I DUNNO...YOU'RE GIVING US A BAD NAME.
...
AND WHAT ABOUT DITTO? WHAT HAPPENS WHEN SHE GETS HURT DURING ONE OF OUR SHOWS?
SHE'S JUST A LITTLE GIRL, D. CAN'T EVEN TALK, AS FAR AS WE KNOW, LET ALONE DEFEND HERSELF.
WHAT'S THE DEAL? WHY IS THERE SO MUCH VIOLENCE AROUND YOU?
ARE YOU GONNA COME CLEAN ABOUT YOUR PAST, OR SHOULD WE JUST CALL IT QUITS NOW, BEFORE WE ALL GET KILLED?
"YOU'RE THE NEW SINGER IN THE BLACK CANARY BAND--BUT NOBODY SEEMS TO KNOW ANYTHING ABOUT YOU..."

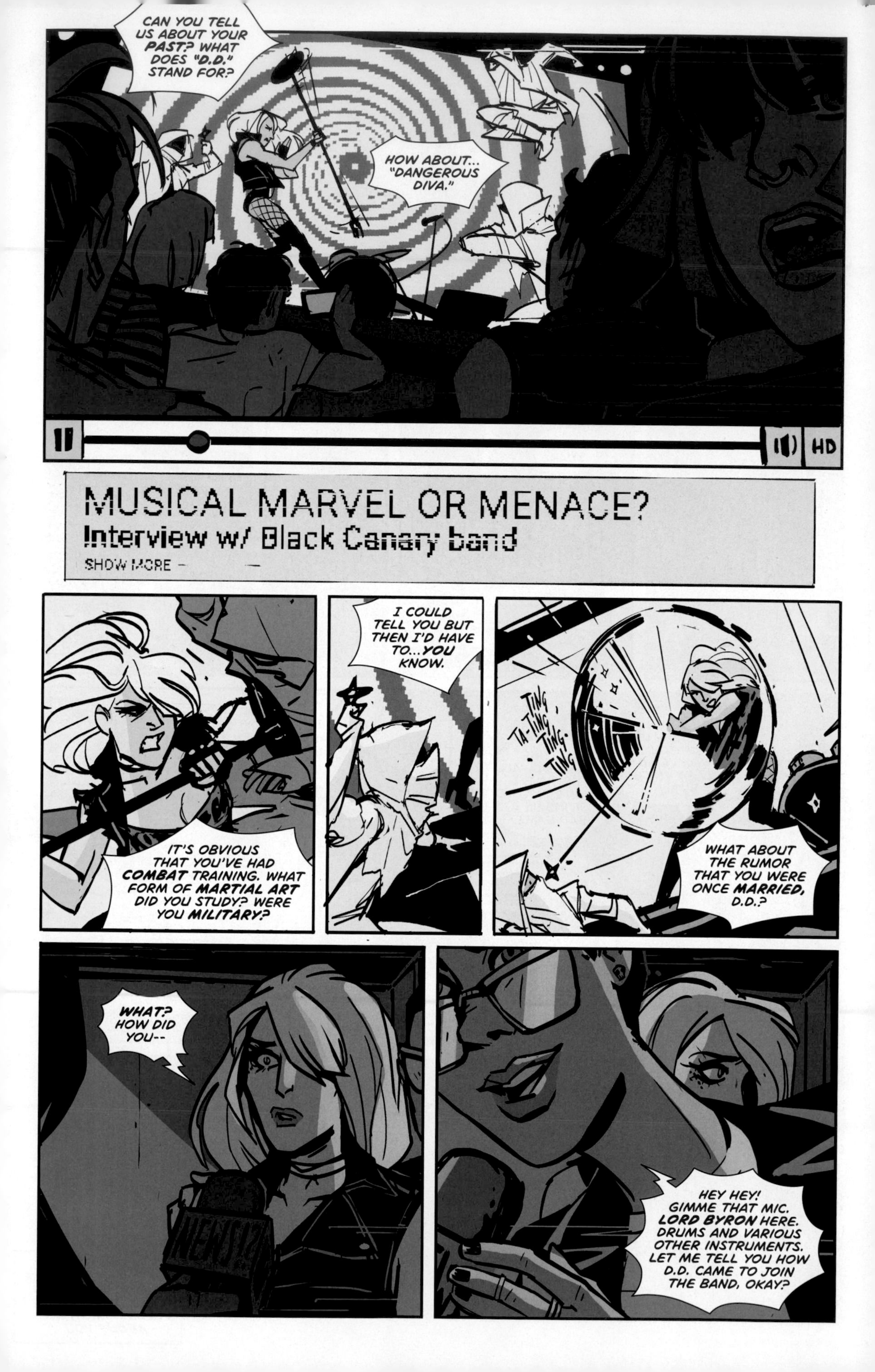
CAN YOU TELL US ABOUT YOUR PAST? WHAT DOES "D.D." STAND FOR?
HOW ABOUT... "DANGEROUS DIVA."
HD
MUSICAL MARVEL OR MENACE?
Interview w/ Black Canary band
SHOW MORE
IT'S OBVIOUS THAT YOU'VE HAD COMBAT TRAINING. WHAT FORM OF MARTIAL ART DID YOU STUDY? WERE YOU MILITARY?
I COULD TELL YOU BUT THEN I'D HAVE TO...YOU KNOW.
TING TA-TING TING TING
WHAT ABOUT THE RUMOR THAT YOU WERE ONCE MARRIED, D.D.?
WHAT? HOW DID YOU--
HEY HEY! GIMME THAT MIC. LORD BYRON HERE. DRUMS AND VARIOUS OTHER INSTRUMENTS. LET ME TELL YOU HOW D.D. CAME TO JOIN THE BAND, OKAY?

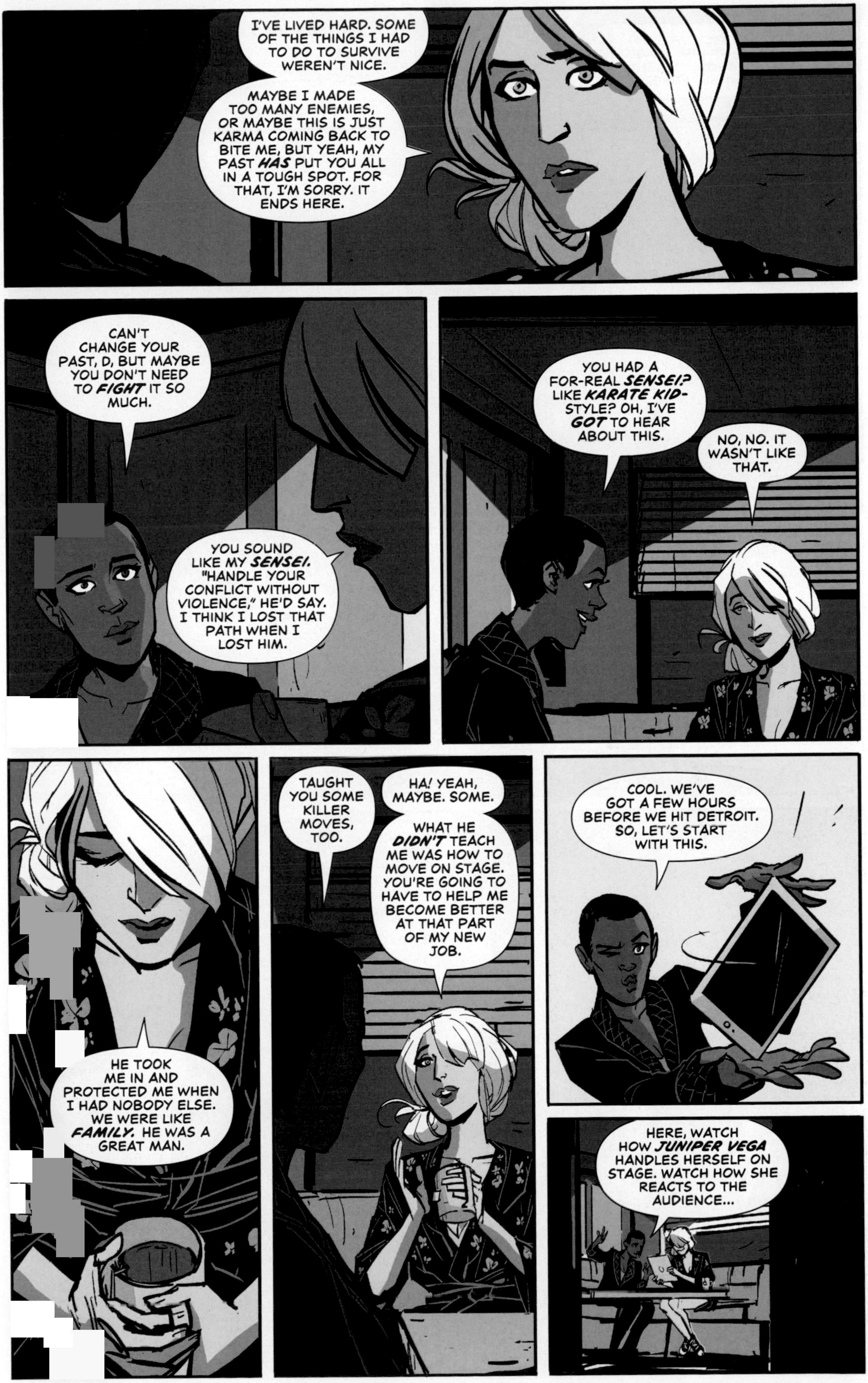
I'VE LIVED HARD. SOME OF THE THINGS I HAD TO DO TO SURVIVE WEREN'T NICE.
MAYBE I MADE TOO MANY ENEMIES, OR MAYBE THIS IS JUST KARMA COMING BACK TO BITE ME, BUT YEAH, MY PAST HAS PUT YOU ALL IN A TOUGH SPOT. FOR THAT, I'M SORRY. IT ENDS HERE.
CAN'T CHANGE YOUR PAST, D, BUT MAYBE YOU DON'T NEED TO FIGHT IT SO MUCH.
YOU SOUND LIKE MY SENSEI. "HANDLE YOUR CONFLICT WITHOUT VIOLENCE," HE'D SAY. I THINK I LOST THAT PATH WHEN I LOST HIM.
YOU HAD A FOR-REAL SENSEI? LIKE KARATE KID-STYLE? OH, I'VE GOT TO HEAR ABOUT THIS.
NO, NO. IT WASN'T LIKE THAT.
HE TOOK ME IN AND PROTECTED ME WHEN I HAD NOBODY ELSE. WE WERE LIKE FAMILY. HE WAS A GREAT MAN.
TAUGHT YOU SOME KILLER MOVES, TOO.
HA! YEAH, MAYBE. SOME.
WHAT HE DIDN'T TEACH ME WAS HOW TO MOVE ON STAGE. YOU'RE GOING TO HAVE TO HELP ME BECOME BETTER AT THAT PART OF MY NEW JOB.
COOL. WE'VE GOT A FEW HOURS BEFORE WE HIT DETROIT. SO, LET'S START WITH THIS.
HERE, WATCH HOW JUNIPER VEGA HANDLES HERSELF ON STAGE. WATCH HOW SHE REACTS TO THE AUDIENCE...

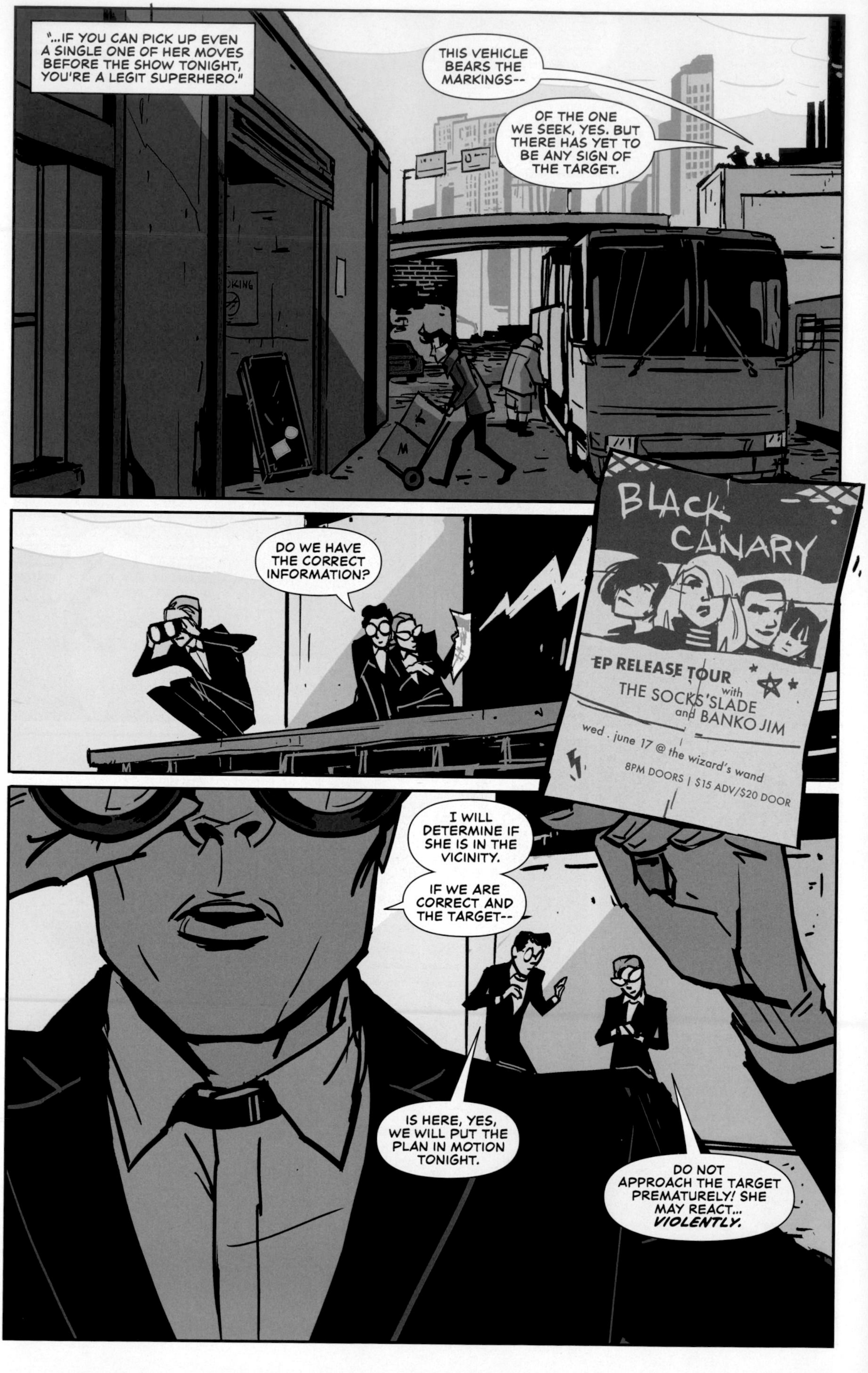
"...IF YOU CAN PICK UP EVEN A SINGLE ONE OF HER MOVES BEFORE THE SHOW TONIGHT, YOU'RE A LEGIT SUPERHERO."
THIS VEHICLE BEARS THE MARKINGS--
OF THE ONE WE SEEK, YES. BUT THERE HAS YET TO BE ANY SIGN OF THE TARGET.
DO WE HAVE THE CORRECT INFORMATION?
BLACK CANARY
EP RELEASE TOUR with THE SOCKS'SLADE and BANKO JIM
wed . june 17 @ the wizard's wand
8PM DOORS | $15 ADV/$20 DOOR
I WILL DETERMINE IF SHE IS IN THE VICINITY.
IF WE ARE CORRECT AND THE TARGET--
IS HERE, YES, WE WILL PUT THE PLAN IN MOTION TONIGHT.
DO NOT APPROACH THE TARGET PREMATURELY! SHE MAY REACT... *VIOLENTLY.*

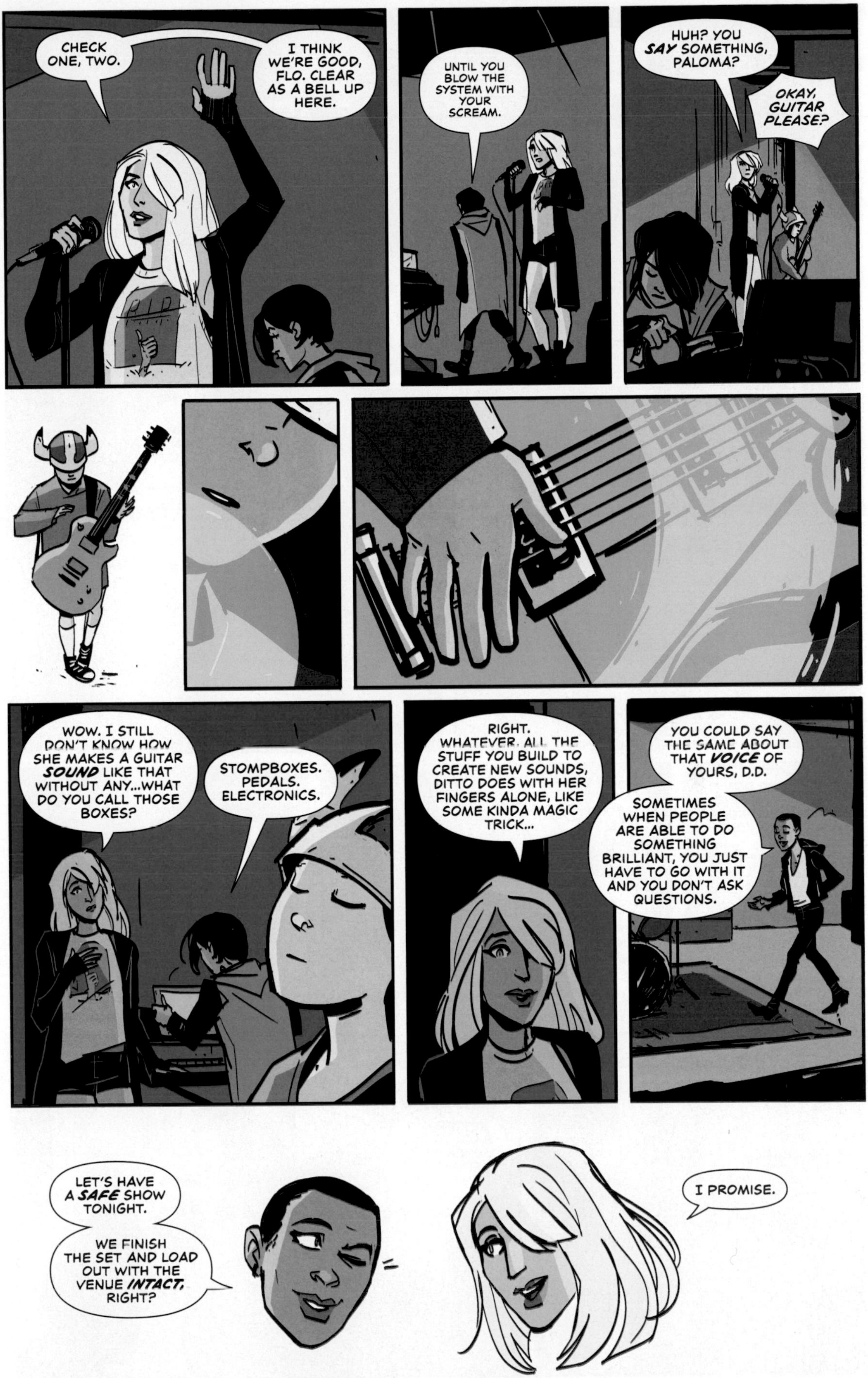
CHECK ONE, TWO.
I THINK WE'RE GOOD, FLO. CLEAR AS A BELL UP HERE.
UNTIL YOU BLOW THE SYSTEM WITH YOUR SCREAM.
HUH? YOU SAY SOMETHING, PALOMA?
OKAY, GUITAR PLEASE?
WOW. I STILL DON'T KNOW HOW SHE MAKES A GUITAR SOUND LIKE THAT WITHOUT ANY...WHAT DO YOU CALL THOSE BOXES?
STOMPBOXES. PEDALS. ELECTRONICS.
RIGHT. WHATEVER. ALL THE STUFF YOU BUILD TO CREATE NEW SOUNDS, DITTO DOES WITH HER FINGERS ALONE, LIKE SOME KINDA MAGIC TRICK...
YOU COULD SAY THE SAME ABOUT THAT VOICE OF YOURS, D.D.
SOMETIMES WHEN PEOPLE ARE ABLE TO DO SOMETHING BRILLIANT, YOU JUST HAVE TO GO WITH IT AND YOU DON'T ASK QUESTIONS.
LET'S HAVE A SAFE SHOW TONIGHT.
WE FINISH THE SET AND LOAD OUT WITH THE VENUE INTACT, RIGHT?
I PROMISE.

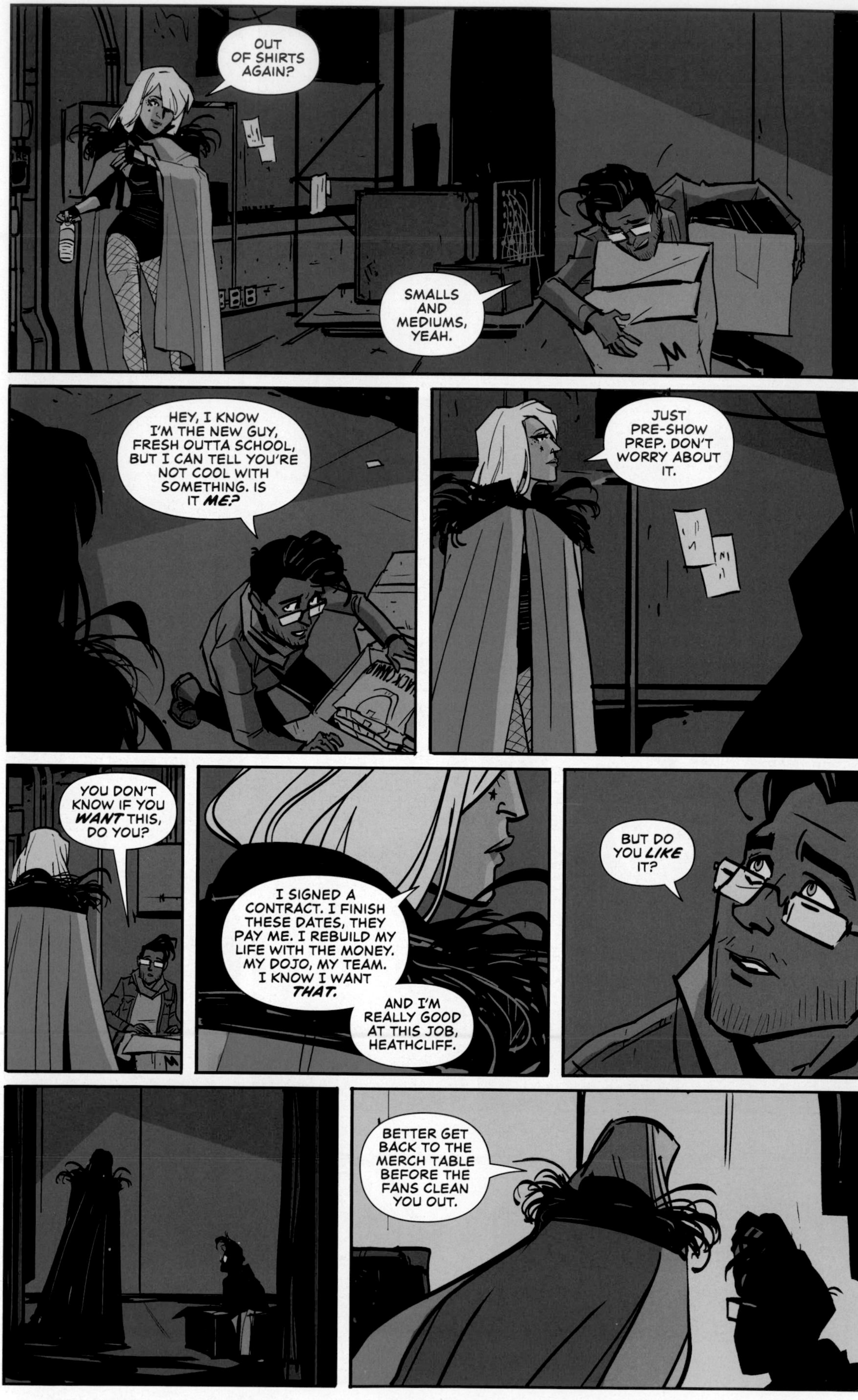
OUT OF SHIRTS AGAIN?
SMALLS AND MEDIUMS, YEAH.
HEY, I KNOW I'M THE NEW GUY, FRESH OUTTA SCHOOL, BUT I CAN TELL YOU'RE NOT COOL WITH SOMETHING. IS IT *ME?*
JUST PRE-SHOW PREP. DON'T WORRY ABOUT IT.
YOU DON'T KNOW IF YOU *WANT* THIS, DO YOU?
I SIGNED A CONTRACT. I FINISH THESE DATES, THEY PAY ME. I REBUILD MY LIFE WITH THE MONEY. MY DOJO, MY TEAM. I KNOW I WANT *THAT.*
AND I'M REALLY GOOD AT THIS JOB, HEATHCLIFF.
BUT DO YOU *LIKE* IT?
BETTER GET BACK TO THE MERCH TABLE BEFORE THE FANS CLEAN YOU OUT.

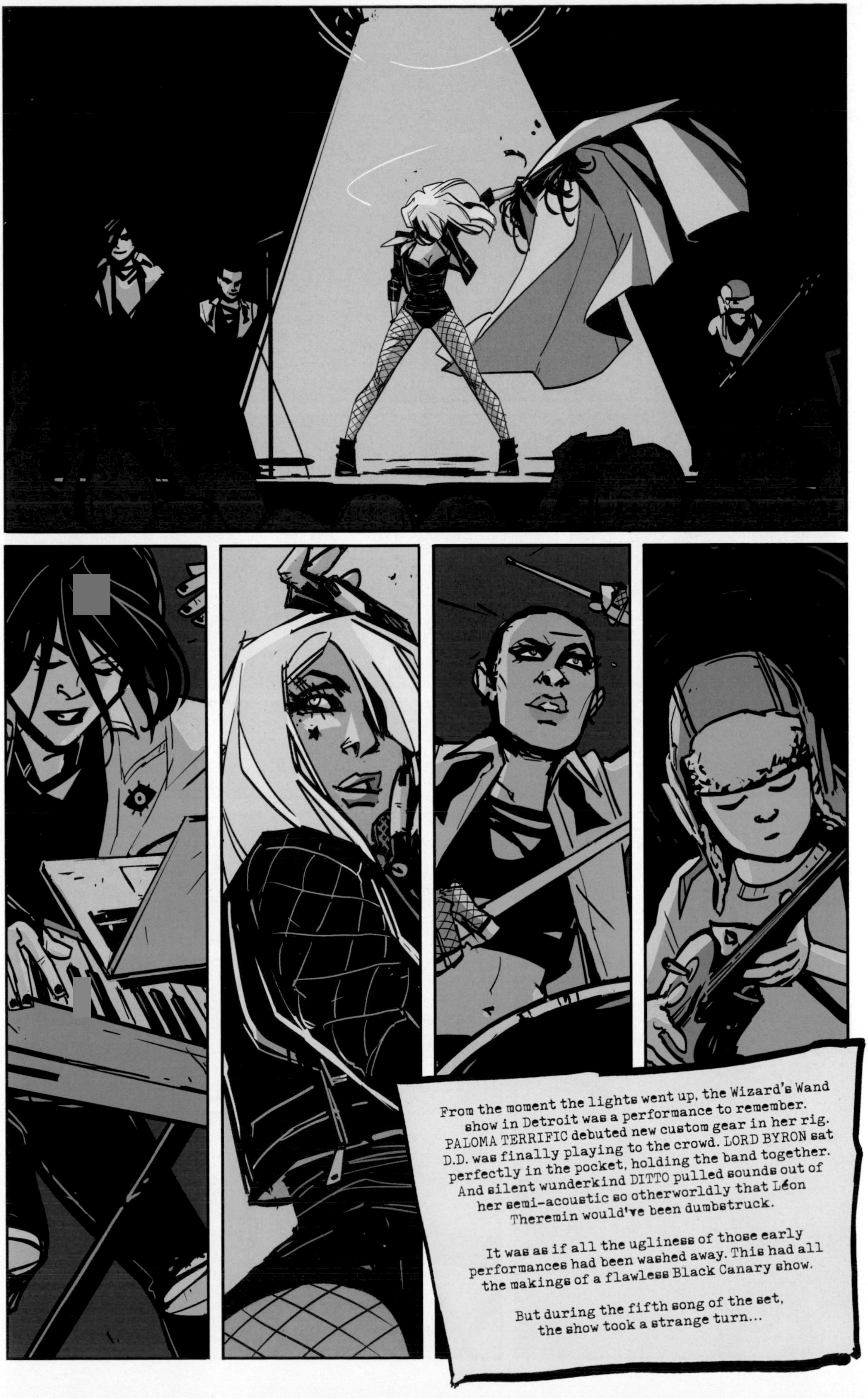
From the moment the lights went up, the Wizard's Wand show in Detroit was a performance to remember. PALOMA TERRIFIC debuted new custom gear in her rig. D.D. was finally playing to the crowd. LORD BYRON sat perfectly in the pocket, holding the band together. And silent wunderkind DITTO pulled sounds out of her semi-acoustic so otherworldly that Léon Theremin would've been dumbstruck.
It was as if all the ugliness of those early performances had been washed away. This had all the makings of a flawless Black Canary show.
But during the fifth song of the set, the show took a strange turn...

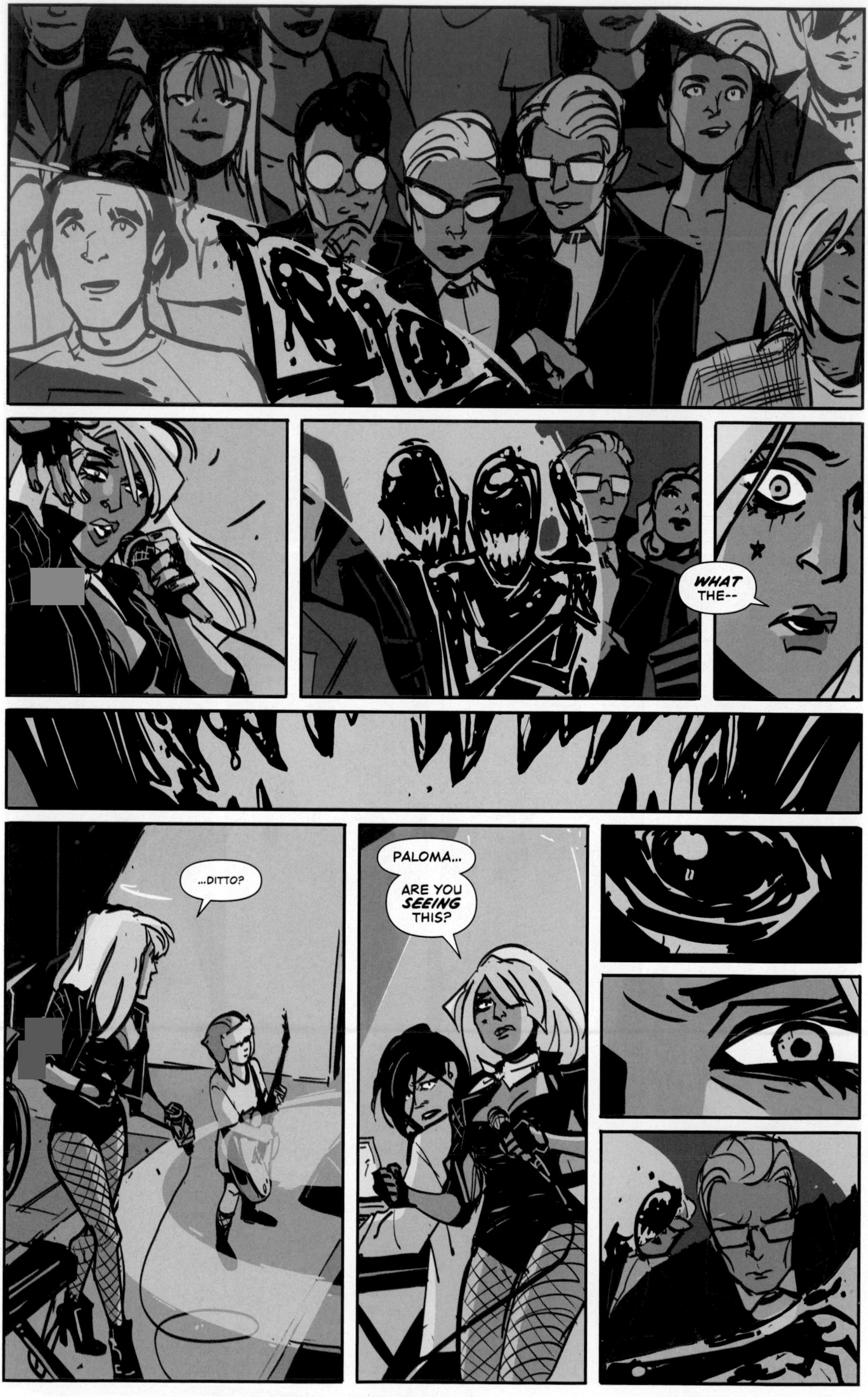
WHAT THE--
...DITTO?
PALOMA...
ARE YOU SEEING THIS?

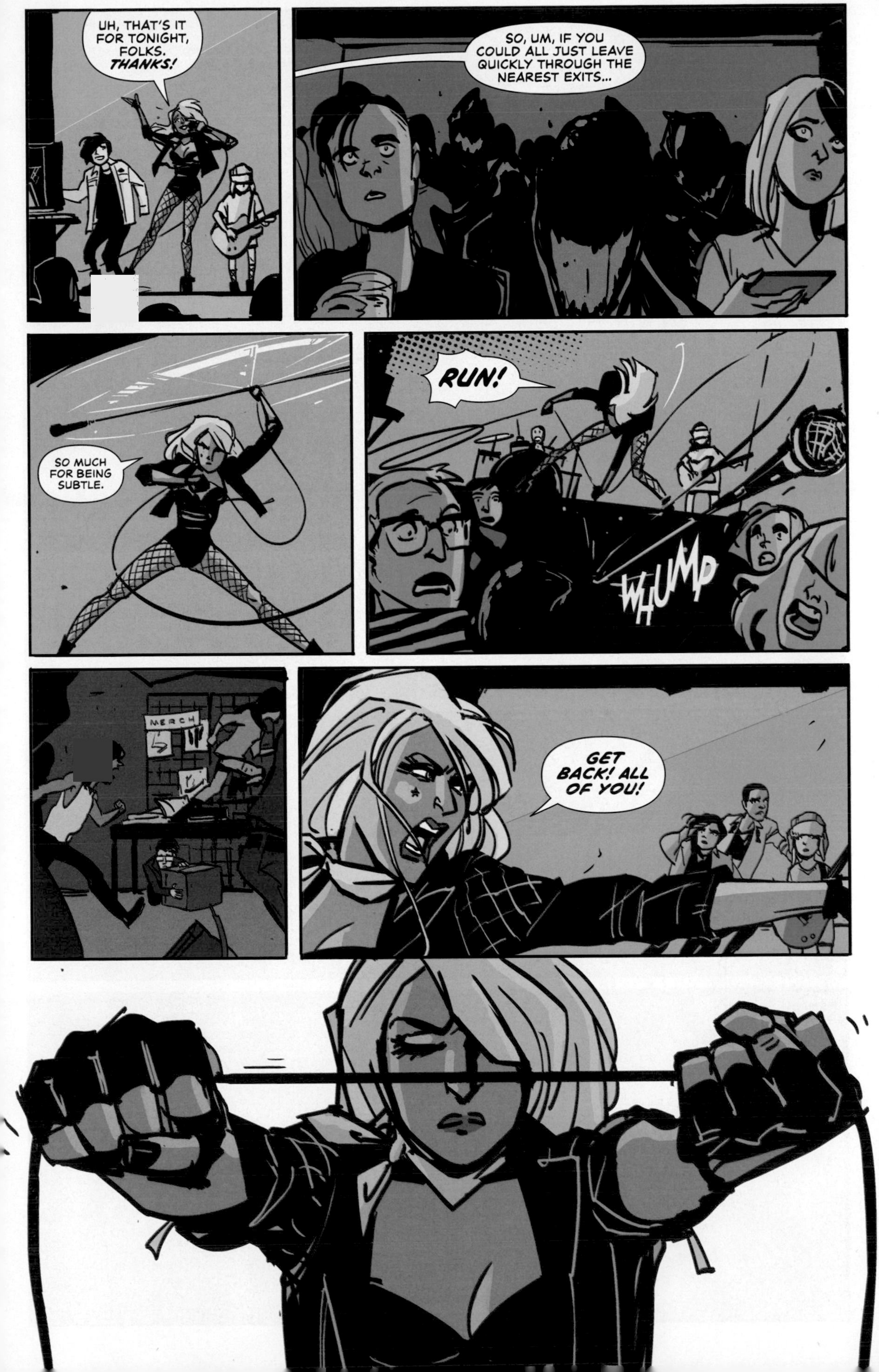
UH, THAT'S IT FOR TONIGHT, FOLKS. THANKS!
SO, UM, IF YOU COULD ALL JUST LEAVE QUICKLY THROUGH THE NEAREST EXITS...
SO MUCH FOR BEING SUBTLE.
RUN!
WHUMP
MERCH
GET BACK! ALL OF YOU!

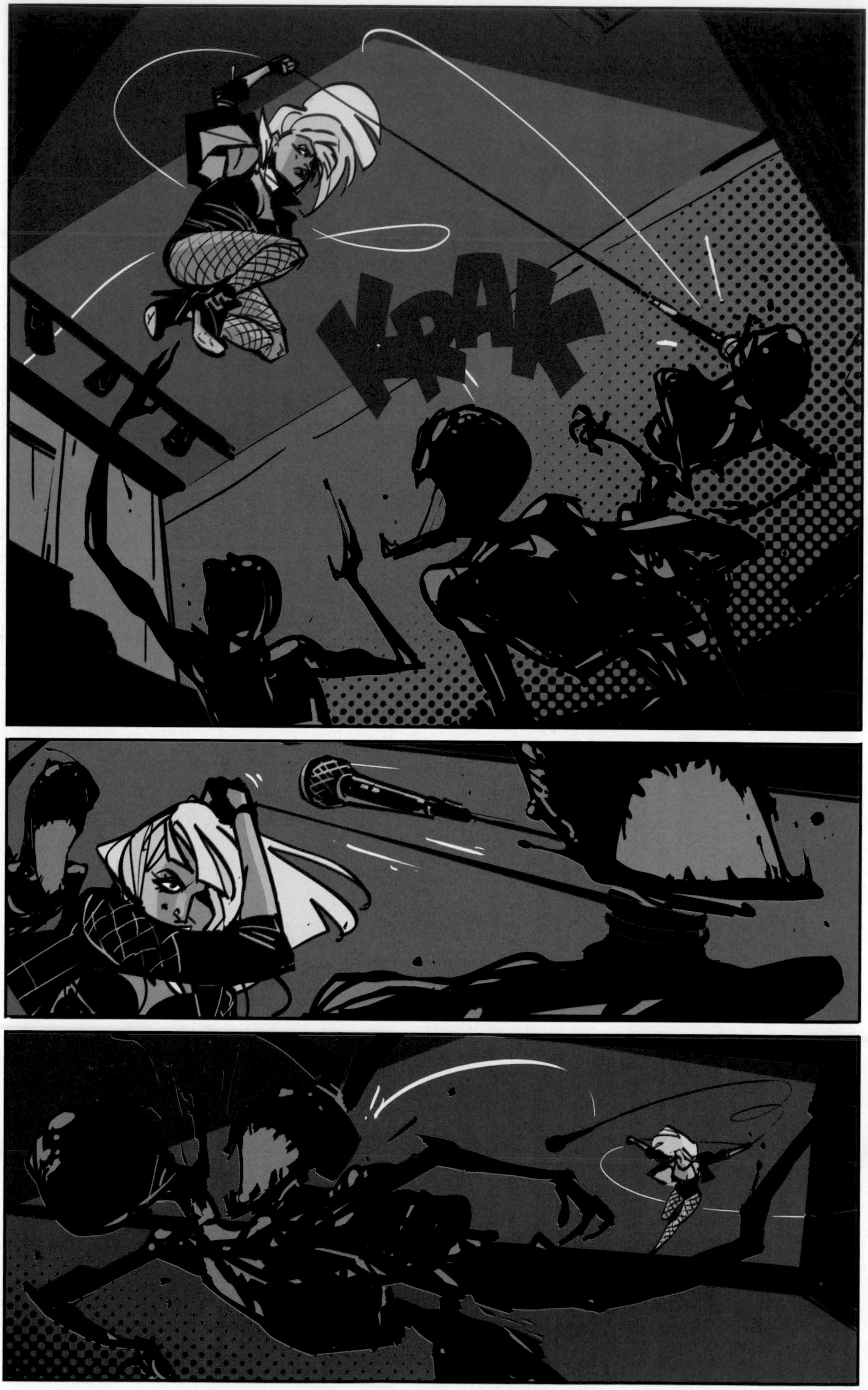
KRAK

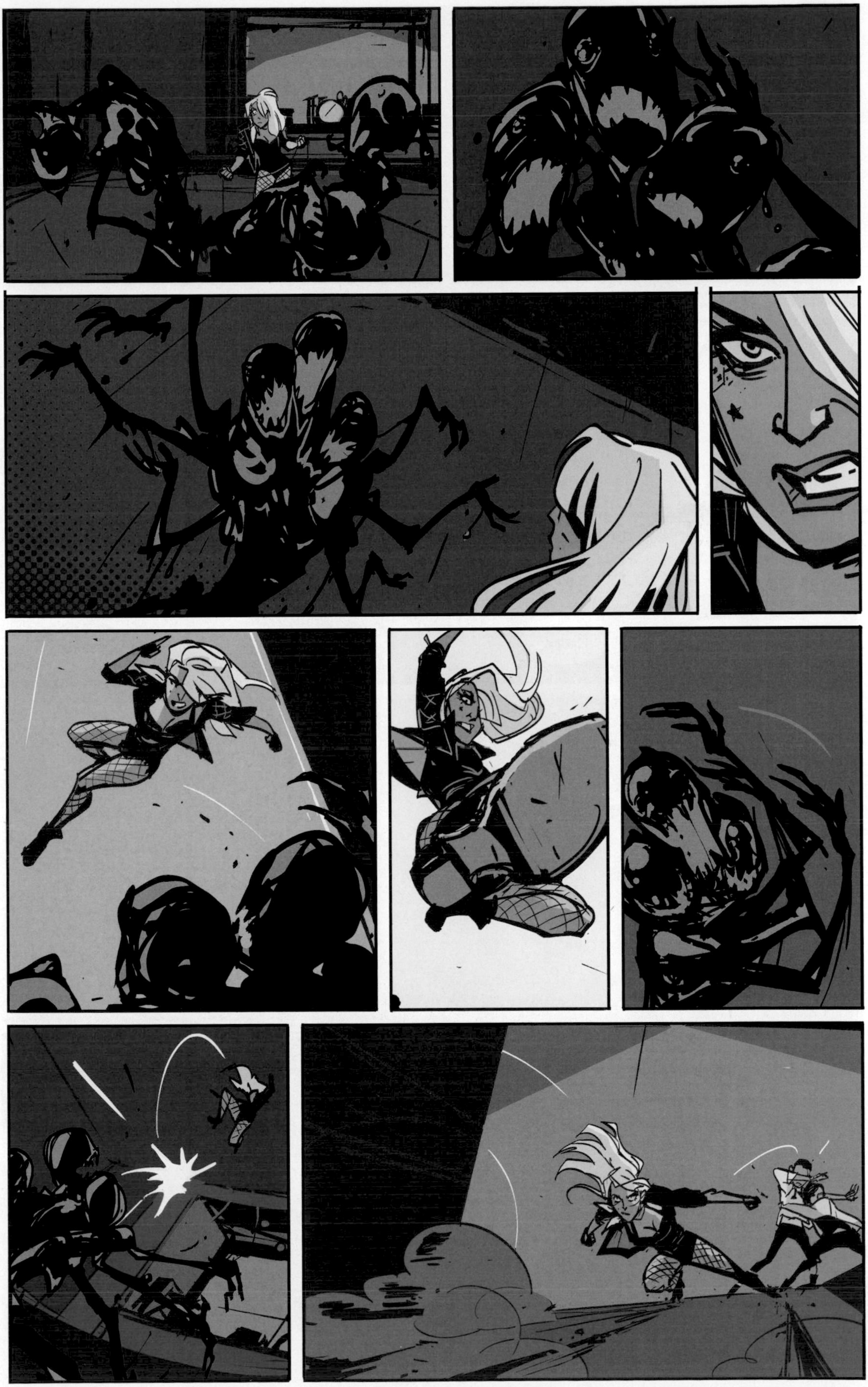

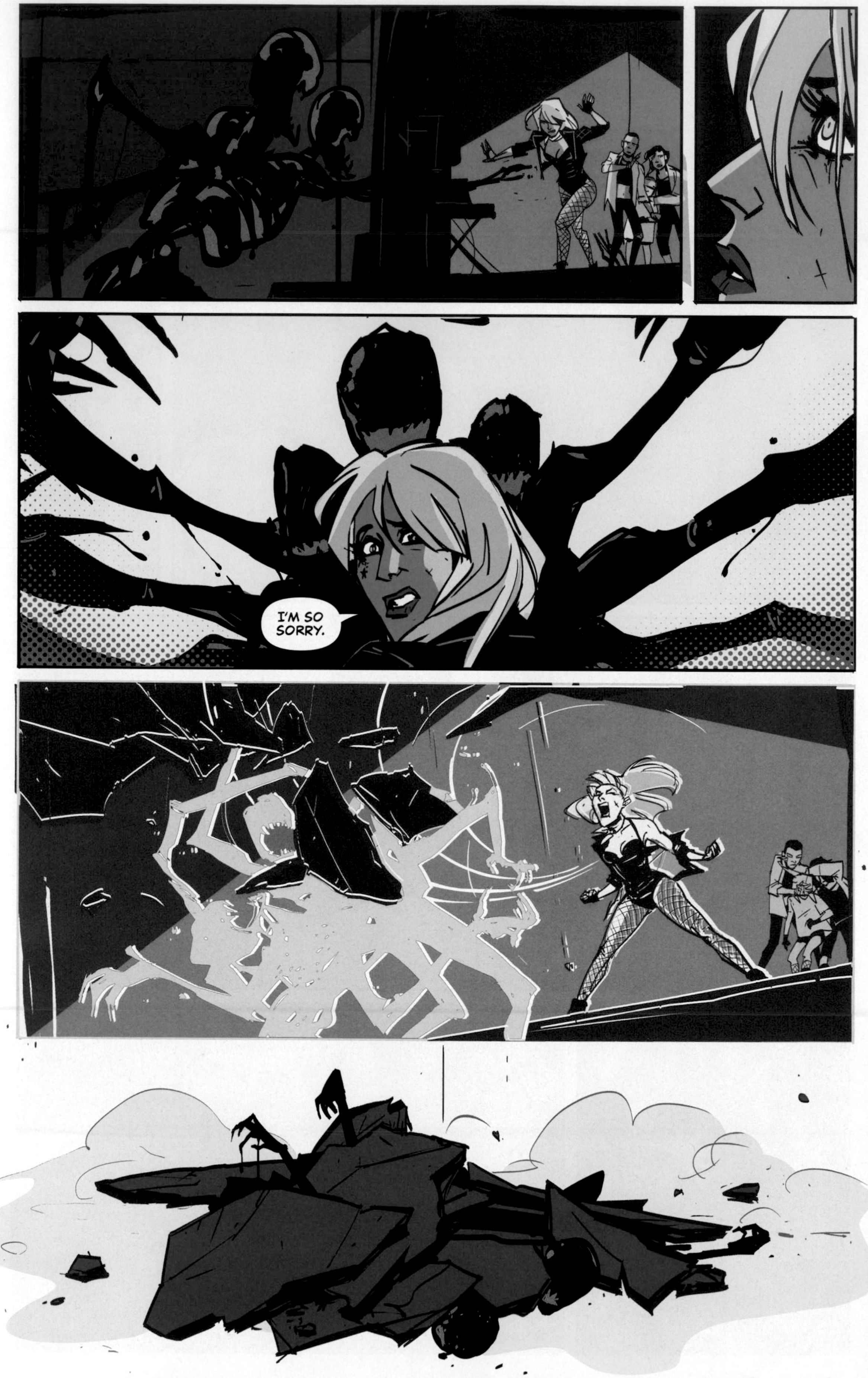
I'M SO SORRY.

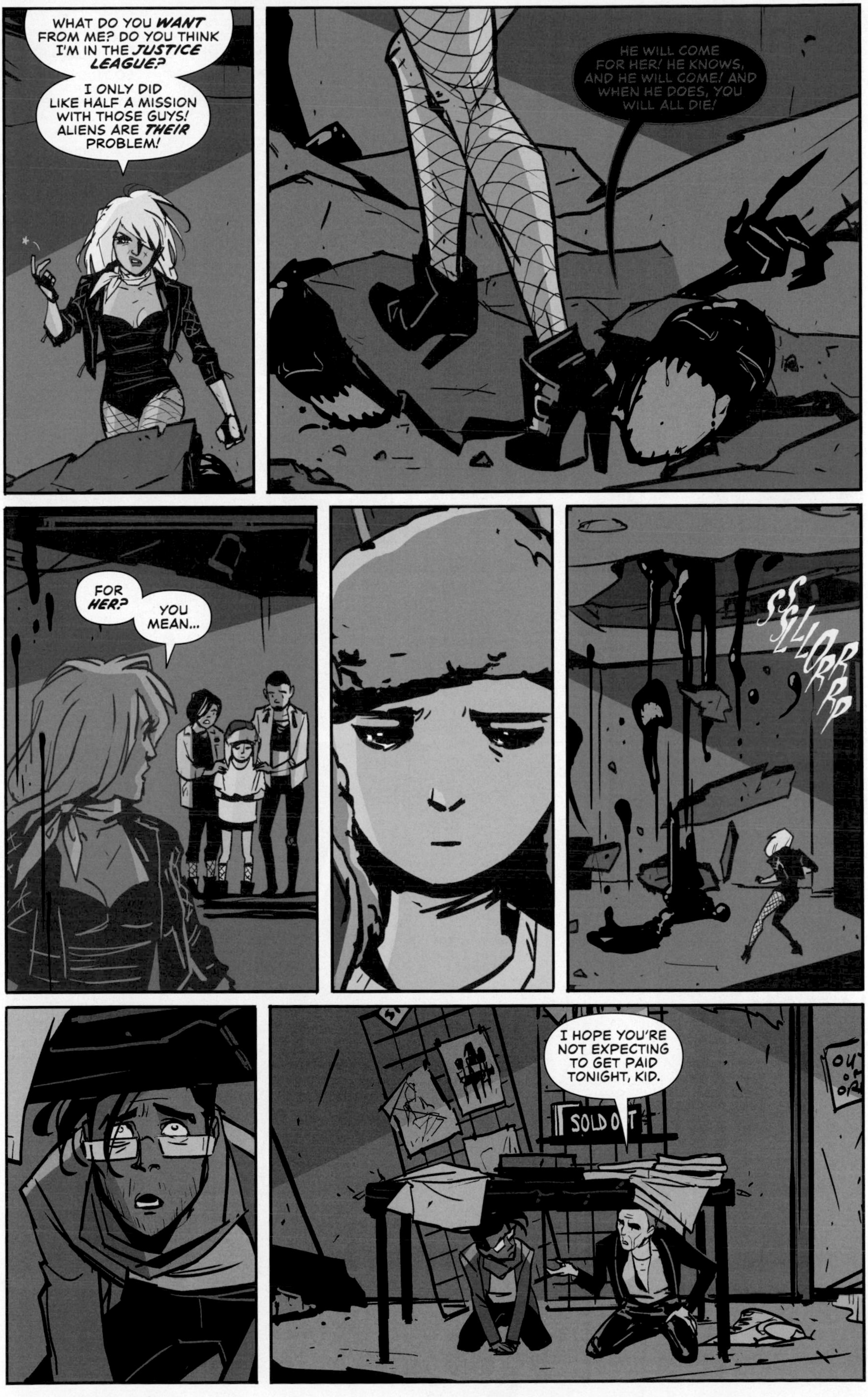
WHAT DO YOU WANT FROM ME? DO YOU THINK I'M IN THE JUSTICE LEAGUE?
I ONLY DID LIKE HALF A MISSION WITH THOSE GUYS! ALIENS ARE THEIR PROBLEM!
HE WILL COME FOR HER! HE KNOWS, AND HE WILL COME! AND WHEN HE DOES, YOU WILL ALL DIE!
FOR HER?
YOU MEAN...
SSLLORRP
I HOPE YOU'RE NOT EXPECTING TO GET PAID TONIGHT, KID.
SOLD OUT

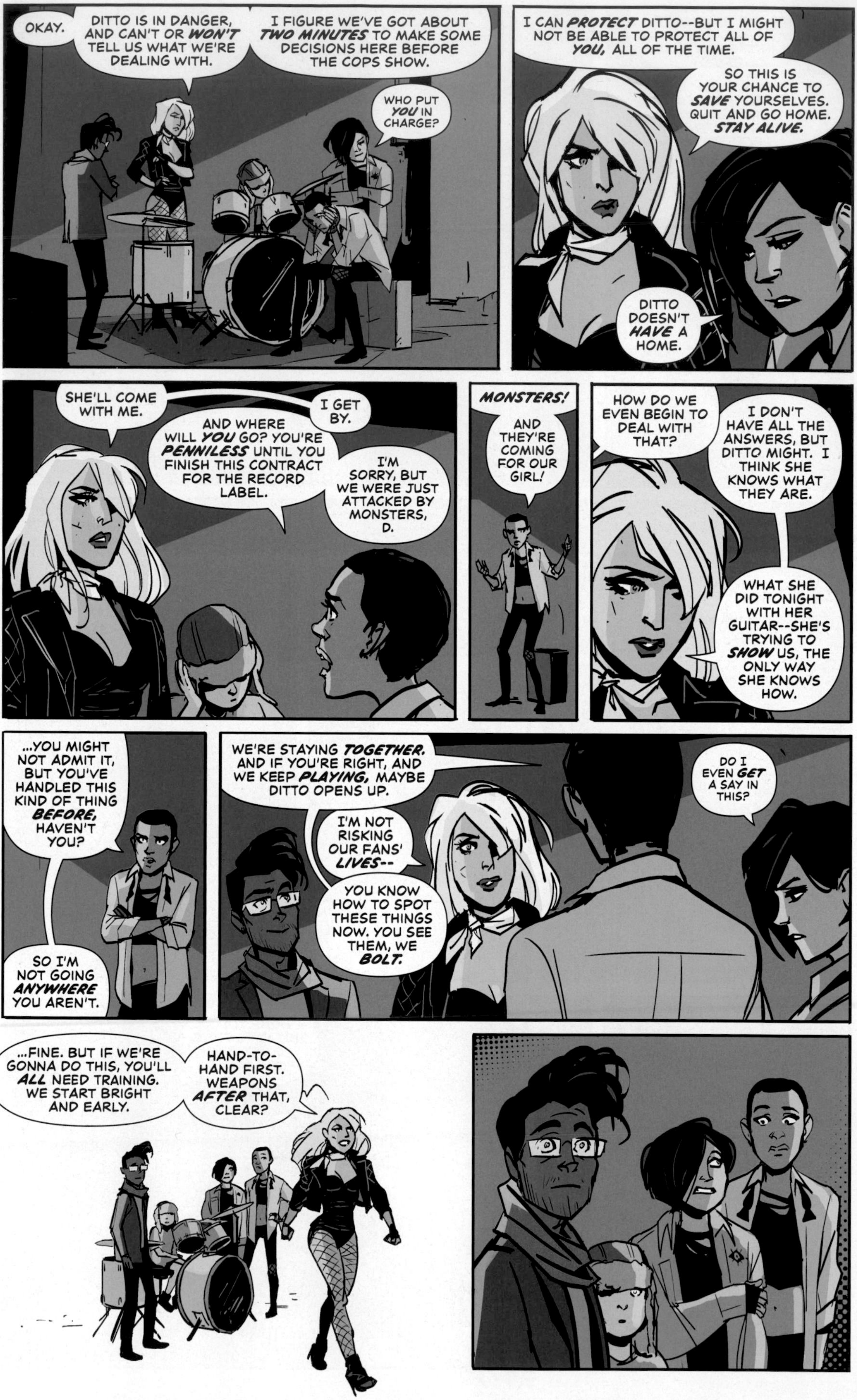
OKAY.
DITTO IS IN DANGER, AND CAN'T OR WON'T TELL US WHAT WE'RE DEALING WITH.
I FIGURE WE'VE GOT ABOUT TWO MINUTES TO MAKE SOME DECISIONS HERE BEFORE THE COPS SHOW.
WHO PUT YOU IN CHARGE?
I CAN PROTECT DITTO--BUT I MIGHT NOT BE ABLE TO PROTECT ALL OF YOU, ALL OF THE TIME.
SO THIS IS YOUR CHANCE TO SAVE YOURSELVES. QUIT AND GO HOME. STAY ALIVE.
DITTO DOESN'T HAVE A HOME.
SHE'LL COME WITH ME.
I GET BY.
AND WHERE WILL YOU GO? YOU'RE PENNILESS UNTIL YOU FINISH THIS CONTRACT FOR THE RECORD LABEL.
I'M SORRY, BUT WE WERE JUST ATTACKED BY MONSTERS, D.
MONSTERS!
AND THEY'RE COMING FOR OUR GIRL!
HOW DO WE EVEN BEGIN TO DEAL WITH THAT?
I DON'T HAVE ALL THE ANSWERS, BUT DITTO MIGHT. I THINK SHE KNOWS WHAT THEY ARE.
WHAT SHE DID TONIGHT WITH HER GUITAR--SHE'S TRYING TO SHOW US, THE ONLY WAY SHE KNOWS HOW.
...YOU MIGHT NOT ADMIT IT, BUT YOU'VE HANDLED THIS KIND OF THING BEFORE, HAVEN'T YOU?
SO I'M NOT GOING ANYWHERE YOU AREN'T.
WE'RE STAYING TOGETHER. AND IF YOU'RE RIGHT, AND WE KEEP PLAYING, MAYBE DITTO OPENS UP.
I'M NOT RISKING OUR FANS' LIVES--
YOU KNOW HOW TO SPOT THESE THINGS NOW. YOU SEE THEM, WE BOLT.
DO I EVEN GET A SAY IN THIS?
...FINE. BUT IF WE'RE GONNA DO THIS, YOU'LL ALL NEED TRAINING. WE START BRIGHT AND EARLY.
HAND-TO-HAND FIRST. WEAPONS AFTER THAT, CLEAR?

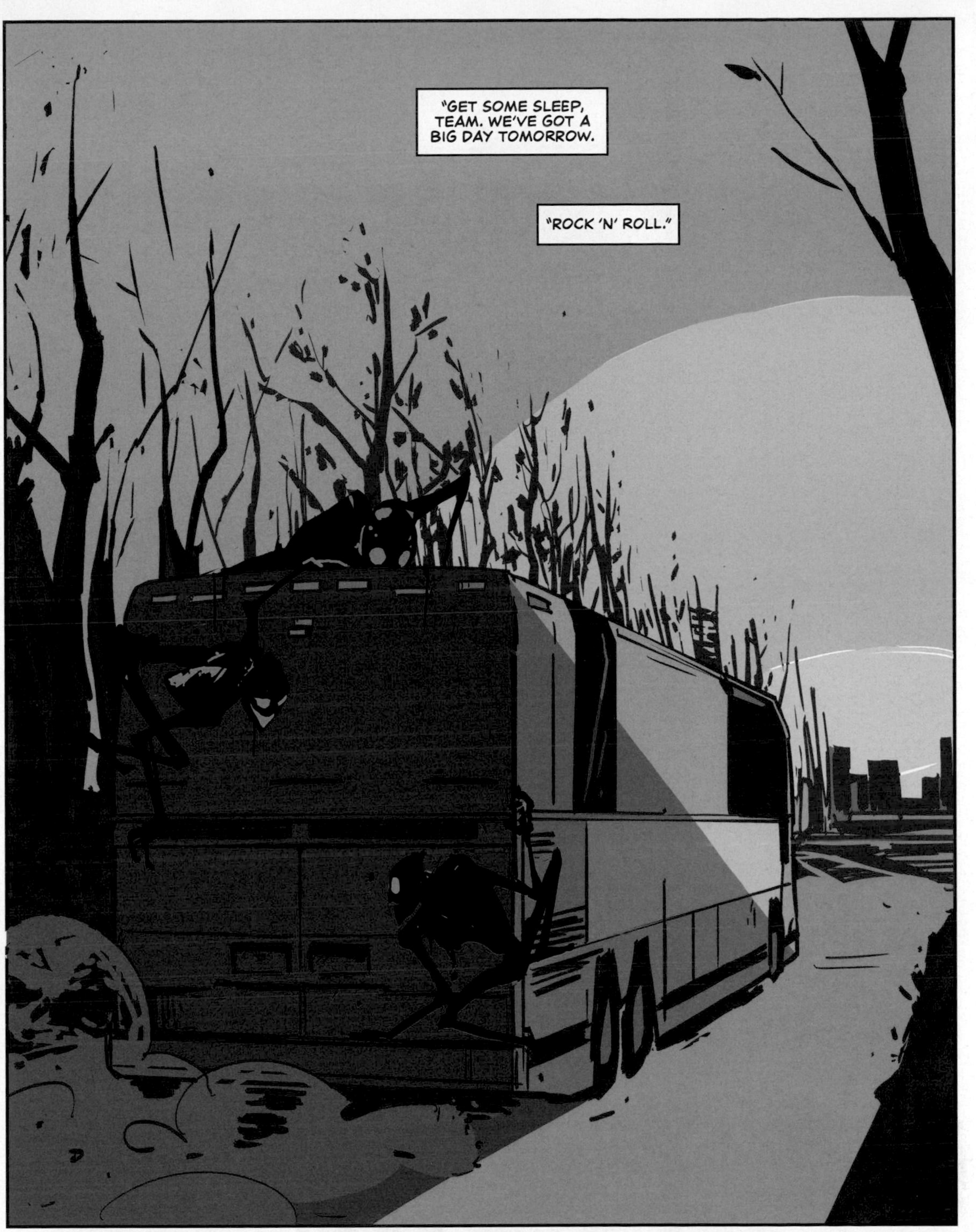
"GET SOME SLEEP, TEAM. WE'VE GOT A BIG DAY TOMORROW.
"ROCK 'N' ROLL."

BLACK CANARY
PLAYLIST: UP NEXT!

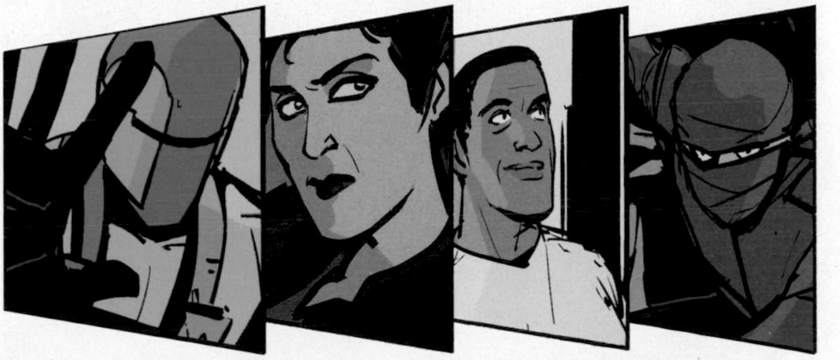

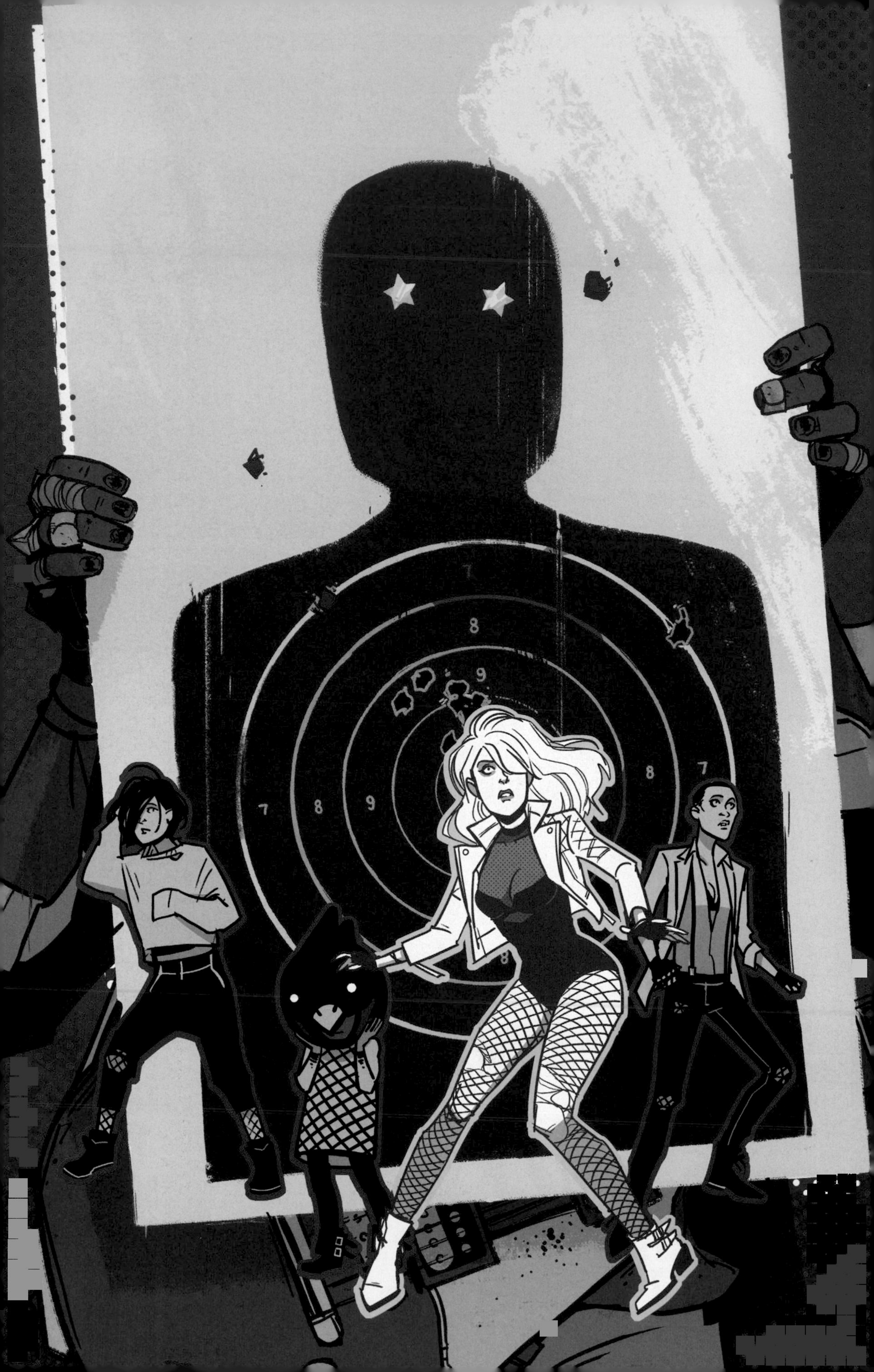

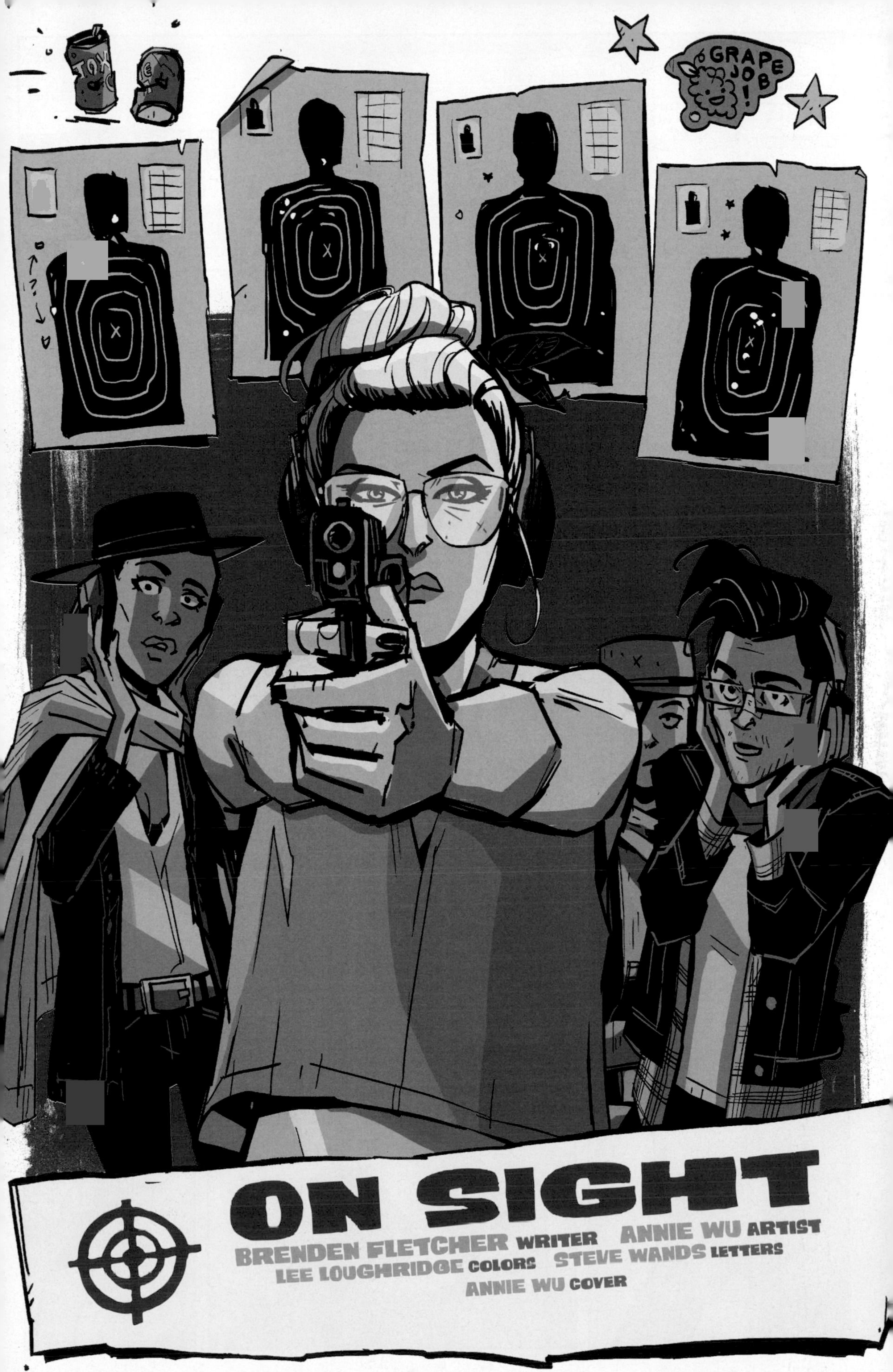
GRAPE JOB!

ON SIGHT

BRENDEN FLETCHER WRITER ANNIE WU ARTIST
LEE LOUGHRIDGE COLORS STEVE WANDS LETTERS
ANNIE WU COVER

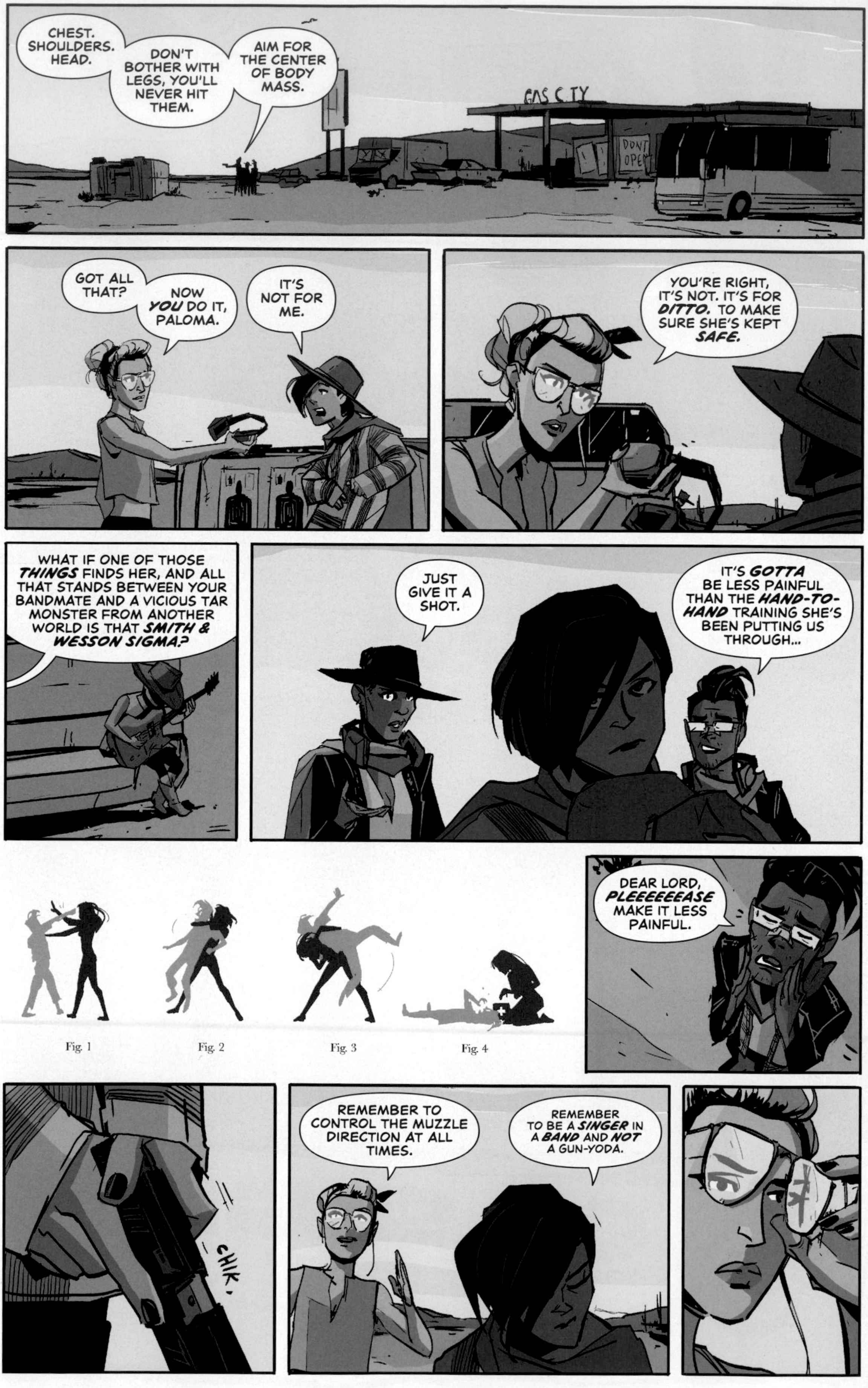
CHEST. SHOULDERS. HEAD.
DON'T BOTHER WITH LEGS, YOU'LL NEVER HIT THEM.
AIM FOR THE CENTER OF BODY MASS.
GAS C TY
DONT OPEN
GOT ALL THAT?
NOW YOU DO IT, PALOMA.
IT'S NOT FOR ME.
YOU'RE RIGHT, IT'S NOT. IT'S FOR DITTO. TO MAKE SURE SHE'S KEPT SAFE.
WHAT IF ONE OF THOSE THINGS FINDS HER, AND ALL THAT STANDS BETWEEN YOUR BANDMATE AND A VICIOUS TAR MONSTER FROM ANOTHER WORLD IS THAT SMITH & WESSON SIGMA?
JUST GIVE IT A SHOT.
IT'S GOTTA BE LESS PAINFUL THAN THE HAND-TO-HAND TRAINING SHE'S BEEN PUTTING US THROUGH...
Fig. 1
Fig. 2
Fig. 3
Fig. 4
DEAR LORD, PLEEEEEEASE MAKE IT LESS PAINFUL.
CHIK
REMEMBER TO CONTROL THE MUZZLE DIRECTION AT ALL TIMES.
REMEMBER TO BE A SINGER IN A BAND AND NOT A GUN-YODA.

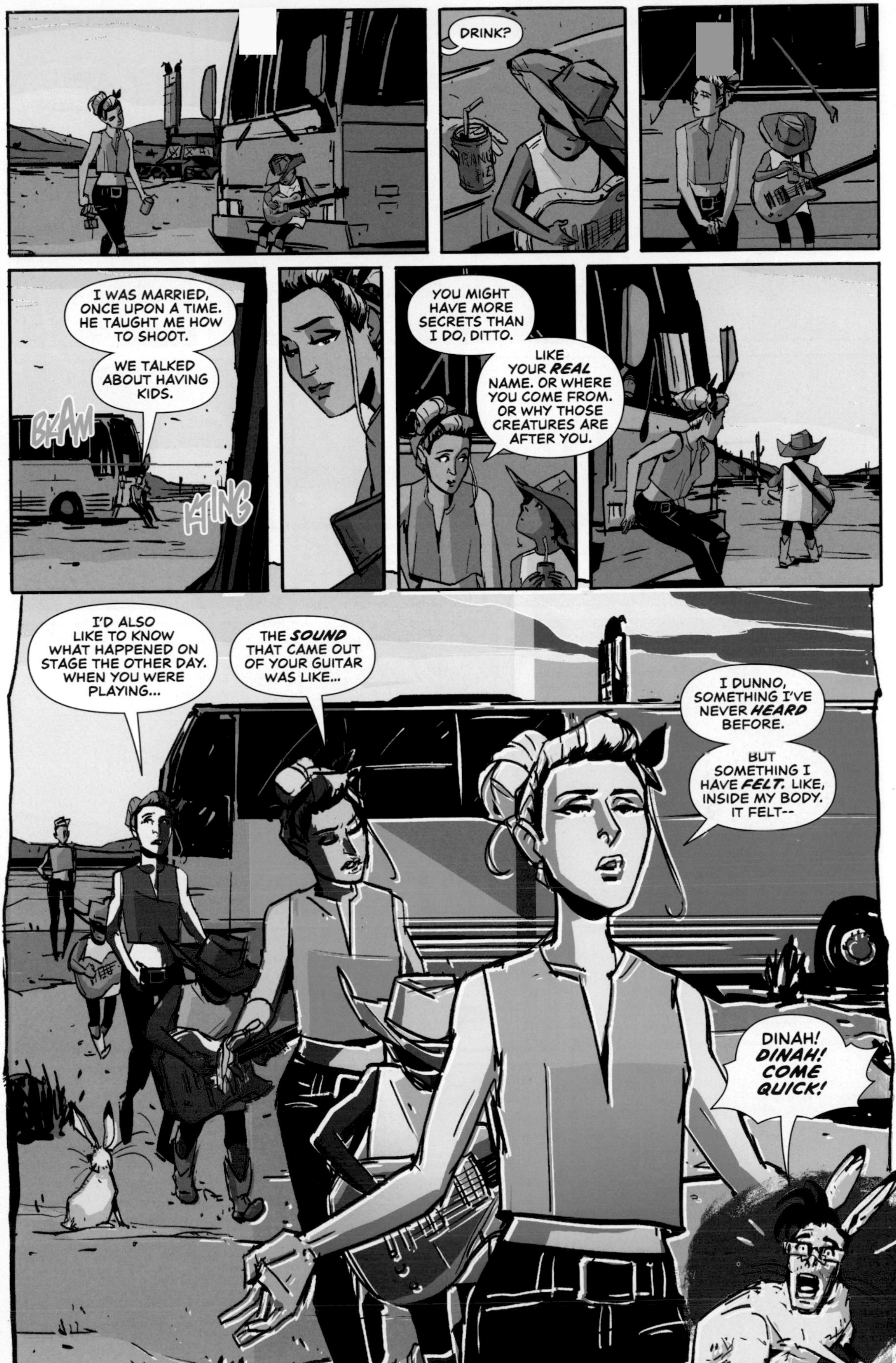
DRINK?
I WAS MARRIED, ONCE UPON A TIME. HE TAUGHT ME HOW TO SHOOT.
WE TALKED ABOUT HAVING KIDS.
BKAM
KTING
YOU MIGHT HAVE MORE SECRETS THAN I DO, DITTO.
LIKE YOUR REAL NAME. OR WHERE YOU COME FROM. OR WHY THOSE CREATURES ARE AFTER YOU.
I'D ALSO LIKE TO KNOW WHAT HAPPENED ON STAGE THE OTHER DAY. WHEN YOU WERE PLAYING...
THE SOUND THAT CAME OUT OF YOUR GUITAR WAS LIKE...
I DUNNO, SOMETHING I'VE NEVER HEARD BEFORE.
BUT SOMETHING I HAVE FELT. LIKE, INSIDE MY BODY. IT FELT--
DINAH! DINAH! COME QUICK!

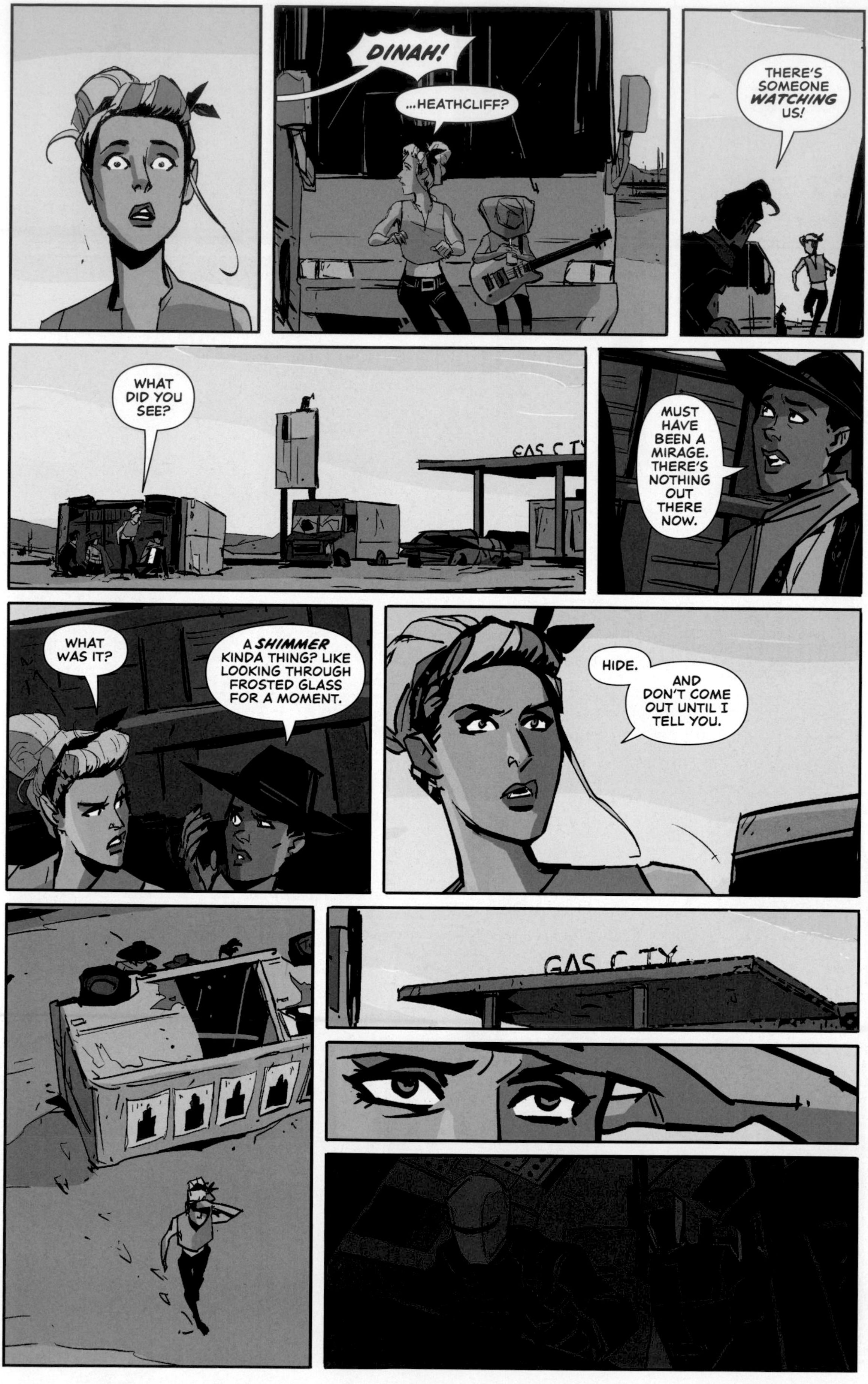

DINAH!
...HEATHCLIFF?
THERE'S SOMEONE WATCHING US!
WHAT DID YOU SEE?
GAS C TY
MUST HAVE BEEN A MIRAGE. THERE'S NOTHING OUT THERE NOW.
WHAT WAS IT?
A SHIMMER KINDA THING? LIKE LOOKING THROUGH FROSTED GLASS FOR A MOMENT.
HIDE.
AND DON'T COME OUT UNTIL I TELL YOU.
GAS C TY

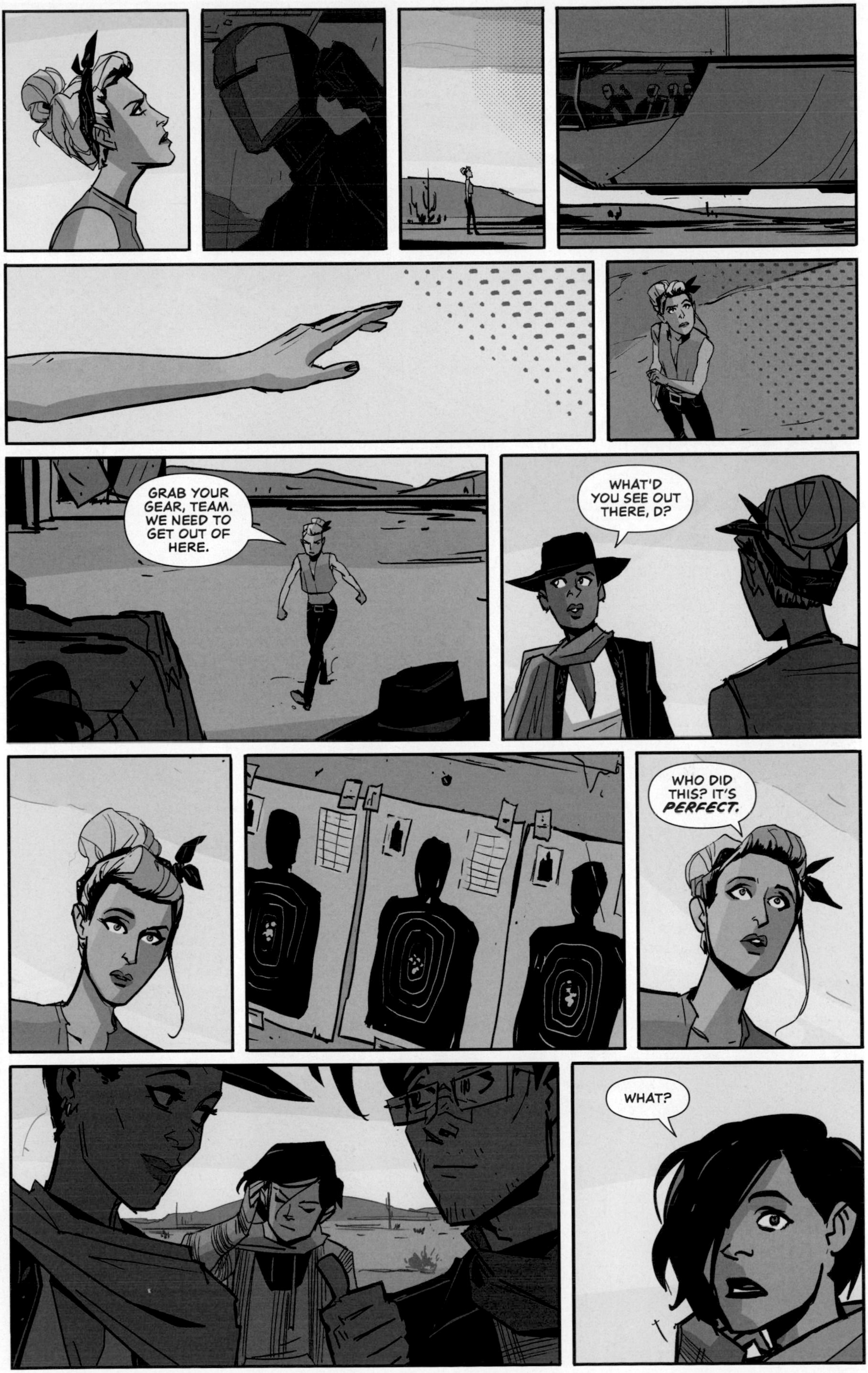
GRAB YOUR GEAR, TEAM. WE NEED TO GET OUT OF HERE.
WHAT'D YOU SEE OUT THERE, D?
WHO DID THIS? IT'S *PERFECT.*
WHAT?

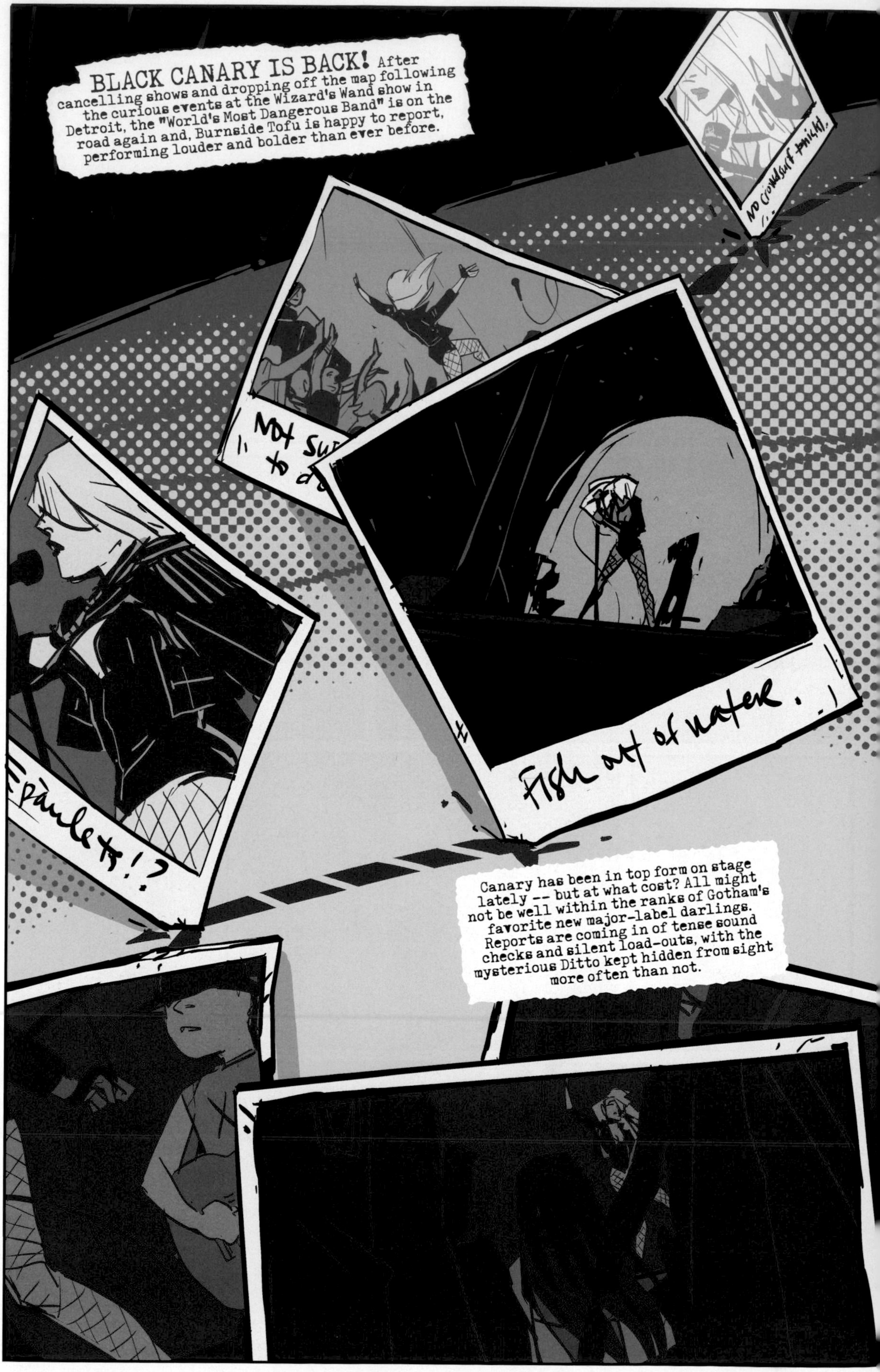
BLACK CANARY IS BACK! After cancelling shows and dropping off the map following the curious events at the Wizard's Wand show in Detroit, the "World's Most Dangerous Band" is on the road again and, Burnside Tofu is happy to report, performing louder and bolder than ever before.
No crowdsurf tonight.
Fish out of water.
Epaulets!?
Canary has been in top form on stage lately -- but at what cost? All might not be well within the ranks of Gotham's favorite new major-label darlings. Reports are coming in of tense sound checks and silent load-outs, with the mysterious Ditto kept hidden from sight more often than not.

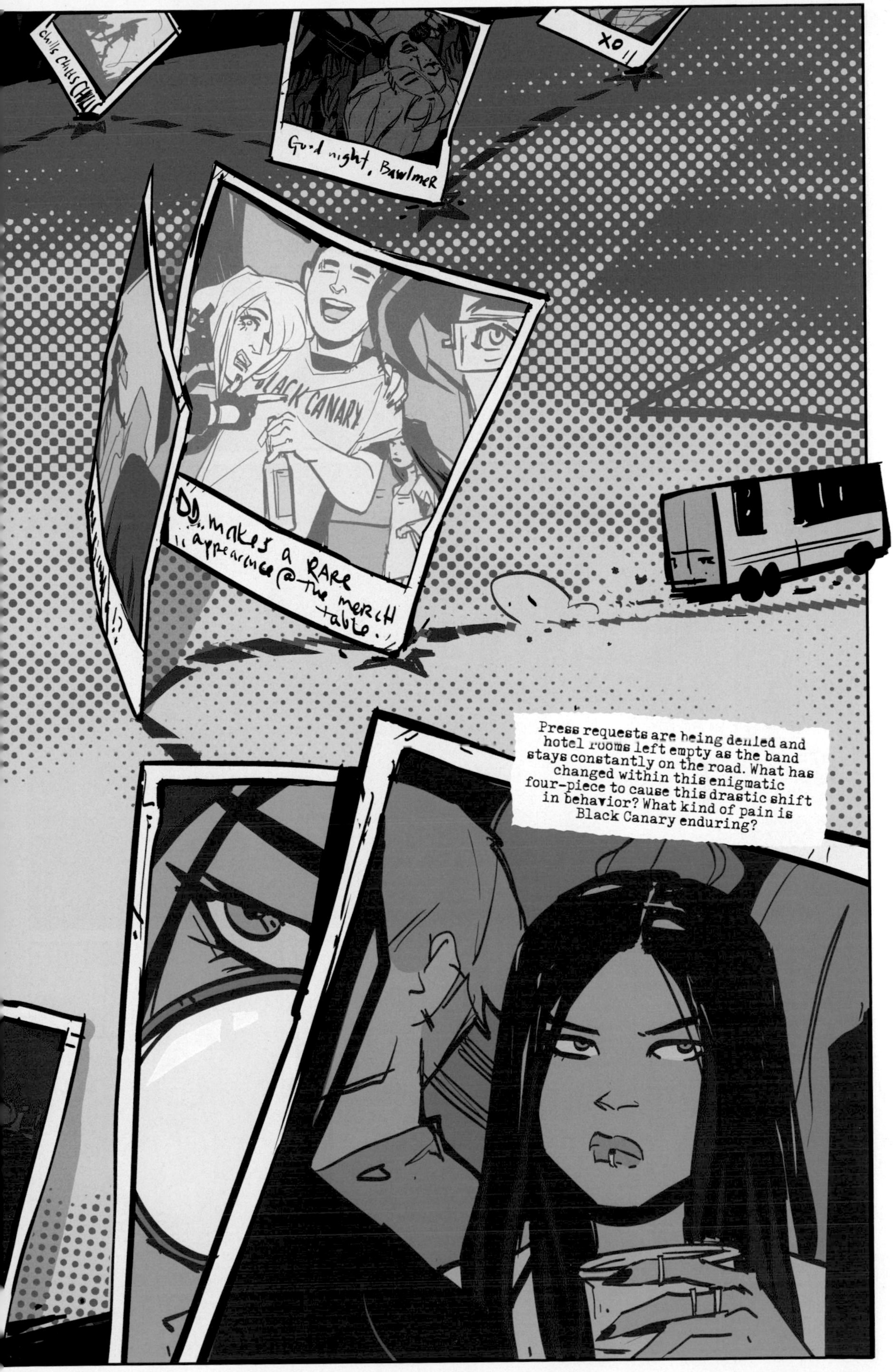
Chills Chills Chill
XO
Good night, Bawlmer
BLACK CANARY
DD makes a RARE appearance @ the merch table.
Press requests are being denied and hotel rooms left empty as the band stays constantly on the road. What has changed within this enigmatic four-piece to cause this drastic shift in behavior? What kind of pain is Black Canary enduring?

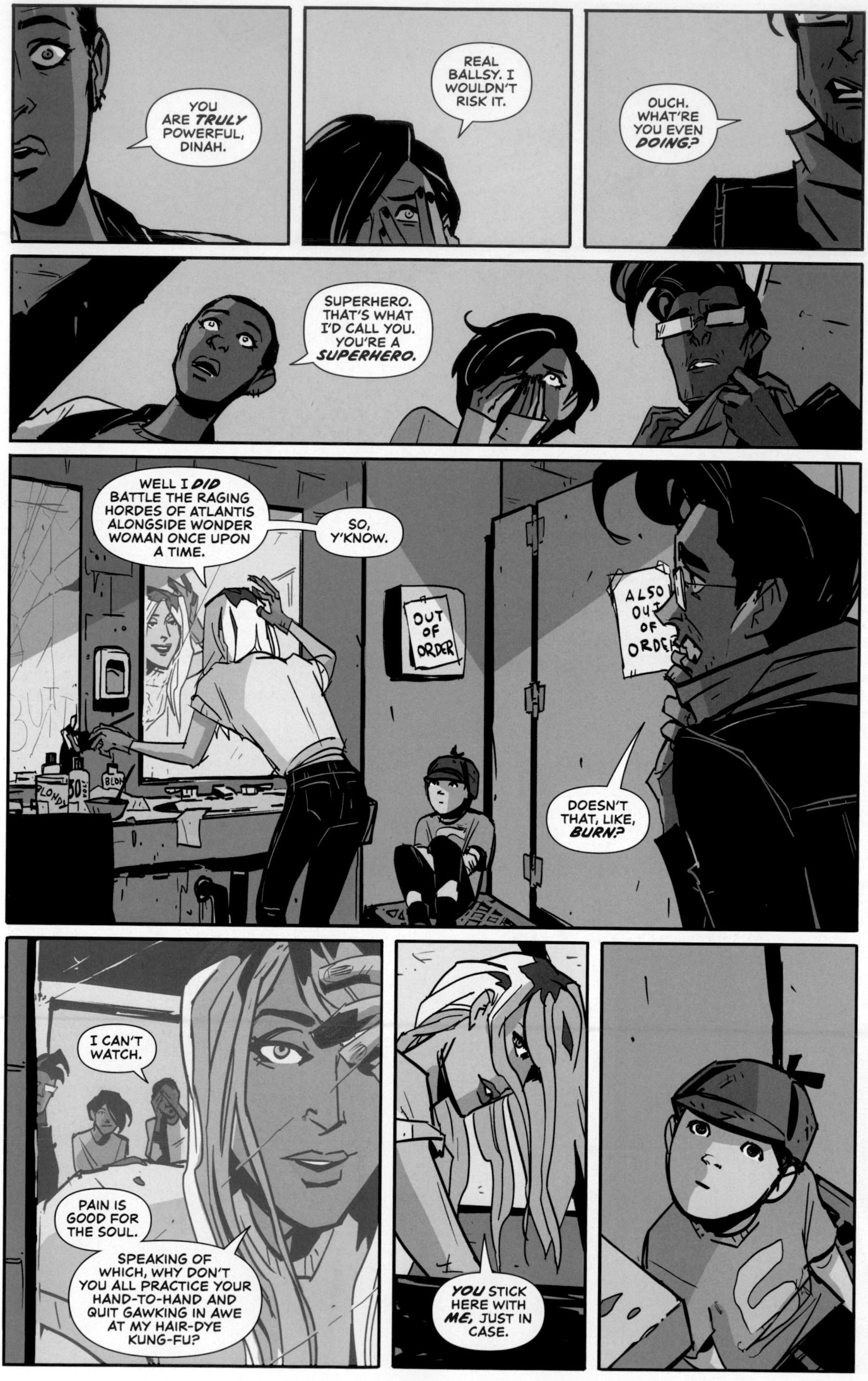
YOU ARE *TRULY* POWERFUL, DINAH.
REAL BALLSY. I WOULDN'T RISK IT.
OUCH. WHAT'RE YOU EVEN *DOING?*
SUPERHERO. THAT'S WHAT I'D CALL YOU. YOU'RE A *SUPERHERO.*
WELL I *DID* BATTLE THE RAGING HORDES OF ATLANTIS ALONGSIDE WONDER WOMAN ONCE UPON A TIME.
SO, Y'KNOW.
OUT OF ORDER
ALSO OUT OF ORDER
BLONDE
DOESN'T THAT, LIKE, *BURN?*
I CAN'T WATCH.
PAIN IS GOOD FOR THE SOUL.
SPEAKING OF WHICH, WHY DON'T YOU ALL PRACTICE YOUR HAND-TO-HAND AND QUIT GAWKING IN AWE AT MY HAIR-DYE KUNG-FU?
YOU STICK HERE WITH *ME,* JUST IN CASE.

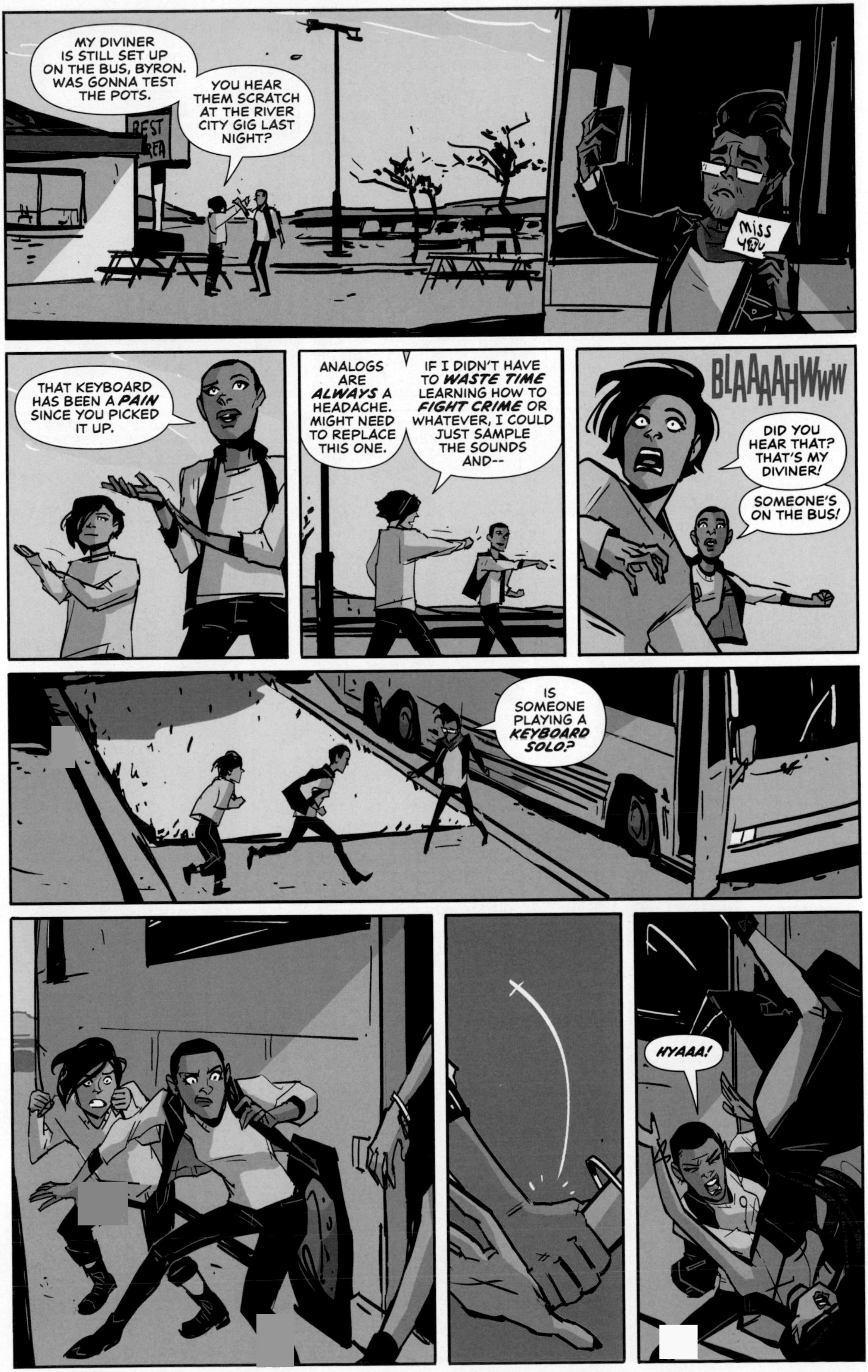
MY DIVINER IS STILL SET UP ON THE BUS, BYRON. WAS GONNA TEST THE POTS.
YOU HEAR THEM SCRATCH AT THE RIVER CITY GIG LAST NIGHT?
REST AREA
MISS YOU
THAT KEYBOARD HAS BEEN A PAIN SINCE YOU PICKED IT UP.
ANALOGS ARE ALWAYS A HEADACHE. MIGHT NEED TO REPLACE THIS ONE.
IF I DIDN'T HAVE TO WASTE TIME LEARNING HOW TO FIGHT CRIME OR WHATEVER, I COULD JUST SAMPLE THE SOUNDS AND--
BLAAAAHWWW
DID YOU HEAR THAT? THAT'S MY DIVINER!
SOMEONE'S ON THE BUS!
IS SOMEONE PLAYING A KEYBOARD SOLO?
HYAAA!

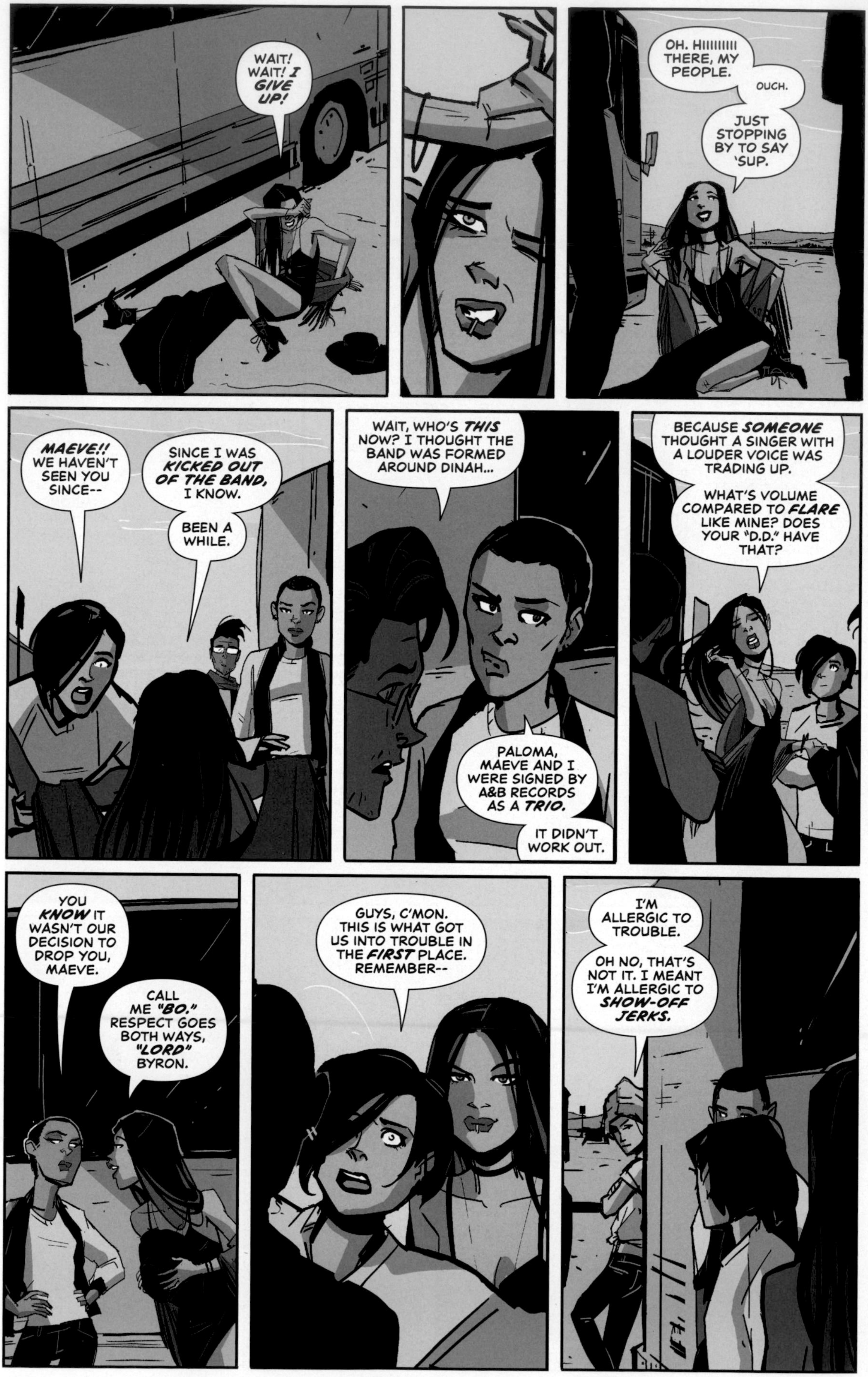
WAIT! WAIT! I GIVE UP!
OH. HIIIIIIIII THERE, MY PEOPLE.
OUCH.
JUST STOPPING BY TO SAY 'SUP.
MAEVE!! WE HAVEN'T SEEN YOU SINCE--
SINCE I WAS KICKED OUT OF THE BAND, I KNOW.
BEEN A WHILE.
WAIT, WHO'S THIS NOW? I THOUGHT THE BAND WAS FORMED AROUND DINAH...
PALOMA, MAEVE AND I WERE SIGNED BY A&B RECORDS AS A TRIO.
IT DIDN'T WORK OUT.
BECAUSE SOMEONE THOUGHT A SINGER WITH A LOUDER VOICE WAS TRADING UP.
WHAT'S VOLUME COMPARED TO FLARE LIKE MINE? DOES YOUR "D.D." HAVE THAT?
YOU KNOW IT WASN'T OUR DECISION TO DROP YOU, MAEVE.
CALL ME "BO." RESPECT GOES BOTH WAYS, "LORD" BYRON.
GUYS, C'MON. THIS IS WHAT GOT US INTO TROUBLE IN THE FIRST PLACE. REMEMBER--
I'M ALLERGIC TO TROUBLE.
OH NO, THAT'S NOT IT. I MEANT I'M ALLERGIC TO SHOW-OFF JERKS.

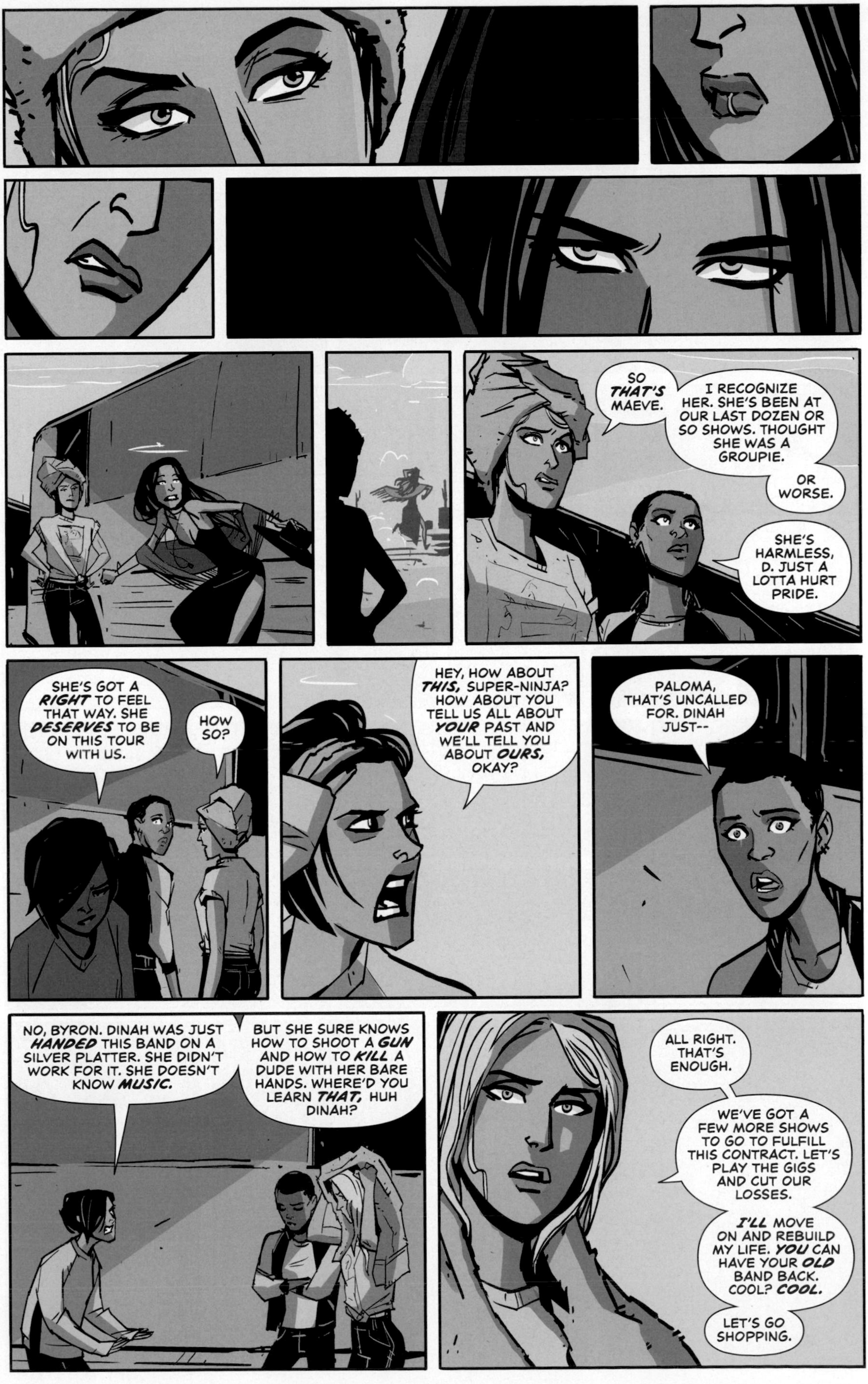

SO *THAT'S* MAEVE.
I RECOGNIZE HER. SHE'S BEEN AT OUR LAST DOZEN OR SO SHOWS. THOUGHT SHE WAS A GROUPIE.
OR WORSE.
SHE'S HARMLESS, D. JUST A LOTTA HURT PRIDE.
SHE'S GOT A *RIGHT* TO FEEL THAT WAY. SHE *DESERVES* TO BE ON THIS TOUR WITH US.
HOW SO?
HEY, HOW ABOUT *THIS,* SUPER-NINJA? HOW ABOUT YOU TELL US ALL ABOUT *YOUR* PAST AND WE'LL TELL YOU ABOUT *OURS,* OKAY?
PALOMA, THAT'S UNCALLED FOR. DINAH JUST--
NO, BYRON. DINAH WAS JUST *HANDED* THIS BAND ON A SILVER PLATTER. SHE DIDN'T WORK FOR IT. SHE DOESN'T KNOW *MUSIC.*
BUT SHE SURE KNOWS HOW TO SHOOT A *GUN* AND HOW TO *KILL* A DUDE WITH HER BARE HANDS. WHERE'D YOU LEARN *THAT,* HUH DINAH?
ALL RIGHT. THAT'S ENOUGH.
WE'VE GOT A FEW MORE SHOWS TO GO TO FULFILL THIS CONTRACT. LET'S PLAY THE GIGS AND CUT OUR LOSSES.
I'LL MOVE ON AND REBUILD MY LIFE. *YOU* CAN HAVE YOUR *OLD* BAND BACK. COOL? *COOL.*
LET'S GO SHOPPING.

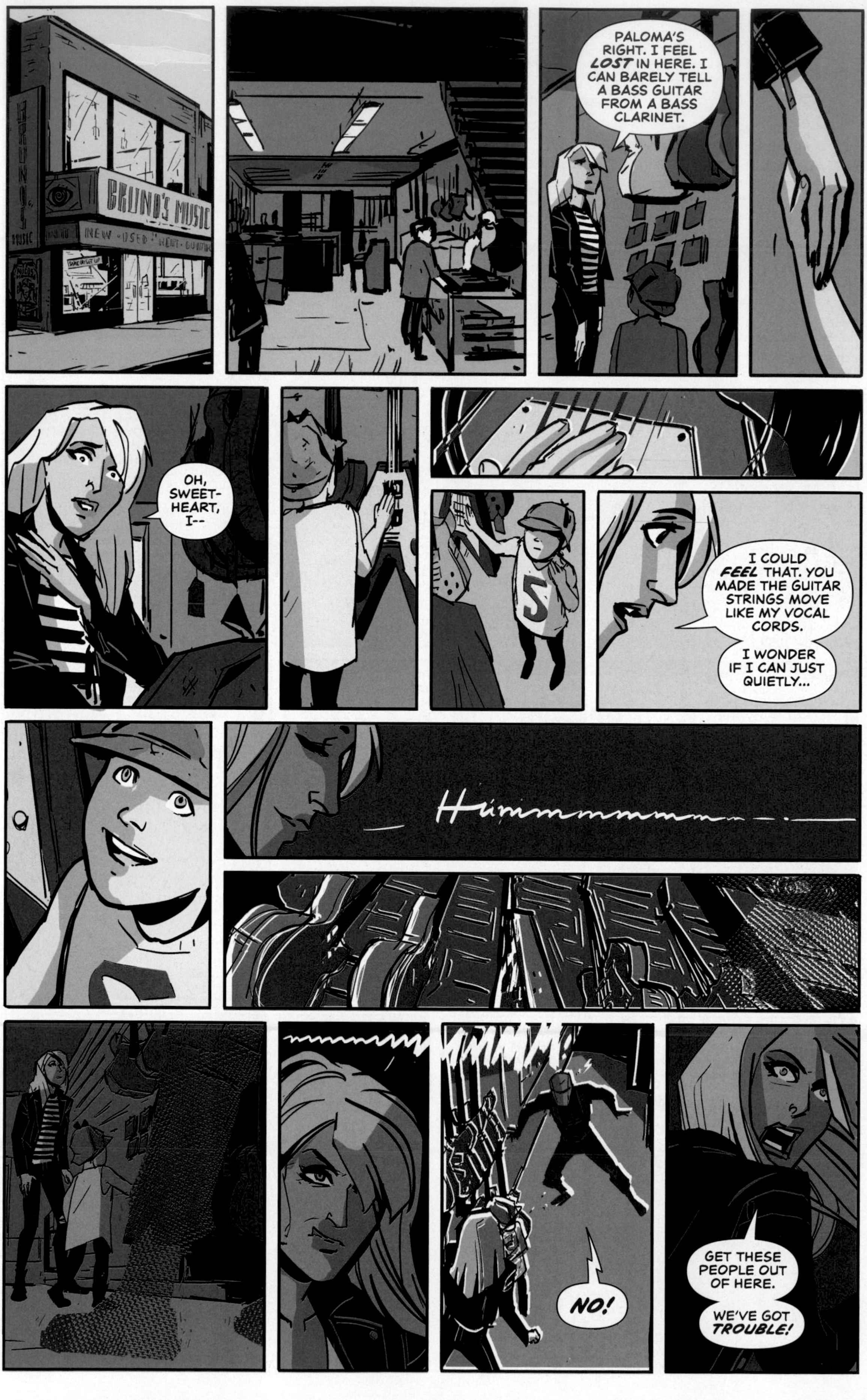
BRUNO'S MUSIC
NEW · USED
PALOMA'S RIGHT. I FEEL *LOST* IN HERE. I CAN BARELY TELL A BASS GUITAR FROM A BASS CLARINET.
OH, SWEET-HEART, I--
I COULD *FEEL* THAT. YOU MADE THE GUITAR STRINGS MOVE LIKE MY VOCAL CORDS.
I WONDER IF I CAN JUST QUIETLY...
Hmmmmmmm
NO!
GET THESE PEOPLE OUT OF HERE.
WE'VE GOT *TROUBLE!*

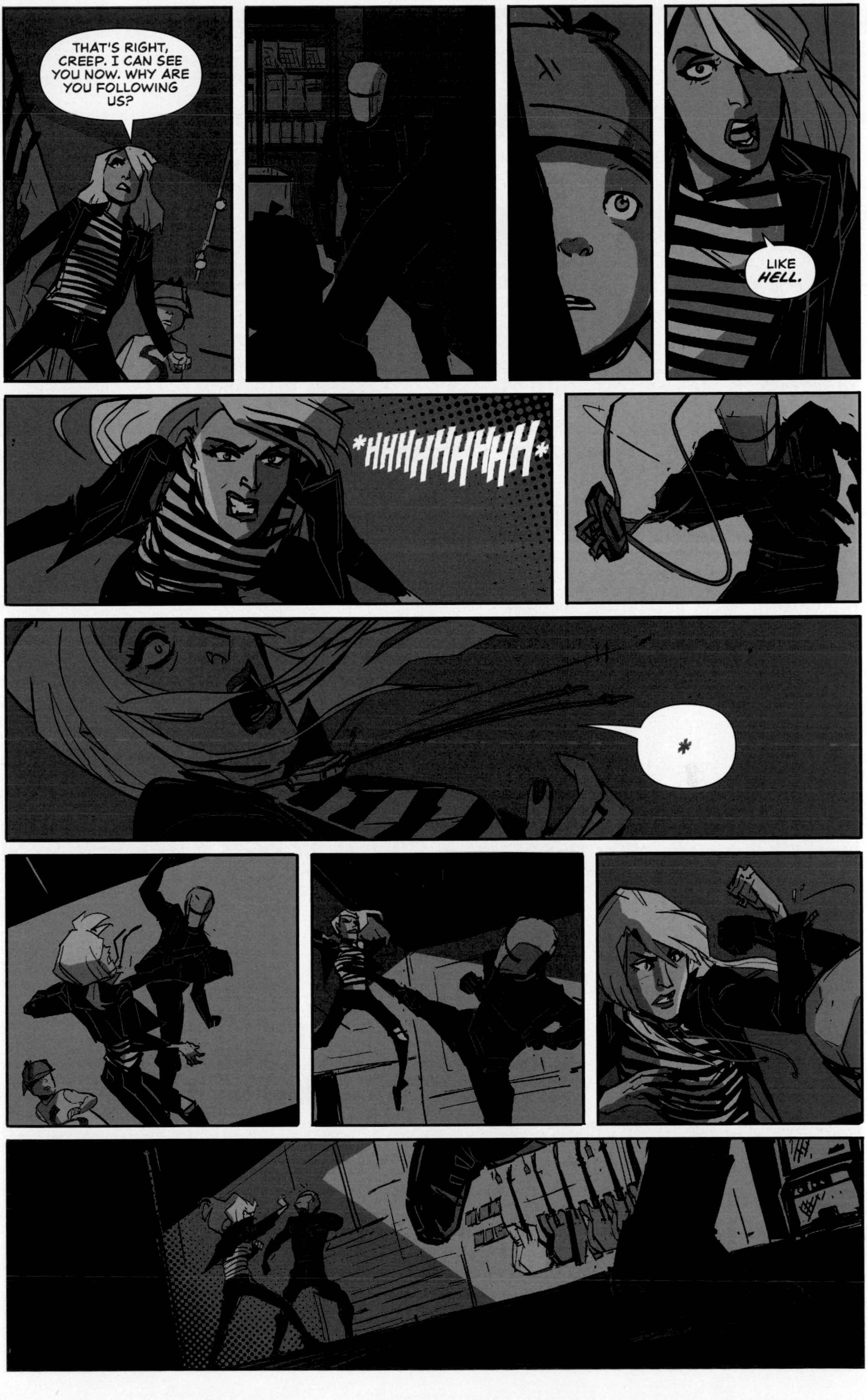
THAT'S RIGHT, CREEP. I CAN SEE YOU NOW. WHY ARE YOU FOLLOWING US?
LIKE *HELL.*
HHHHHHHHH
*

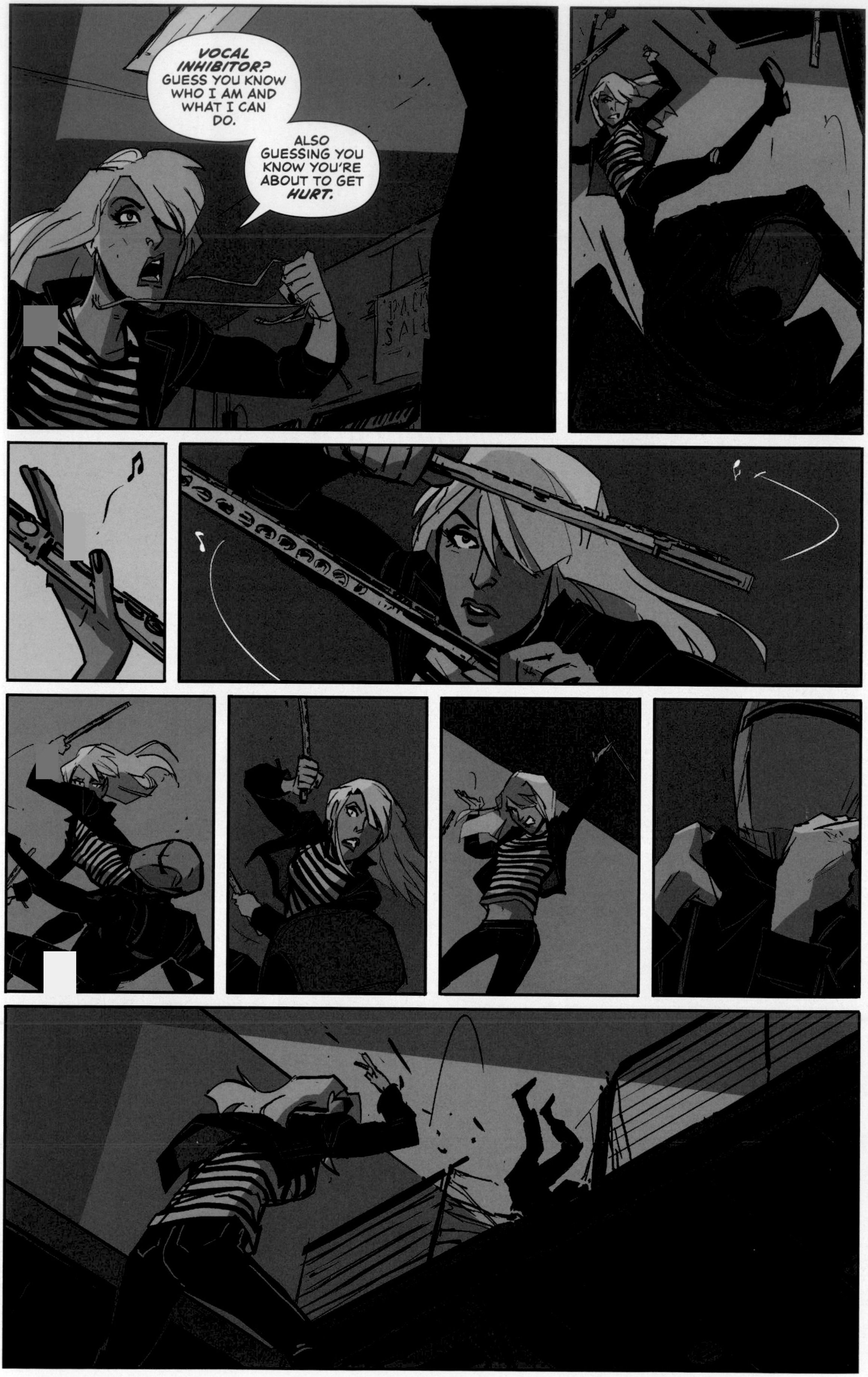
VOCAL INHIBITOR? GUESS YOU KNOW WHO I AM AND WHAT I CAN DO.
ALSO GUESSING YOU KNOW YOU'RE ABOUT TO GET HURT.

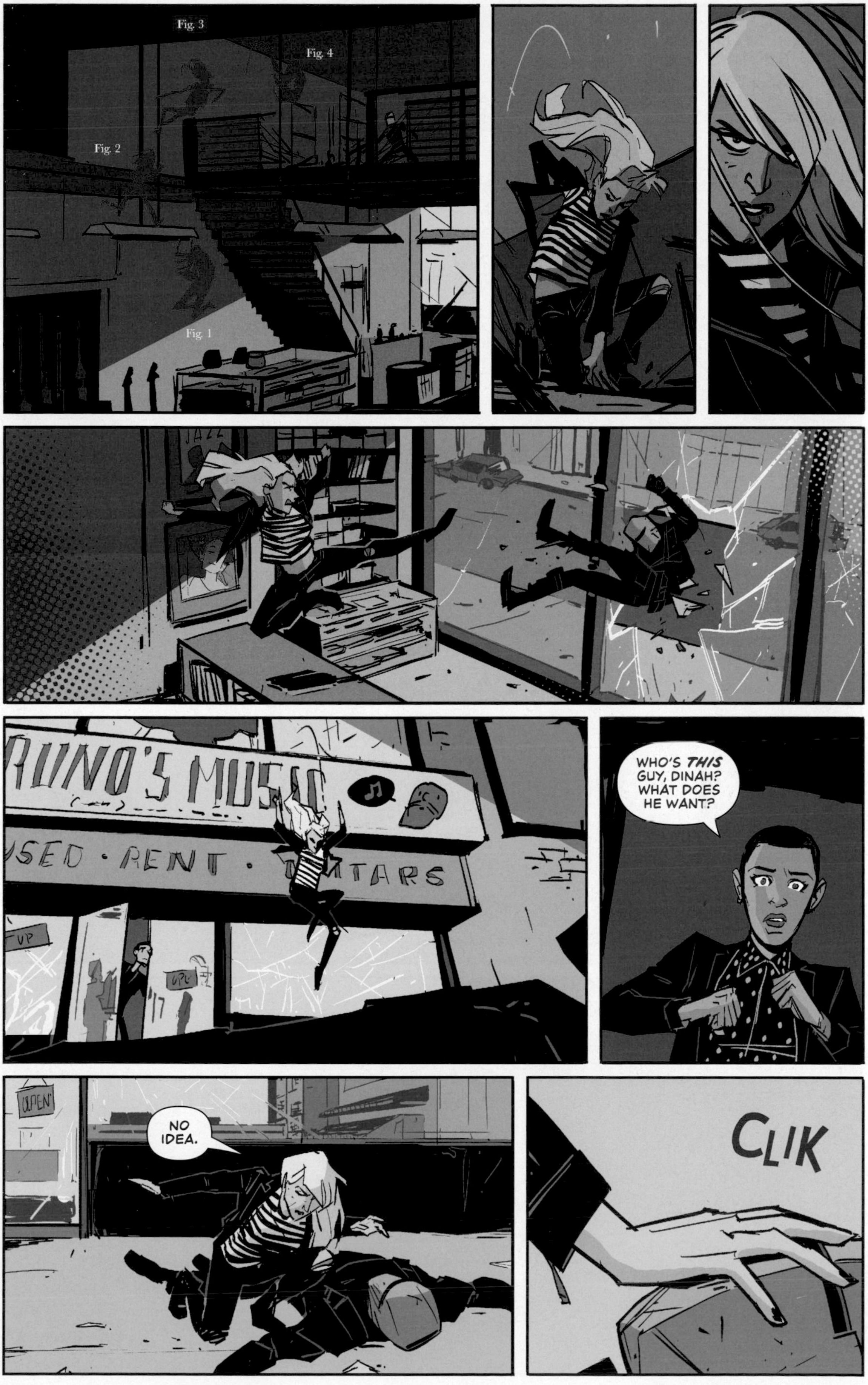
Fig. 3
Fig. 4
Fig. 2
Fig. 1
WHO'S *THIS* GUY, DINAH? WHAT DOES HE WANT?
OPEN
NO IDEA.
CLIK

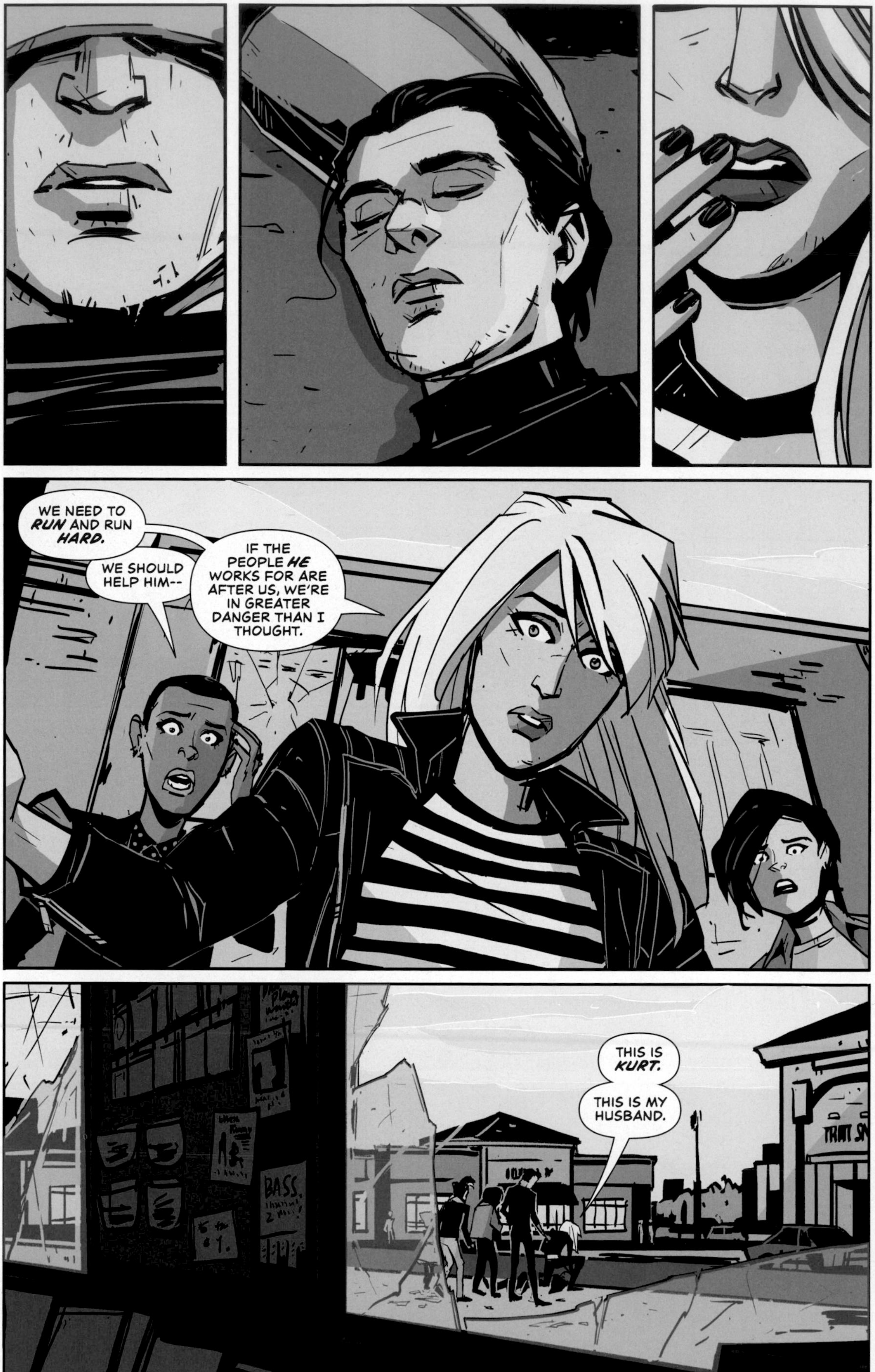
WE NEED TO RUN AND RUN HARD.
WE SHOULD HELP HIM--
IF THE PEOPLE HE WORKS FOR ARE AFTER US, WE'RE IN GREATER DANGER THAN I THOUGHT.
THIS IS KURT.
THIS IS MY HUSBAND.

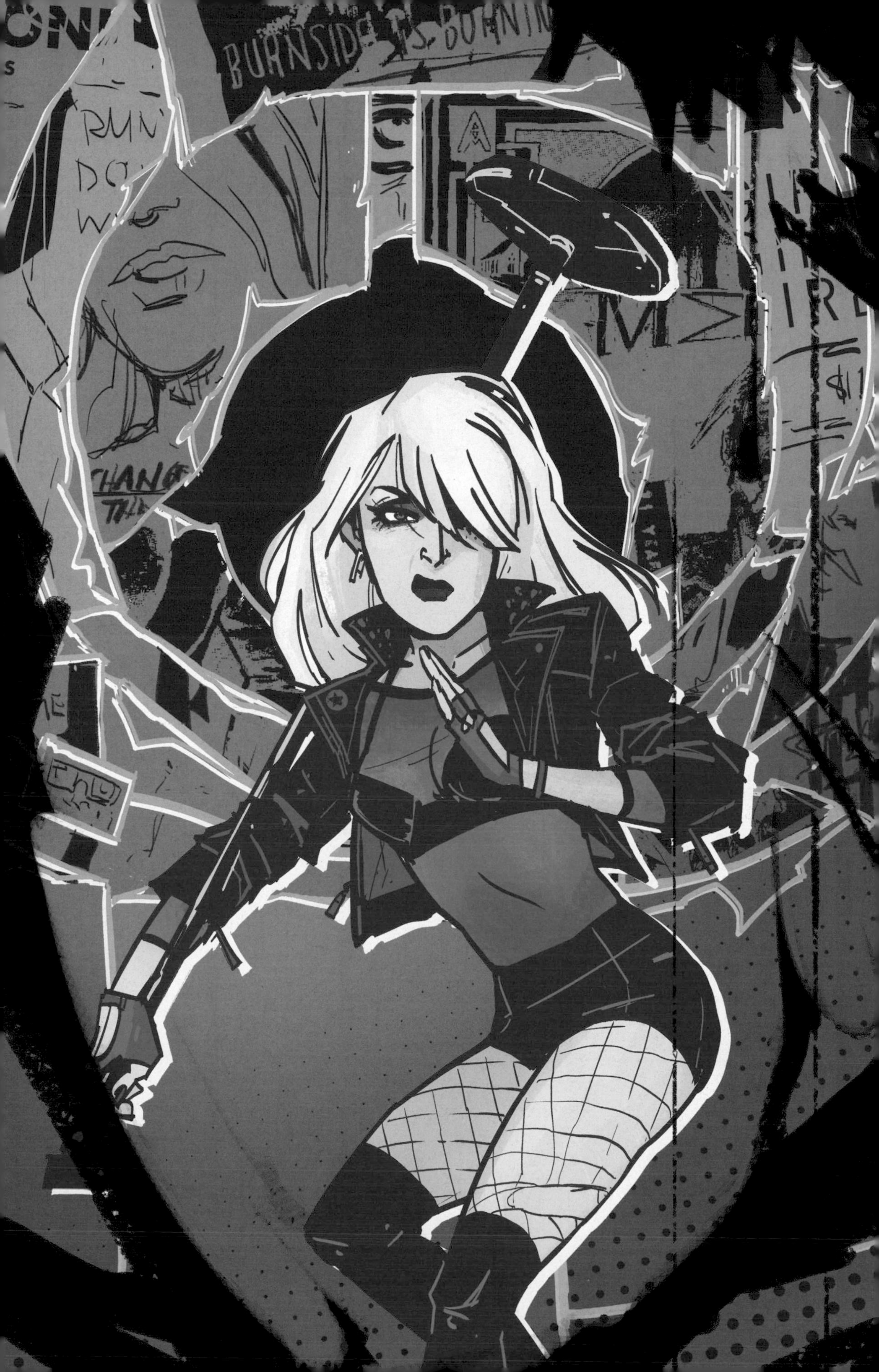

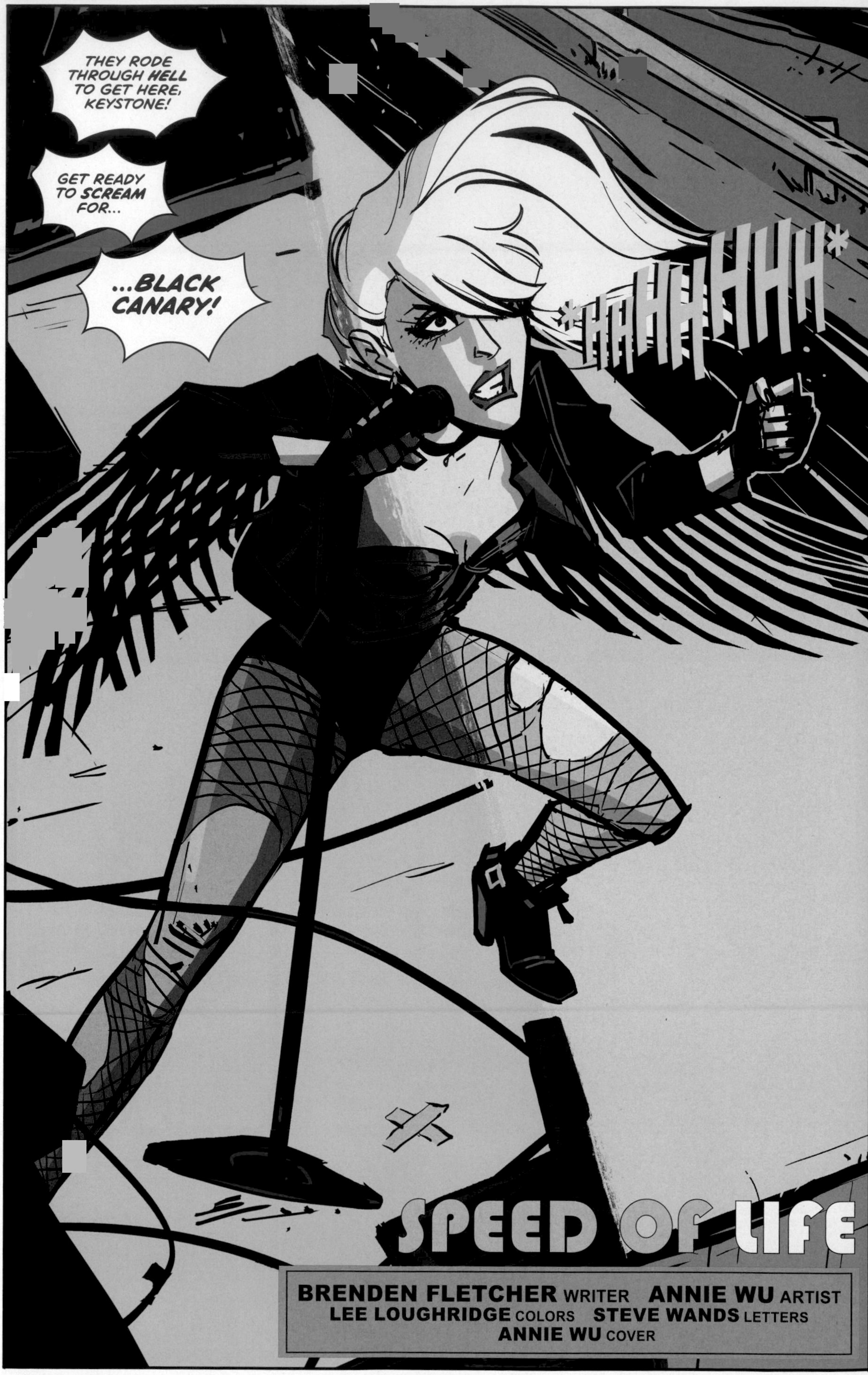

THEY RODE THROUGH HELL TO GET HERE, KEYSTONE!
GET READY TO SCREAM FOR...
...BLACK CANARY!
HAHHHHHH
SPEED OF LIFE
BRENDEN FLETCHER WRITER ANNIE WU ARTIST
LEE LOUGHRIDGE COLORS STEVE WANDS LETTERS
ANNIE WU COVER

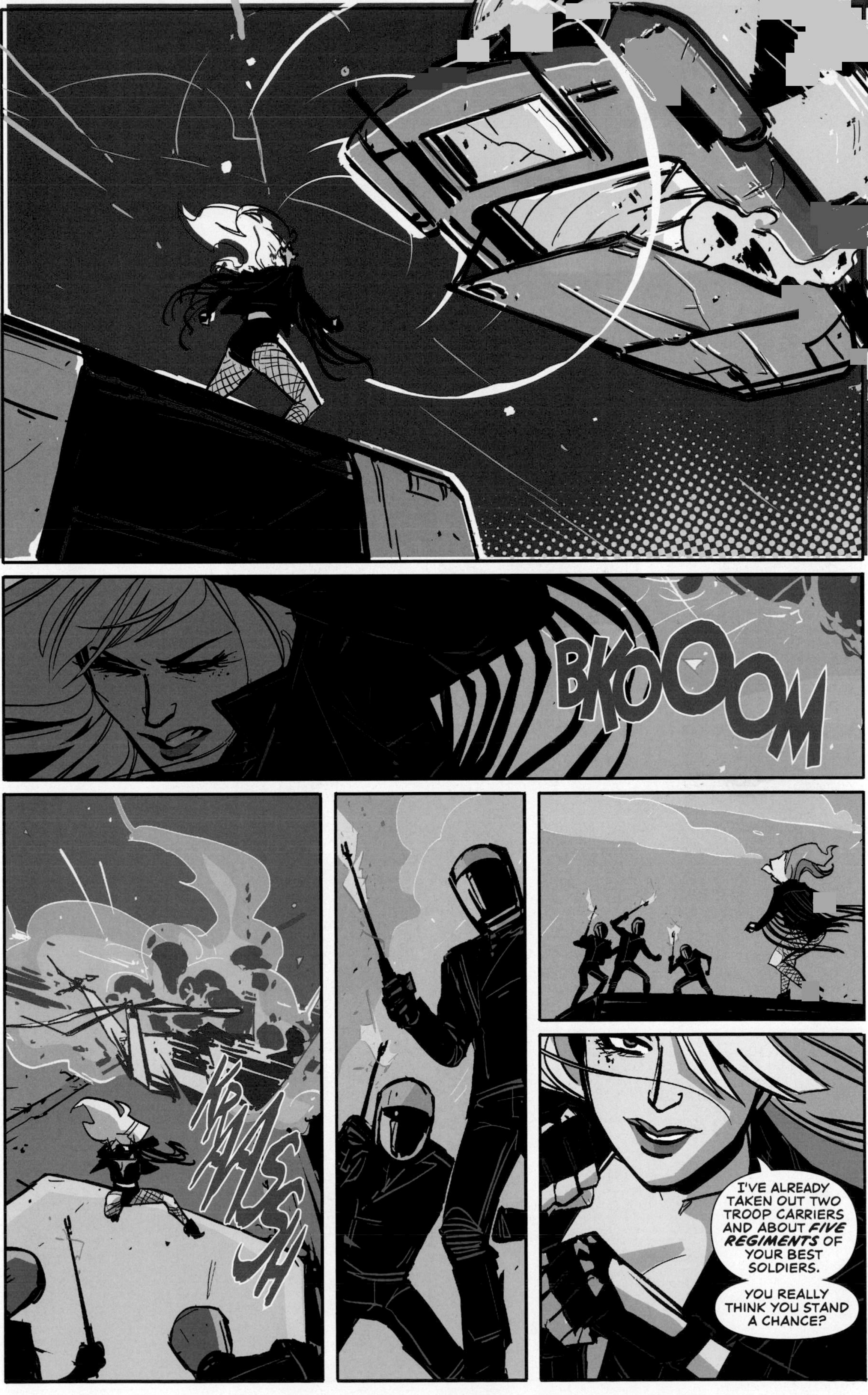
BKOOOM
I'VE ALREADY TAKEN OUT TWO TROOP CARRIERS AND ABOUT *FIVE REGIMENTS* OF YOUR BEST SOLDIERS.
YOU REALLY THINK YOU STAND A CHANCE?

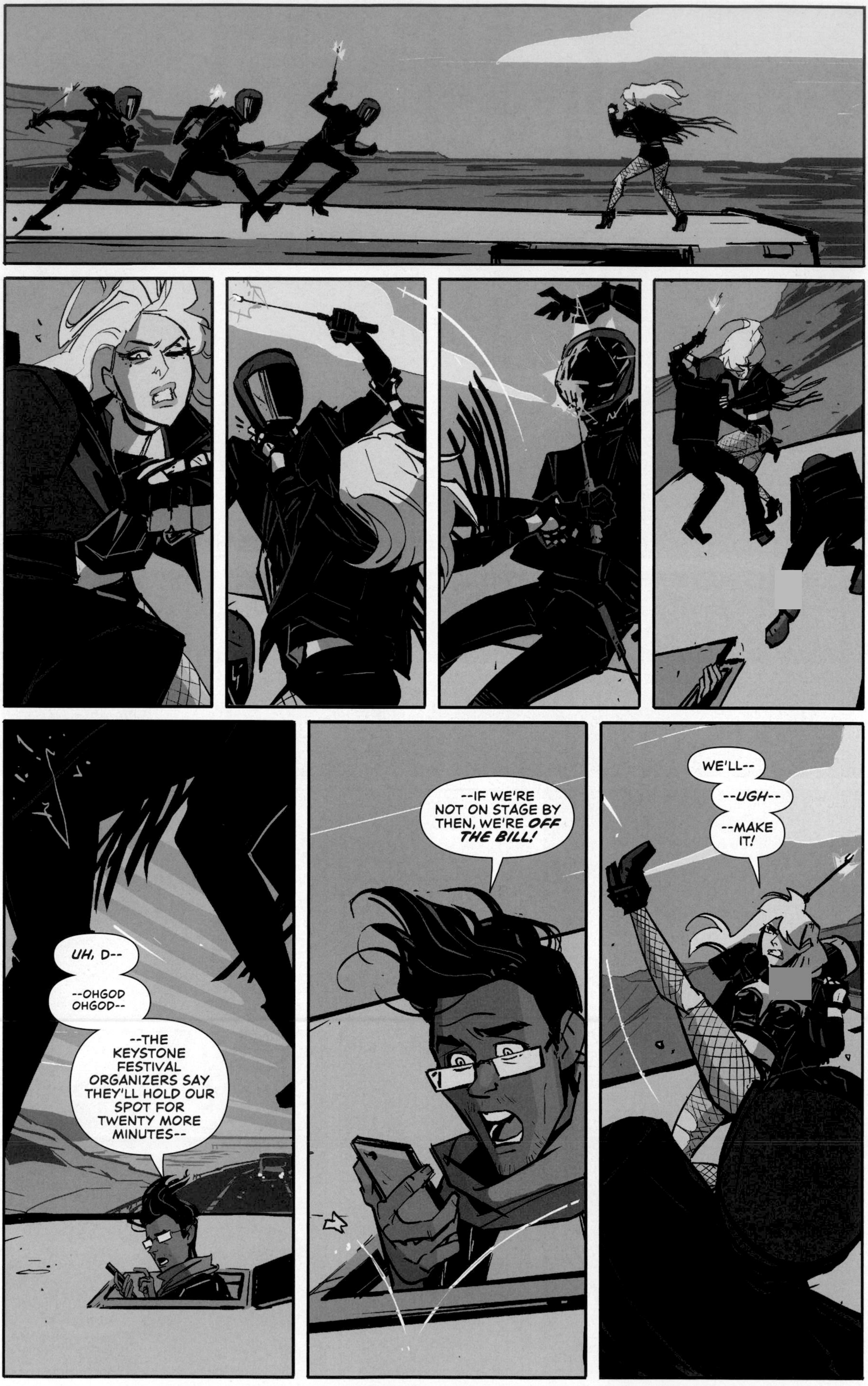
UH, D--
--OHGOD OHGOD--
--THE KEYSTONE FESTIVAL ORGANIZERS SAY THEY'LL HOLD OUR SPOT FOR TWENTY MORE MINUTES--
--IF WE'RE NOT ON STAGE BY THEN, WE'RE *OFF THE BILL!*
WE'LL--
--*UGH*--
--MAKE IT!

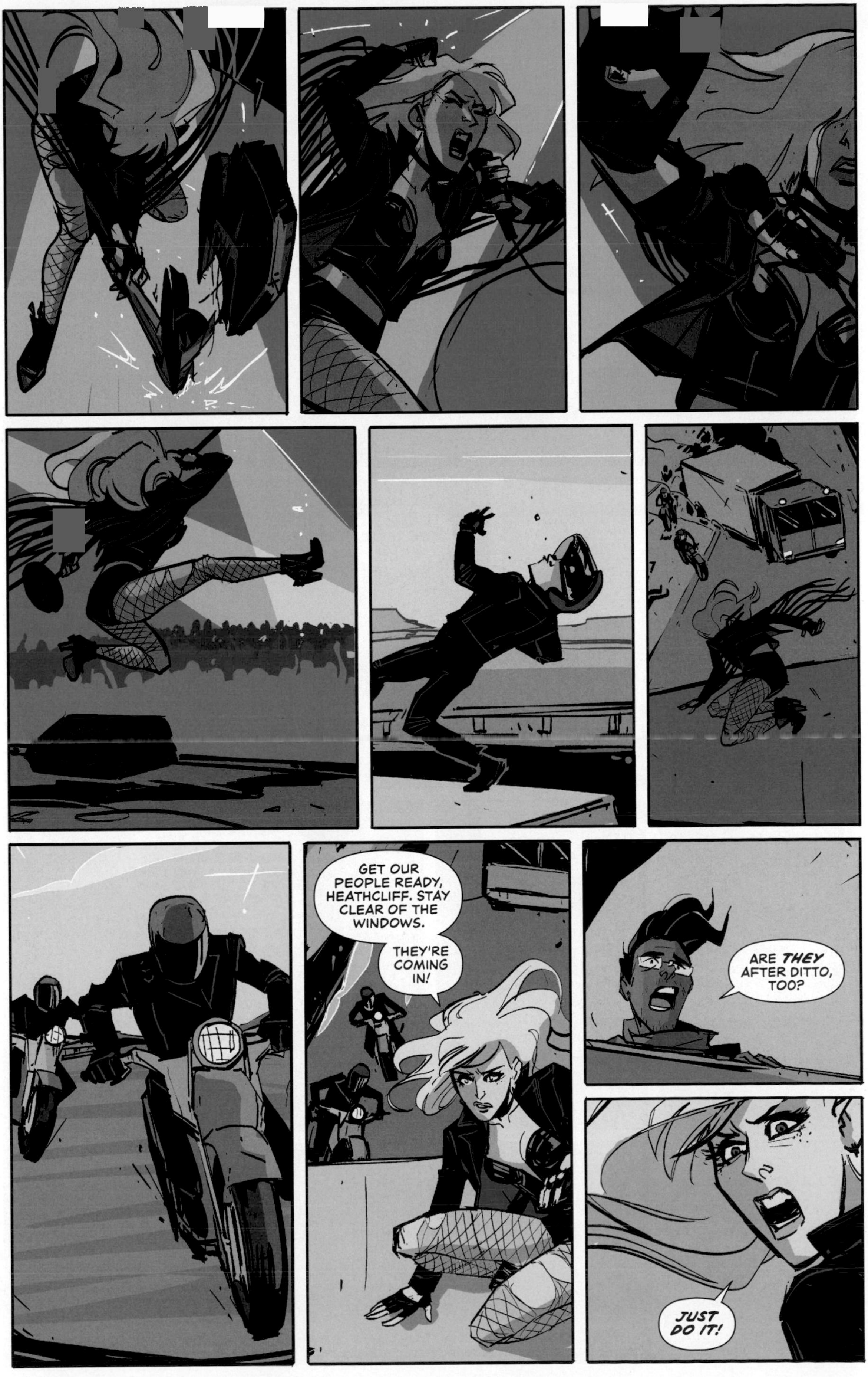
GET OUR PEOPLE READY, HEATHCLIFF. STAY CLEAR OF THE WINDOWS.
THEY'RE COMING IN!
ARE *THEY* AFTER DITTO, TOO?
JUST DO IT!

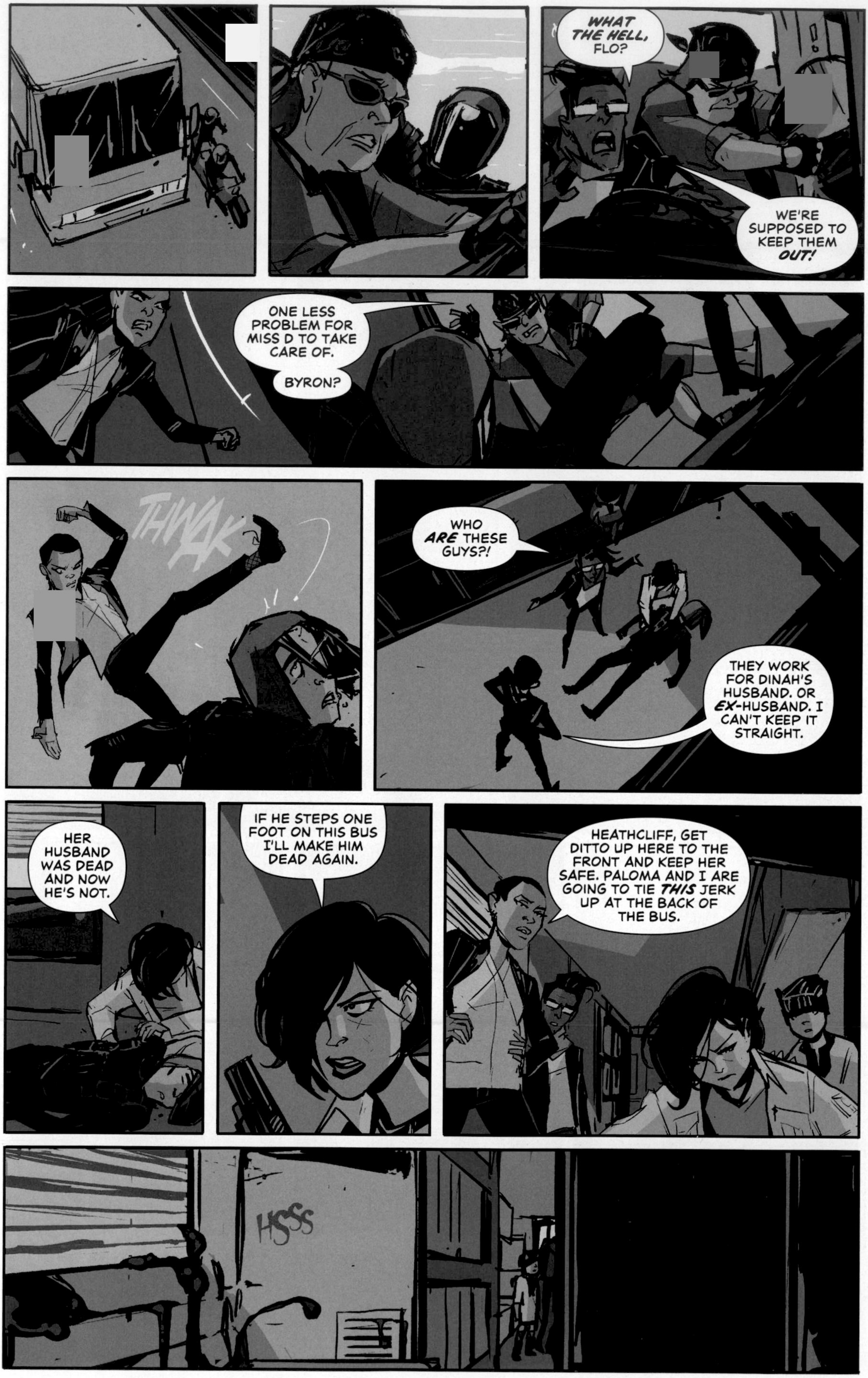
WHAT THE HELL, FLO?
WE'RE SUPPOSED TO KEEP THEM OUT!
ONE LESS PROBLEM FOR MISS D TO TAKE CARE OF.
BYRON?
THWAK
WHO ARE THESE GUYS?!
THEY WORK FOR DINAH'S HUSBAND. OR EX-HUSBAND. I CAN'T KEEP IT STRAIGHT.
HER HUSBAND WAS DEAD AND NOW HE'S NOT.
IF HE STEPS ONE FOOT ON THIS BUS I'LL MAKE HIM DEAD AGAIN.
HEATHCLIFF, GET DITTO UP HERE TO THE FRONT AND KEEP HER SAFE. PALOMA AND I ARE GOING TO TIE THIS JERK UP AT THE BACK OF THE BUS.
HSSS

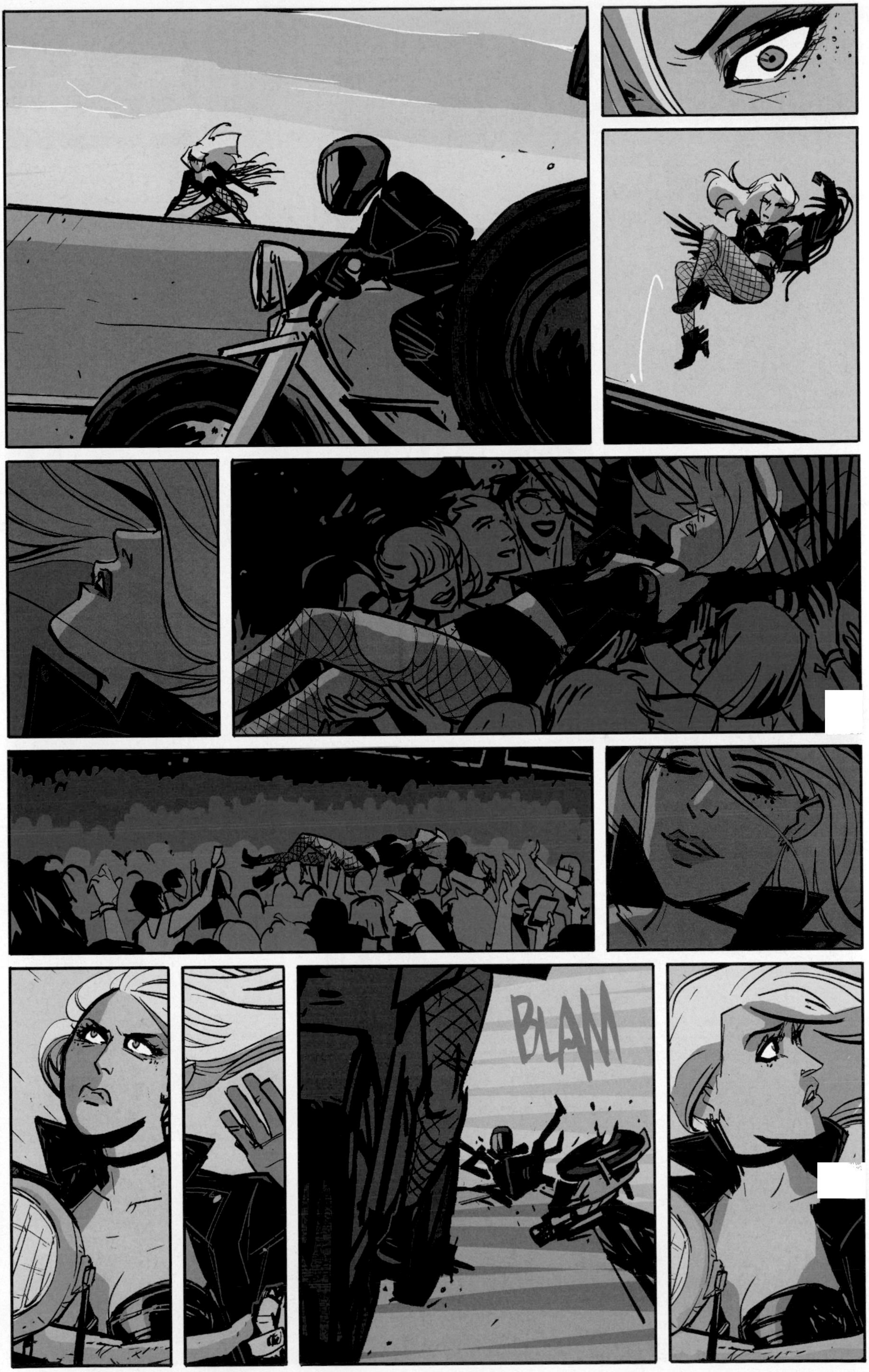
BLAM

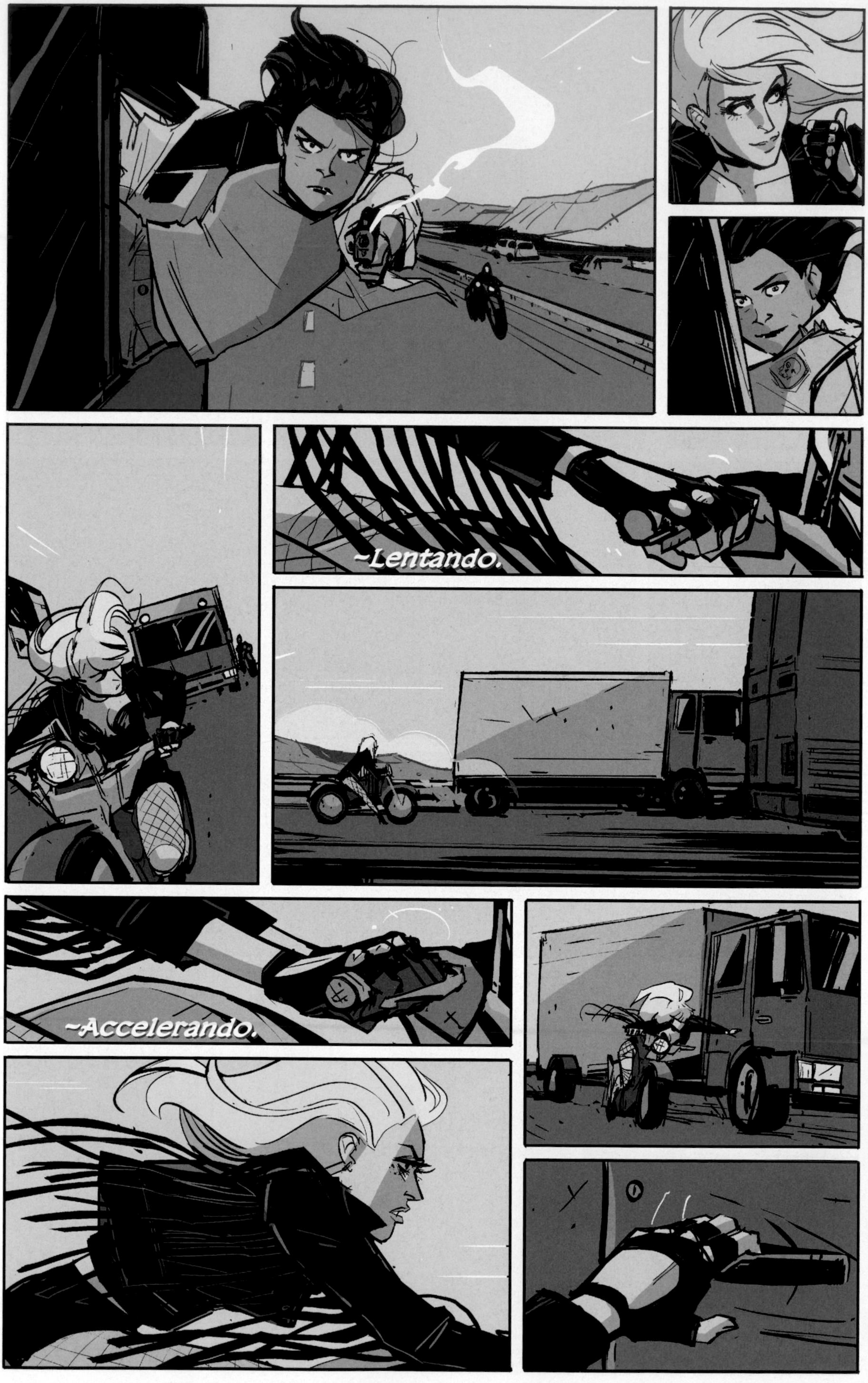
~Lentando.
~Accelerando.

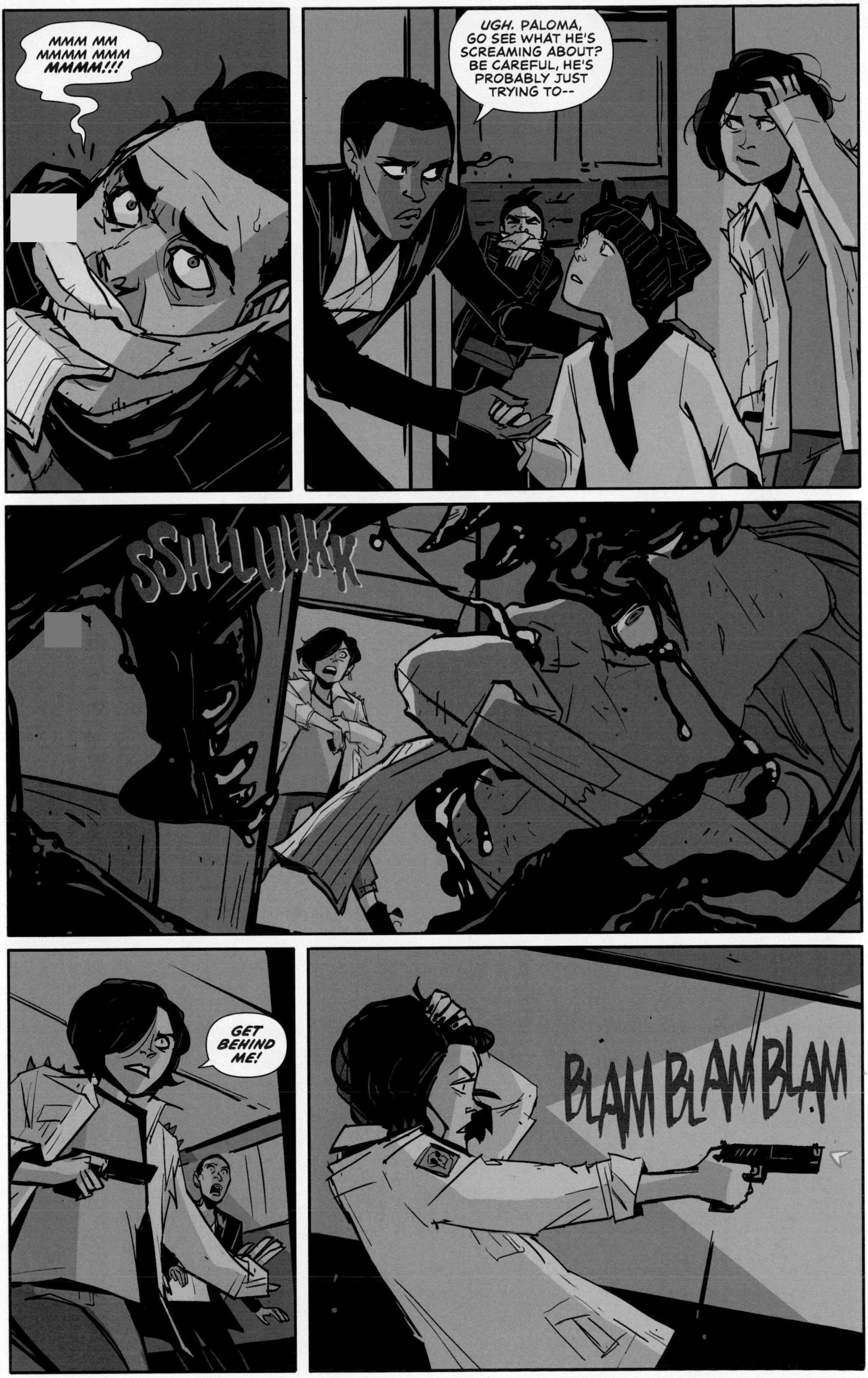
MMM MM
MMMM MMM
MMMM!!!
UGH. PALOMA, GO SEE WHAT HE'S SCREAMING ABOUT? BE CAREFUL, HE'S PROBABLY JUST TRYING TO--
SSHLLUUKK
GET BEHIND ME!
BLAM BLAM BLAM

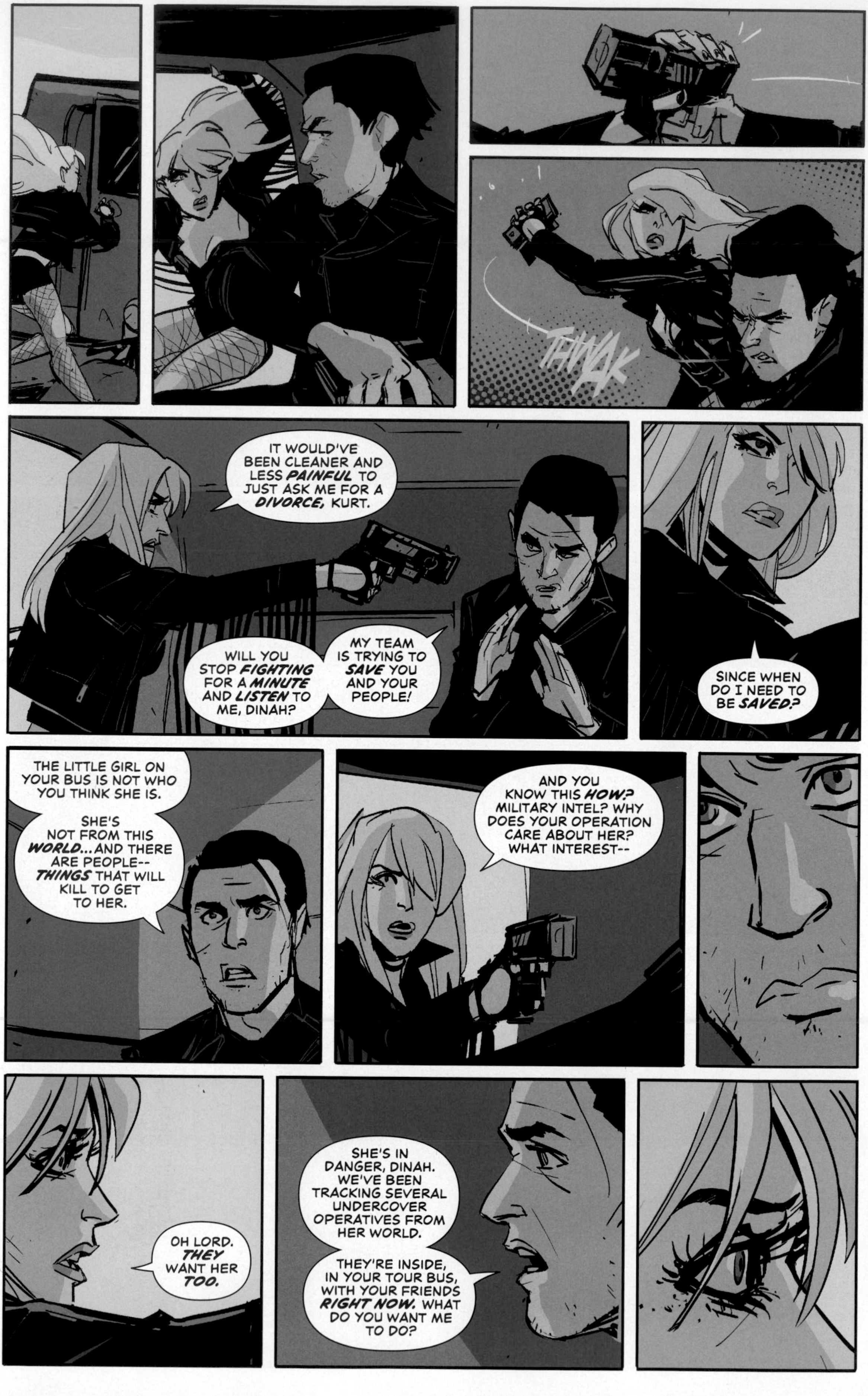
THWAK
IT WOULD'VE BEEN CLEANER AND LESS PAINFUL TO JUST ASK ME FOR A DIVORCE, KURT.
WILL YOU STOP FIGHTING FOR A MINUTE AND LISTEN TO ME, DINAH?
MY TEAM IS TRYING TO SAVE YOU AND YOUR PEOPLE!
SINCE WHEN DO I NEED TO BE SAVED?
THE LITTLE GIRL ON YOUR BUS IS NOT WHO YOU THINK SHE IS.
SHE'S NOT FROM THIS WORLD...AND THERE ARE PEOPLE-- THINGS THAT WILL KILL TO GET TO HER.
AND YOU KNOW THIS HOW? MILITARY INTEL? WHY DOES YOUR OPERATION CARE ABOUT HER? WHAT INTEREST--
OH LORD. THEY WANT HER TOO.
SHE'S IN DANGER, DINAH. WE'VE BEEN TRACKING SEVERAL UNDERCOVER OPERATIVES FROM HER WORLD.
THEY'RE INSIDE, IN YOUR TOUR BUS, WITH YOUR FRIENDS RIGHT NOW. WHAT DO YOU WANT ME TO DO?

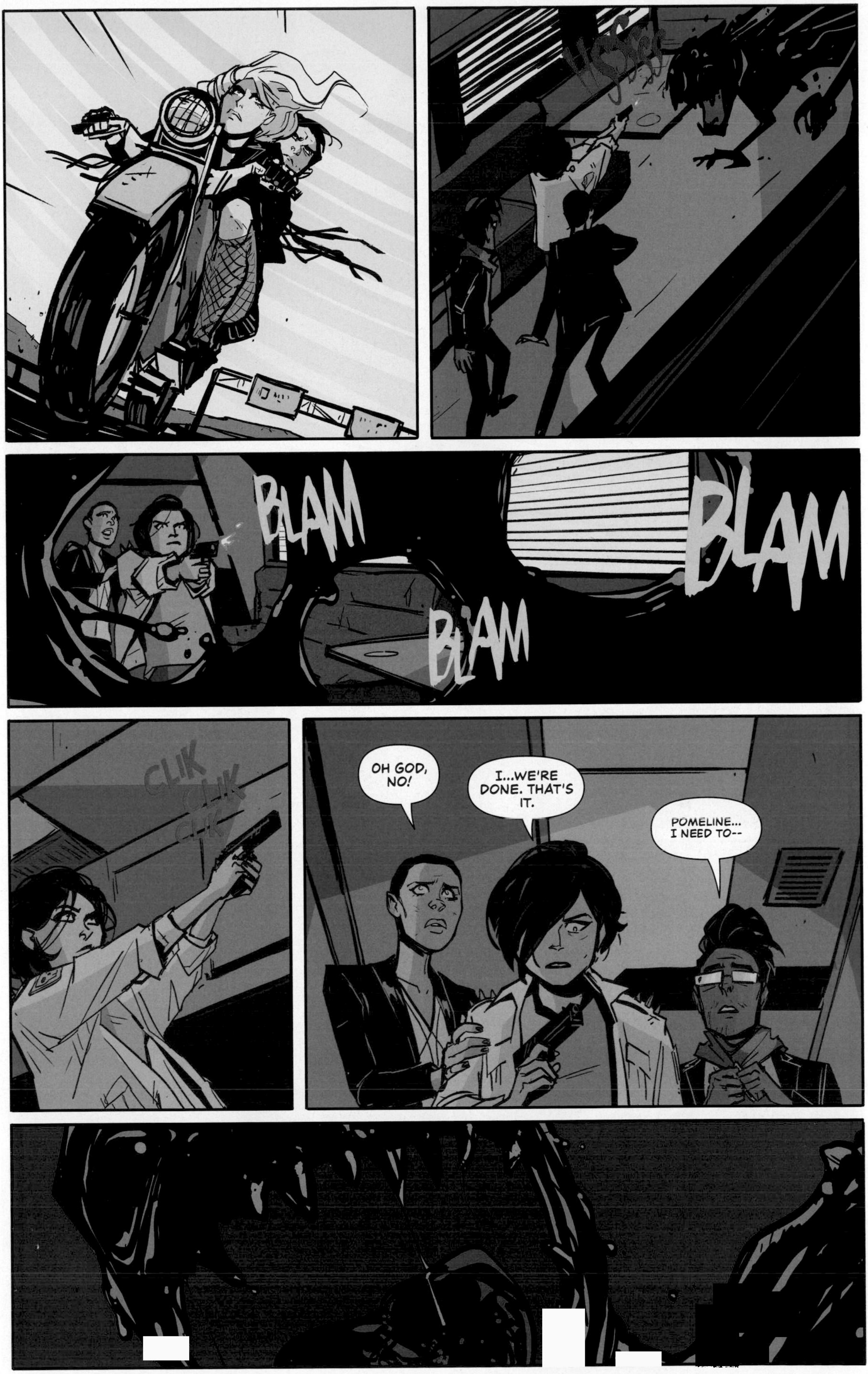
HSSSS
BLAM
BLAM
BLAM
CLIK
CLIK
CLIK
OH GOD, NO!
I...WE'RE DONE. THAT'S IT.
POMELINE... I NEED TO--

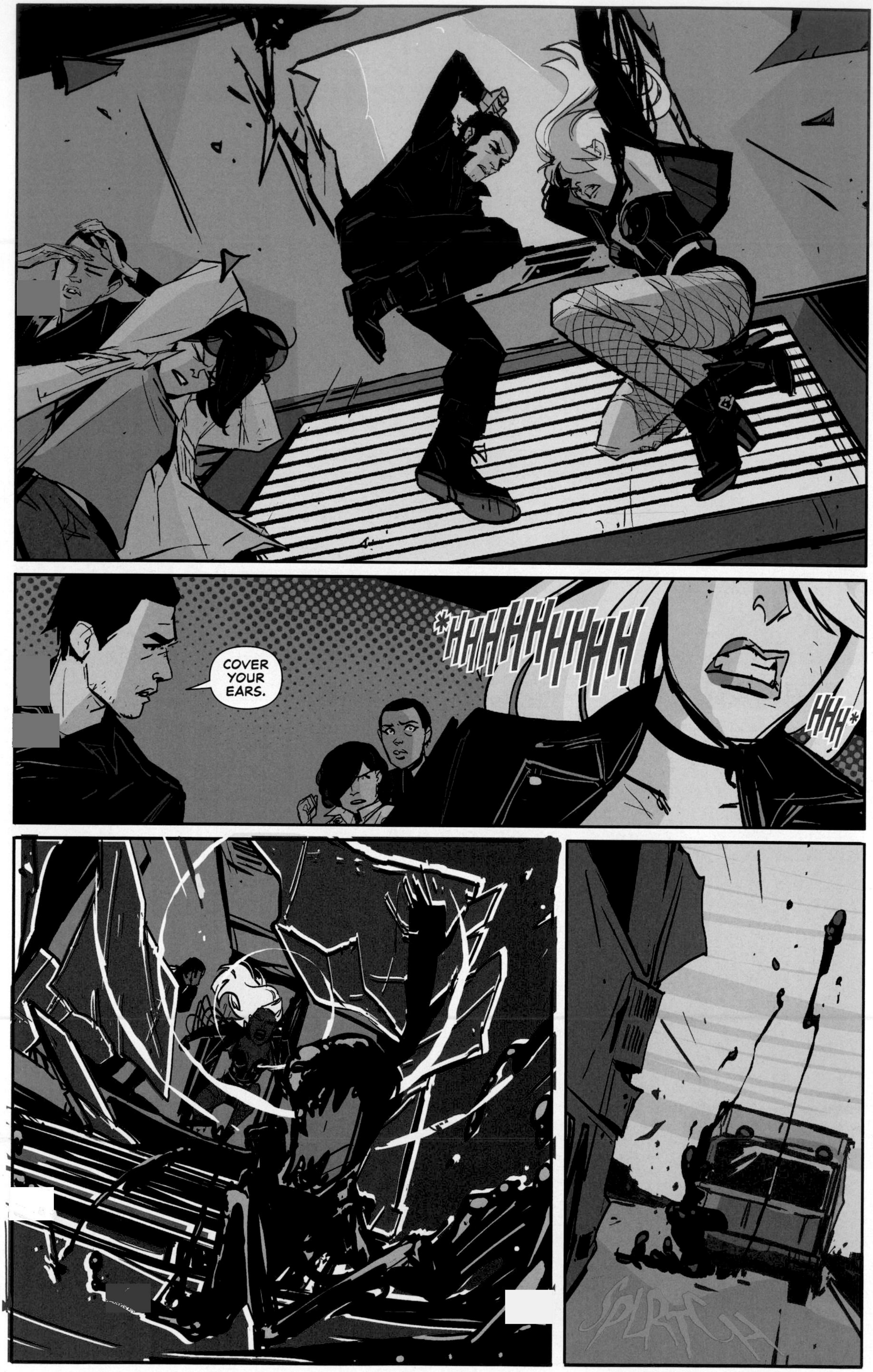
COVER YOUR EARS.
*HHHHHHHHHH
HHH*

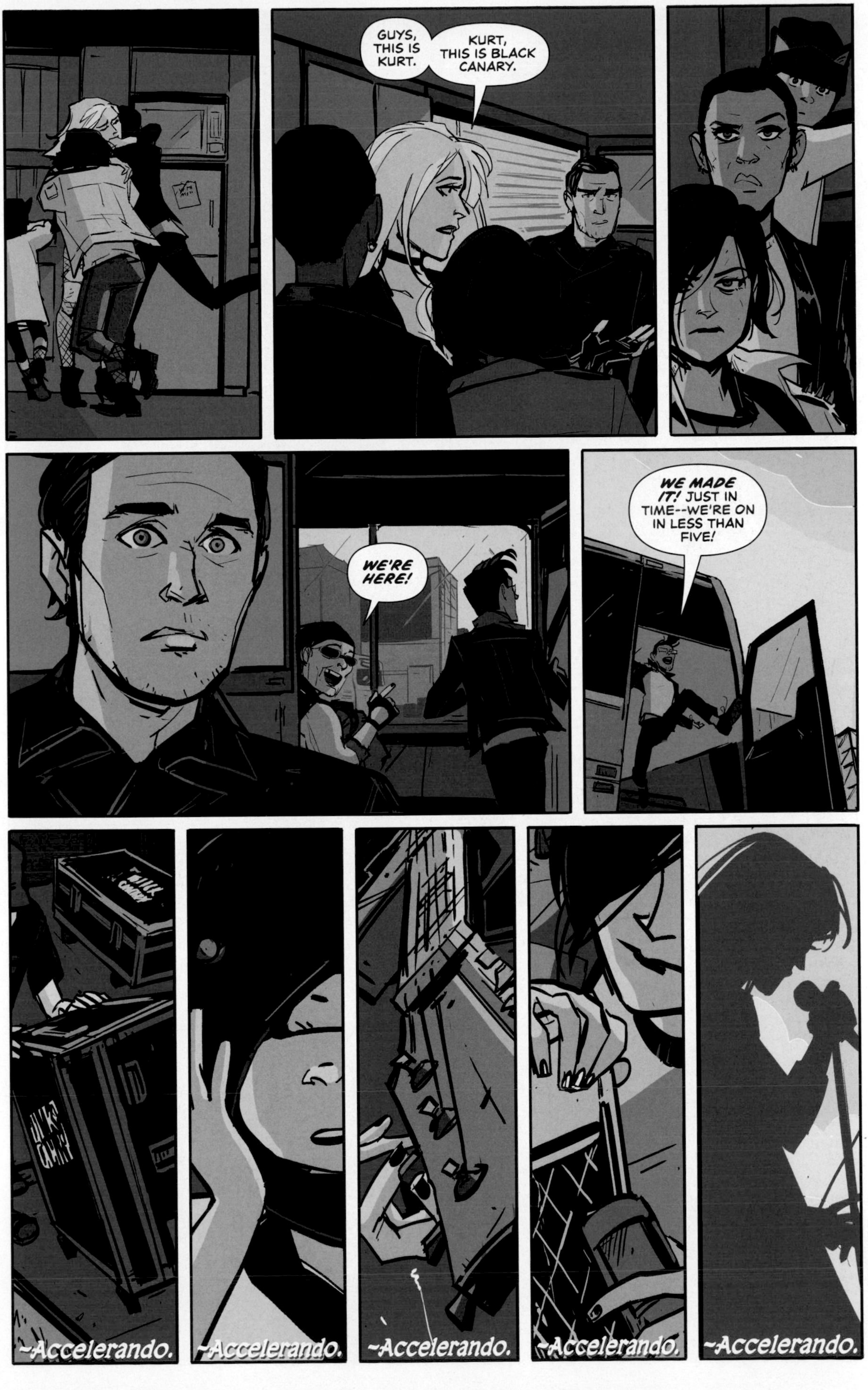
GUYS, THIS IS KURT.
KURT, THIS IS BLACK CANARY.
WE'RE HERE!
WE MADE IT! JUST IN TIME--WE'RE ON IN LESS THAN FIVE!
~Accelerando.
~Accelerando.
~Accelerando.
~Accelerando.
~Accelerando.

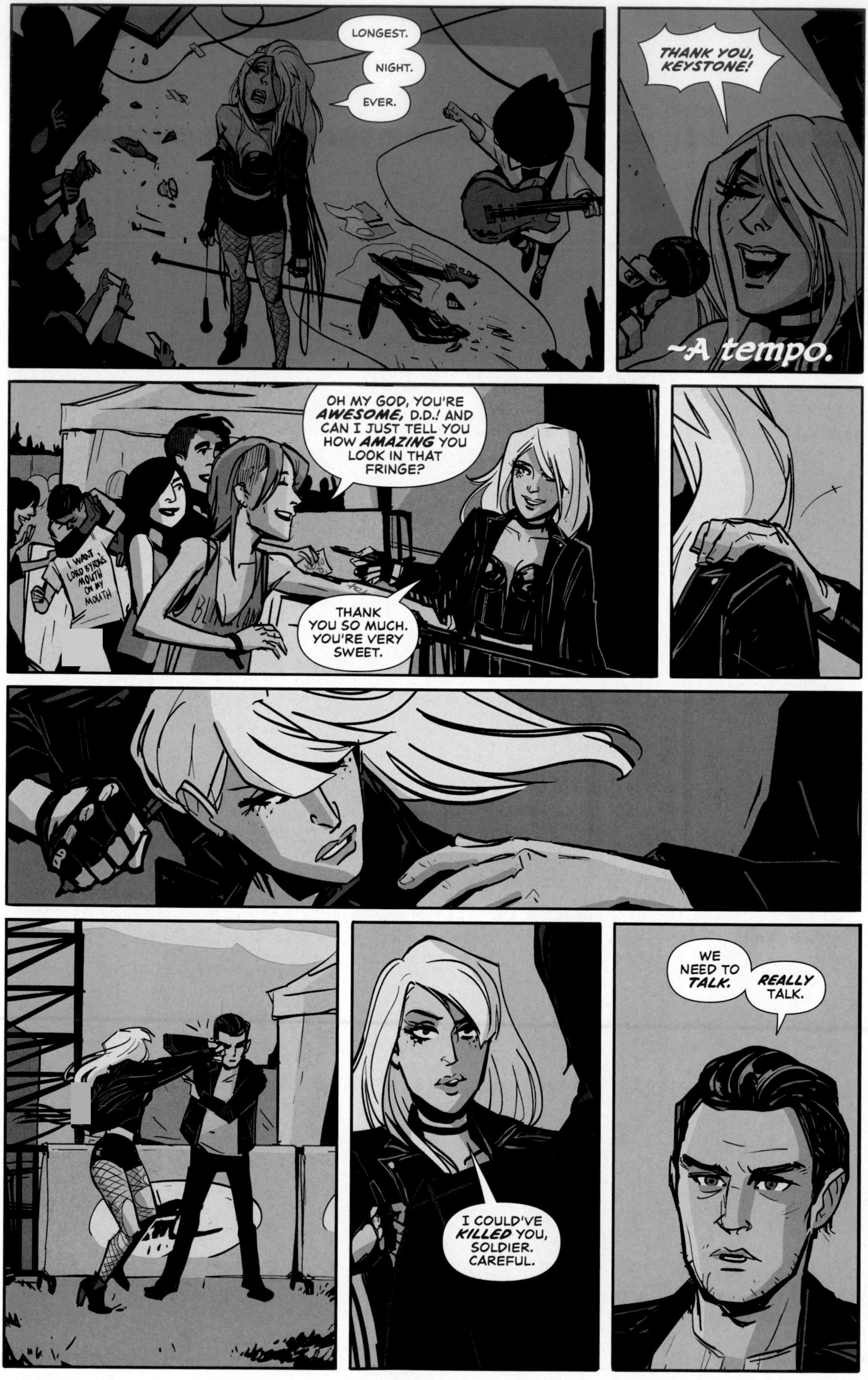
LONGEST.
NIGHT.
EVER.
THANK YOU, KEYSTONE!
~A tempo.
OH MY GOD, YOU'RE AWESOME, D.D.! AND CAN I JUST TELL YOU HOW AMAZING YOU LOOK IN THAT FRINGE?
I WANT LORD BYRON'S MOUTH ON MY MOUTH
THANK YOU SO MUCH. YOU'RE VERY SWEET.
I COULD'VE KILLED YOU, SOLDIER. CAREFUL.
WE NEED TO TALK.
REALLY TALK.

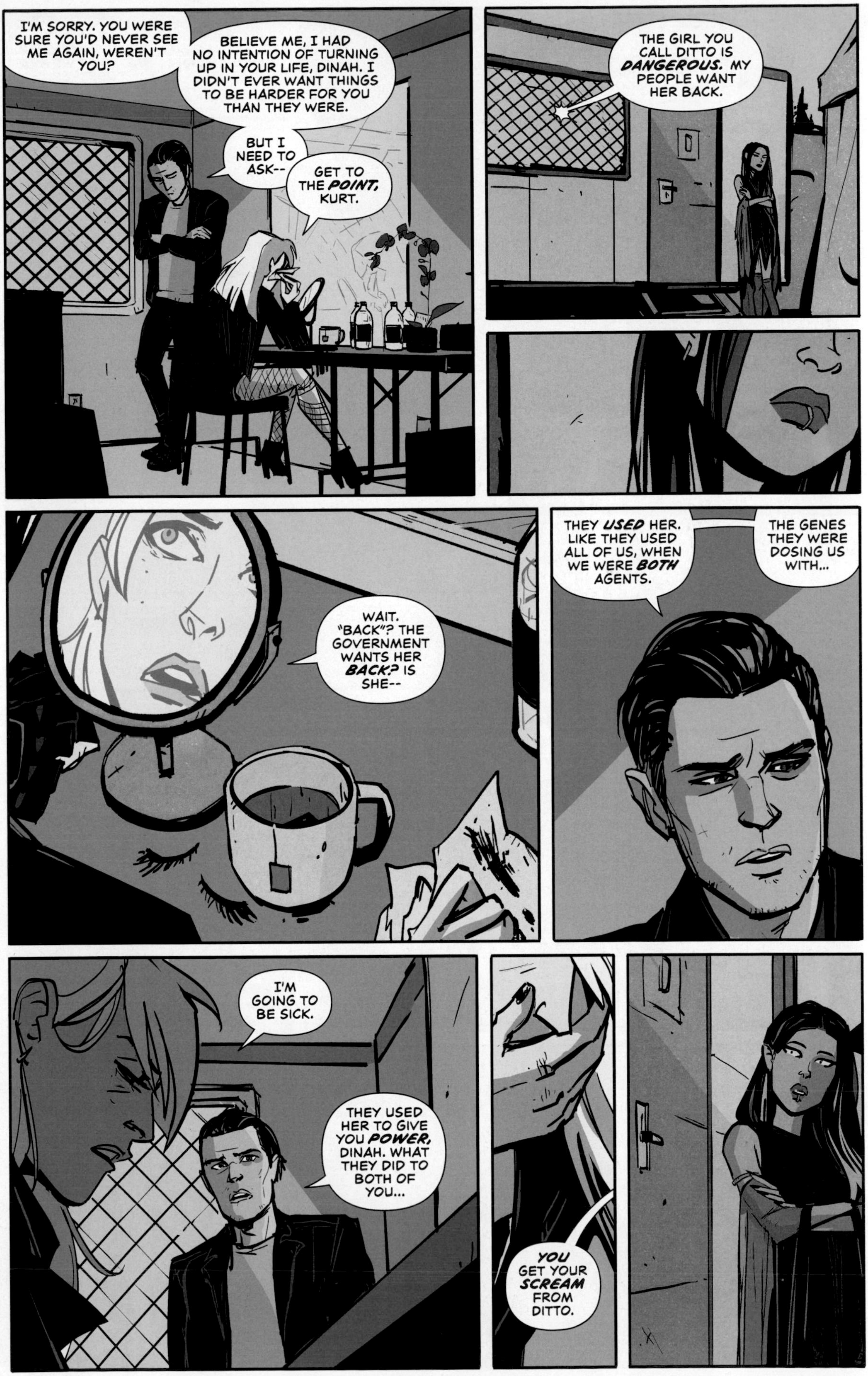
I'M SORRY. YOU WERE SURE YOU'D NEVER SEE ME AGAIN, WEREN'T YOU?
BELIEVE ME, I HAD NO INTENTION OF TURNING UP IN YOUR LIFE, DINAH. I DIDN'T EVER WANT THINGS TO BE HARDER FOR YOU THAN THEY WERE.
BUT I NEED TO ASK--
GET TO THE *POINT,* KURT.
THE GIRL YOU CALL DITTO IS *DANGEROUS.* MY PEOPLE WANT HER BACK.
WAIT. "BACK"? THE GOVERNMENT WANTS HER *BACK?* IS SHE--
THEY *USED* HER. LIKE THEY USED ALL OF US, WHEN WE WERE *BOTH* AGENTS.
THE GENES THEY WERE DOSING US WITH...
I'M GOING TO BE SICK.
THEY USED HER TO GIVE YOU *POWER,* DINAH. WHAT THEY DID TO BOTH OF YOU...
YOU GET YOUR *SCREAM* FROM DITTO.

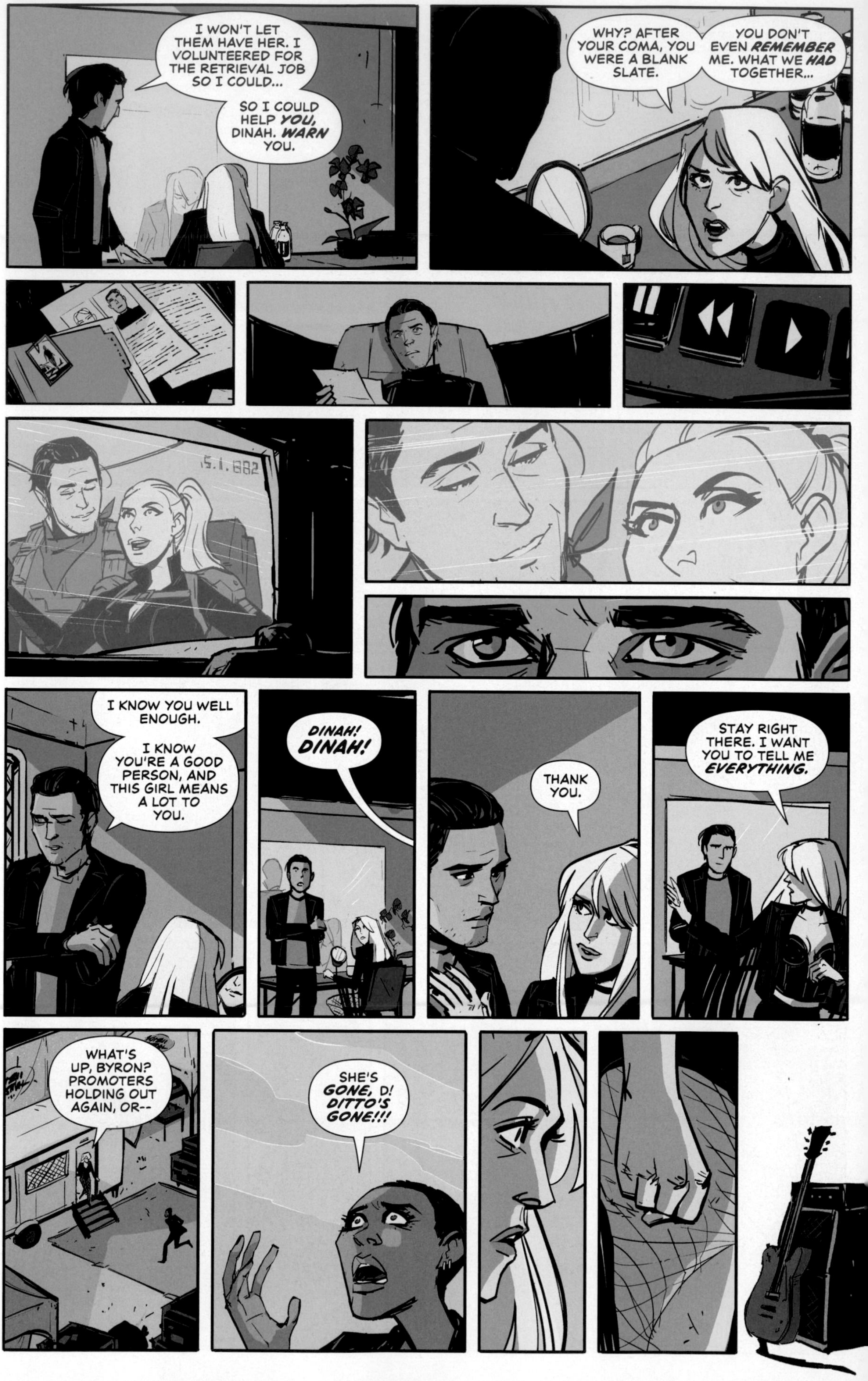

I WON'T LET THEM HAVE HER. I VOLUNTEERED FOR THE RETRIEVAL JOB SO I COULD...
SO I COULD HELP *YOU,* DINAH. *WARN* YOU.
WHY? AFTER YOUR COMA, YOU WERE A BLANK SLATE.
YOU DON'T EVEN *REMEMBER* ME. WHAT WE *HAD* TOGETHER...
S.I. 882
I KNOW YOU WELL ENOUGH.
I KNOW YOU'RE A GOOD PERSON, AND THIS GIRL MEANS A LOT TO YOU.
DINAH! DINAH!
THANK YOU.
STAY RIGHT THERE. I WANT YOU TO TELL ME *EVERYTHING.*
WHAT'S UP, BYRON? PROMOTERS HOLDING OUT AGAIN, OR--
SHE'S *GONE,* D! *DITTO'S GONE!!!*

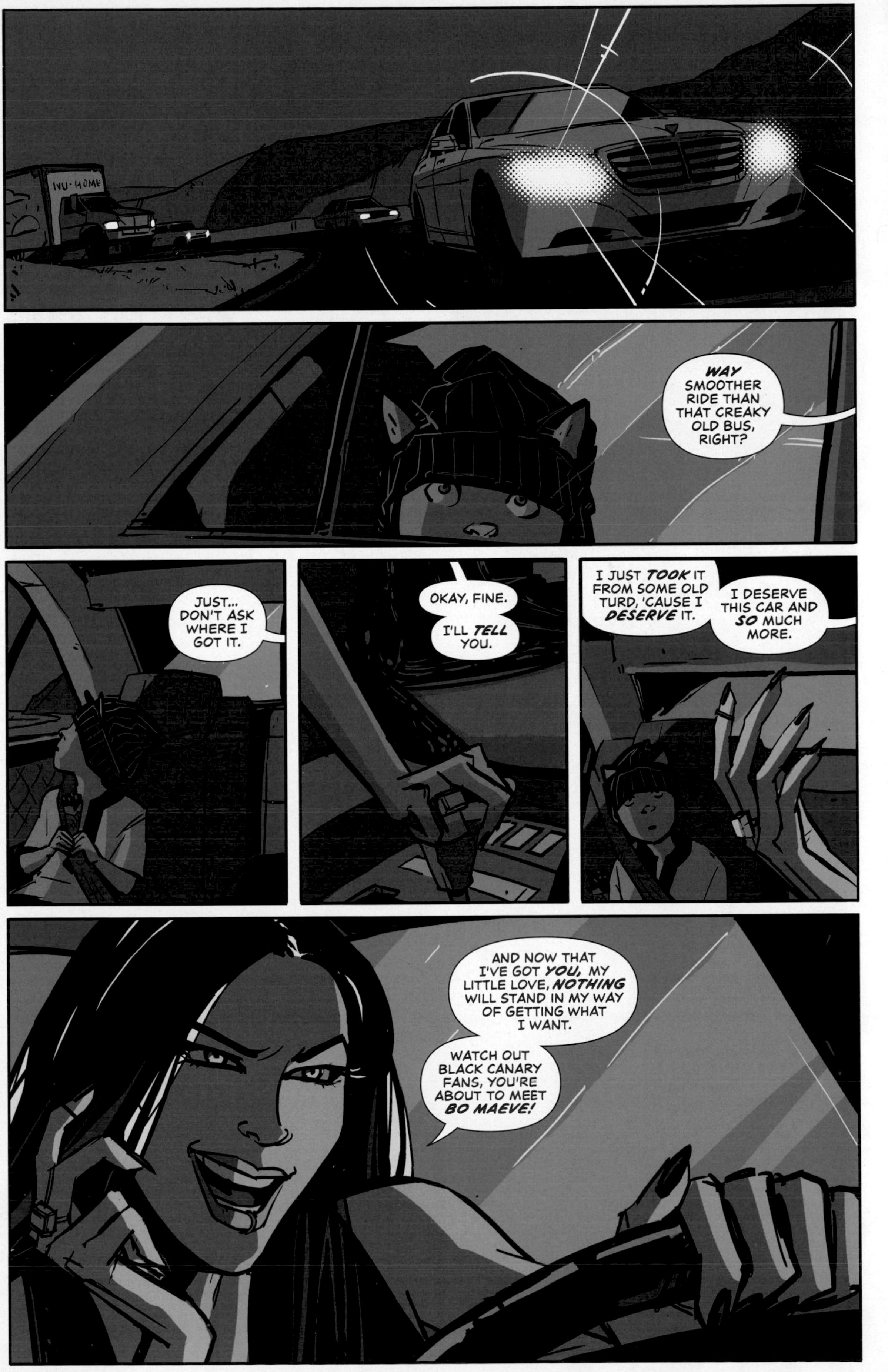
NU-HOME
WAY SMOOTHER RIDE THAN THAT CREAKY OLD BUS, RIGHT?
JUST... DON'T ASK WHERE I GOT IT.
OKAY, FINE.
I'LL TELL YOU.
I JUST TOOK IT FROM SOME OLD TURD, 'CAUSE I DESERVE IT.
I DESERVE THIS CAR AND SO MUCH MORE.
AND NOW THAT I'VE GOT YOU, MY LITTLE LOVE, NOTHING WILL STAND IN MY WAY OF GETTING WHAT I WANT.
WATCH OUT BLACK CANARY FANS, YOU'RE ABOUT TO MEET BO MAEVE!

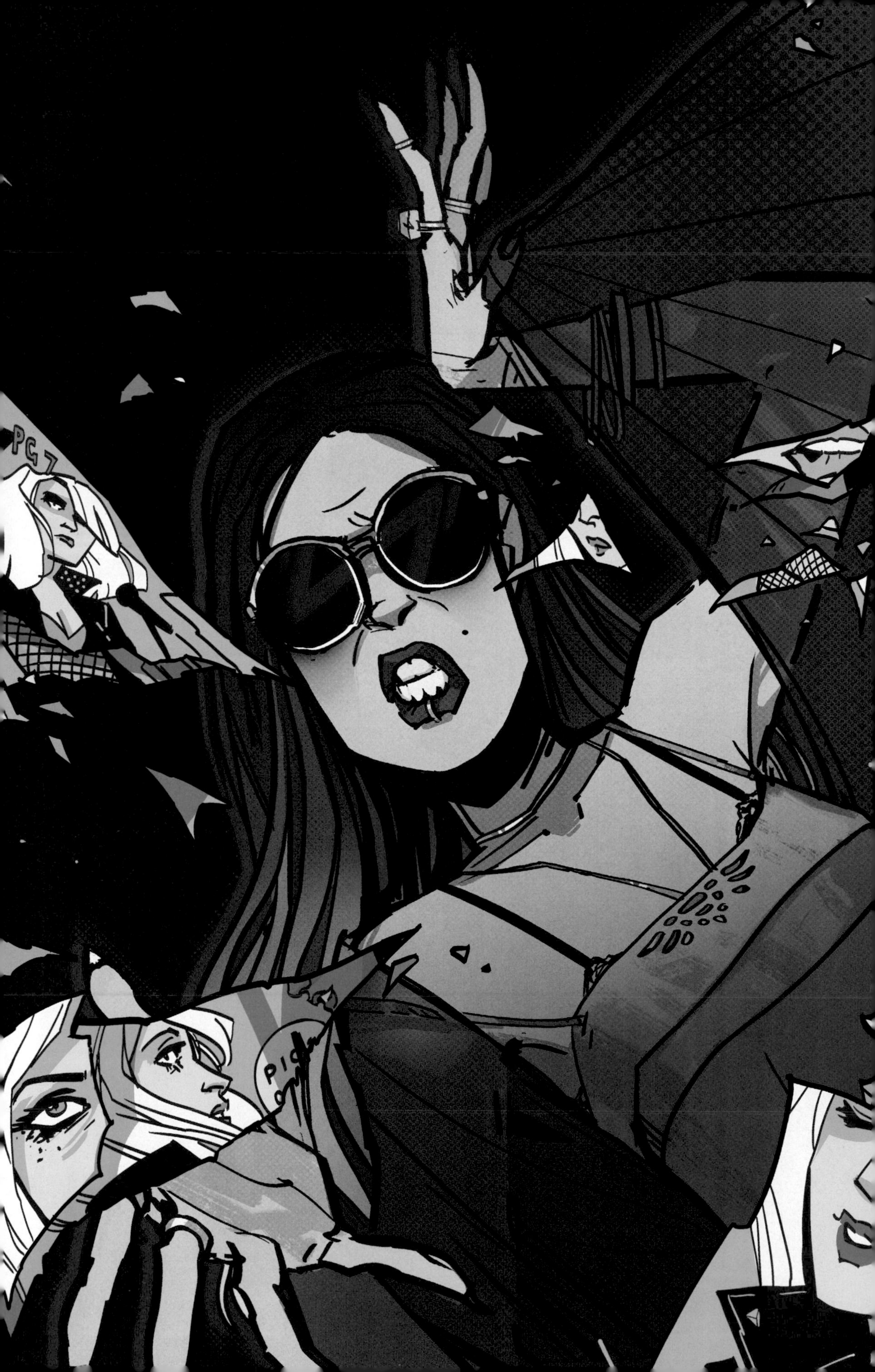

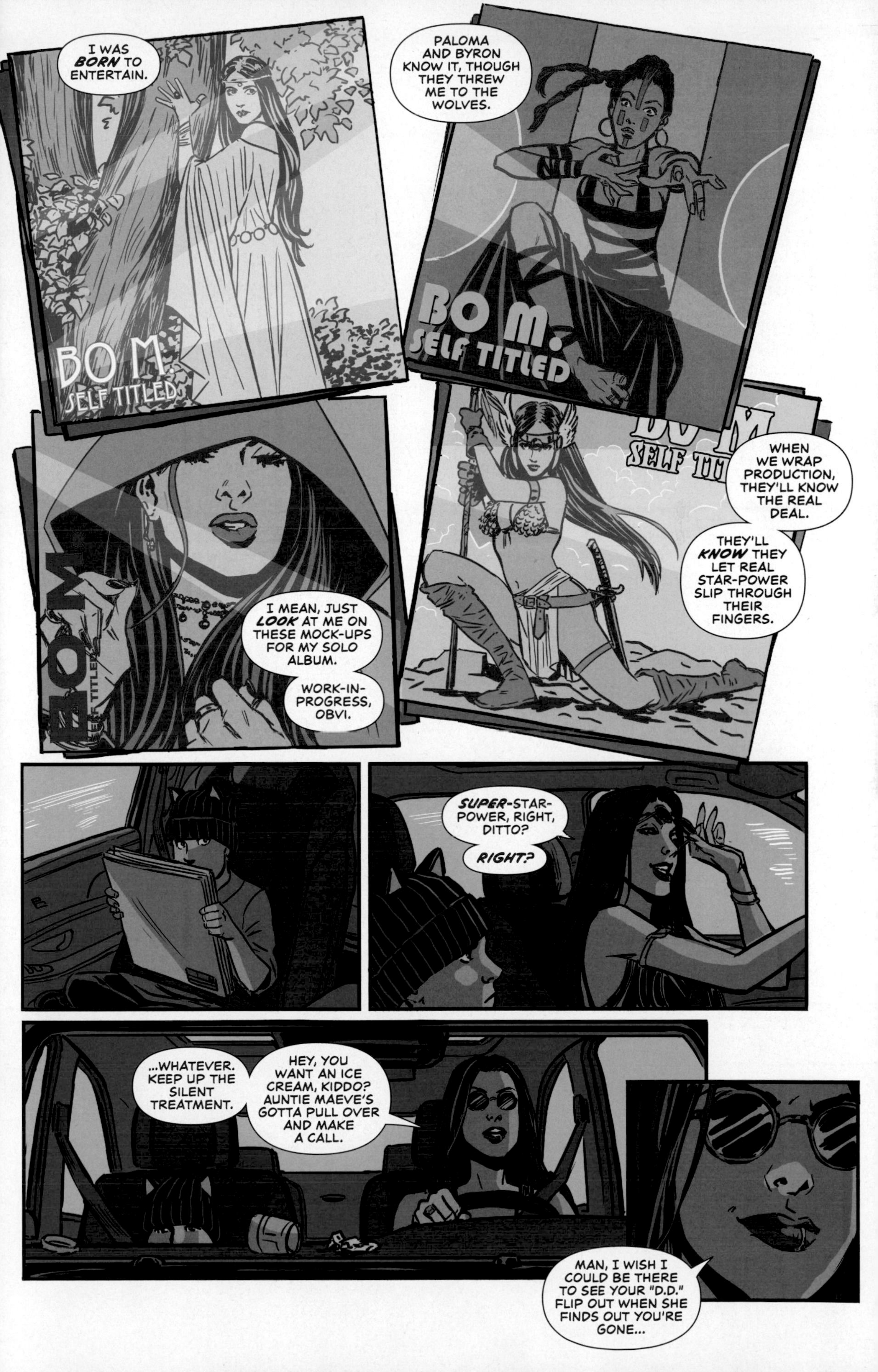

I WAS BORN TO ENTERTAIN.
BO M. SELF TITLED
PALOMA AND BYRON KNOW IT, THOUGH THEY THREW ME TO THE WOLVES.
BO M. SELF TITLED
I MEAN, JUST LOOK AT ME ON THESE MOCK-UPS FOR MY SOLO ALBUM.
WORK-IN-PROGRESS, OBVI.
WHEN WE WRAP PRODUCTION, THEY'LL KNOW THE REAL DEAL.
THEY'LL KNOW THEY LET REAL STAR-POWER SLIP THROUGH THEIR FINGERS.
SUPER-STAR-POWER, RIGHT, DITTO?
RIGHT?
...WHATEVER. KEEP UP THE SILENT TREATMENT.
HEY, YOU WANT AN ICE CREAM, KIDDO? AUNTIE MAEVE'S GOTTA PULL OVER AND MAKE A CALL.
MAN, I WISH I COULD BE THERE TO SEE YOUR "D.D." FLIP OUT WHEN SHE FINDS OUT YOU'RE GONE...

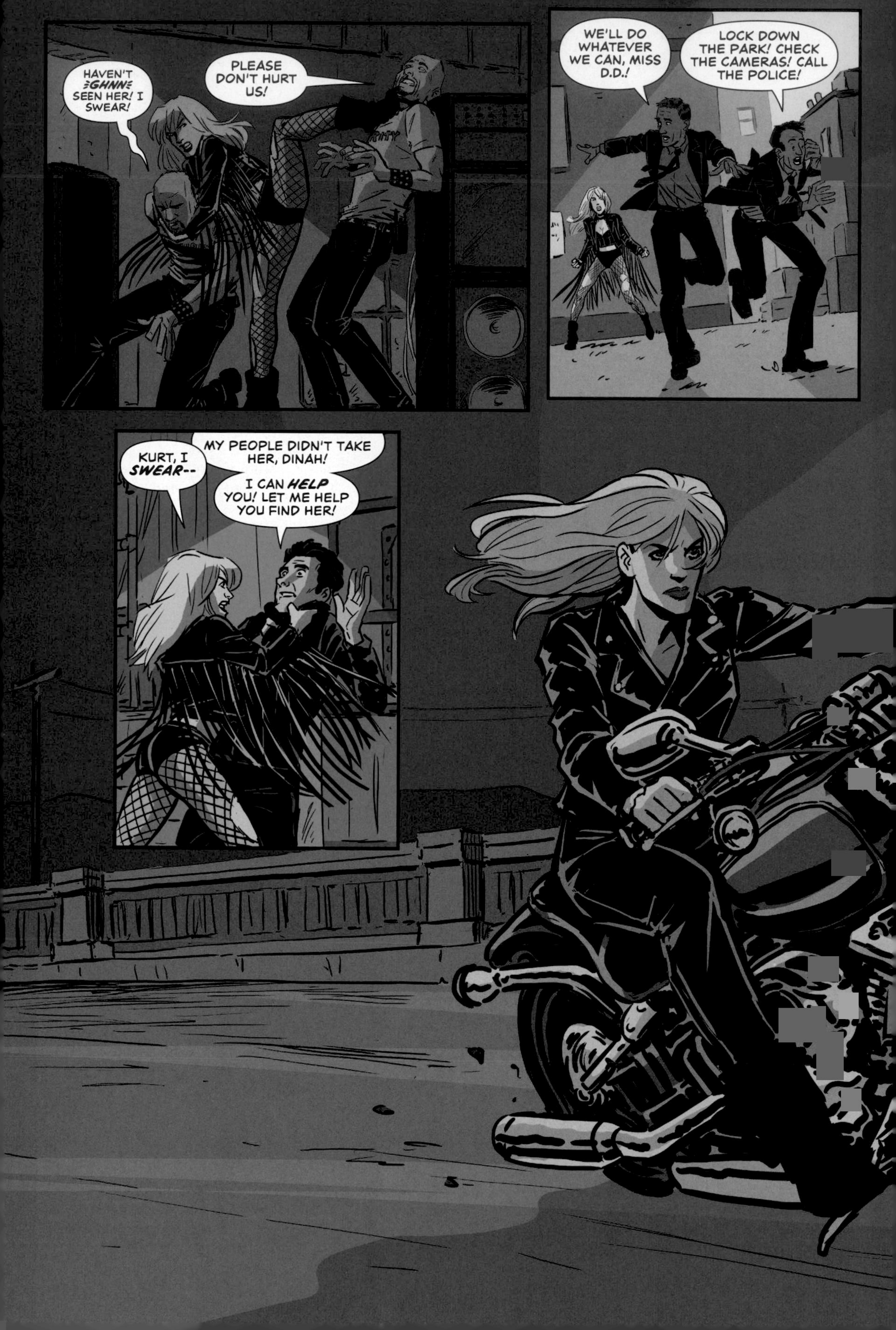
HAVEN'T *GHNN* SEEN HER! I SWEAR!
PLEASE DON'T HURT US!
WE'LL DO WHATEVER WE CAN, MISS D.D.!
LOCK DOWN THE PARK! CHECK THE CAMERAS! CALL THE POLICE!
KURT, I *SWEAR--*
MY PEOPLE DIDN'T TAKE HER, DINAH!
I CAN *HELP* YOU! LET ME HELP YOU FIND HER!

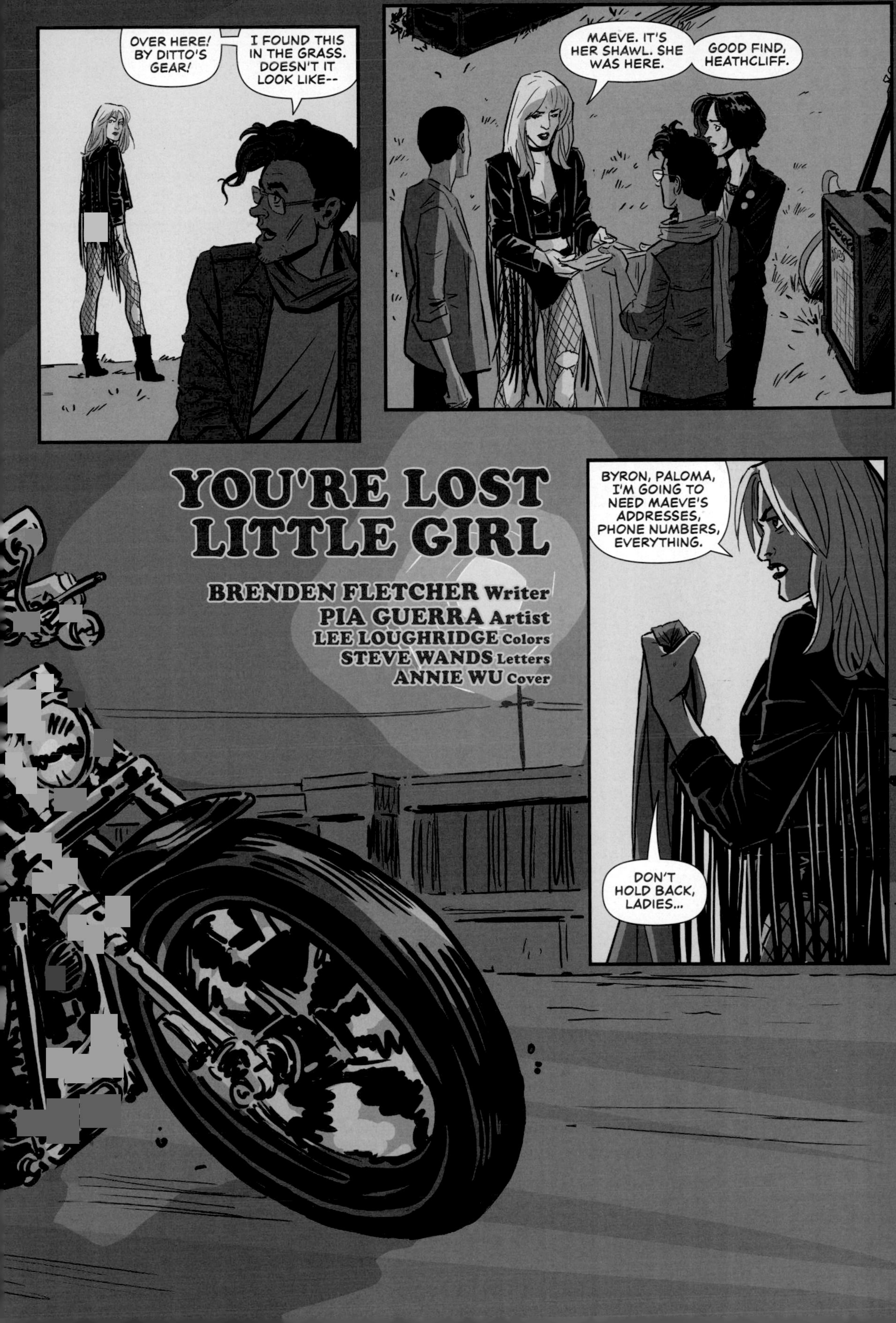

OVER HERE! BY DITTO'S GEAR!
I FOUND THIS IN THE GRASS. DOESN'T IT LOOK LIKE--
MAEVE. IT'S HER SHAWL. SHE WAS HERE.
GOOD FIND, HEATHCLIFF.
YOU'RE LOST LITTLE GIRL
BRENDEN FLETCHER Writer
PIA GUERRA Artist
LEE LOUGHRIDGE Colors
STEVE WANDS Letters
ANNIE WU Cover
BYRON, PALOMA, I'M GOING TO NEED MAEVE'S ADDRESSES, PHONE NUMBERS, EVERYTHING.
DON'T HOLD BACK, LADIES...

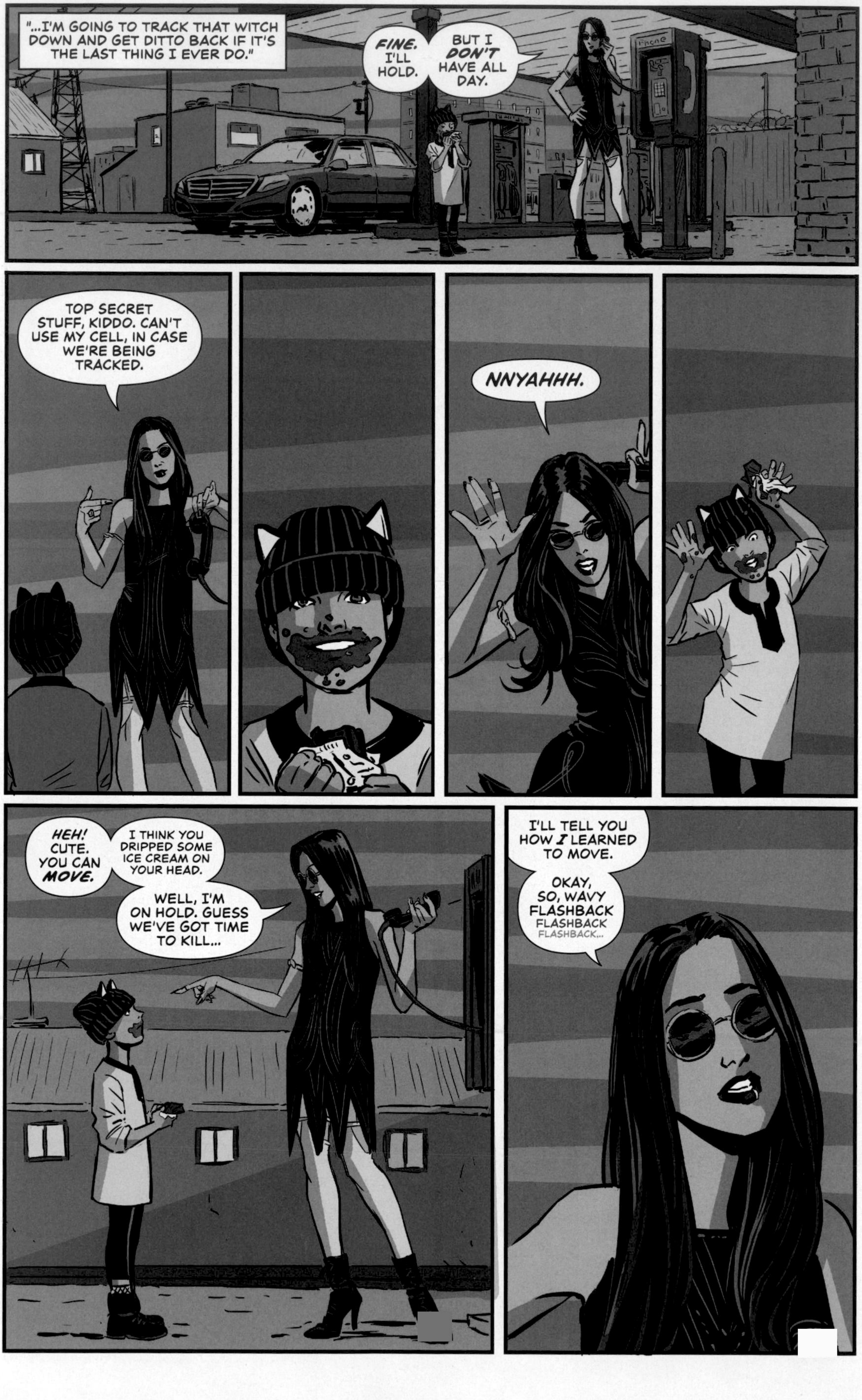
"...I'M GOING TO TRACK THAT WITCH DOWN AND GET DITTO BACK IF IT'S THE LAST THING I EVER DO."
FINE. I'LL HOLD.
BUT I DON'T HAVE ALL DAY.
PHONE
TOP SECRET STUFF, KIDDO. CAN'T USE MY CELL, IN CASE WE'RE BEING TRACKED.
NNYAHHH.
HEH! CUTE. YOU CAN MOVE.
I THINK YOU DRIPPED SOME ICE CREAM ON YOUR HEAD.
WELL, I'M ON HOLD. GUESS WE'VE GOT TIME TO KILL...
I'LL TELL YOU HOW I LEARNED TO MOVE.
OKAY, SO, WAVY FLASHBACK FLASHBACK FLASHBACK...

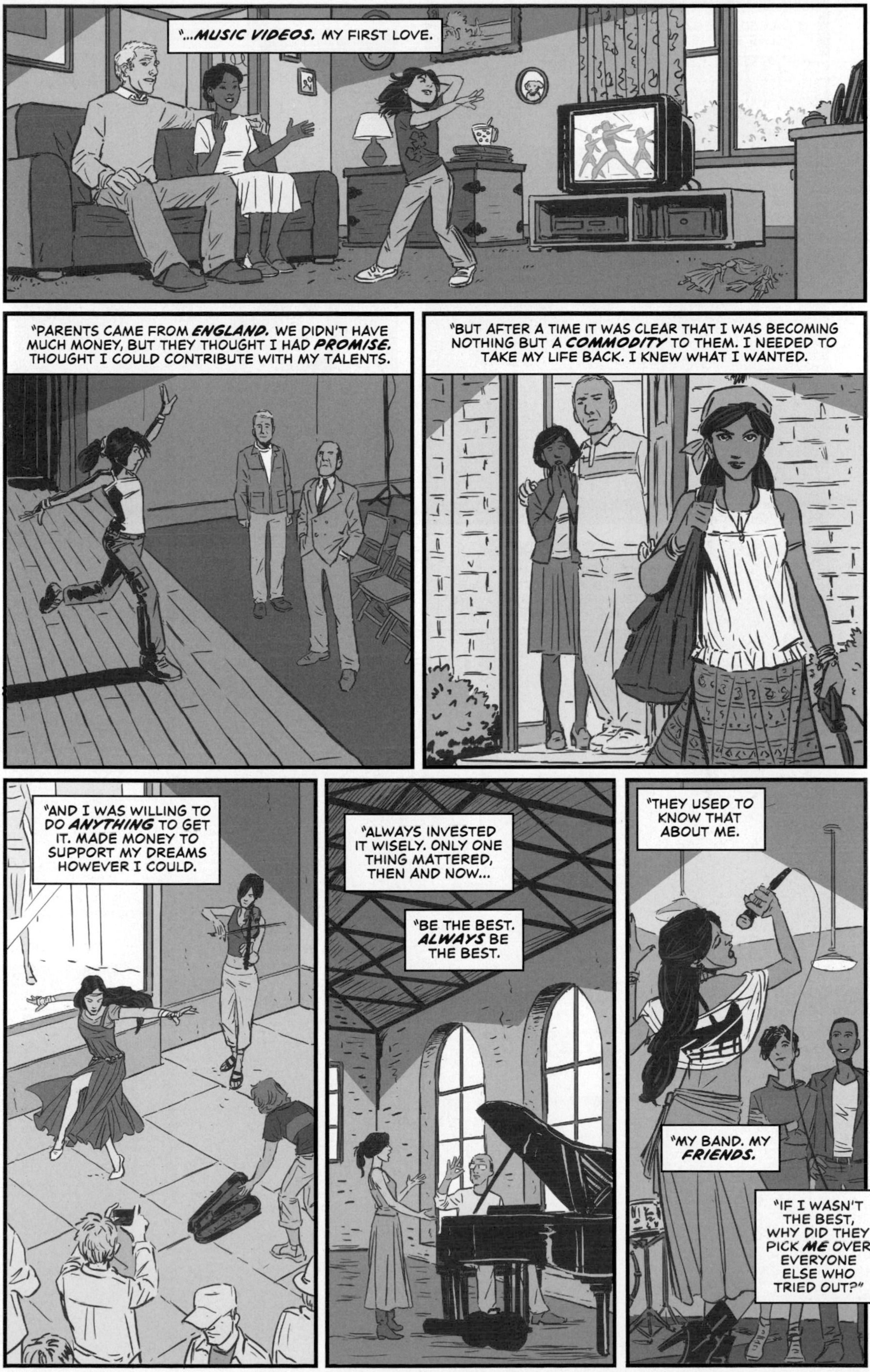
"...MUSIC VIDEOS. MY FIRST LOVE.
"PARENTS CAME FROM ENGLAND. WE DIDN'T HAVE MUCH MONEY, BUT THEY THOUGHT I HAD PROMISE. THOUGHT I COULD CONTRIBUTE WITH MY TALENTS.
"BUT AFTER A TIME IT WAS CLEAR THAT I WAS BECOMING NOTHING BUT A COMMODITY TO THEM. I NEEDED TO TAKE MY LIFE BACK. I KNEW WHAT I WANTED.
"AND I WAS WILLING TO DO ANYTHING TO GET IT. MADE MONEY TO SUPPORT MY DREAMS HOWEVER I COULD.
"ALWAYS INVESTED IT WISELY. ONLY ONE THING MATTERED, THEN AND NOW...
"BE THE BEST. ALWAYS BE THE BEST.
"THEY USED TO KNOW THAT ABOUT ME.
"MY BAND. MY FRIENDS.
"IF I WASN'T THE BEST, WHY DID THEY PICK ME OVER EVERYONE ELSE WHO TRIED OUT?"

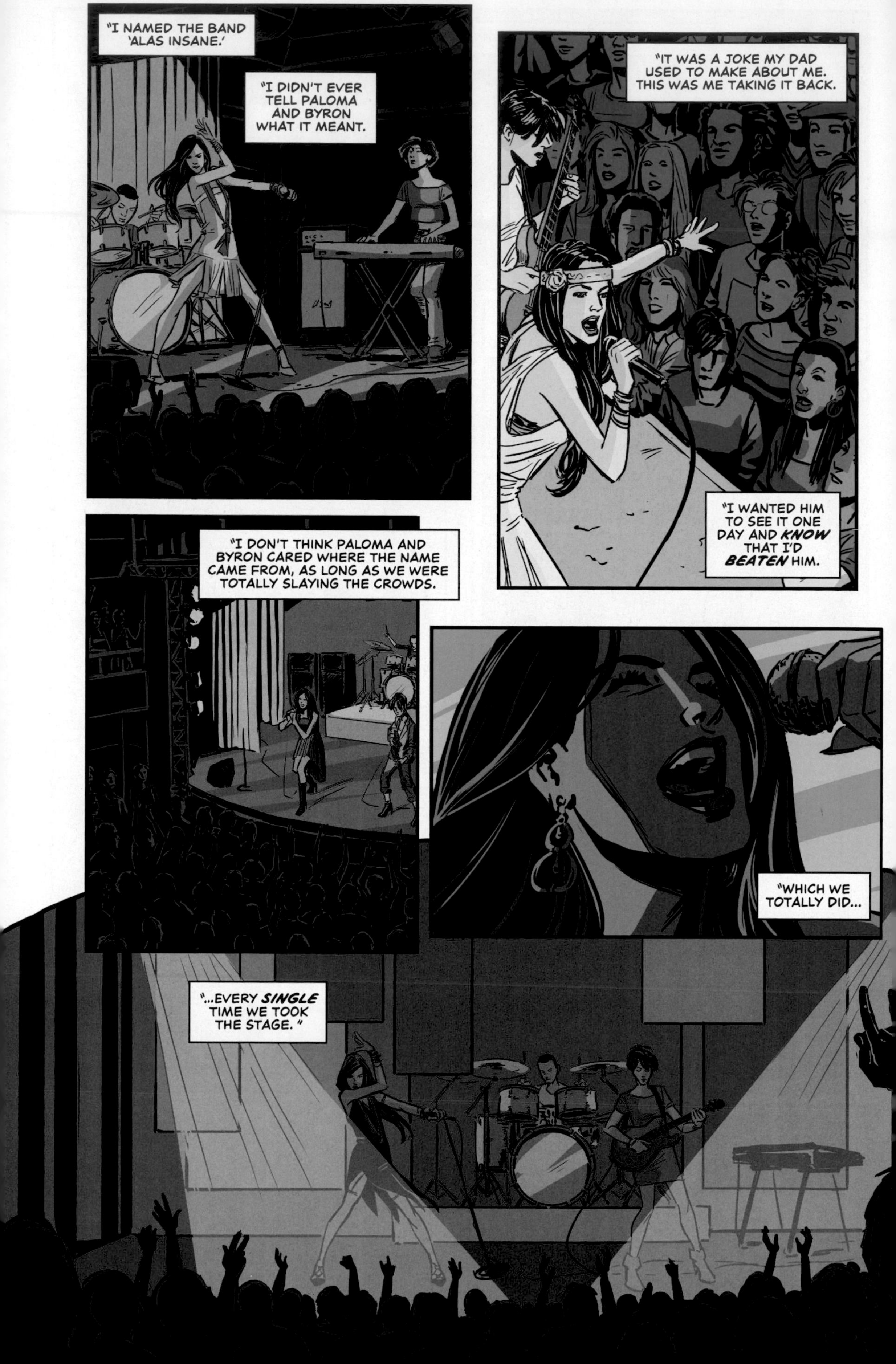
"I NAMED THE BAND 'ALAS INSANE.'
"I DIDN'T EVER TELL PALOMA AND BYRON WHAT IT MEANT.
"IT WAS A JOKE MY DAD USED TO MAKE ABOUT ME. THIS WAS ME TAKING IT BACK.
"I WANTED HIM TO SEE IT ONE DAY AND *KNOW* THAT I'D *BEATEN* HIM.
"I DON'T THINK PALOMA AND BYRON CARED WHERE THE NAME CAME FROM, AS LONG AS WE WERE TOTALLY SLAYING THE CROWDS.
"WHICH WE TOTALLY DID...
"...EVERY *SINGLE* TIME WE TOOK THE STAGE."

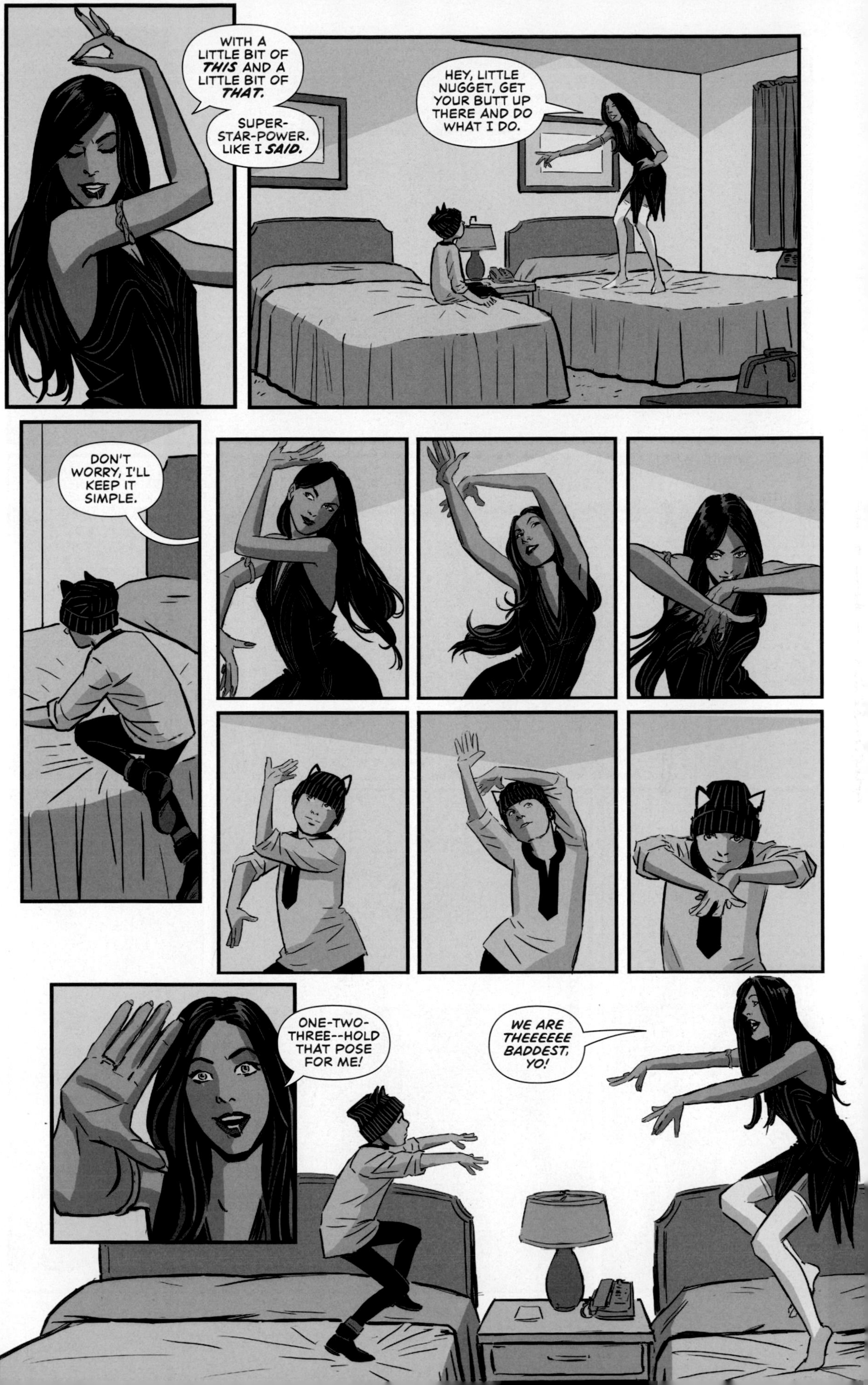
WITH A LITTLE BIT OF *THIS* AND A LITTLE BIT OF *THAT.*
SUPER-STAR-POWER. LIKE I *SAID.*
HEY, LITTLE NUGGET, GET YOUR BUTT UP THERE AND DO WHAT I DO.
DON'T WORRY, I'LL KEEP IT SIMPLE.
ONE-TWO-THREE--HOLD THAT POSE FOR ME!
WE ARE THEEEEEE BADDEST, YO!

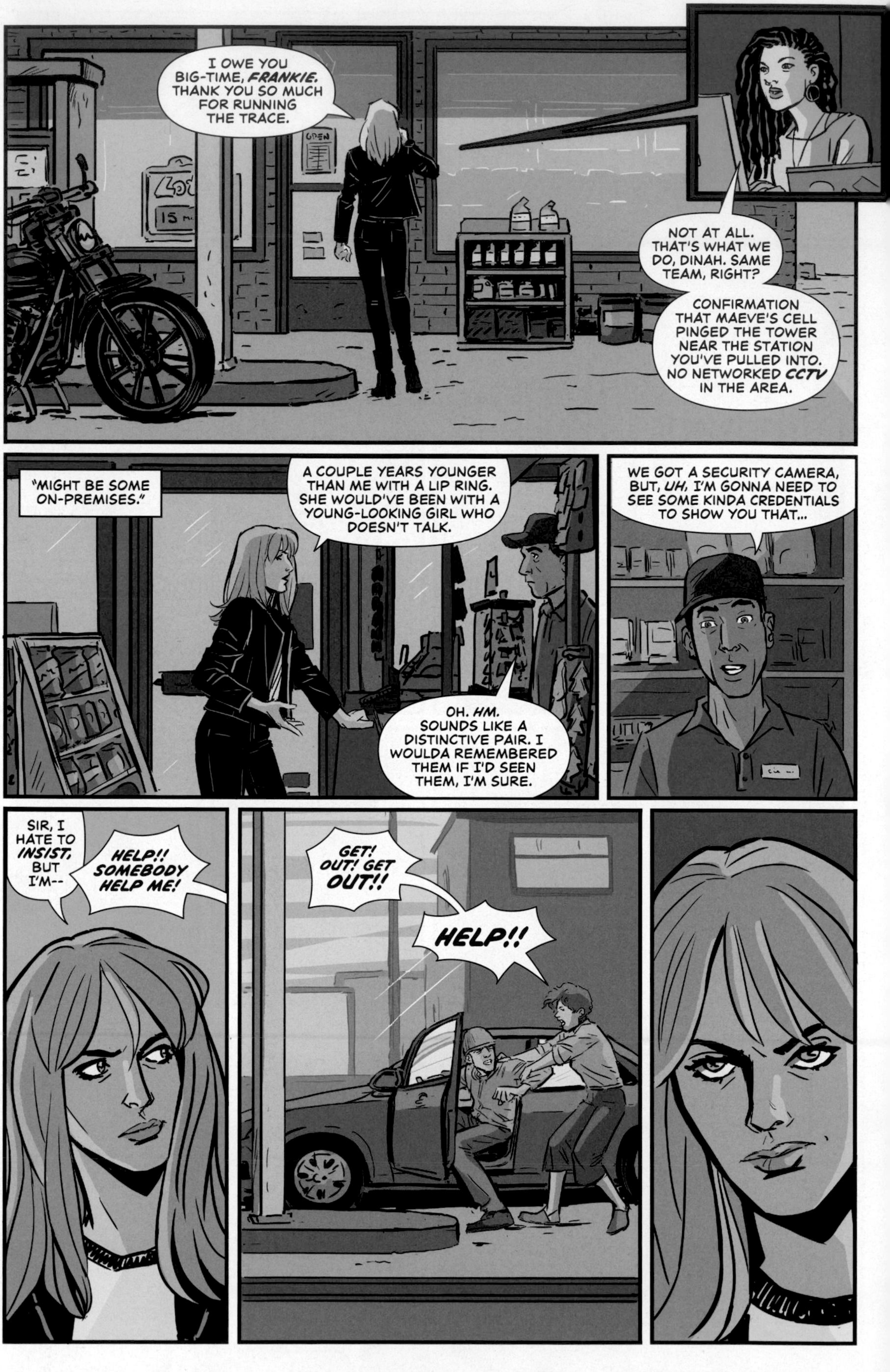

I OWE YOU BIG-TIME, FRANKIE. THANK YOU SO MUCH FOR RUNNING THE TRACE.
OPEN
NOT AT ALL. THAT'S WHAT WE DO, DINAH. SAME TEAM, RIGHT?
CONFIRMATION THAT MAEVE'S CELL PINGED THE TOWER NEAR THE STATION YOU'VE PULLED INTO. NO NETWORKED CCTV IN THE AREA.
"MIGHT BE SOME ON-PREMISES."
A COUPLE YEARS YOUNGER THAN ME WITH A LIP RING. SHE WOULD'VE BEEN WITH A YOUNG-LOOKING GIRL WHO DOESN'T TALK.
OH. HM. SOUNDS LIKE A DISTINCTIVE PAIR. I WOULDA REMEMBERED THEM IF I'D SEEN THEM, I'M SURE.
WE GOT A SECURITY CAMERA, BUT, UH, I'M GONNA NEED TO SEE SOME KINDA CREDENTIALS TO SHOW YOU THAT...
SIR, I HATE TO INSIST, BUT I'M--
HELP!! SOMEBODY HELP ME!
GET! OUT! GET OUT!!
HELP!!

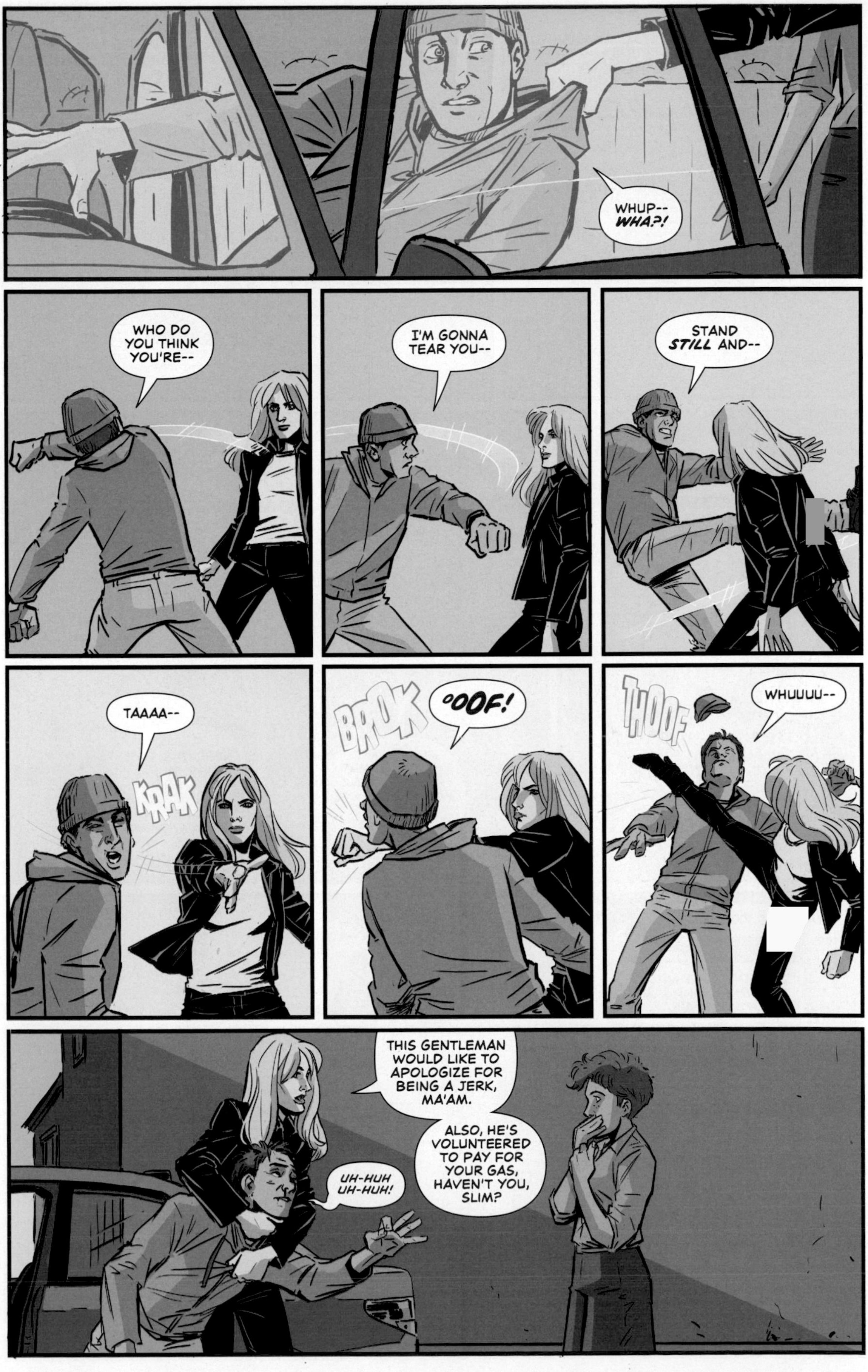
WHUP--
WHA?!
WHO DO YOU THINK YOU'RE--
I'M GONNA TEAR YOU--
STAND STILL AND--
TAAAA--
KRAK
BROK
OOF!
THOOF
WHUUUU--
THIS GENTLEMAN WOULD LIKE TO APOLOGIZE FOR BEING A JERK, MA'AM.
ALSO, HE'S VOLUNTEERED TO PAY FOR YOUR GAS, HAVEN'T YOU, SLIM?
UH-HUH UH-HUH!

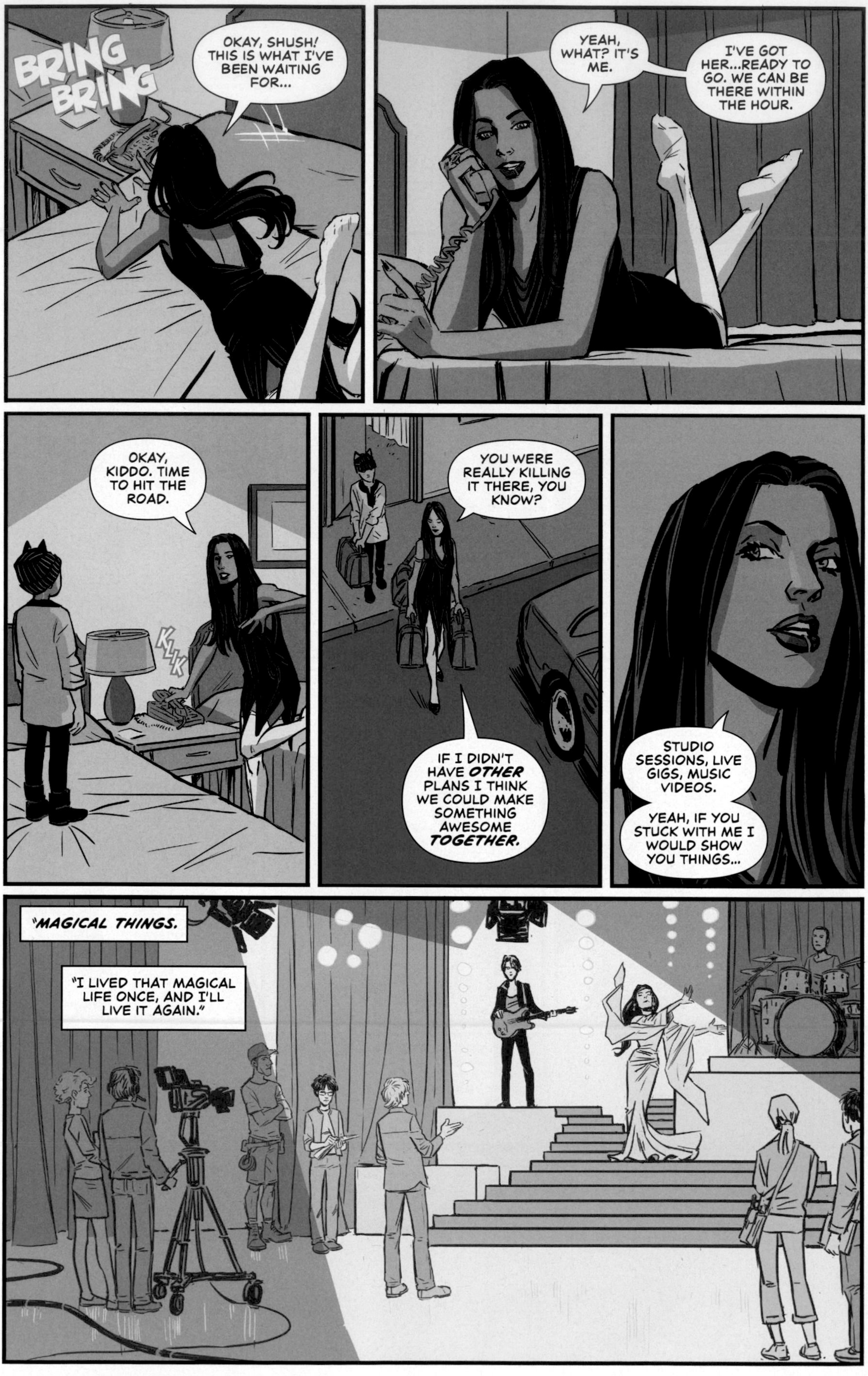
BRING BRING
OKAY, SHUSH! THIS IS WHAT I'VE BEEN WAITING FOR...
YEAH, WHAT? IT'S ME.
I'VE GOT HER...READY TO GO. WE CAN BE THERE WITHIN THE HOUR.
OKAY, KIDDO. TIME TO HIT THE ROAD.
KLIK
YOU WERE REALLY KILLING IT THERE, YOU KNOW?
IF I DIDN'T HAVE OTHER PLANS I THINK WE COULD MAKE SOMETHING AWESOME TOGETHER.
STUDIO SESSIONS, LIVE GIGS, MUSIC VIDEOS.
YEAH, IF YOU STUCK WITH ME I WOULD SHOW YOU THINGS...
"MAGICAL THINGS.
"I LIVED THAT MAGICAL LIFE ONCE, AND I'LL LIVE IT AGAIN."

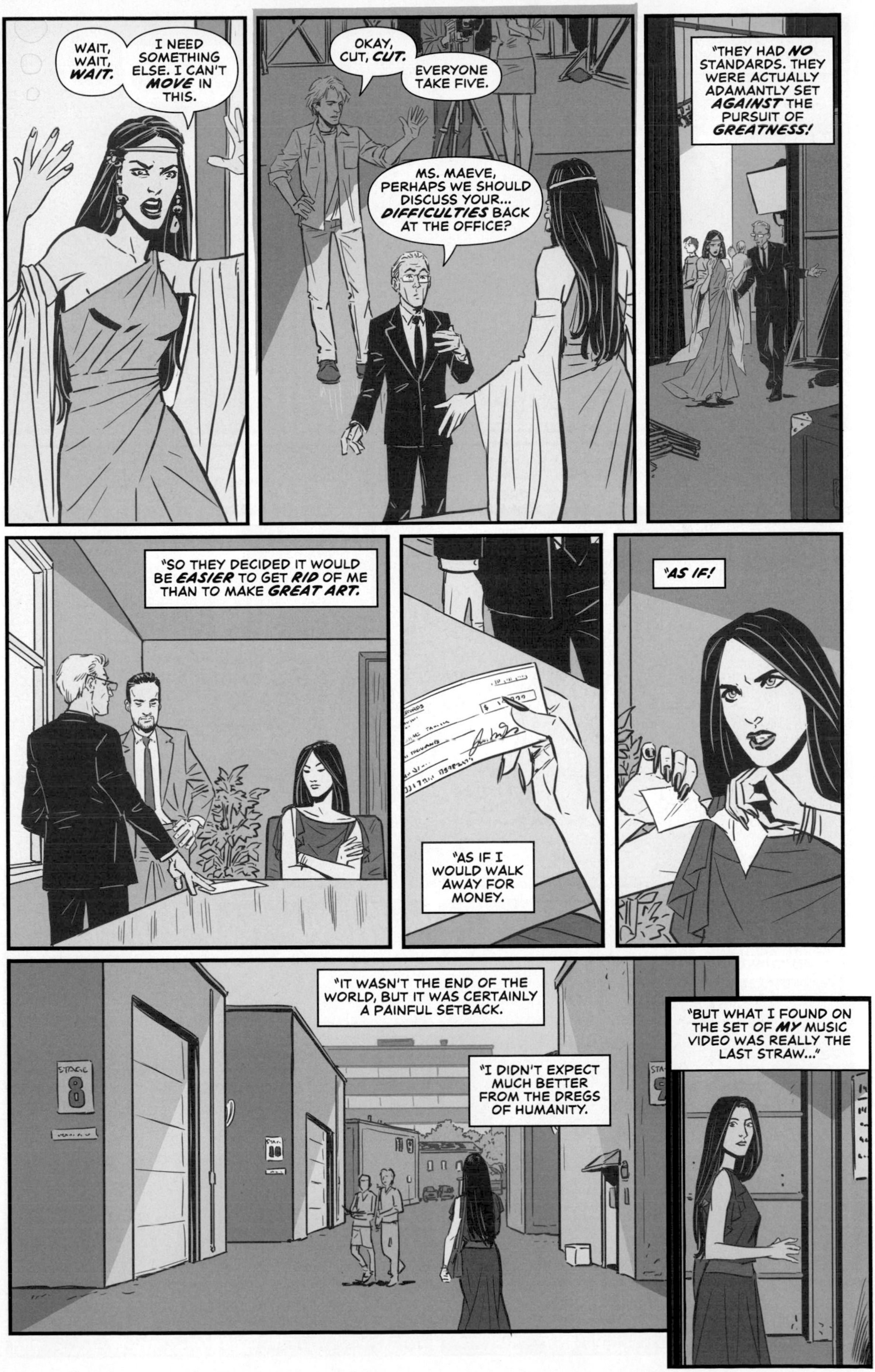

WAIT, WAIT, WAIT.
I NEED SOMETHING ELSE. I CAN'T MOVE IN THIS.
OKAY, CUT, CUT.
EVERYONE TAKE FIVE.
MS. MAEVE, PERHAPS WE SHOULD DISCUSS YOUR... DIFFICULTIES BACK AT THE OFFICE?
"THEY HAD NO STANDARDS. THEY WERE ACTUALLY ADAMANTLY SET AGAINST THE PURSUIT OF GREATNESS!
"SO THEY DECIDED IT WOULD BE EASIER TO GET RID OF ME THAN TO MAKE GREAT ART.
"AS IF I WOULD WALK AWAY FOR MONEY.
"AS IF!
"IT WASN'T THE END OF THE WORLD, BUT IT WAS CERTAINLY A PAINFUL SETBACK.
"I DIDN'T EXPECT MUCH BETTER FROM THE DREGS OF HUMANITY.
STAGE 8
"BUT WHAT I FOUND ON THE SET OF MY MUSIC VIDEO WAS REALLY THE LAST STRAW..."

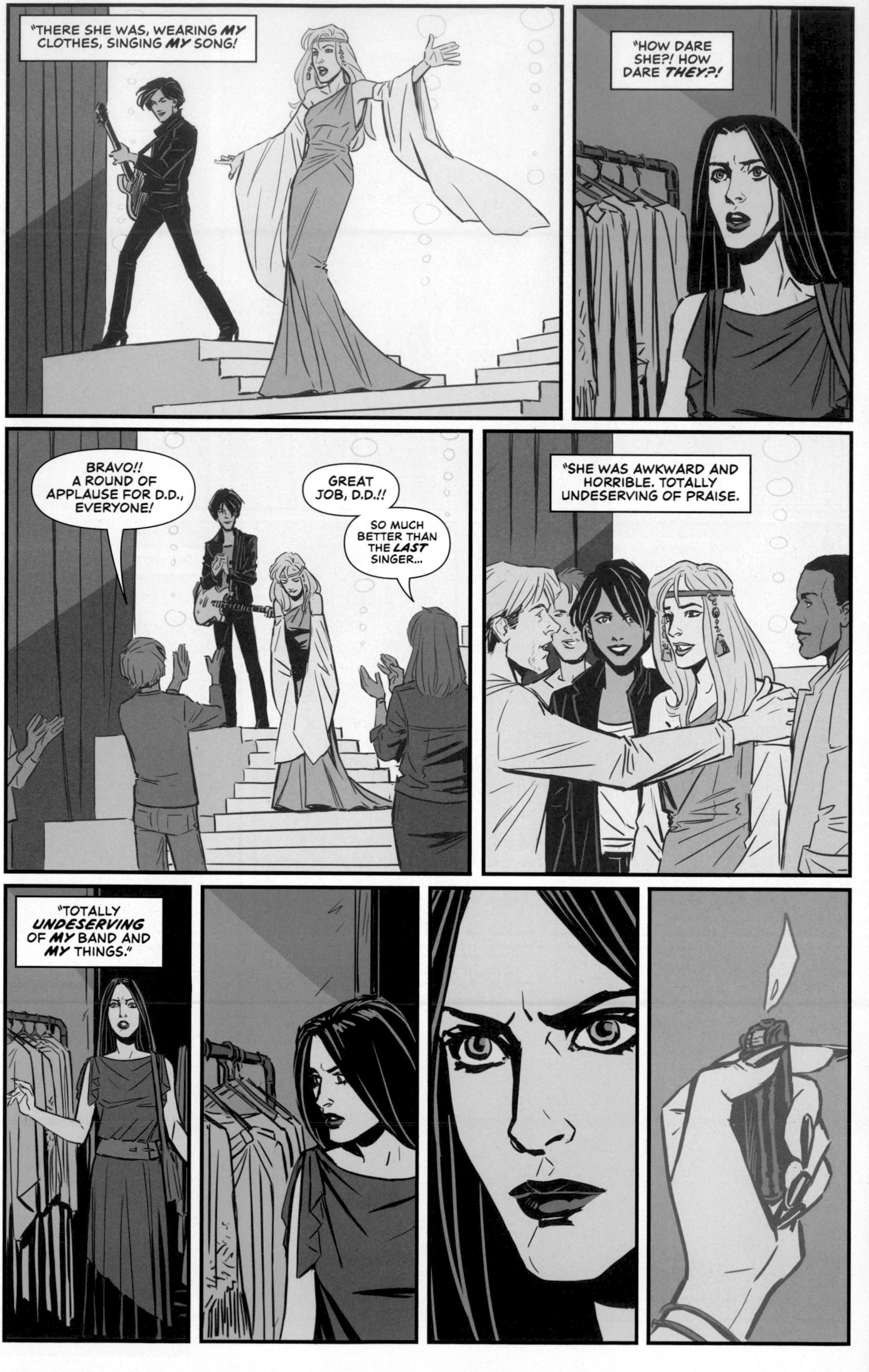
"THERE SHE WAS, WEARING *MY* CLOTHES, SINGING *MY* SONG!
"HOW DARE SHE?! HOW DARE *THEY?!*
BRAVO!! A ROUND OF APPLAUSE FOR D.D., EVERYONE!
GREAT JOB, D.D.!!
SO MUCH BETTER THAN THE *LAST* SINGER...
"SHE WAS AWKWARD AND HORRIBLE. TOTALLY UNDESERVING OF PRAISE.
"TOTALLY *UNDESERVING* OF *MY* BAND AND *MY* THINGS."

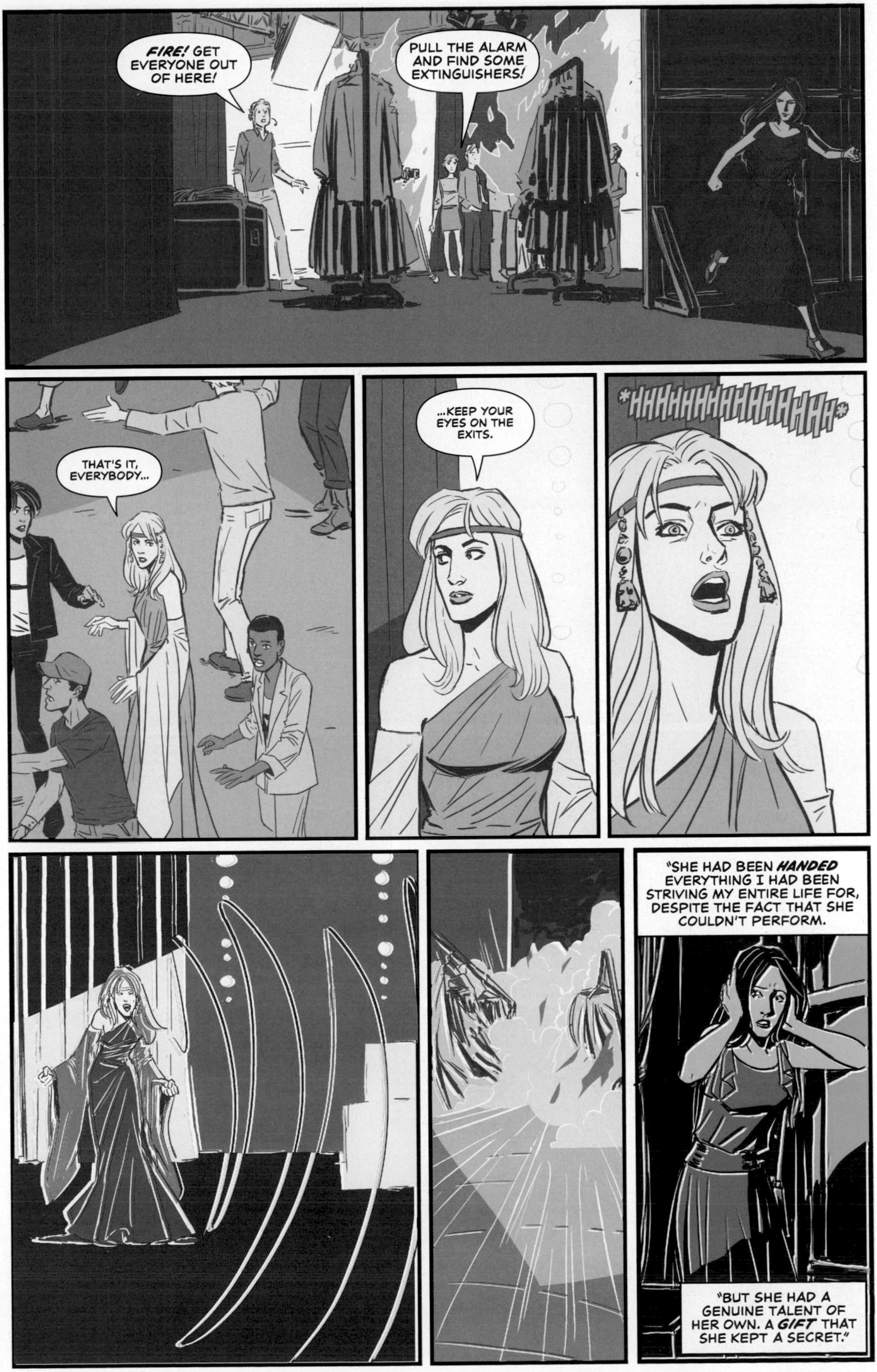
FIRE! GET EVERYONE OUT OF HERE!
PULL THE ALARM AND FIND SOME EXTINGUISHERS!
THAT'S IT, EVERYBODY...
...KEEP YOUR EYES ON THE EXITS.
HHHHHHHHHHHHHHH
"SHE HAD BEEN HANDED EVERYTHING I HAD BEEN STRIVING MY ENTIRE LIFE FOR, DESPITE THE FACT THAT SHE COULDN'T PERFORM.
"BUT SHE HAD A GENUINE TALENT OF HER OWN. A GIFT THAT SHE KEPT A SECRET."

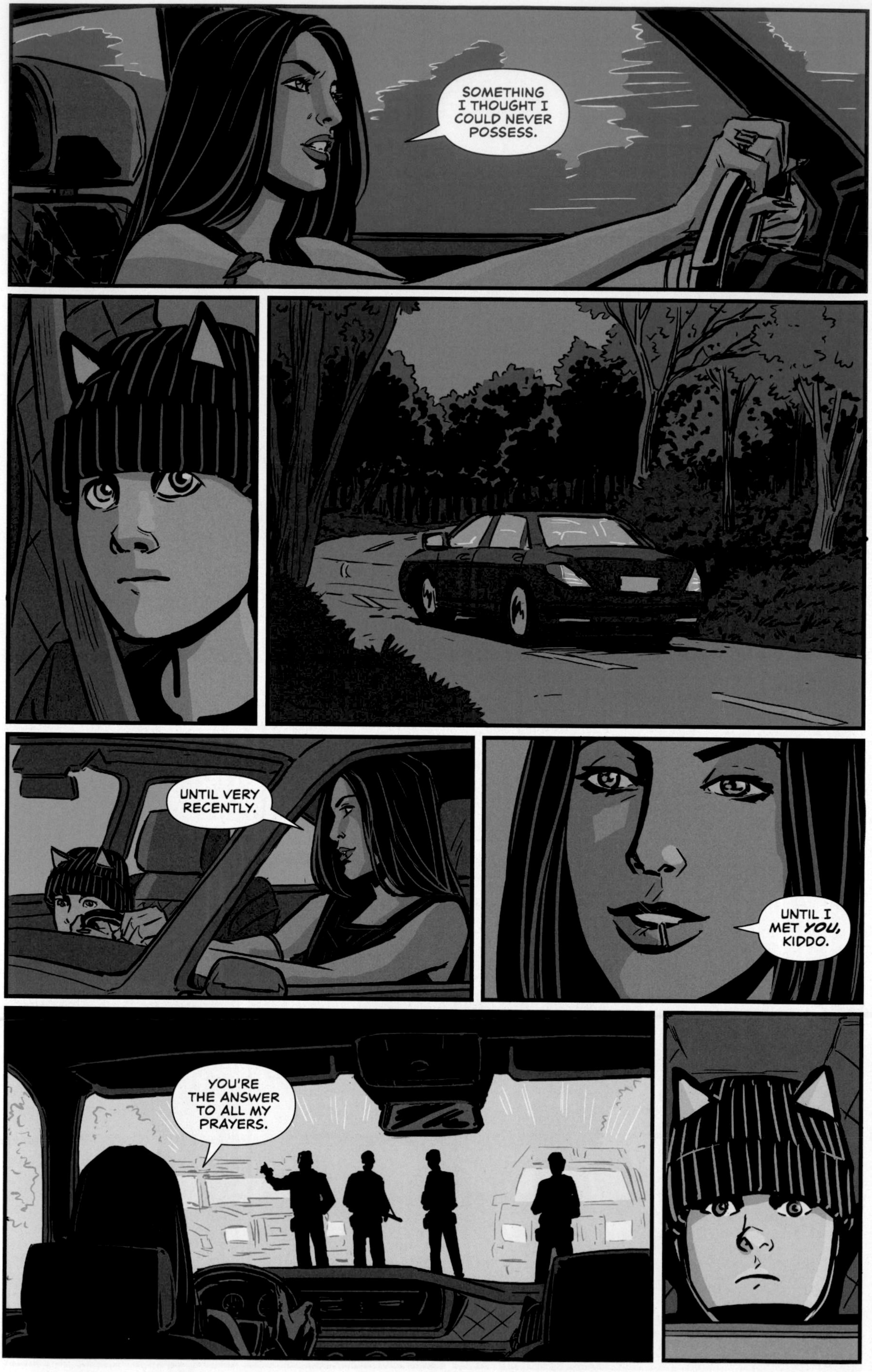
SOMETHING I THOUGHT I COULD NEVER POSSESS.
UNTIL VERY RECENTLY.
UNTIL I MET *YOU,* KIDDO.
YOU'RE THE ANSWER TO ALL MY PRAYERS.

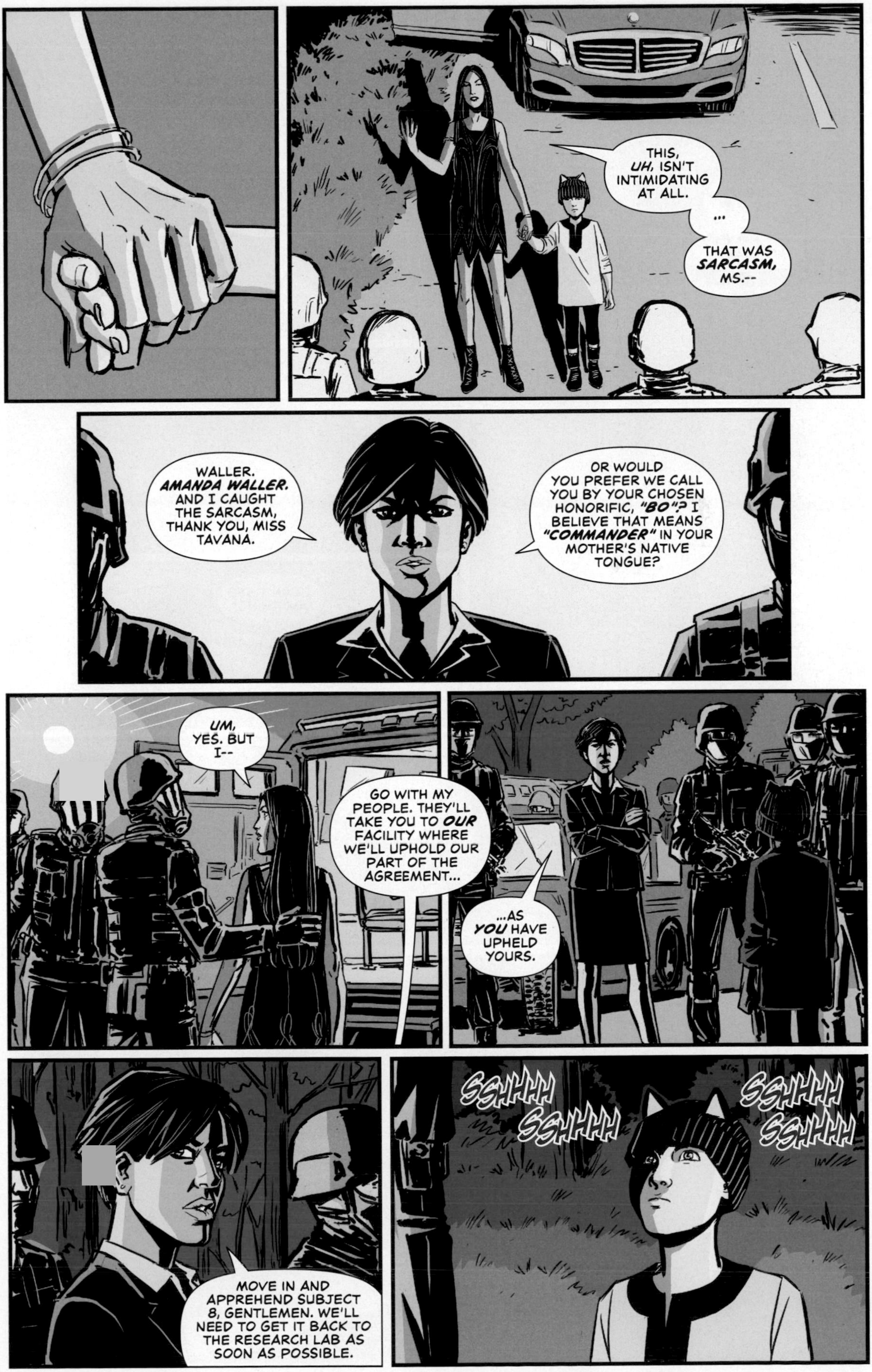
THIS, *UH,* ISN'T INTIMIDATING AT ALL.
...
THAT WAS *SARCASM,* MS.--
WALLER. *AMANDA WALLER.* AND I CAUGHT THE SARCASM, THANK YOU, MISS TAVANA.
OR WOULD YOU PREFER WE CALL YOU BY YOUR CHOSEN HONORIFIC, *"BO"?* I BELIEVE THAT MEANS *"COMMANDER"* IN YOUR MOTHER'S NATIVE TONGUE?
UM, YES. BUT I--
GO WITH MY PEOPLE. THEY'LL TAKE YOU TO *OUR* FACILITY WHERE WE'LL UPHOLD OUR PART OF THE AGREEMENT...
...AS *YOU* HAVE UPHELD YOURS.
MOVE IN AND APPREHEND SUBJECT 8, GENTLEMEN. WE'LL NEED TO GET IT BACK TO THE RESEARCH LAB AS SOON AS POSSIBLE.
SSHHHH SSHHHH
SSHHHHH SSHHHH

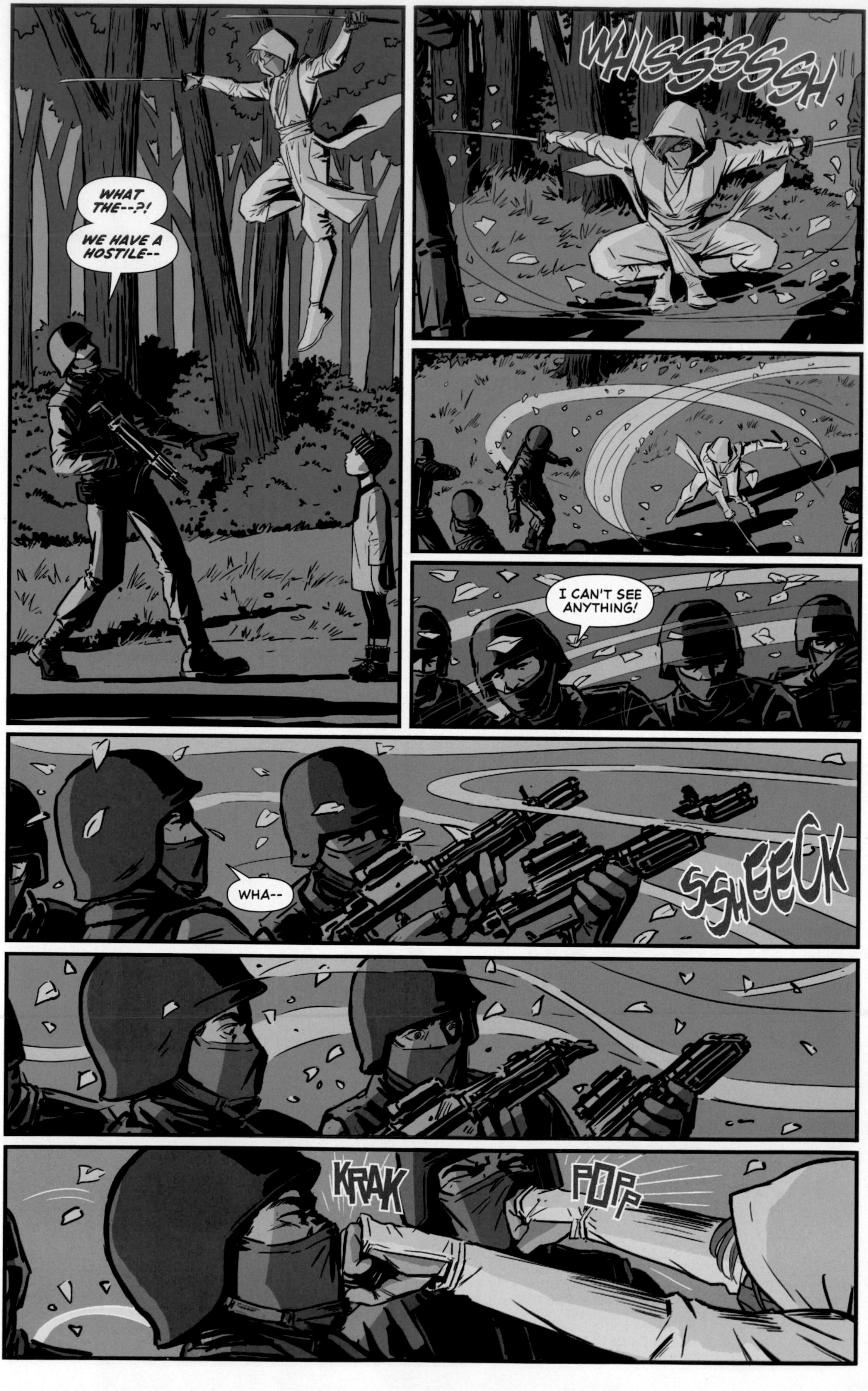
WHAT THE--?!
WE HAVE A HOSTILE--
WHISSSSSH
I CAN'T SEE ANYTHING!
WHA--
SSHEECK
KRAK
POPP

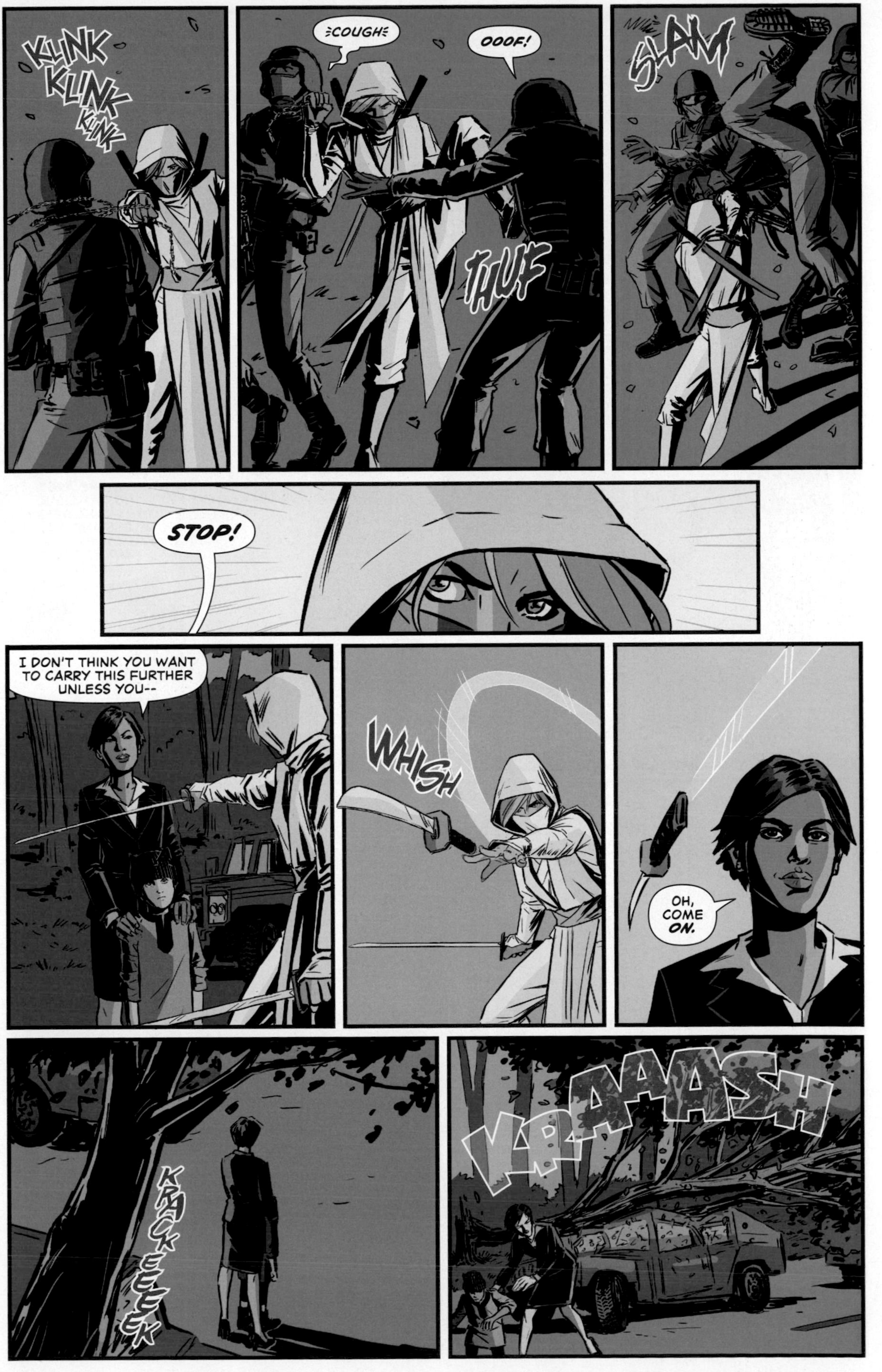
KLINK
KLINK
KLINK
COUGH
OOOF!
THUF
SLAM
STOP!
I DON'T THINK YOU WANT TO CARRY THIS FURTHER UNLESS YOU--
WHISH
OH, COME ON.
KRACKEEEEK
KRAAAASH

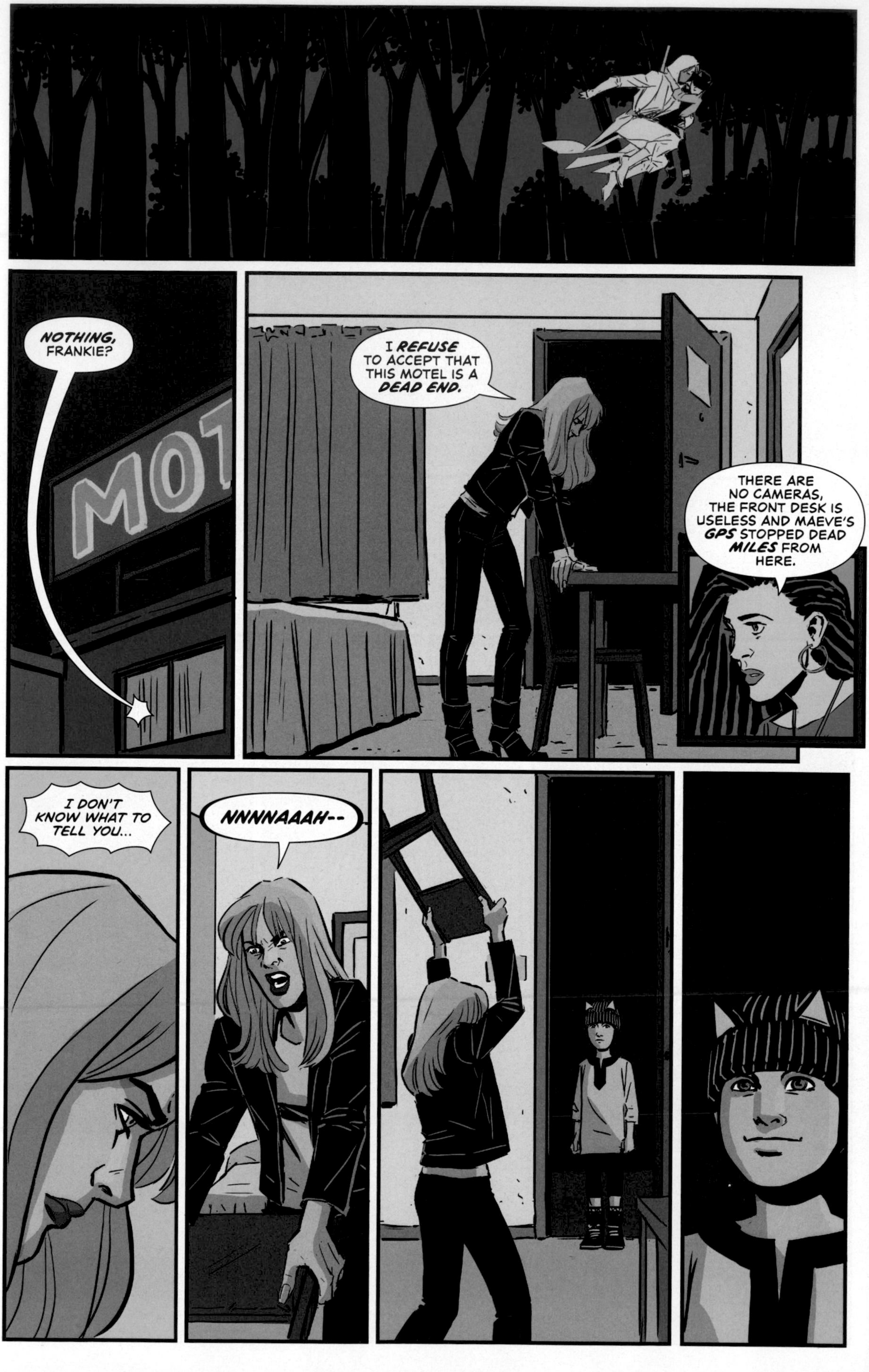
NOTHING, FRANKIE?
MOT
I REFUSE TO ACCEPT THAT THIS MOTEL IS A DEAD END.
THERE ARE NO CAMERAS, THE FRONT DESK IS USELESS AND MAEVE'S GPS STOPPED DEAD MILES FROM HERE.
I DON'T KNOW WHAT TO TELL YOU...
NNNNAAAH--

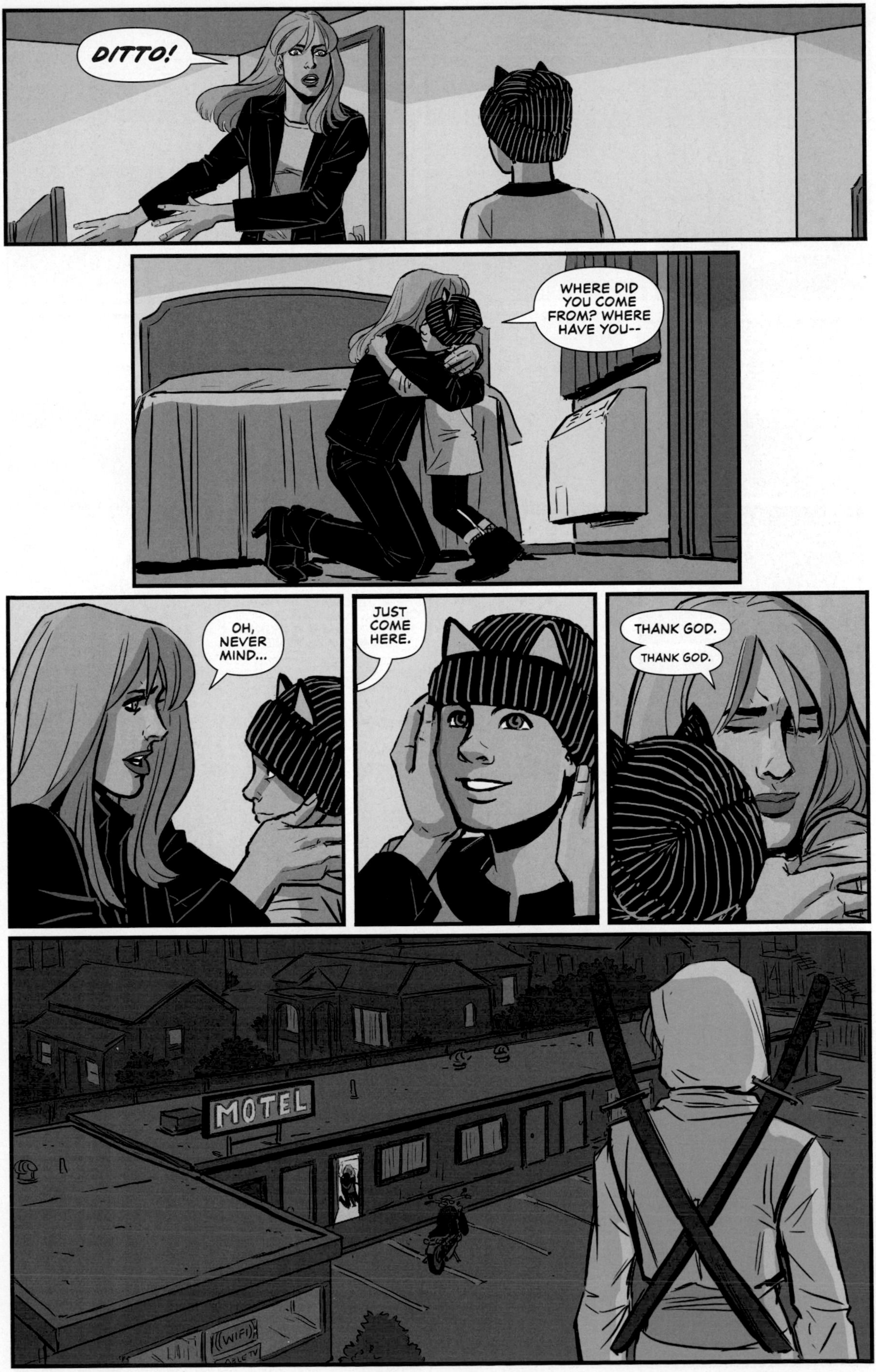
DITTO!
WHERE DID YOU COME FROM? WHERE HAVE YOU--
OH, NEVER MIND...
JUST COME HERE.
THANK GOD.
THANK GOD.
MOTEL

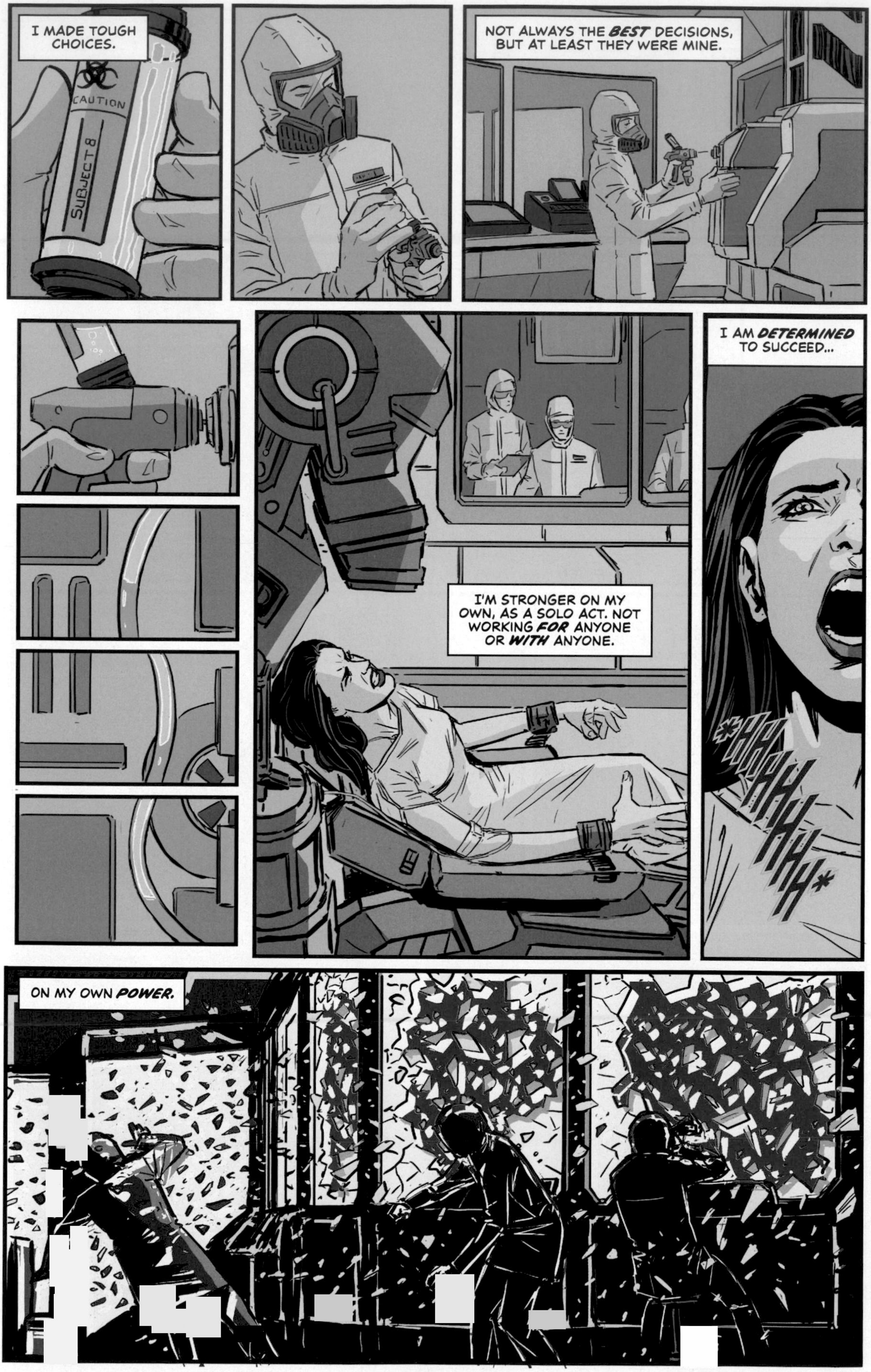
I MADE TOUGH CHOICES.
CAUTION
SUBJECT 8
NOT ALWAYS THE BEST DECISIONS, BUT AT LEAST THEY WERE MINE.
I'M STRONGER ON MY OWN, AS A SOLO ACT. NOT WORKING FOR ANYONE OR WITH ANYONE.
I AM DETERMINED TO SUCCEED...
HHHHHHHHH
ON MY OWN POWER.

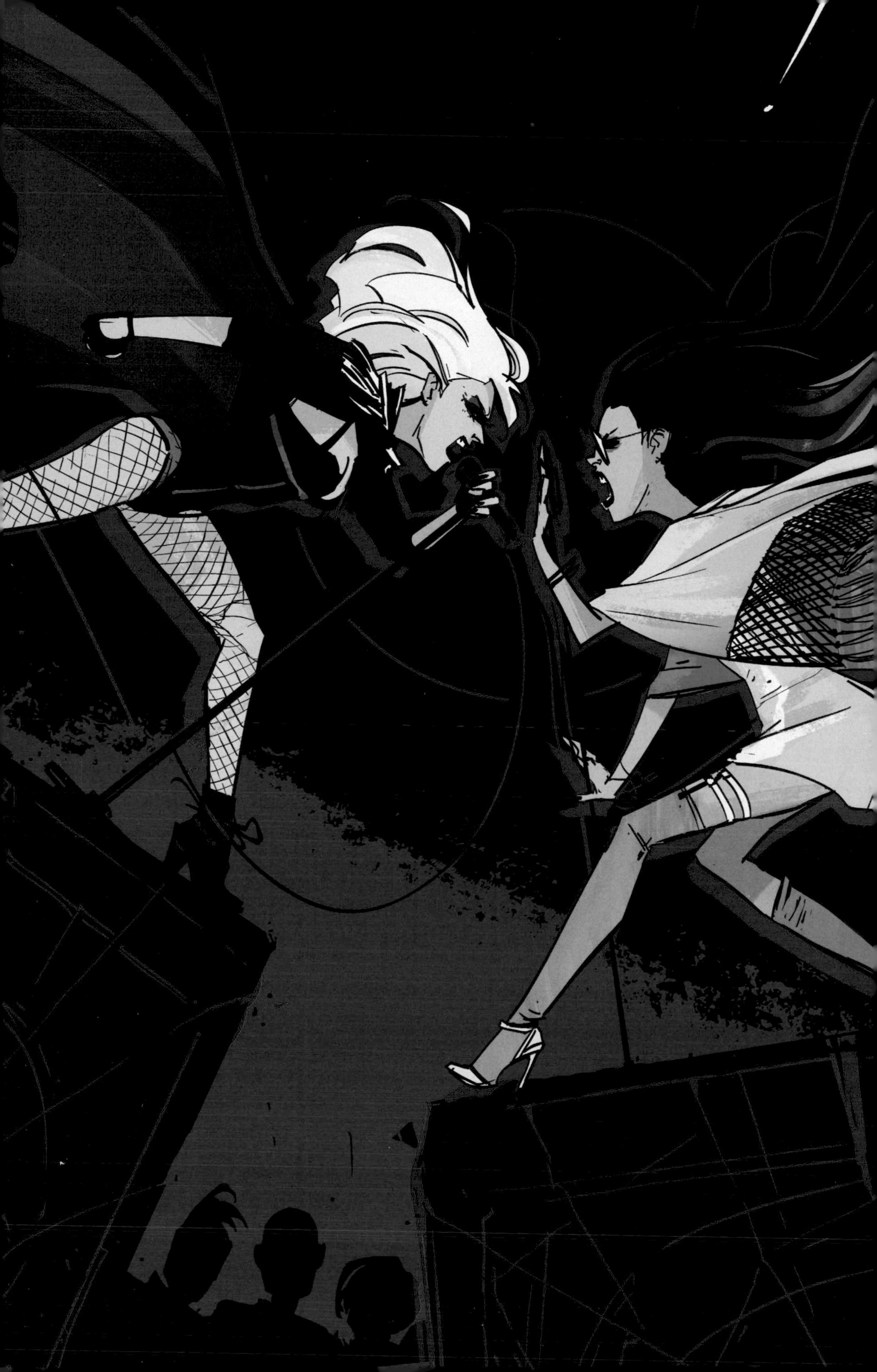

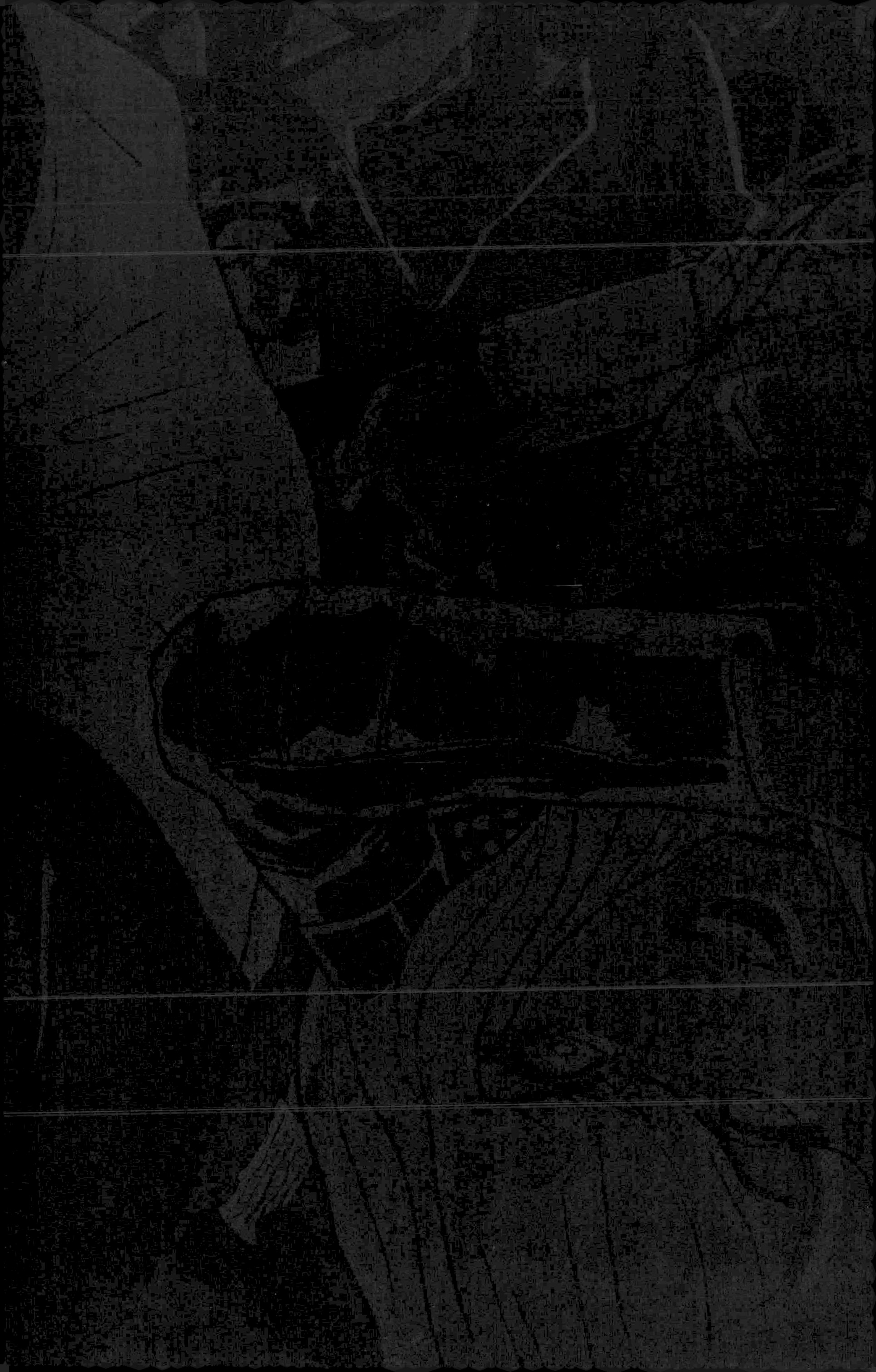

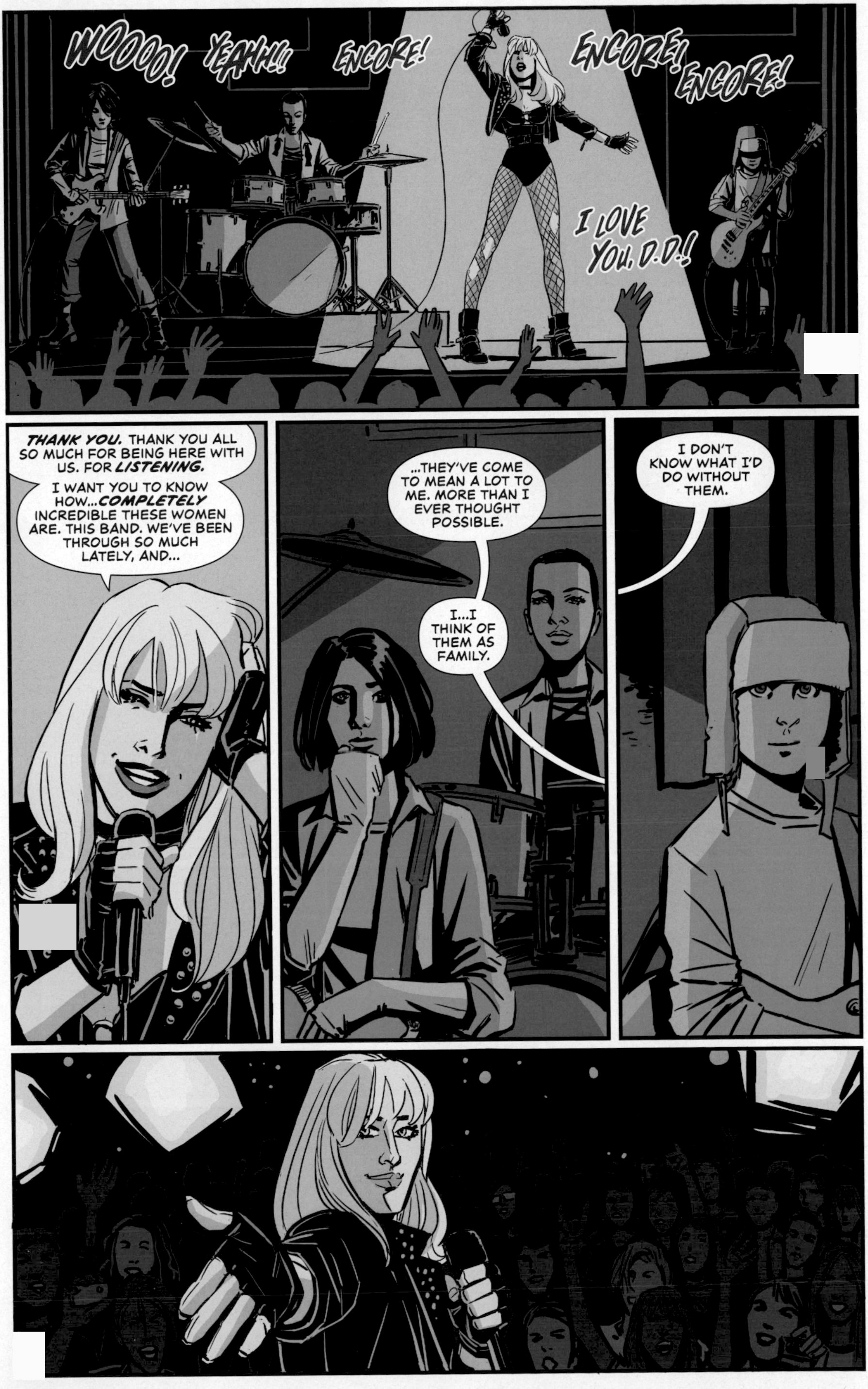
WOOOO!
YEAHH!!
ENCORE!
ENCORE! ENCORE!
I LOVE YOU, D.D.!
THANK YOU. THANK YOU ALL SO MUCH FOR BEING HERE WITH US. FOR LISTENING.
I WANT YOU TO KNOW HOW...COMPLETELY INCREDIBLE THESE WOMEN ARE. THIS BAND. WE'VE BEEN THROUGH SO MUCH LATELY, AND...
...THEY'VE COME TO MEAN A LOT TO ME. MORE THAN I EVER THOUGHT POSSIBLE.
I...I THINK OF THEM AS FAMILY.
I DON'T KNOW WHAT I'D DO WITHOUT THEM.

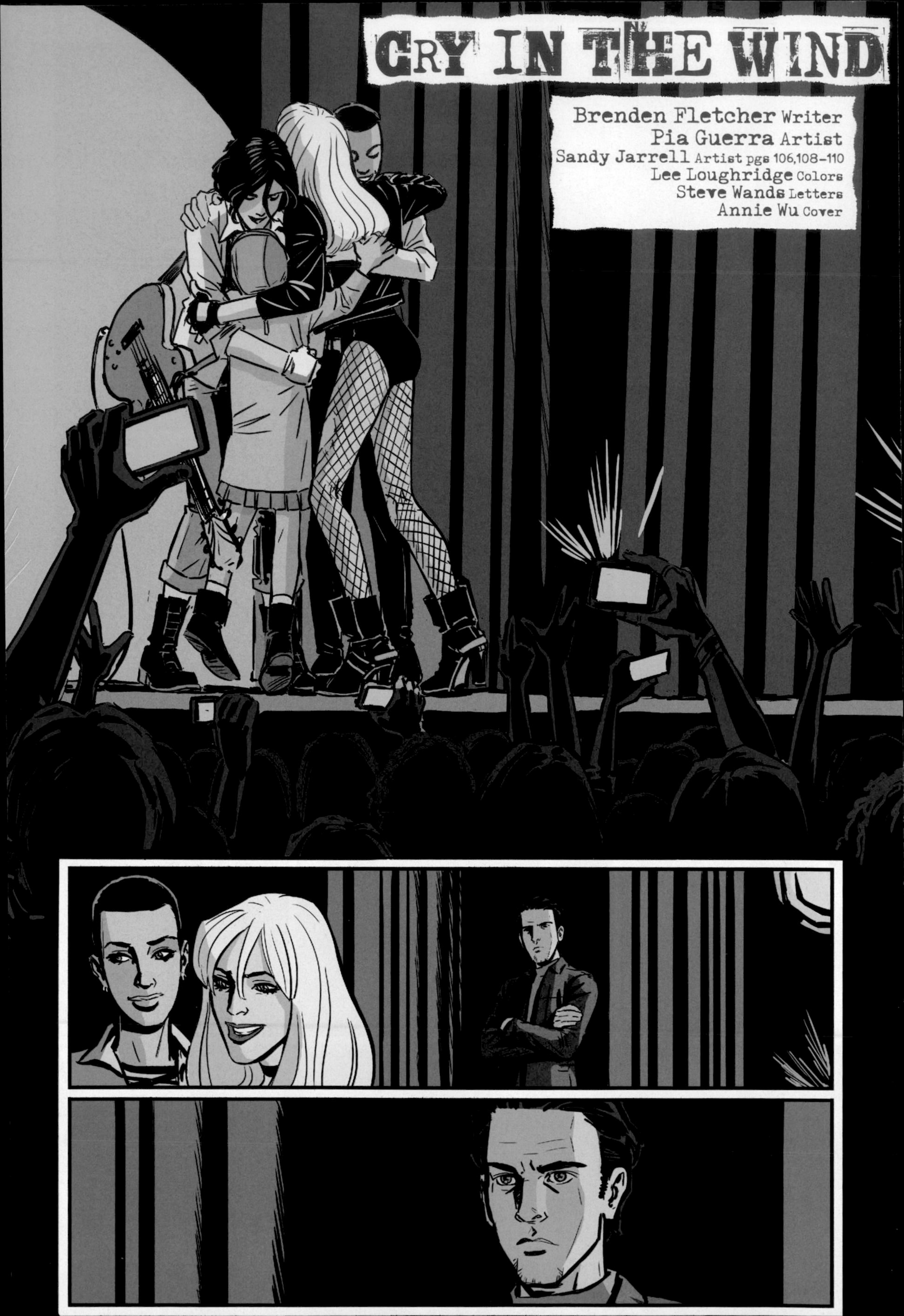
CRY IN THE WIND
Brenden Fletcher Writer
Pia Guerra Artist
Sandy Jarrell Artist pgs 106,108-110
Lee Loughridge Colors
Steve Wands Letters
Annie Wu Cover

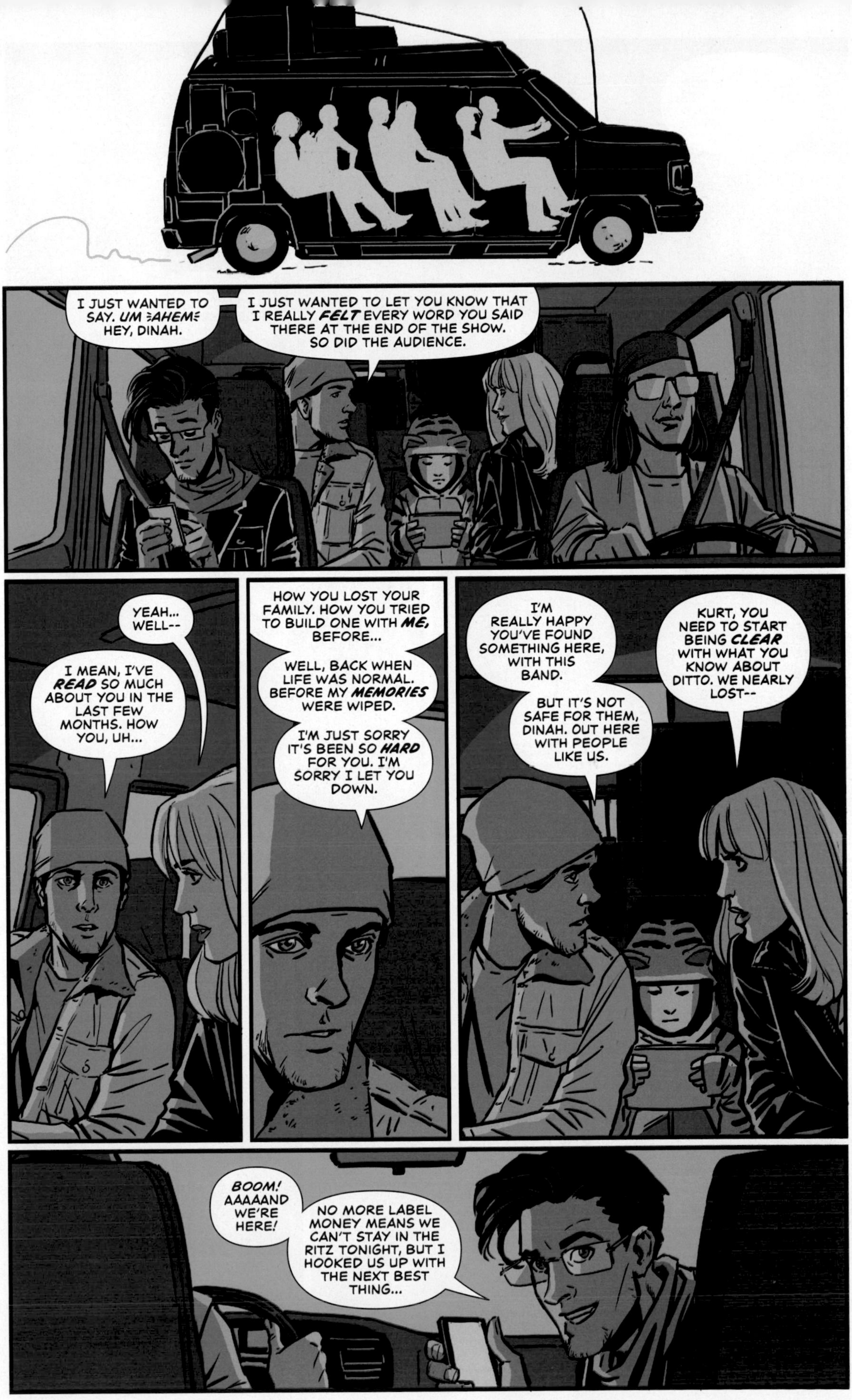
I JUST WANTED TO SAY. UM *AHEM* HEY, DINAH.
I JUST WANTED TO LET YOU KNOW THAT I REALLY FELT EVERY WORD YOU SAID THERE AT THE END OF THE SHOW. SO DID THE AUDIENCE.
YEAH... WELL--
I MEAN, I'VE READ SO MUCH ABOUT YOU IN THE LAST FEW MONTHS. HOW YOU, UH...
HOW YOU LOST YOUR FAMILY. HOW YOU TRIED TO BUILD ONE WITH ME, BEFORE...
WELL, BACK WHEN LIFE WAS NORMAL. BEFORE MY MEMORIES WERE WIPED.
I'M JUST SORRY IT'S BEEN SO HARD FOR YOU. I'M SORRY I LET YOU DOWN.
I'M REALLY HAPPY YOU'VE FOUND SOMETHING HERE, WITH THIS BAND.
BUT IT'S NOT SAFE FOR THEM, DINAH. OUT HERE WITH PEOPLE LIKE US.
KURT, YOU NEED TO START BEING CLEAR WITH WHAT YOU KNOW ABOUT DITTO. WE NEARLY LOST--
BOOM! AAAAAND WE'RE HERE!
NO MORE LABEL MONEY MEANS WE CAN'T STAY IN THE RITZ TONIGHT, BUT I HOOKED US UP WITH THE NEXT BEST THING...

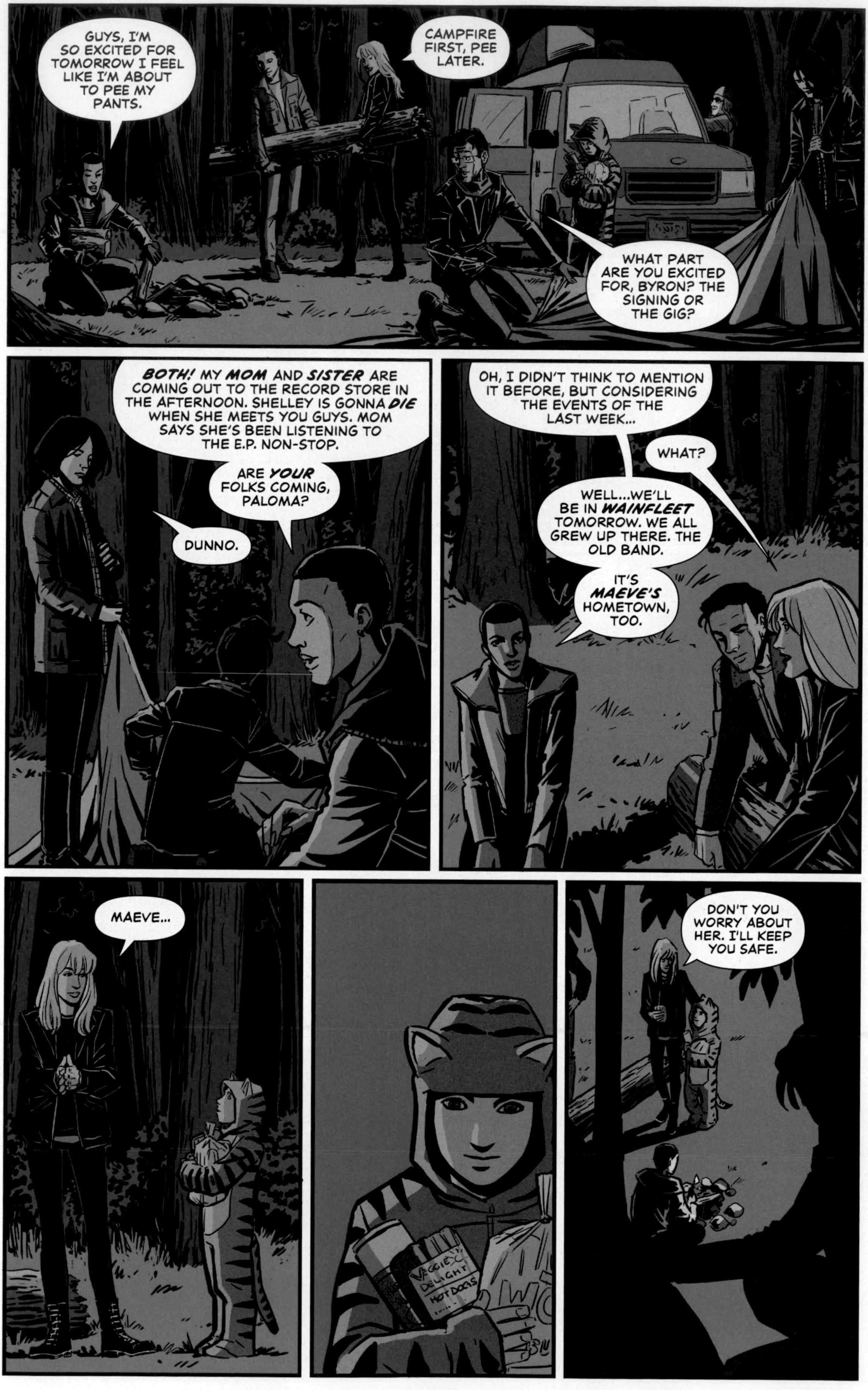
GUYS, I'M SO EXCITED FOR TOMORROW I FEEL LIKE I'M ABOUT TO PEE MY PANTS.
CAMPFIRE FIRST, PEE LATER.
WHAT PART ARE YOU EXCITED FOR, BYRON? THE SIGNING OR THE GIG?
BOTH! MY MOM AND SISTER ARE COMING OUT TO THE RECORD STORE IN THE AFTERNOON. SHELLEY IS GONNA DIE WHEN SHE MEETS YOU GUYS. MOM SAYS SHE'S BEEN LISTENING TO THE E.P. NON-STOP.
ARE YOUR FOLKS COMING, PALOMA?
DUNNO.
OH, I DIDN'T THINK TO MENTION IT BEFORE, BUT CONSIDERING THE EVENTS OF THE LAST WEEK...
WHAT?
WELL...WE'LL BE IN WAINFLEET TOMORROW. WE ALL GREW UP THERE. THE OLD BAND.
IT'S MAEVE'S HOMETOWN, TOO.
MAEVE...
VEGGIE DELIGHT
HOT DOGS
DON'T YOU WORRY ABOUT HER. I'LL KEEP YOU SAFE.

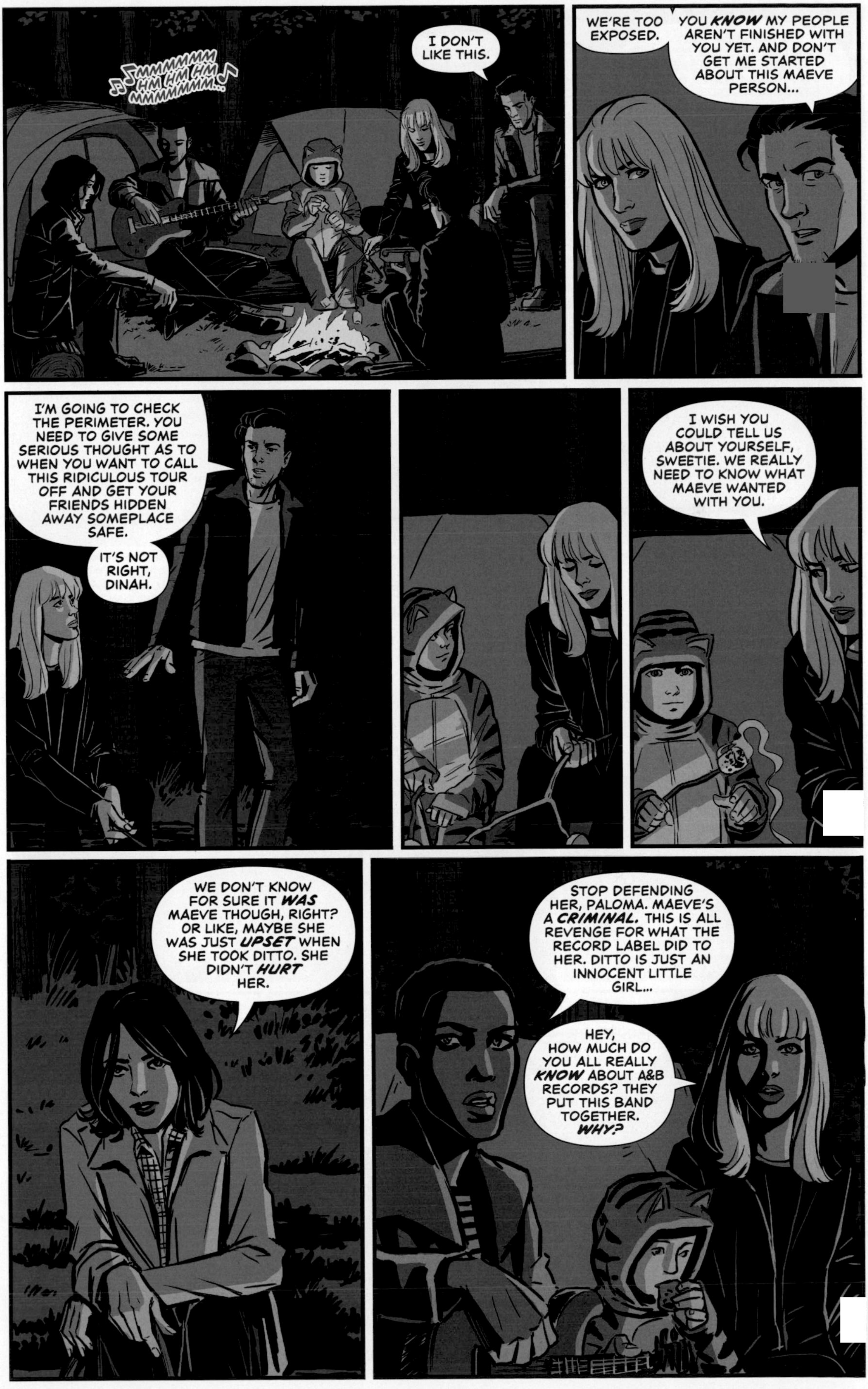
♪MMMMMMM HM HM HM MMMMMMM...♪
I DON'T LIKE THIS.
WE'RE TOO EXPOSED.
YOU *KNOW* MY PEOPLE AREN'T FINISHED WITH YOU YET. AND DON'T GET ME STARTED ABOUT THIS MAEVE PERSON...
I'M GOING TO CHECK THE PERIMETER. YOU NEED TO GIVE SOME SERIOUS THOUGHT AS TO WHEN YOU WANT TO CALL THIS RIDICULOUS TOUR OFF AND GET YOUR FRIENDS HIDDEN AWAY SOMEPLACE SAFE.
IT'S NOT RIGHT, DINAH.
I WISH YOU COULD TELL US ABOUT YOURSELF, SWEETIE. WE REALLY NEED TO KNOW WHAT MAEVE WANTED WITH YOU.
WE DON'T KNOW FOR SURE IT *WAS* MAEVE THOUGH, RIGHT? OR LIKE, MAYBE SHE WAS JUST *UPSET* WHEN SHE TOOK DITTO. SHE DIDN'T *HURT* HER.
STOP DEFENDING HER, PALOMA. MAEVE'S A *CRIMINAL.* THIS IS ALL REVENGE FOR WHAT THE RECORD LABEL DID TO HER. DITTO IS JUST AN INNOCENT LITTLE GIRL...
HEY, HOW MUCH DO YOU ALL REALLY *KNOW* ABOUT A&B RECORDS? THEY PUT THIS BAND TOGETHER. *WHY?*

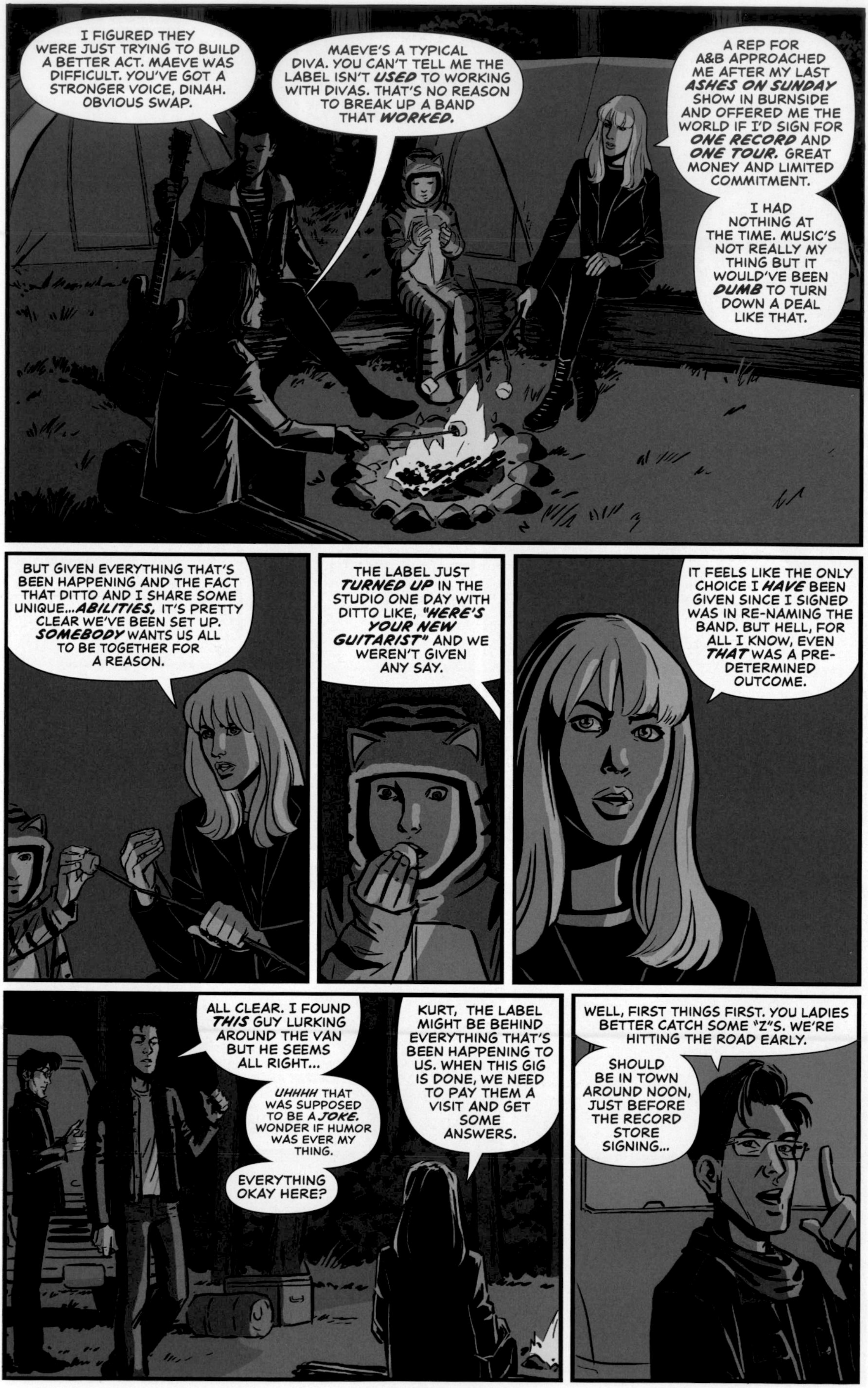
I FIGURED THEY WERE JUST TRYING TO BUILD A BETTER ACT. MAEVE WAS DIFFICULT. YOU'VE GOT A STRONGER VOICE, DINAH. OBVIOUS SWAP.
MAEVE'S A TYPICAL DIVA. YOU CAN'T TELL ME THE LABEL ISN'T USED TO WORKING WITH DIVAS. THAT'S NO REASON TO BREAK UP A BAND THAT WORKED.
A REP FOR A&B APPROACHED ME AFTER MY LAST ASHES ON SUNDAY SHOW IN BURNSIDE AND OFFERED ME THE WORLD IF I'D SIGN FOR ONE RECORD AND ONE TOUR. GREAT MONEY AND LIMITED COMMITMENT.
I HAD NOTHING AT THE TIME. MUSIC'S NOT REALLY MY THING BUT IT WOULD'VE BEEN DUMB TO TURN DOWN A DEAL LIKE THAT.
BUT GIVEN EVERYTHING THAT'S BEEN HAPPENING AND THE FACT THAT DITTO AND I SHARE SOME UNIQUE...ABILITIES, IT'S PRETTY CLEAR WE'VE BEEN SET UP. SOMEBODY WANTS US ALL TO BE TOGETHER FOR A REASON.
THE LABEL JUST TURNED UP IN THE STUDIO ONE DAY WITH DITTO LIKE, "HERE'S YOUR NEW GUITARIST" AND WE WEREN'T GIVEN ANY SAY.
IT FEELS LIKE THE ONLY CHOICE I HAVE BEEN GIVEN SINCE I SIGNED WAS IN RE-NAMING THE BAND. BUT HELL, FOR ALL I KNOW, EVEN THAT WAS A PRE-DETERMINED OUTCOME.
ALL CLEAR. I FOUND THIS GUY LURKING AROUND THE VAN BUT HE SEEMS ALL RIGHT...
UHHHH THAT WAS SUPPOSED TO BE A JOKE. WONDER IF HUMOR WAS EVER MY THING.
EVERYTHING OKAY HERE?
KURT, THE LABEL MIGHT BE BEHIND EVERYTHING THAT'S BEEN HAPPENING TO US. WHEN THIS GIG IS DONE, WE NEED TO PAY THEM A VISIT AND GET SOME ANSWERS.
WELL, FIRST THINGS FIRST. YOU LADIES BETTER CATCH SOME "Z"S. WE'RE HITTING THE ROAD EARLY.
SHOULD BE IN TOWN AROUND NOON, JUST BEFORE THE RECORD STORE SIGNING...

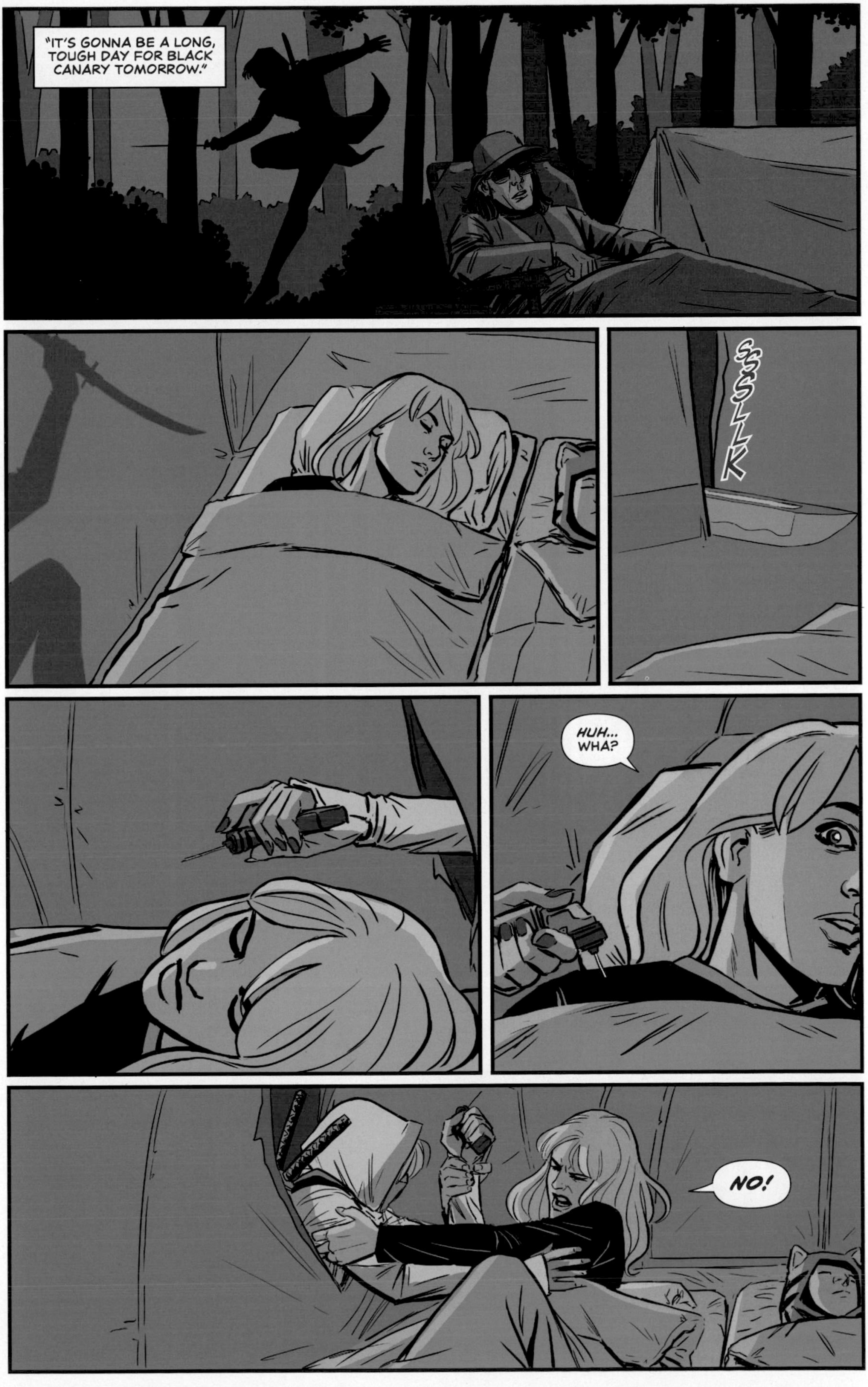
"IT'S GONNA BE A LONG, TOUGH DAY FOR BLACK CANARY TOMORROW."
SSSLLK
HUH... WHA?
NO!

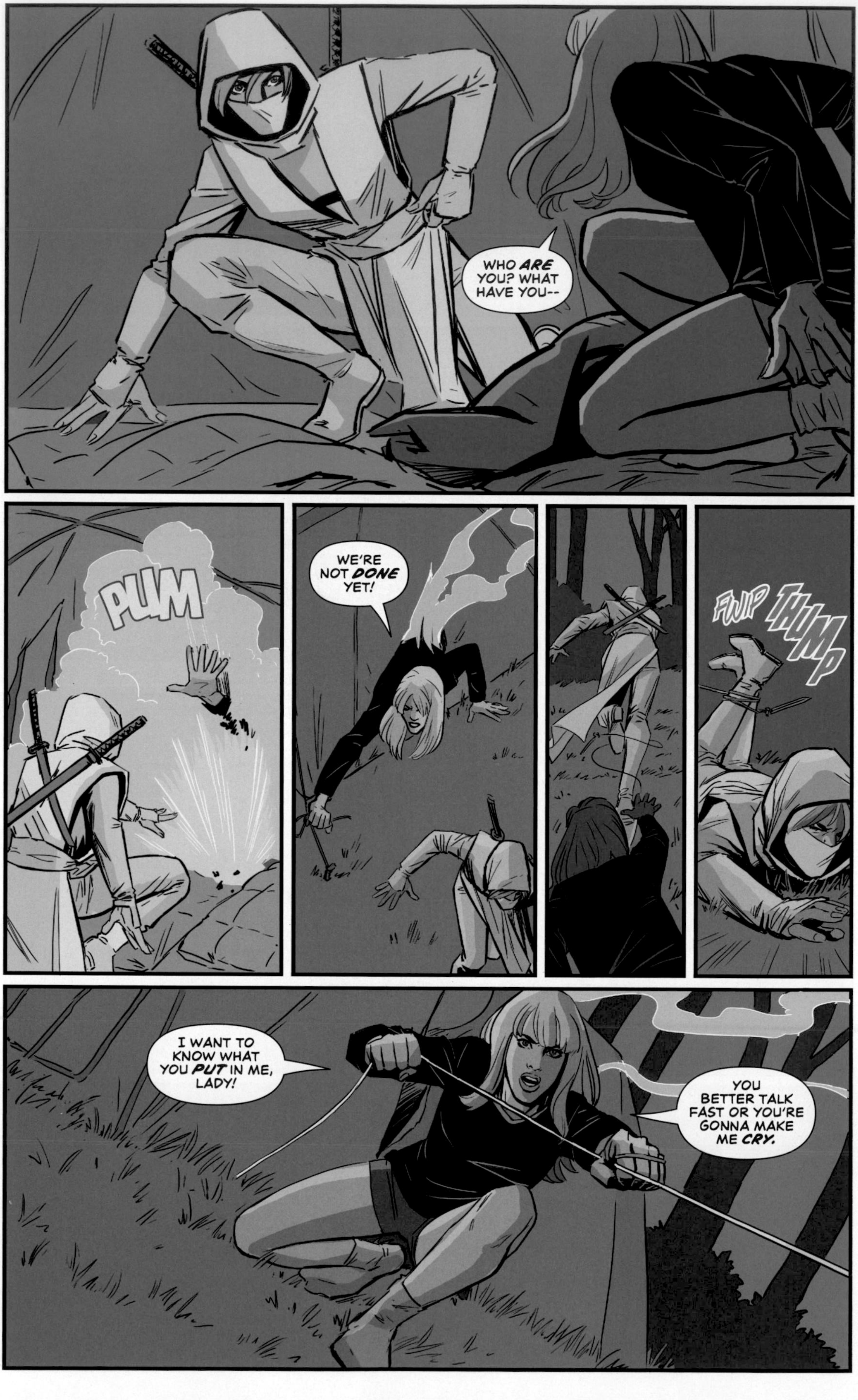

WHO *ARE* YOU? WHAT HAVE YOU--
PUM
WE'RE NOT *DONE* YET!
FWIP
THUMP
I WANT TO KNOW WHAT YOU *PUT* IN ME, LADY!
YOU BETTER TALK FAST OR YOU'RE GONNA MAKE ME *CRY.*

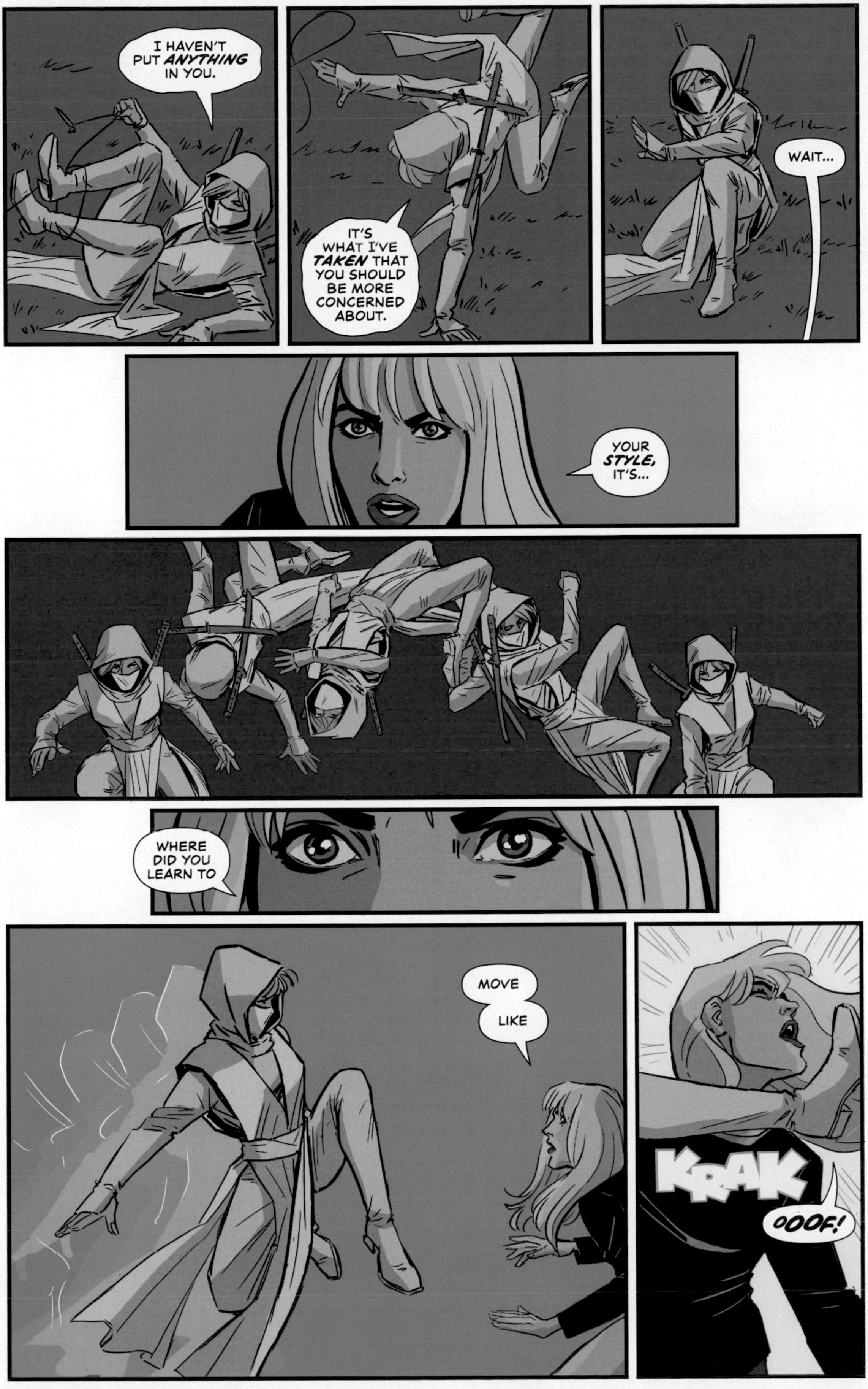

I HAVEN'T PUT ANYTHING IN YOU.
IT'S WHAT I'VE TAKEN THAT YOU SHOULD BE MORE CONCERNED ABOUT.
WAIT...
YOUR STYLE, IT'S...
WHERE DID YOU LEARN TO
MOVE
LIKE
KRAK
OOOF!

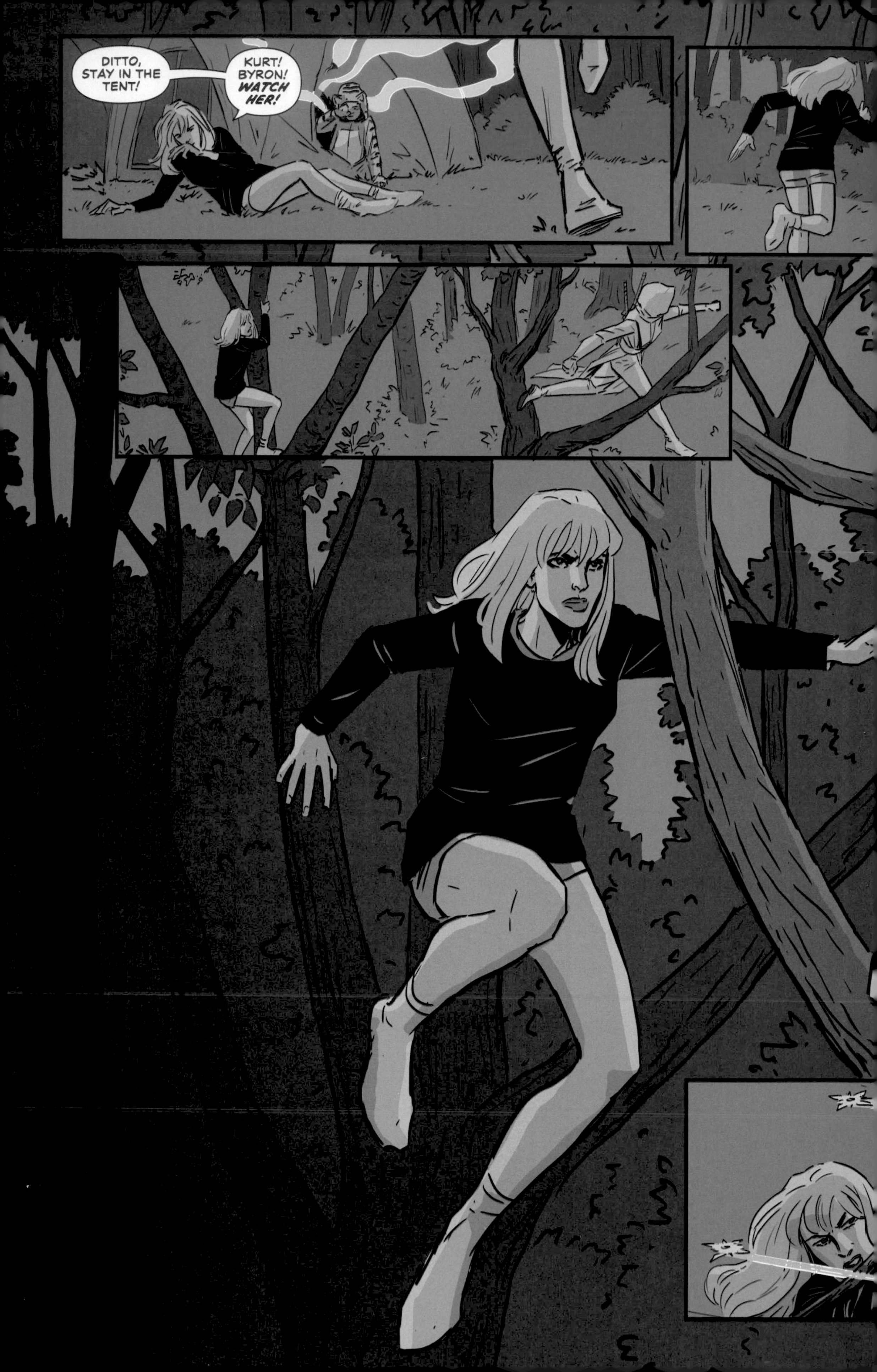
DITTO, STAY IN THE TENT!
KURT! BYRON! WATCH HER!

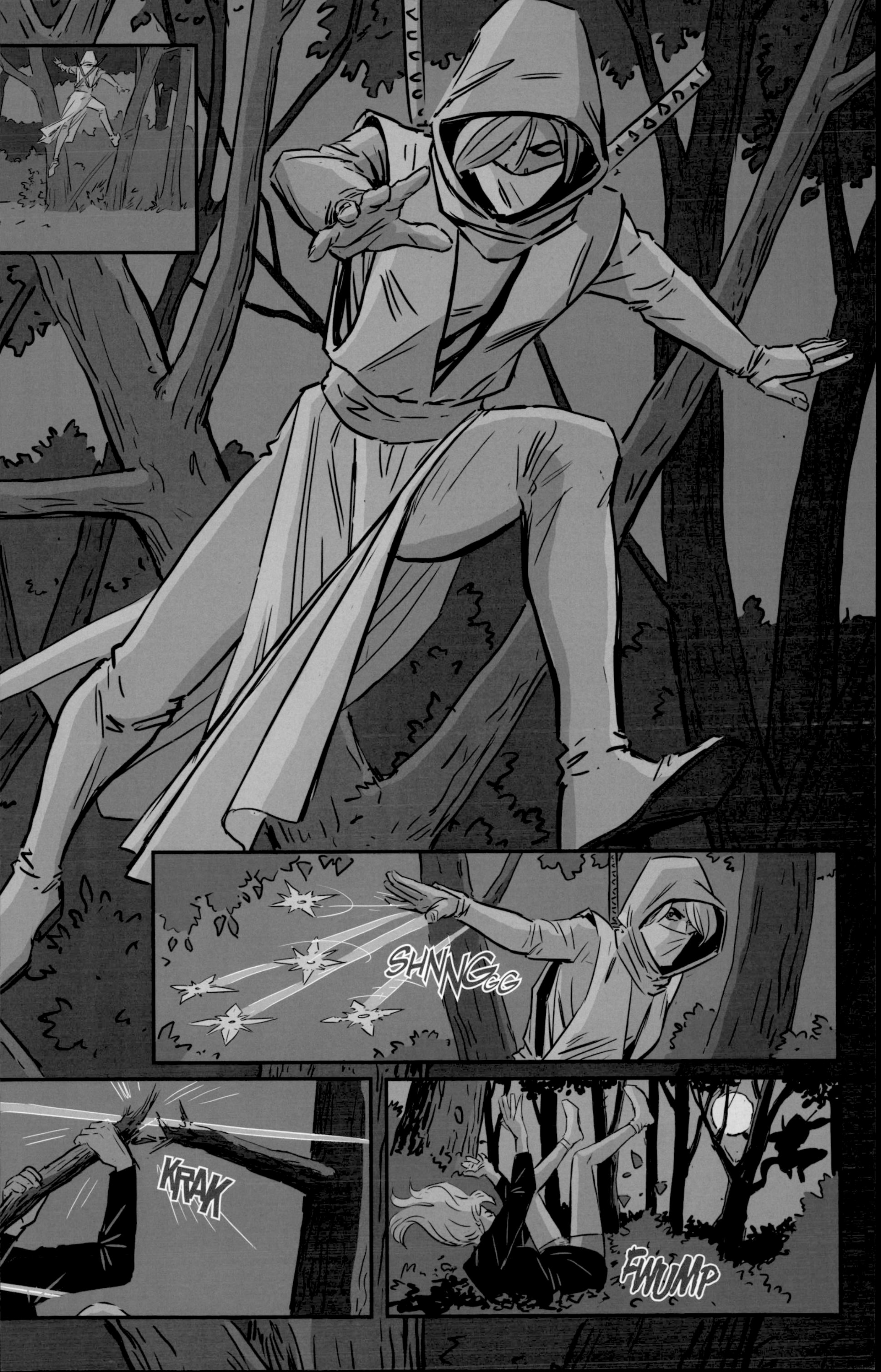
SHNNGee
KRAK
FWUMP

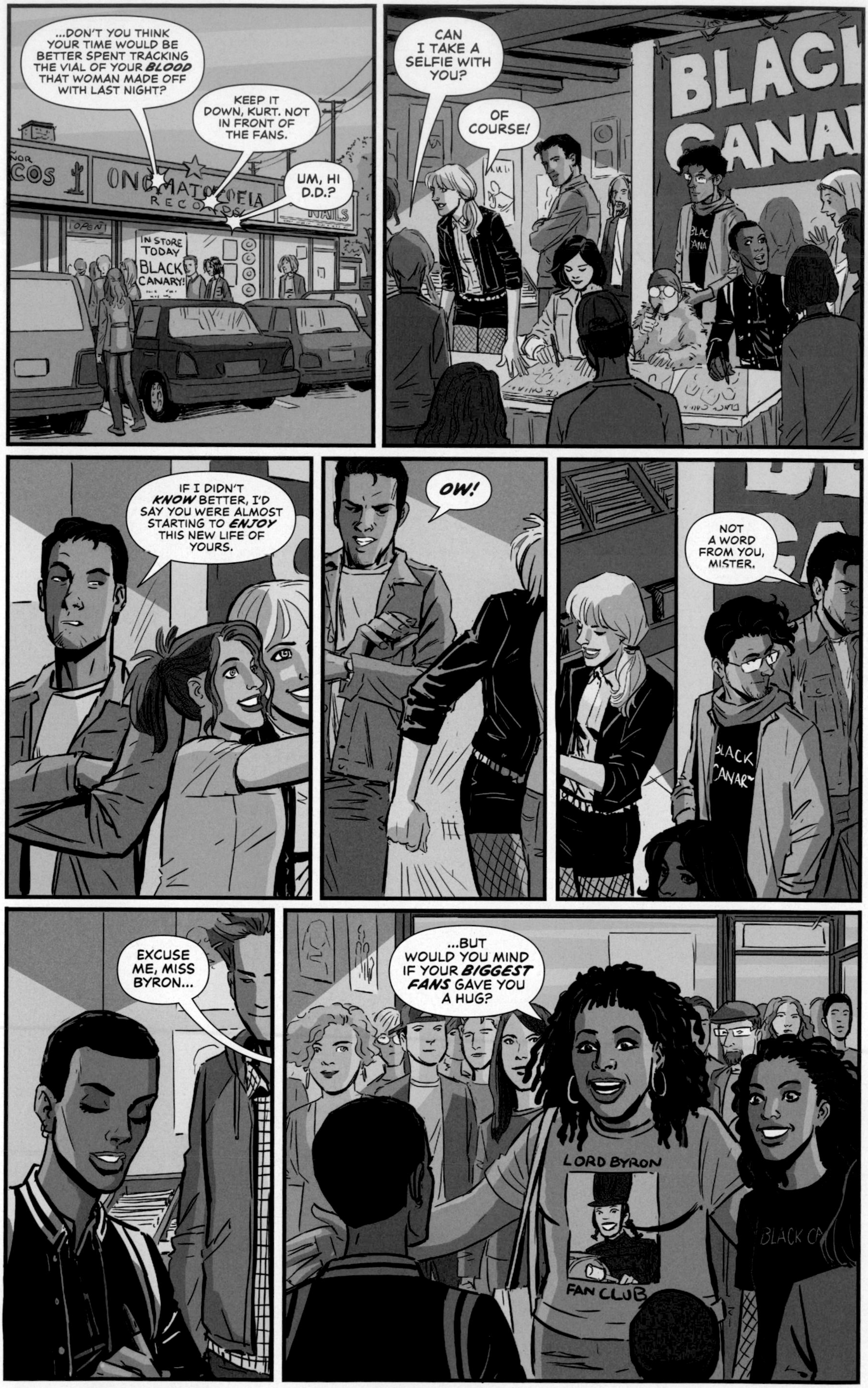
...DON'T YOU THINK YOUR TIME WOULD BE BETTER SPENT TRACKING THE VIAL OF YOUR BLOOD THAT WOMAN MADE OFF WITH LAST NIGHT?
KEEP IT DOWN, KURT. NOT IN FRONT OF THE FANS.
UM, HI D.D.?
ONOMATOPOEIA RECORDS
NAILS
OPEN
IN STORE TODAY BLACK CANARY!
CAN I TAKE A SELFIE WITH YOU?
OF COURSE!
BLACK CANA
IF I DIDN'T KNOW BETTER, I'D SAY YOU WERE ALMOST STARTING TO ENJOY THIS NEW LIFE OF YOURS.
OW!
NOT A WORD FROM YOU, MISTER.
BLACK CANARY
EXCUSE ME, MISS BYRON...
...BUT WOULD YOU MIND IF YOUR BIGGEST FANS GAVE YOU A HUG?
LORD BYRON
FAN CLUB
BLACK CA

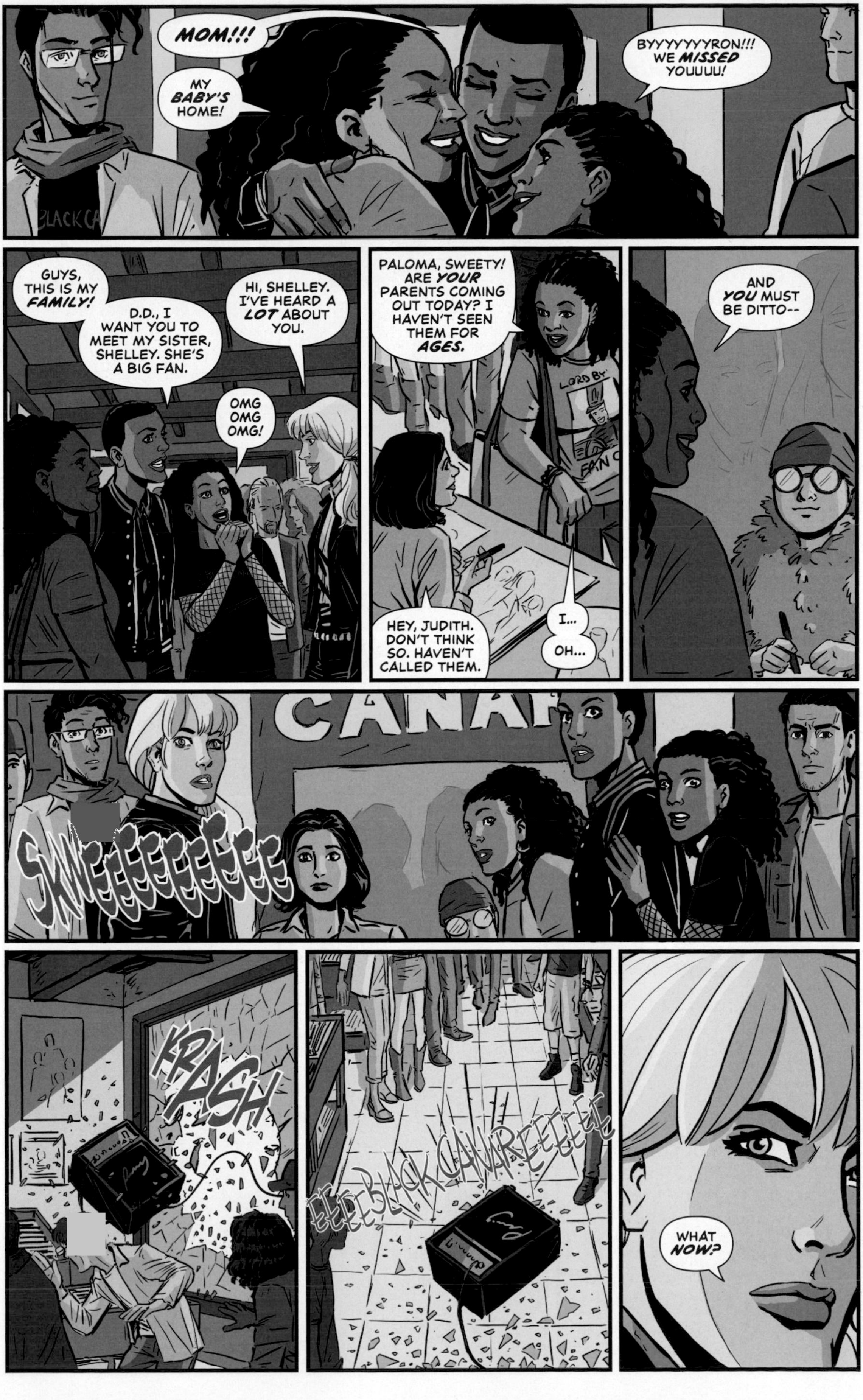

MOM!!!
MY BABY'S HOME!
BYYYYYYYRON!!! WE MISSED YOUUUU!
GUYS, THIS IS MY FAMILY!
D.D., I WANT YOU TO MEET MY SISTER, SHELLEY. SHE'S A BIG FAN.
HI, SHELLEY. I'VE HEARD A LOT ABOUT YOU.
OMG OMG OMG!
PALOMA, SWEETY! ARE YOUR PARENTS COMING OUT TODAY? I HAVEN'T SEEN THEM FOR AGES.
LORD BY
FAN C
HEY, JUDITH. DON'T THINK SO. HAVEN'T CALLED THEM.
I...
OH...
AND YOU MUST BE DITTO--
CANA
SKWEEEEEEEEEE
KRASH
EEEEBLACK CANAREEEEEE
WHAT NOW?

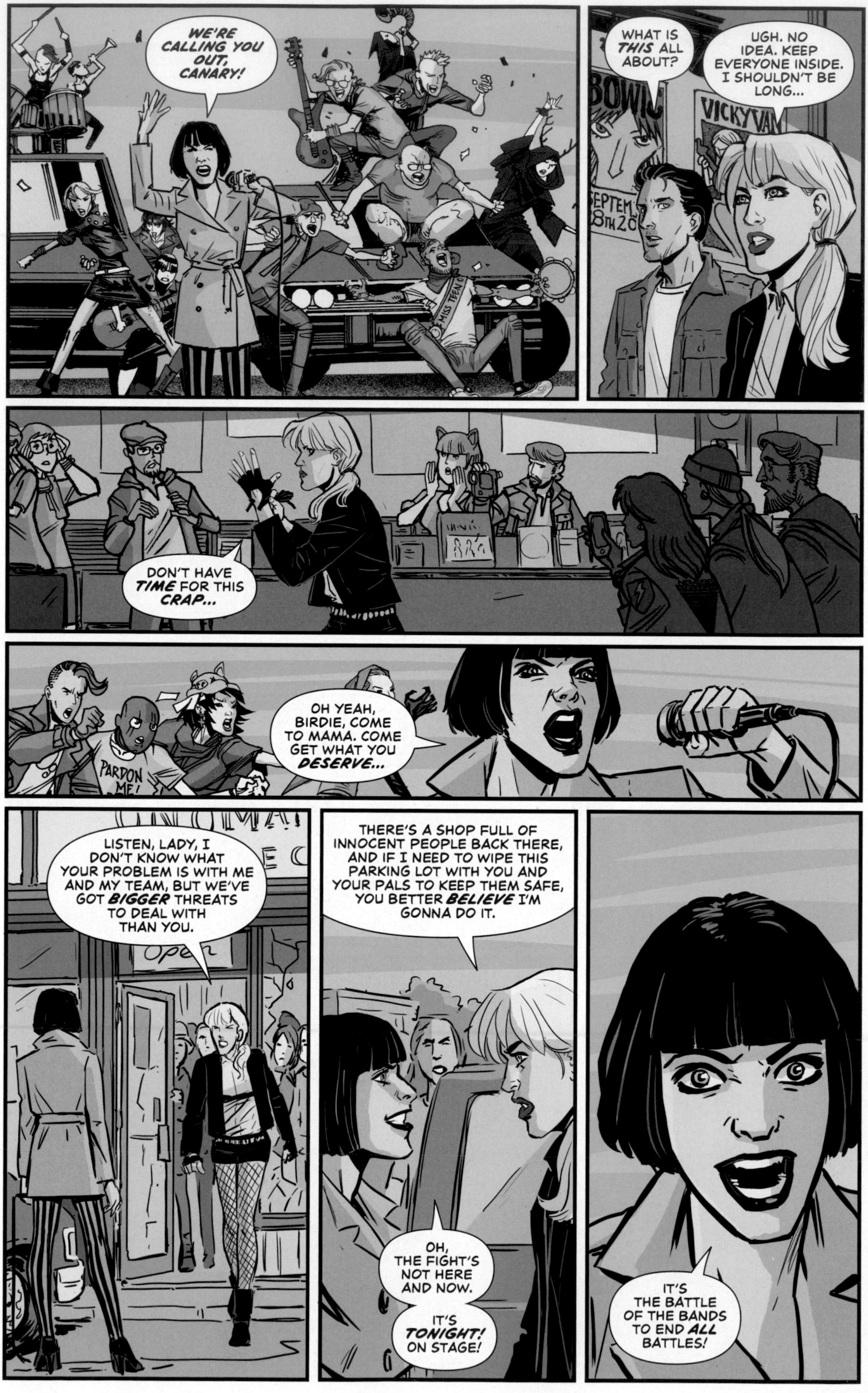
WE'RE CALLING YOU OUT, CANARY!
MISS TEEN
WHAT IS THIS ALL ABOUT?
UGH. NO IDEA. KEEP EVERYONE INSIDE. I SHOULDN'T BE LONG...
VICKY VAN
DON'T HAVE TIME FOR THIS CRAP...
PARDON ME!
OH YEAH, BIRDIE, COME TO MAMA. COME GET WHAT YOU DESERVE...
LISTEN, LADY, I DON'T KNOW WHAT YOUR PROBLEM IS WITH ME AND MY TEAM, BUT WE'VE GOT BIGGER THREATS TO DEAL WITH THAN YOU.
Open
THERE'S A SHOP FULL OF INNOCENT PEOPLE BACK THERE, AND IF I NEED TO WIPE THIS PARKING LOT WITH YOU AND YOUR PALS TO KEEP THEM SAFE, YOU BETTER BELIEVE I'M GONNA DO IT.
OH, THE FIGHT'S NOT HERE AND NOW.
IT'S TONIGHT! ON STAGE!
IT'S THE BATTLE OF THE BANDS TO END ALL BATTLES!

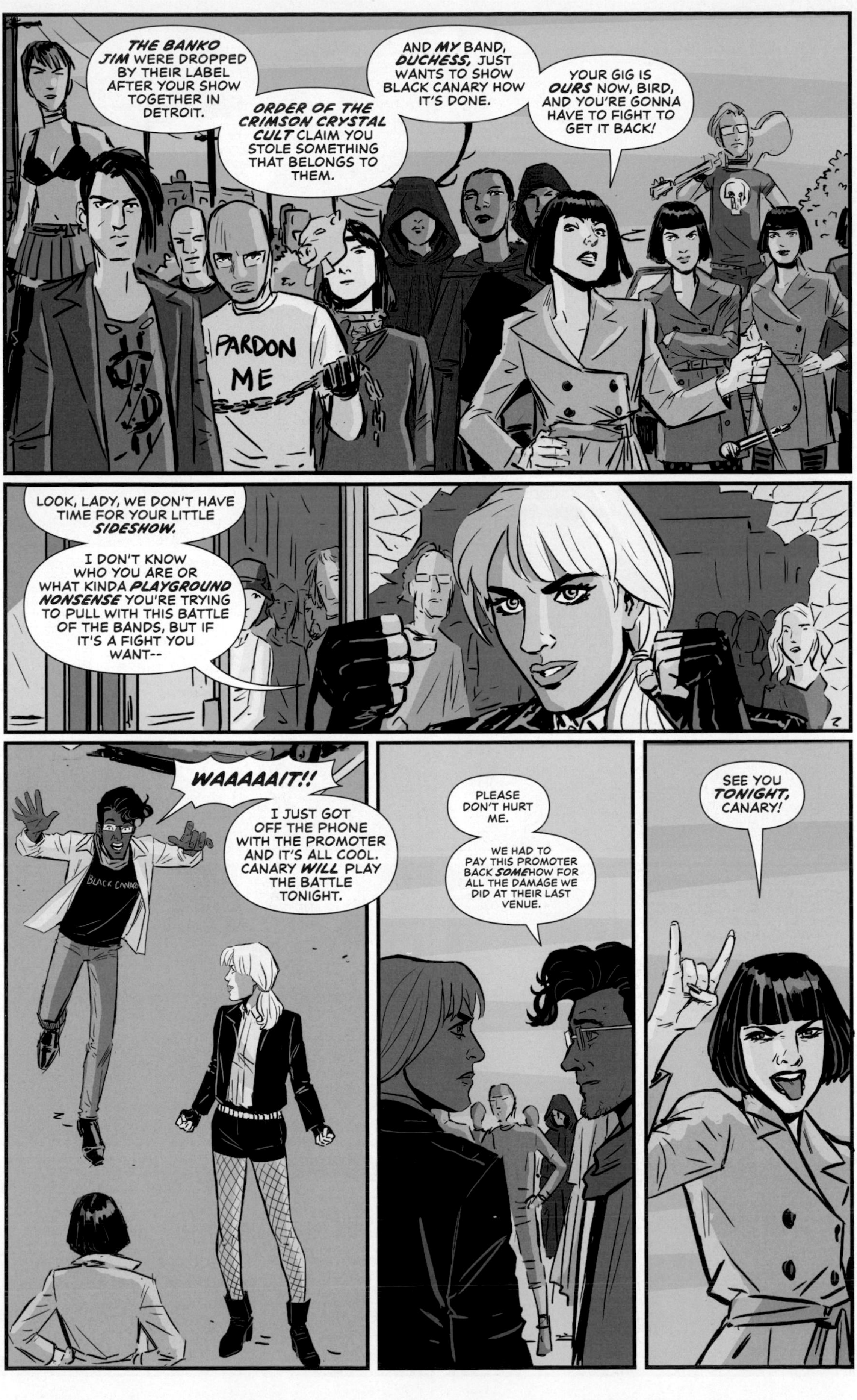
THE BANKO JIM WERE DROPPED BY THEIR LABEL AFTER YOUR SHOW TOGETHER IN DETROIT.
ORDER OF THE CRIMSON CRYSTAL CULT CLAIM YOU STOLE SOMETHING THAT BELONGS TO THEM.
AND MY BAND, DUCHESS, JUST WANTS TO SHOW BLACK CANARY HOW IT'S DONE.
YOUR GIG IS OURS NOW, BIRD, AND YOU'RE GONNA HAVE TO FIGHT TO GET IT BACK!
PARDON ME
LOOK, LADY, WE DON'T HAVE TIME FOR YOUR LITTLE SIDESHOW.
I DON'T KNOW WHO YOU ARE OR WHAT KINDA PLAYGROUND NONSENSE YOU'RE TRYING TO PULL WITH THIS BATTLE OF THE BANDS, BUT IF IT'S A FIGHT YOU WANT--
WAAAAAIT!!
I JUST GOT OFF THE PHONE WITH THE PROMOTER AND IT'S ALL COOL. CANARY WILL PLAY THE BATTLE TONIGHT.
BLACK CANARY
PLEASE DON'T HURT ME.
WE HAD TO PAY THIS PROMOTER BACK SOMEHOW FOR ALL THE DAMAGE WE DID AT THEIR LAST VENUE.
SEE YOU TONIGHT, CANARY!

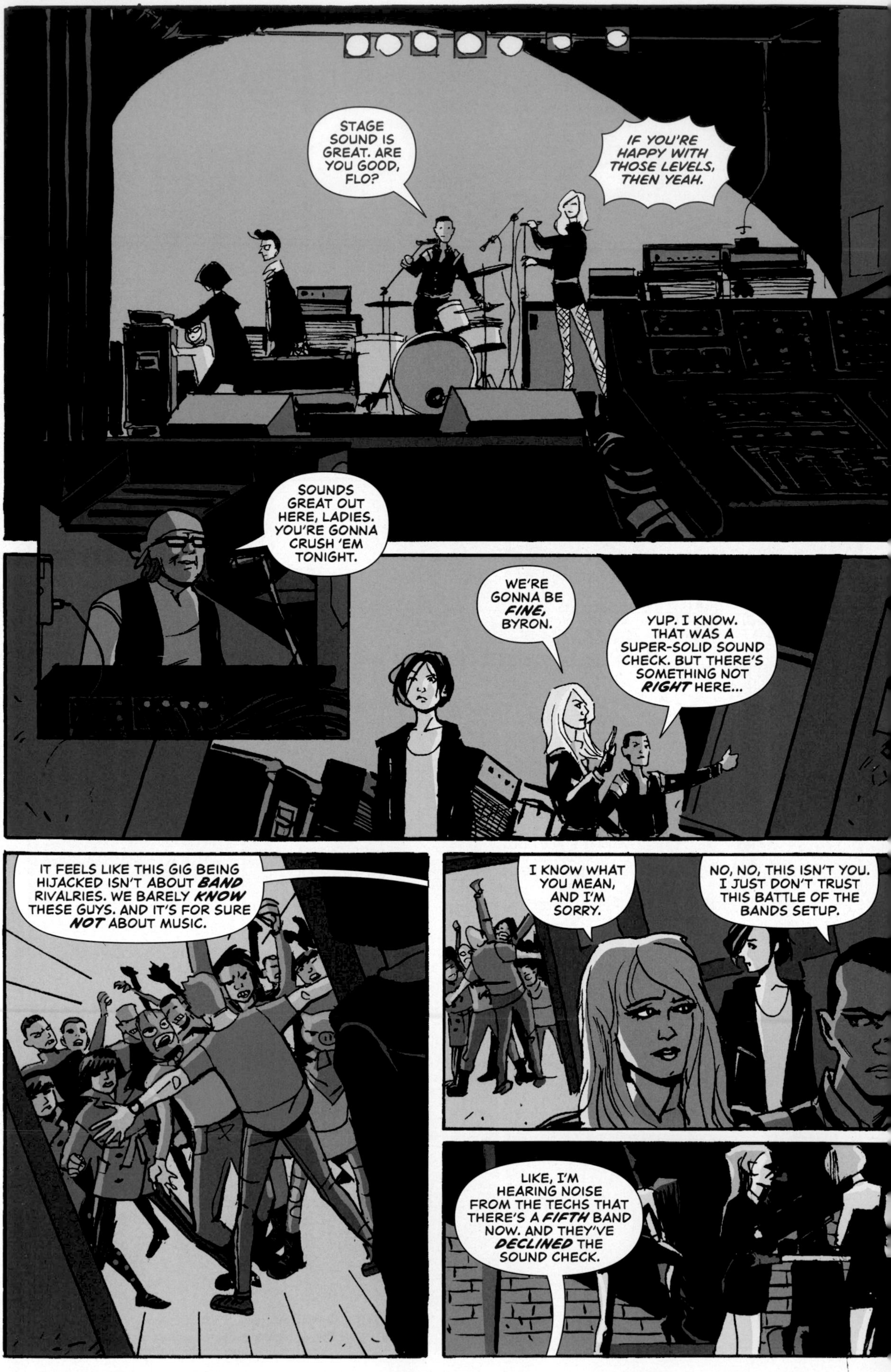
STAGE SOUND IS GREAT. ARE YOU GOOD, FLO?
IF YOU'RE HAPPY WITH THOSE LEVELS, THEN YEAH.
SOUNDS GREAT OUT HERE, LADIES. YOU'RE GONNA CRUSH 'EM TONIGHT.
WE'RE GONNA BE FINE, BYRON.
YUP. I KNOW. THAT WAS A SUPER-SOLID SOUND CHECK. BUT THERE'S SOMETHING NOT RIGHT HERE...
IT FEELS LIKE THIS GIG BEING HIJACKED ISN'T ABOUT BAND RIVALRIES. WE BARELY KNOW THESE GUYS. AND IT'S FOR SURE NOT ABOUT MUSIC.
I KNOW WHAT YOU MEAN, AND I'M SORRY.
NO, NO, THIS ISN'T YOU. I JUST DON'T TRUST THIS BATTLE OF THE BANDS SETUP.
LIKE, I'M HEARING NOISE FROM THE TECHS THAT THERE'S A FIFTH BAND NOW. AND THEY'VE DECLINED THE SOUND CHECK.

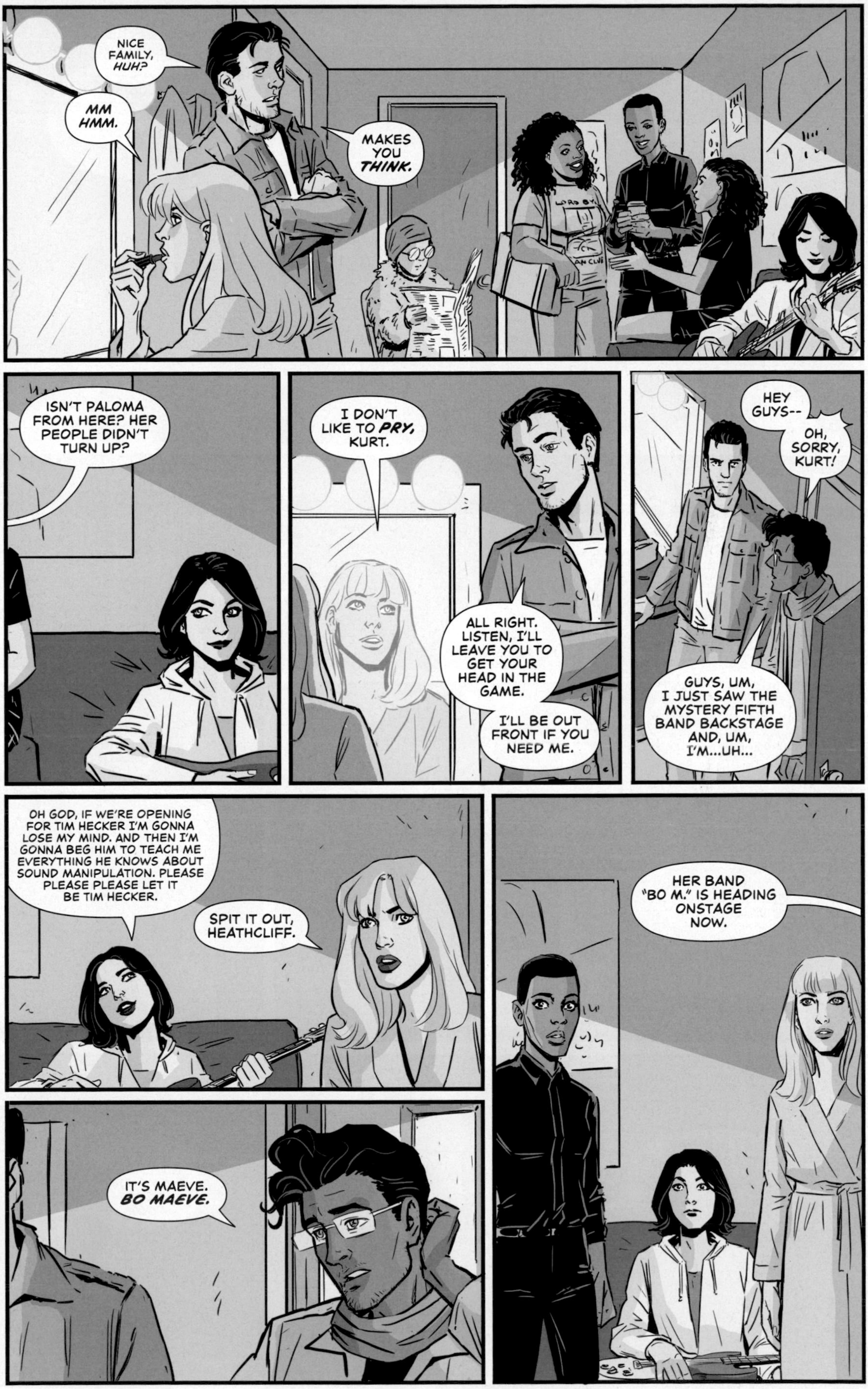
NICE FAMILY, HUH?
MM HMM.
MAKES YOU THINK.
ISN'T PALOMA FROM HERE? HER PEOPLE DIDN'T TURN UP?
I DON'T LIKE TO PRY, KURT.
ALL RIGHT. LISTEN, I'LL LEAVE YOU TO GET YOUR HEAD IN THE GAME.
I'LL BE OUT FRONT IF YOU NEED ME.
HEY GUYS--
OH, SORRY, KURT!
GUYS, UM, I JUST SAW THE MYSTERY FIFTH BAND BACKSTAGE AND, UM, I'M...UH...
OH GOD, IF WE'RE OPENING FOR TIM HECKER I'M GONNA LOSE MY MIND. AND THEN I'M GONNA BEG HIM TO TEACH ME EVERYTHING HE KNOWS ABOUT SOUND MANIPULATION. PLEASE PLEASE PLEASE LET IT BE TIM HECKER.
SPIT IT OUT, HEATHCLIFF.
IT'S MAEVE. BO MAEVE.
HER BAND "BO M." IS HEADING ONSTAGE NOW.

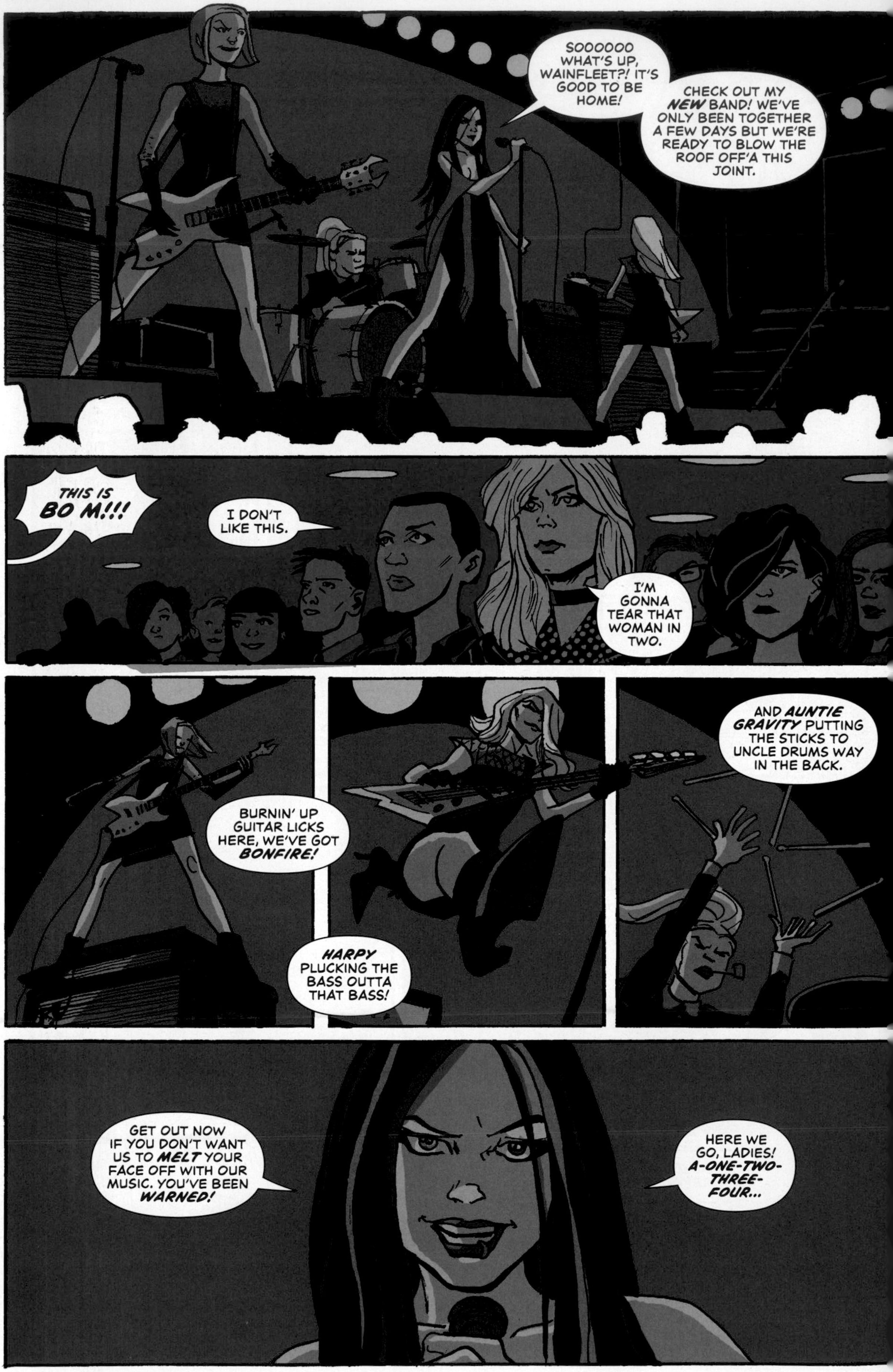
SOOOOOO WHAT'S UP, WAINFLEET?! IT'S GOOD TO BE HOME!
CHECK OUT MY NEW BAND! WE'VE ONLY BEEN TOGETHER A FEW DAYS BUT WE'RE READY TO BLOW THE ROOF OFF'A THIS JOINT.
THIS IS BO M!!!
I DON'T LIKE THIS.
I'M GONNA TEAR THAT WOMAN IN TWO.
BURNIN' UP GUITAR LICKS HERE, WE'VE GOT BONFIRE!
HARPY PLUCKING THE BASS OUTTA THAT BASS!
AND AUNTIE GRAVITY PUTTING THE STICKS TO UNCLE DRUMS WAY IN THE BACK.
GET OUT NOW IF YOU DON'T WANT US TO MELT YOUR FACE OFF WITH OUR MUSIC. YOU'VE BEEN WARNED!
HERE WE GO, LADIES! A-ONE-TWO-THREE-FOUR...

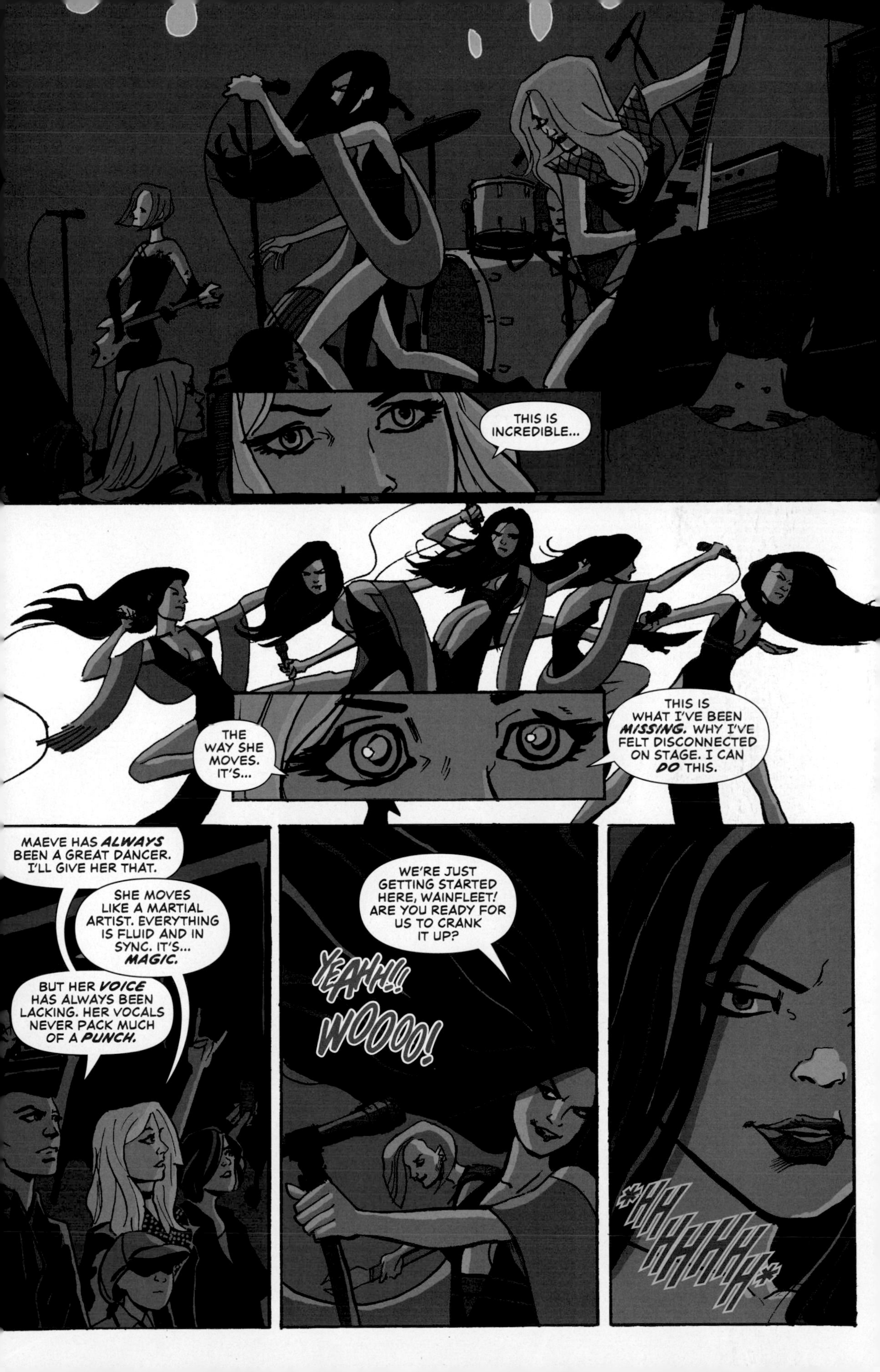

THIS IS INCREDIBLE...
THE WAY SHE MOVES. IT'S...
THIS IS WHAT I'VE BEEN MISSING. WHY I'VE FELT DISCONNECTED ON STAGE. I CAN DO THIS.
MAEVE HAS ALWAYS BEEN A GREAT DANCER. I'LL GIVE HER THAT.
SHE MOVES LIKE A MARTIAL ARTIST. EVERYTHING IS FLUID AND IN SYNC. IT'S... MAGIC.
BUT HER VOICE HAS ALWAYS BEEN LACKING. HER VOCALS NEVER PACK MUCH OF A PUNCH.
WE'RE JUST GETTING STARTED HERE, WAINFLEET! ARE YOU READY FOR US TO CRANK IT UP?
YEAHH!!!
WOOOO!
HHHHHH

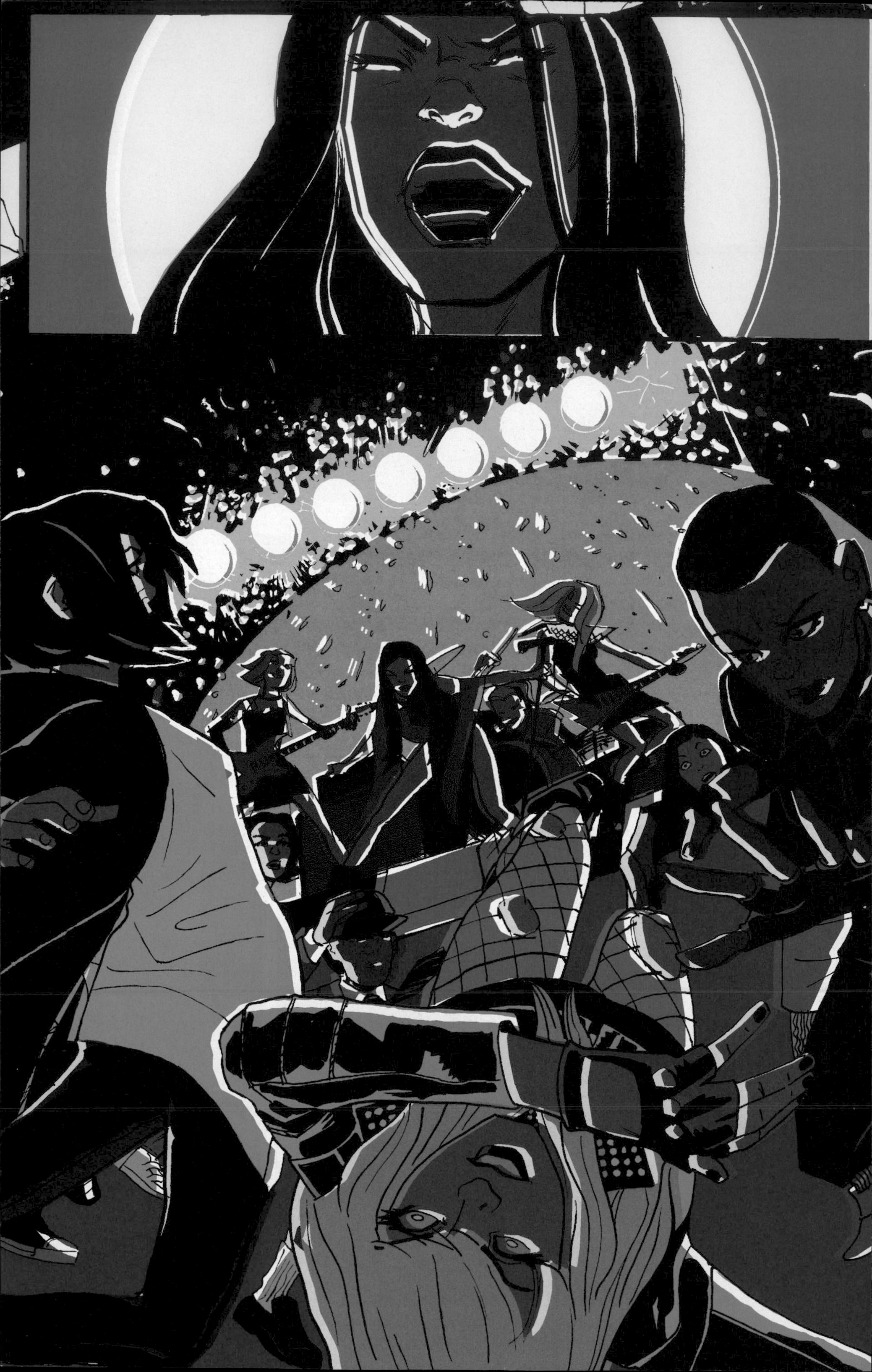

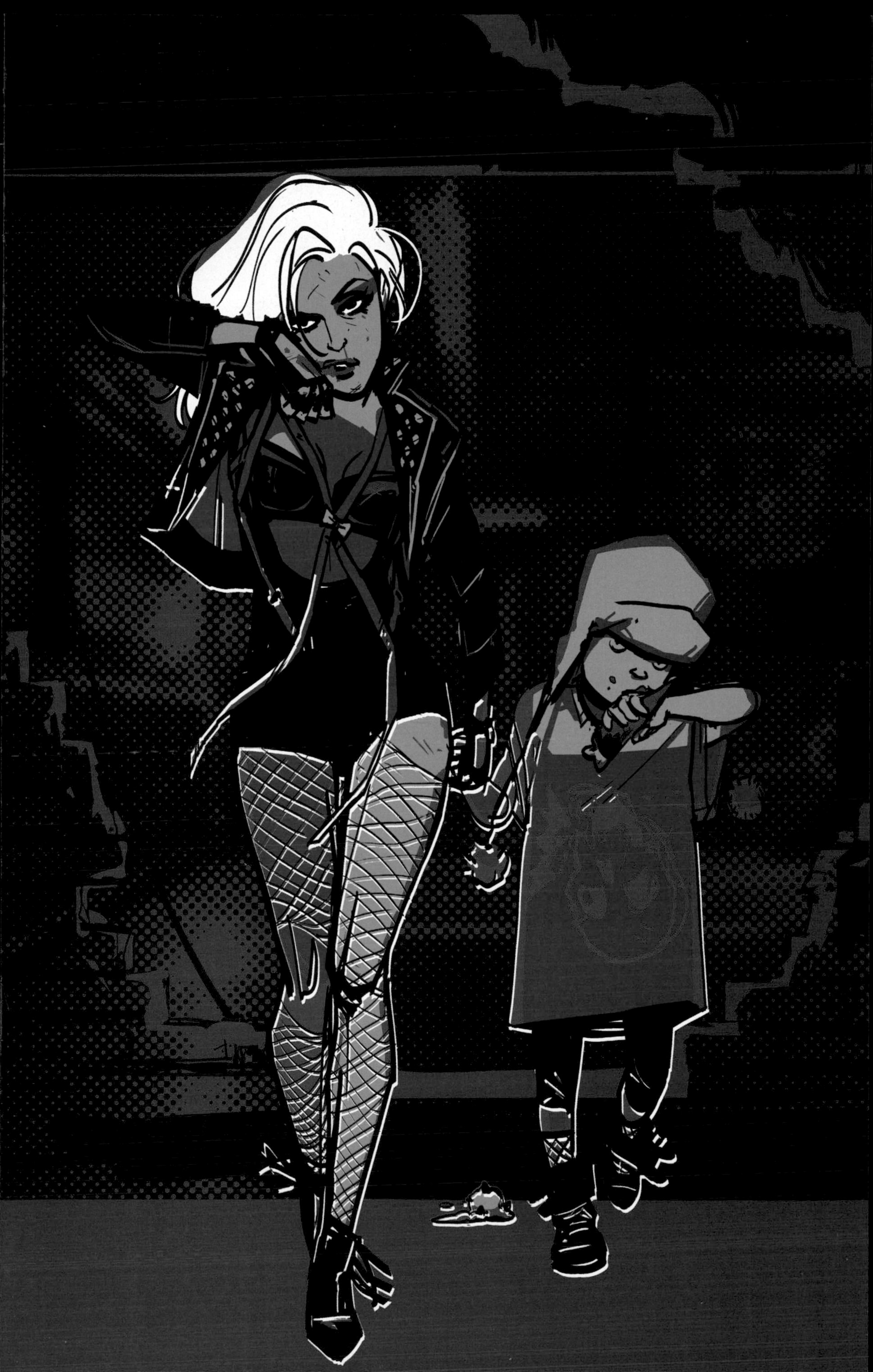

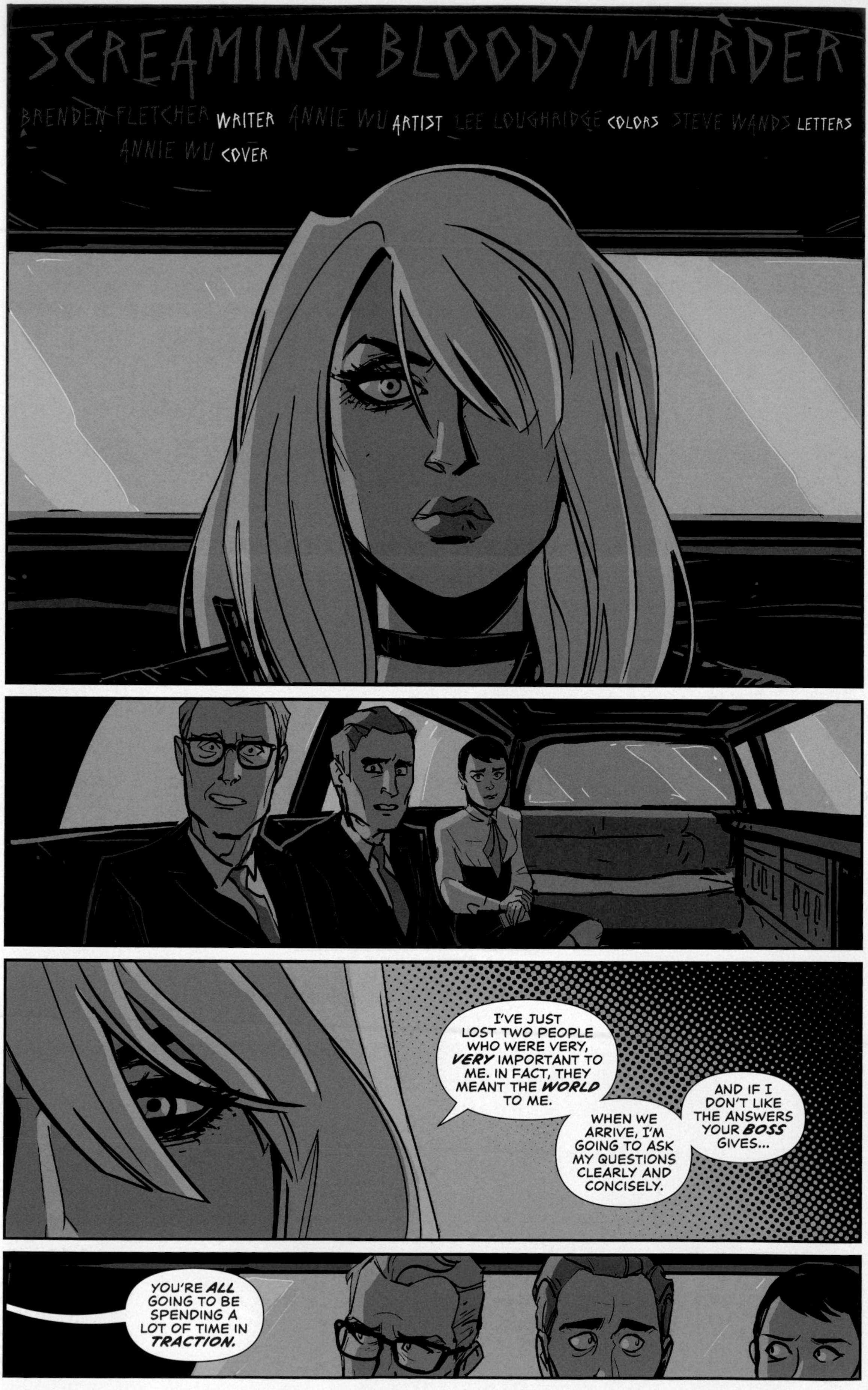
SCREAMING BLOODY MURDER
BRENDEN FLETCHER WRITER ANNIE WU ARTIST LEE LOUGHRIDGE COLORS STEVE WANDS LETTERS
ANNIE WU COVER
I'VE JUST LOST TWO PEOPLE WHO WERE VERY, VERY IMPORTANT TO ME. IN FACT, THEY MEANT THE WORLD TO ME.
WHEN WE ARRIVE, I'M GOING TO ASK MY QUESTIONS CLEARLY AND CONCISELY.
AND IF I DON'T LIKE THE ANSWERS YOUR BOSS GIVES...
YOU'RE ALL GOING TO BE SPENDING A LOT OF TIME IN TRACTION.

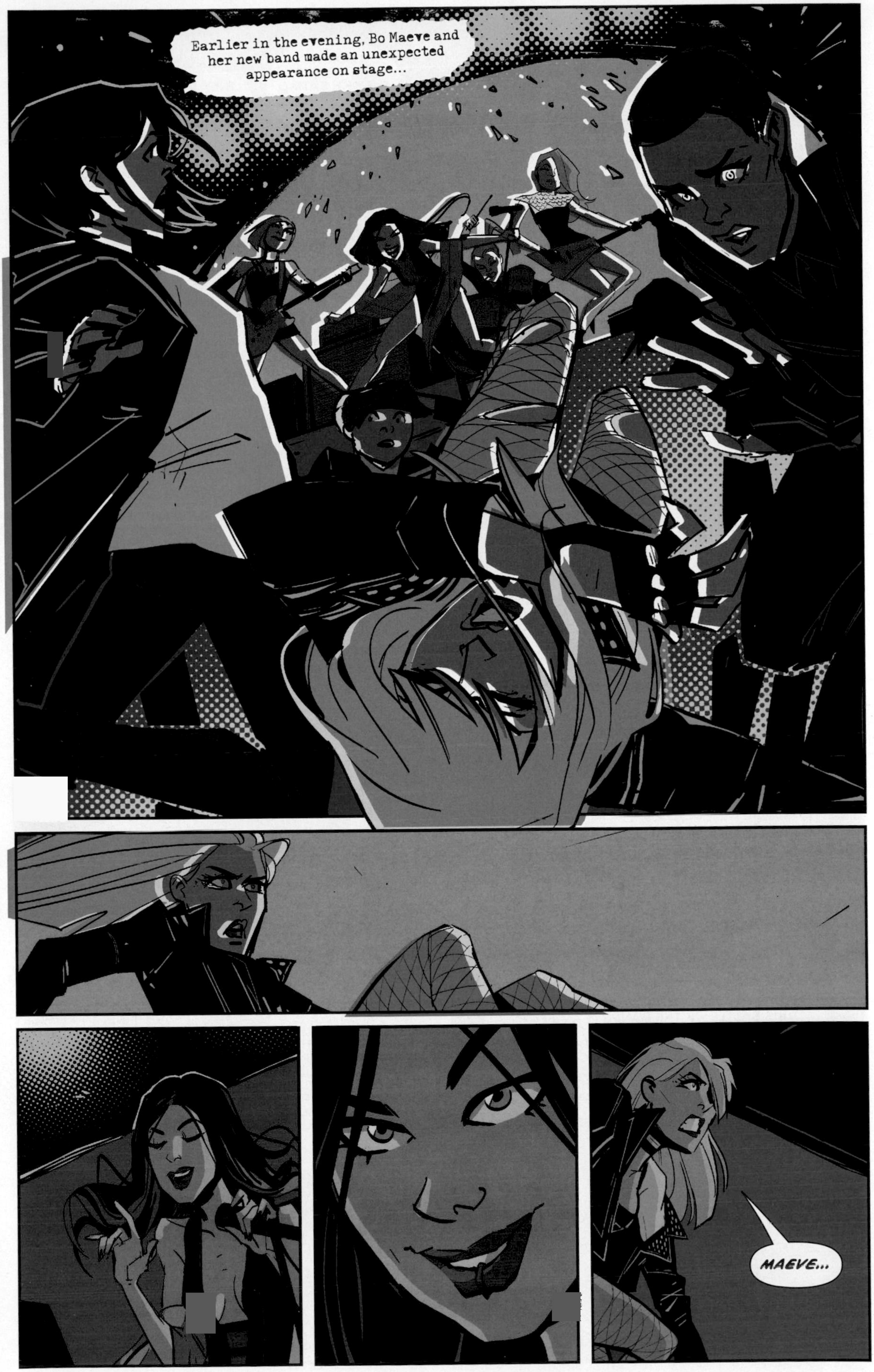
Earlier in the evening, Bo Maeve and her new band made an unexpected appearance on stage...
MAEVE...

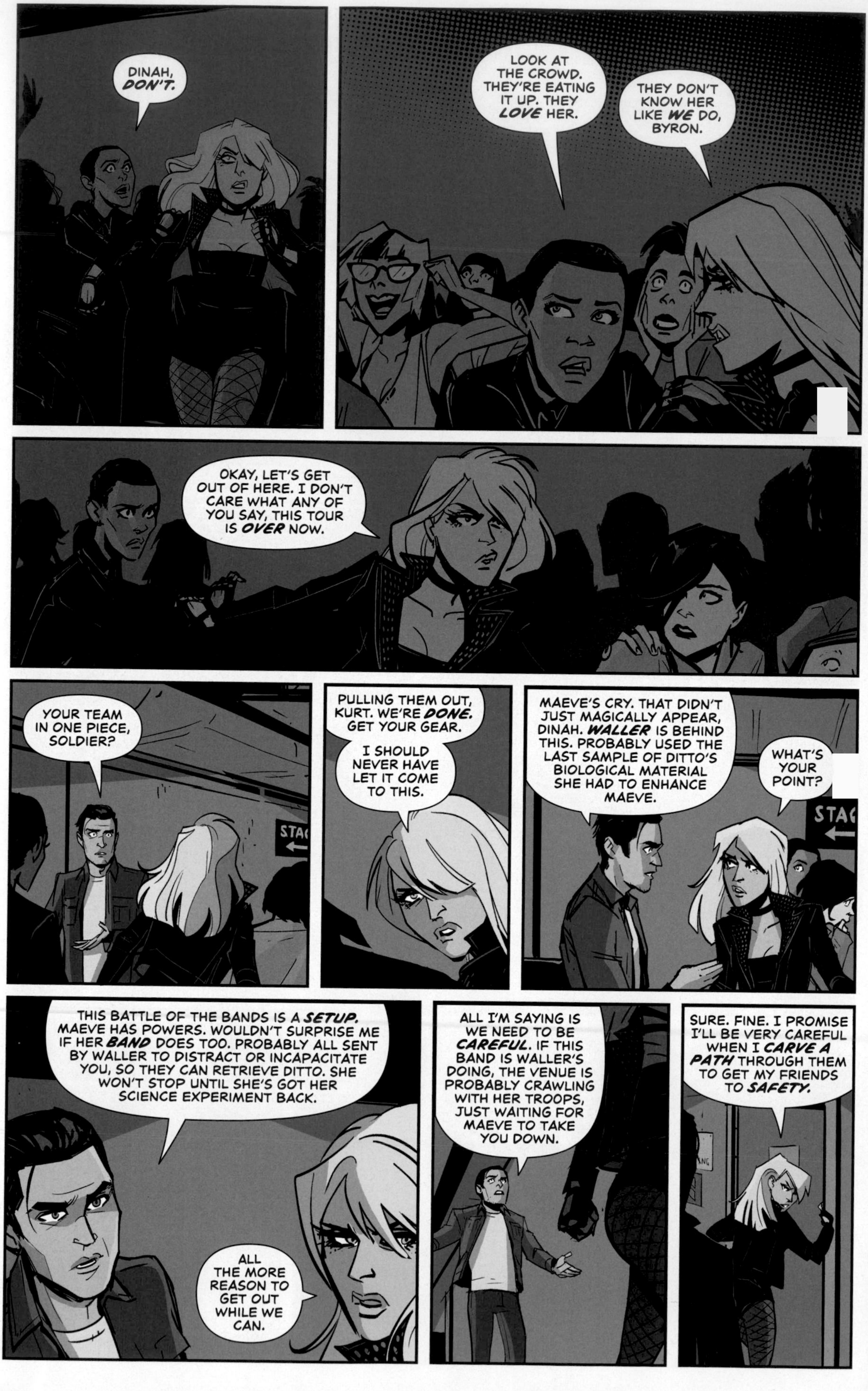
DINAH, DON'T.
LOOK AT THE CROWD. THEY'RE EATING IT UP. THEY LOVE HER.
THEY DON'T KNOW HER LIKE WE DO, BYRON.
OKAY, LET'S GET OUT OF HERE. I DON'T CARE WHAT ANY OF YOU SAY, THIS TOUR IS OVER NOW.
YOUR TEAM IN ONE PIECE, SOLDIER?
PULLING THEM OUT, KURT. WE'RE DONE. GET YOUR GEAR.
I SHOULD NEVER HAVE LET IT COME TO THIS.
MAEVE'S CRY. THAT DIDN'T JUST MAGICALLY APPEAR, DINAH. WALLER IS BEHIND THIS. PROBABLY USED THE LAST SAMPLE OF DITTO'S BIOLOGICAL MATERIAL SHE HAD TO ENHANCE MAEVE.
WHAT'S YOUR POINT?
THIS BATTLE OF THE BANDS IS A SETUP. MAEVE HAS POWERS. WOULDN'T SURPRISE ME IF HER BAND DOES TOO. PROBABLY ALL SENT BY WALLER TO DISTRACT OR INCAPACITATE YOU, SO THEY CAN RETRIEVE DITTO. SHE WON'T STOP UNTIL SHE'S GOT HER SCIENCE EXPERIMENT BACK.
ALL THE MORE REASON TO GET OUT WHILE WE CAN.
ALL I'M SAYING IS WE NEED TO BE CAREFUL. IF THIS BAND IS WALLER'S DOING, THE VENUE IS PROBABLY CRAWLING WITH HER TROOPS, JUST WAITING FOR MAEVE TO TAKE YOU DOWN.
SURE. FINE. I PROMISE I'LL BE VERY CAREFUL WHEN I CARVE A PATH THROUGH THEM TO GET MY FRIENDS TO SAFETY.

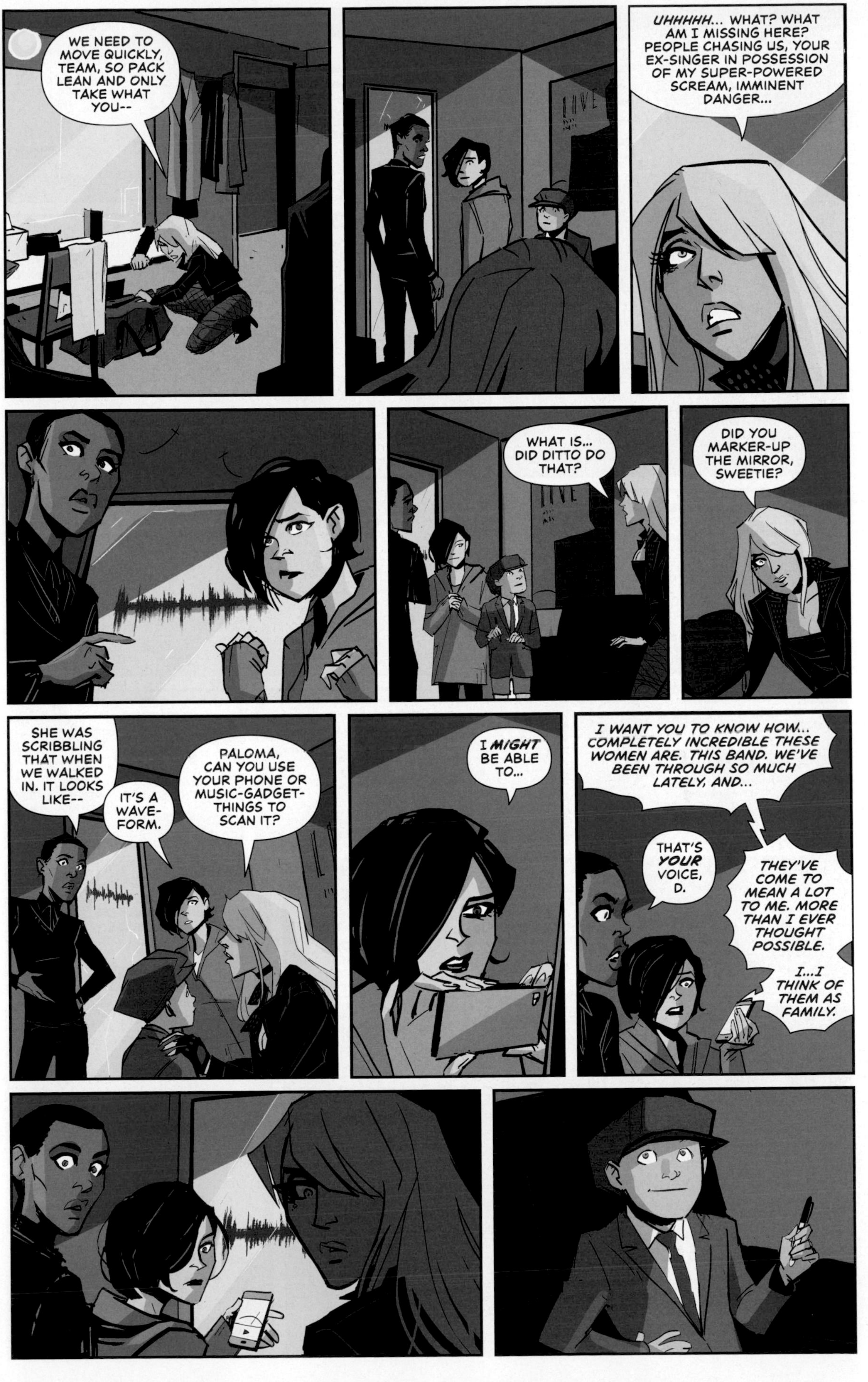
WE NEED TO MOVE QUICKLY, TEAM, SO PACK LEAN AND ONLY TAKE WHAT YOU--
UHHHHH... WHAT? WHAT AM I MISSING HERE? PEOPLE CHASING US, YOUR EX-SINGER IN POSSESSION OF MY SUPER-POWERED SCREAM, IMMINENT DANGER...
WHAT IS... DID DITTO DO THAT?
DID YOU MARKER-UP THE MIRROR, SWEETIE?
SHE WAS SCRIBBLING THAT WHEN WE WALKED IN. IT LOOKS LIKE--
IT'S A WAVE-FORM.
PALOMA, CAN YOU USE YOUR PHONE OR MUSIC-GADGET-THINGS TO SCAN IT?
I MIGHT BE ABLE TO...
I WANT YOU TO KNOW HOW... COMPLETELY INCREDIBLE THESE WOMEN ARE. THIS BAND. WE'VE BEEN THROUGH SO MUCH LATELY, AND...
THAT'S YOUR VOICE, D.
THEY'VE COME TO MEAN A LOT TO ME. MORE THAN I EVER THOUGHT POSSIBLE.
I...I THINK OF THEM AS FAMILY.

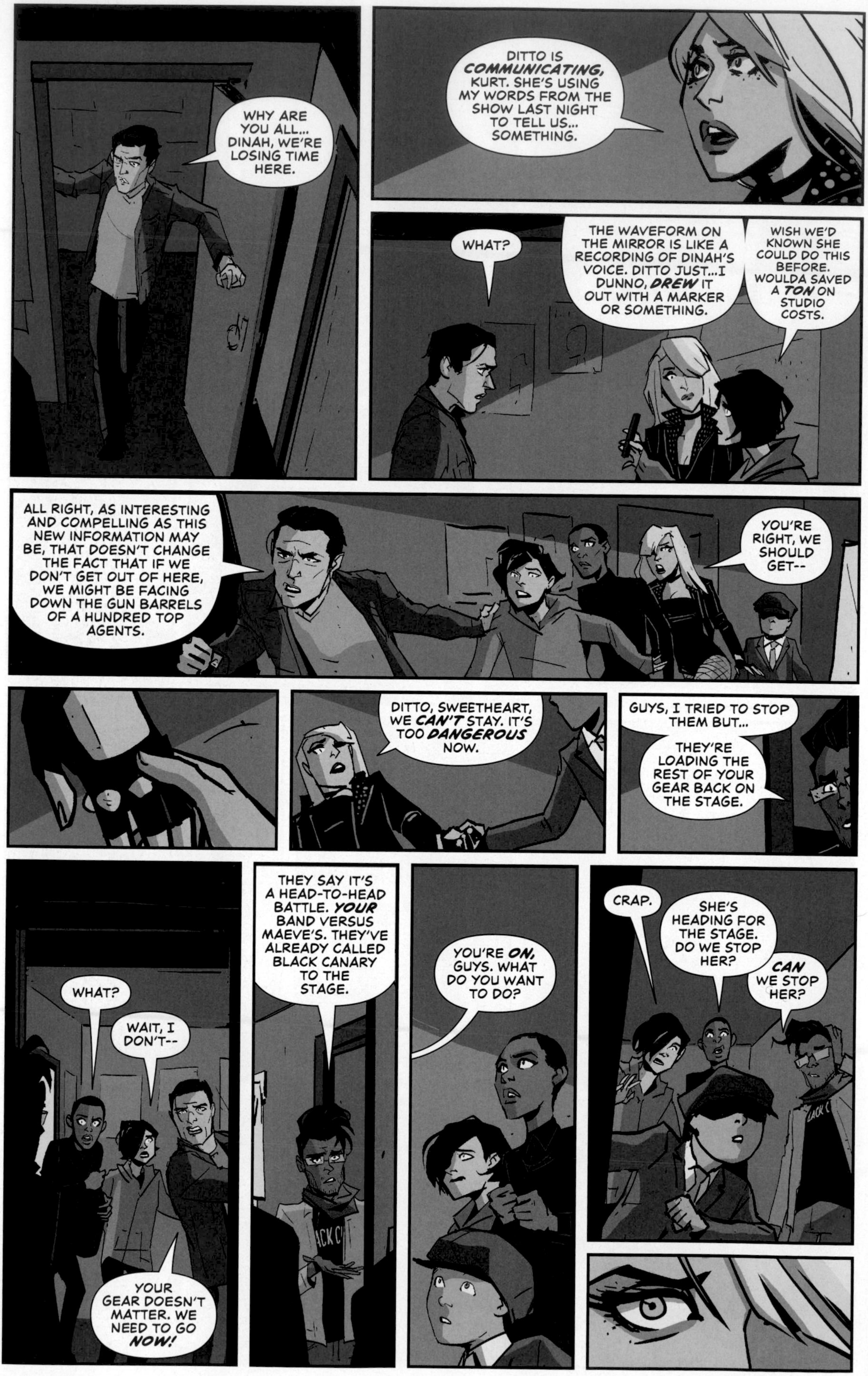
WHY ARE YOU ALL... DINAH, WE'RE LOSING TIME HERE.
DITTO IS *COMMUNICATING,* KURT. SHE'S USING MY WORDS FROM THE SHOW LAST NIGHT TO TELL US... SOMETHING.
WHAT?
THE WAVEFORM ON THE MIRROR IS LIKE A RECORDING OF DINAH'S VOICE. DITTO JUST...I DUNNO, *DREW* IT OUT WITH A MARKER OR SOMETHING.
WISH WE'D KNOWN SHE COULD DO THIS BEFORE. WOULDA SAVED A *TON* ON STUDIO COSTS.
ALL RIGHT, AS INTERESTING AND COMPELLING AS THIS NEW INFORMATION MAY BE, THAT DOESN'T CHANGE THE FACT THAT IF WE DON'T GET OUT OF HERE, WE MIGHT BE FACING DOWN THE GUN BARRELS OF A HUNDRED TOP AGENTS.
YOU'RE RIGHT, WE SHOULD GET--
DITTO, SWEETHEART, WE *CAN'T* STAY. IT'S TOO *DANGEROUS* NOW.
GUYS, I TRIED TO STOP THEM BUT...
THEY'RE LOADING THE REST OF YOUR GEAR BACK ON THE STAGE.
WHAT?
WAIT, I DON'T--
YOUR GEAR DOESN'T MATTER. WE NEED TO GO *NOW!*
THEY SAY IT'S A HEAD-TO-HEAD BATTLE. *YOUR* BAND VERSUS MAEVE'S. THEY'VE ALREADY CALLED BLACK CANARY TO THE STAGE.
YOU'RE *ON,* GUYS. WHAT DO YOU WANT TO DO?
CRAP.
SHE'S HEADING FOR THE STAGE. DO WE STOP HER?
CAN WE STOP HER?

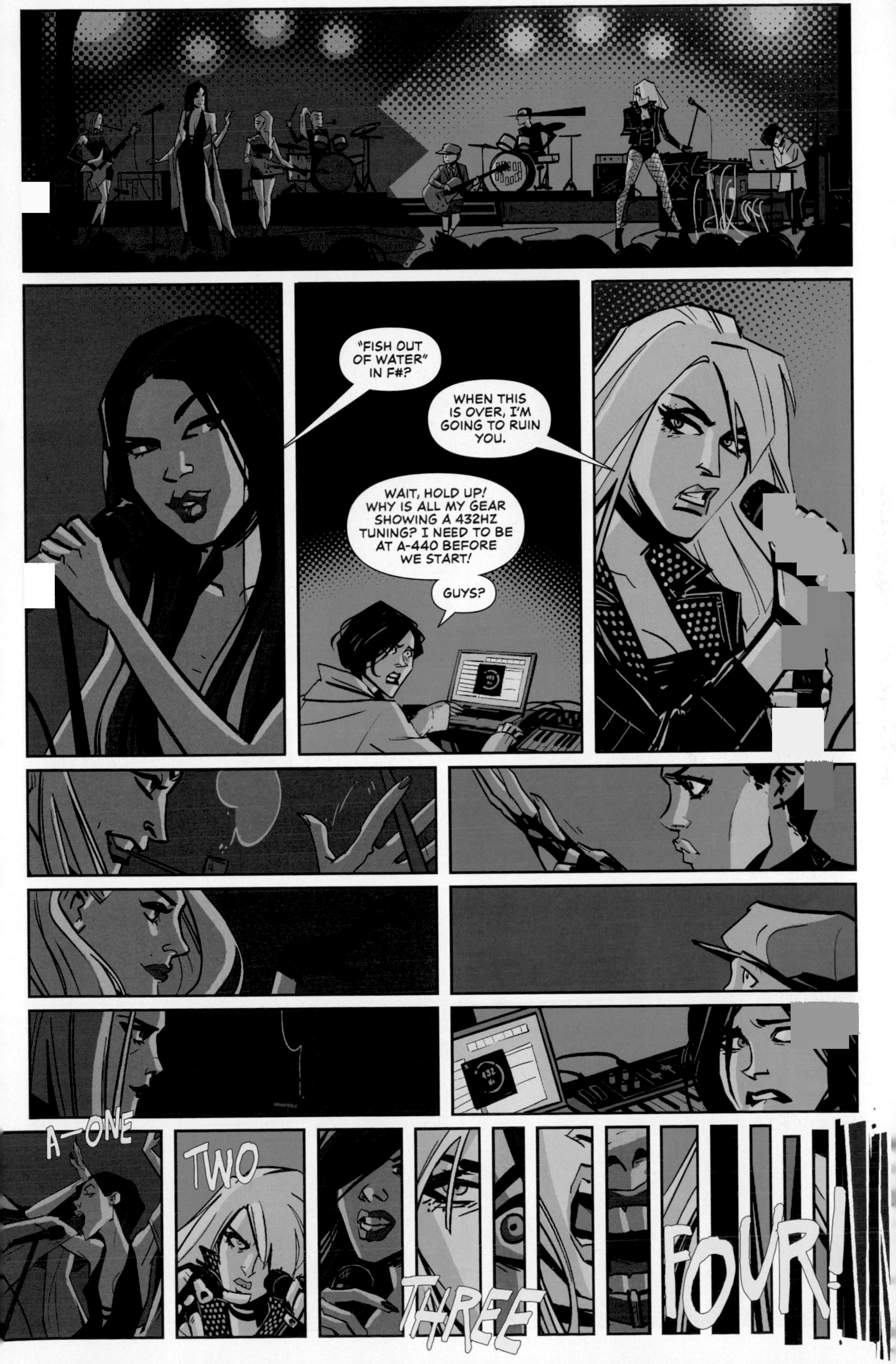

"FISH OUT OF WATER" IN F#?
WHEN THIS IS OVER, I'M GOING TO RUIN YOU.
WAIT, HOLD UP! WHY IS ALL MY GEAR SHOWING A 432HZ TUNING? I NEED TO BE AT A-440 BEFORE WE START!
GUYS?
A-ONE
TWO
THREE
FOUR!

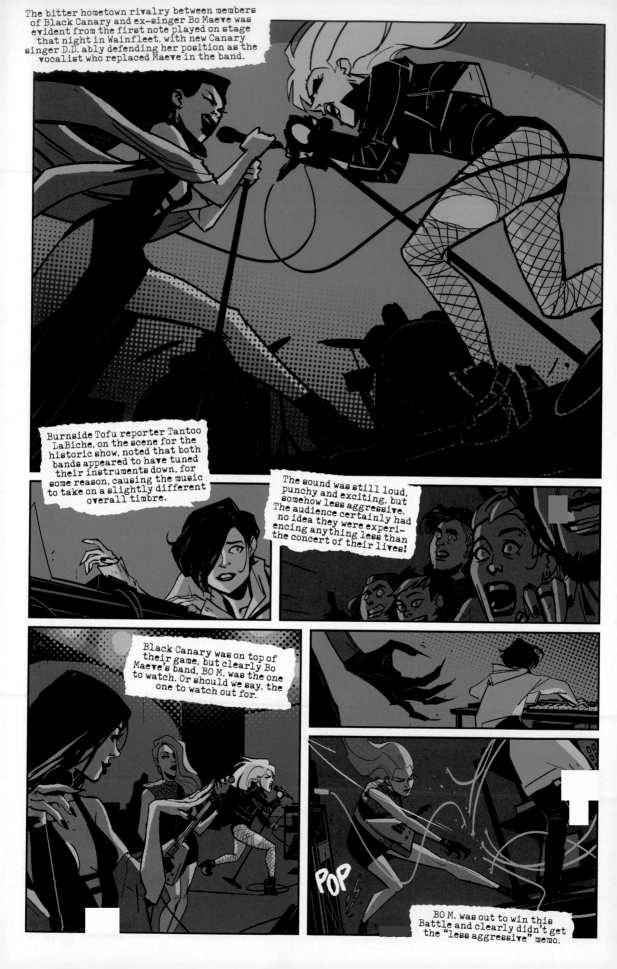

The bitter hometown rivalry between members of Black Canary and ex-singer Bo Maeve was evident from the first note played on stage that night in Wainfleet, with new Canary singer D.D. ably defending her position as the vocalist who replaced Maeve in the band.

Burnside Tofu reporter Tantoo LaBiche, on the scene for the historic show, noted that both bands appeared to have tuned their instruments down, for some reason, causing the music to take on a slightly different overall timbre.

The sound was still loud, punchy and exciting, but somehow less aggressive. The audience certainly had no idea they were experiencing anything less than the concert of their lives!

Black Canary was on top of their game, but clearly Bo Maeve's band, BO M. was the one to watch. Or should we say, the one to watch out for.

POP

BO M. was out to win this Battle and clearly didn't get the "less aggressive" memo.

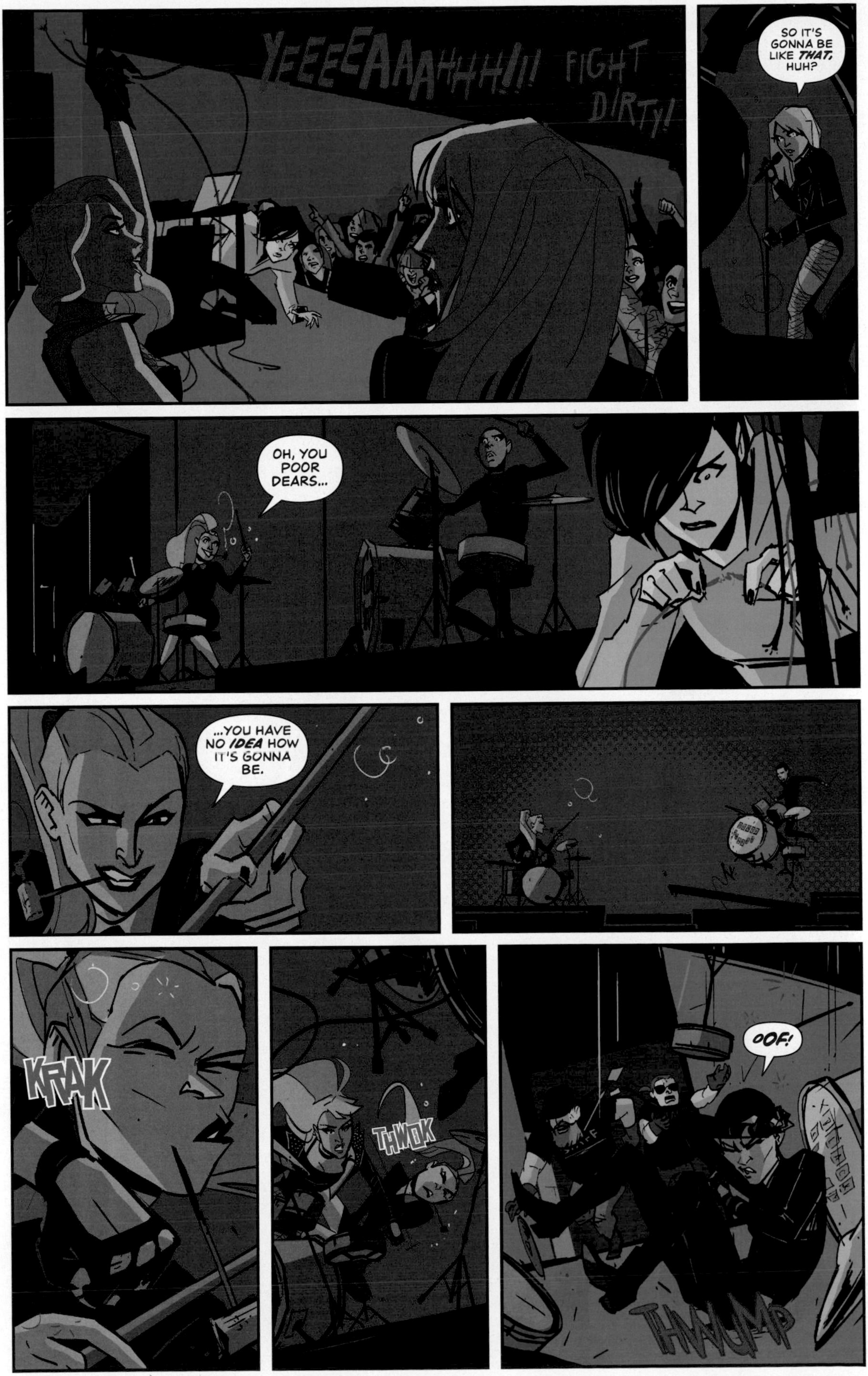

YEEEEAAAHHH!!! FIGHT DIRTY!
SO IT'S GONNA BE LIKE *THAT*, HUH?
OH, YOU POOR DEARS...
...YOU HAVE NO *IDEA* HOW IT'S GONNA BE.
KRAK
THWOK
OOF!
THWUMP

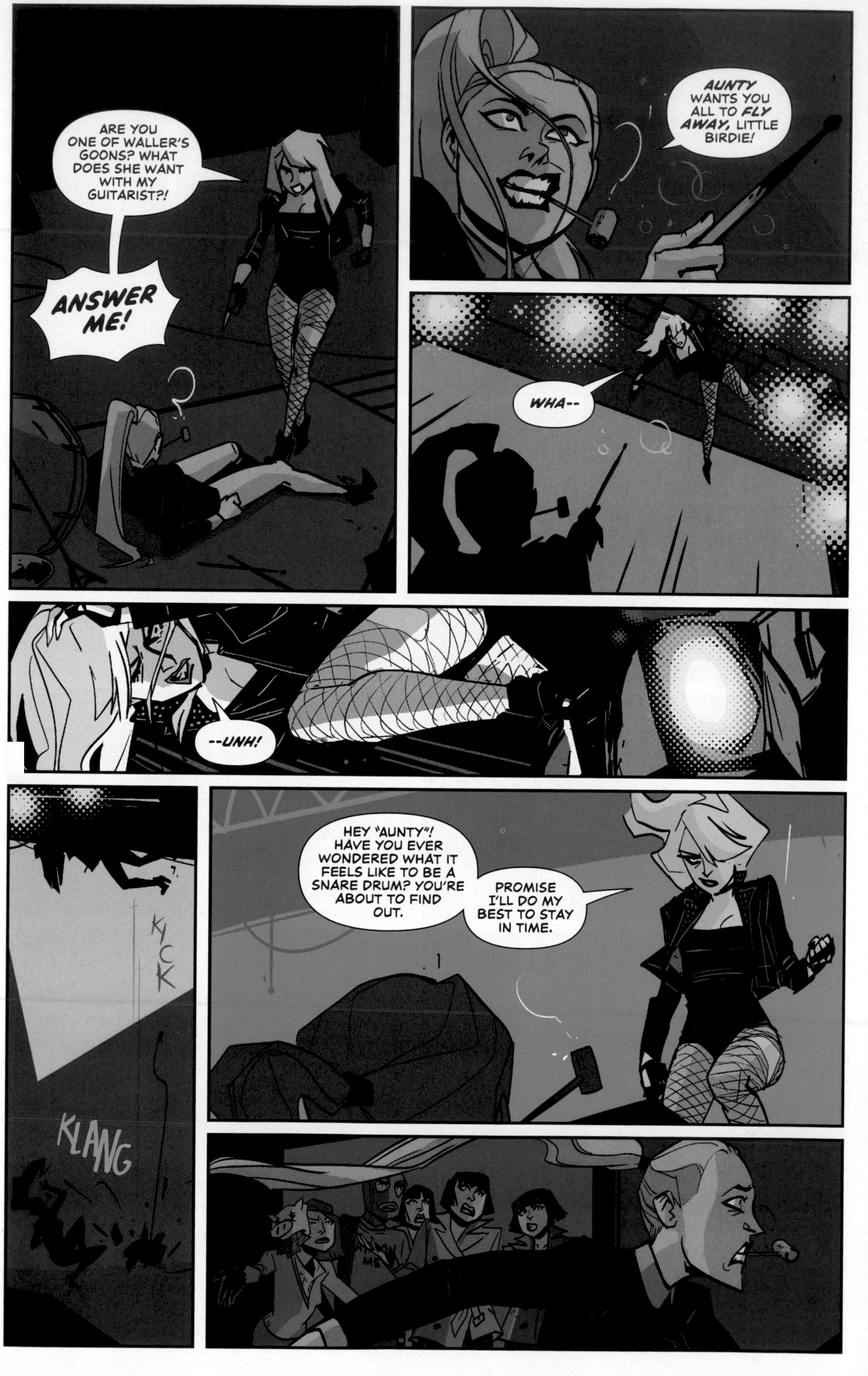
ARE YOU ONE OF WALLER'S GOONS? WHAT DOES SHE WANT WITH MY GUITARIST?!
ANSWER ME!
AUNTY WANTS YOU ALL TO FLY AWAY, LITTLE BIRDIE!
WHA--
--UNH!
KICK
KLANG
HEY "AUNTY"! HAVE YOU EVER WONDERED WHAT IT FEELS LIKE TO BE A SNARE DRUM? YOU'RE ABOUT TO FIND OUT.
PROMISE I'LL DO MY BEST TO STAY IN TIME.

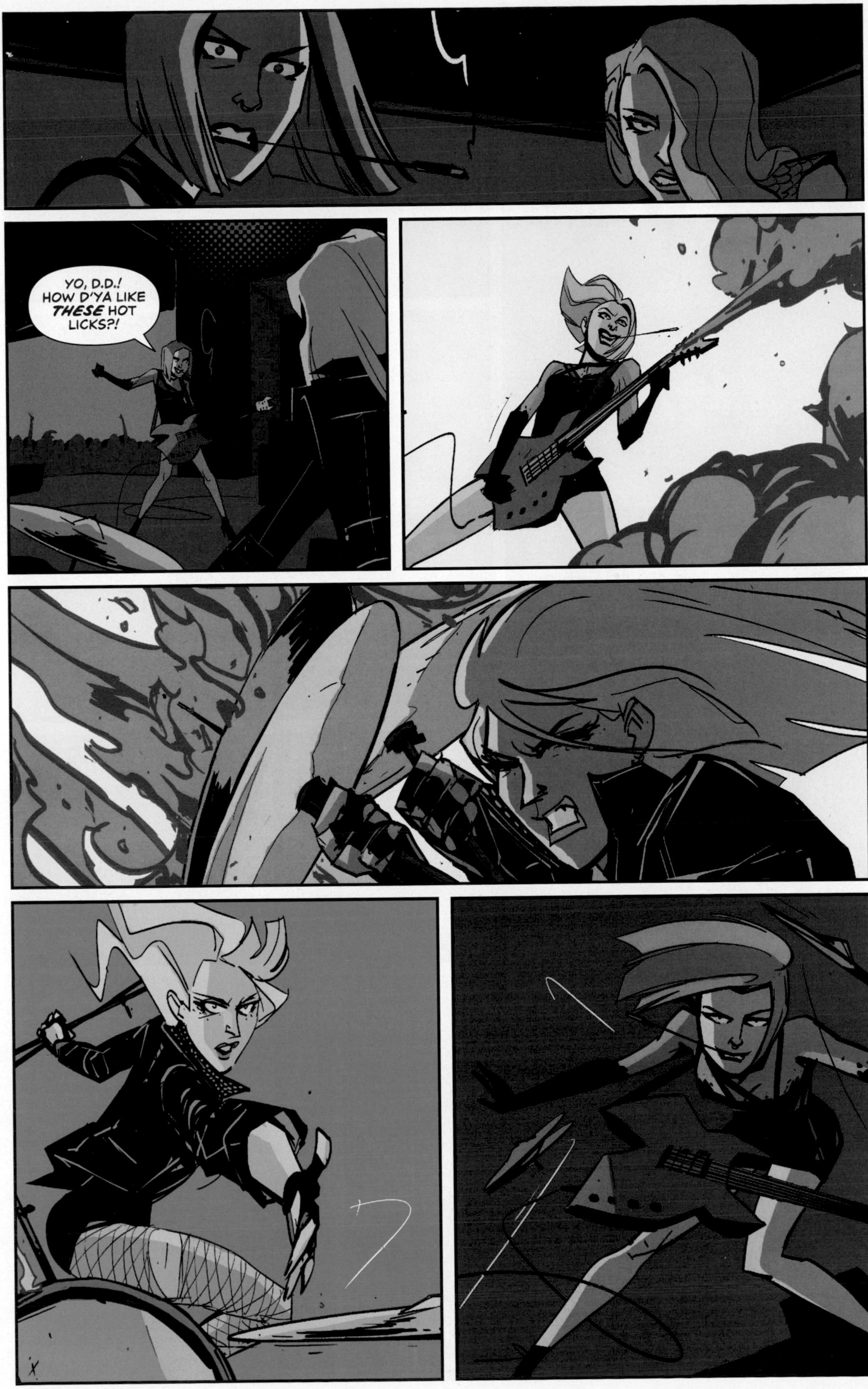
YO, D.D.! HOW D'YA LIKE *THESE* HOT LICKS?!

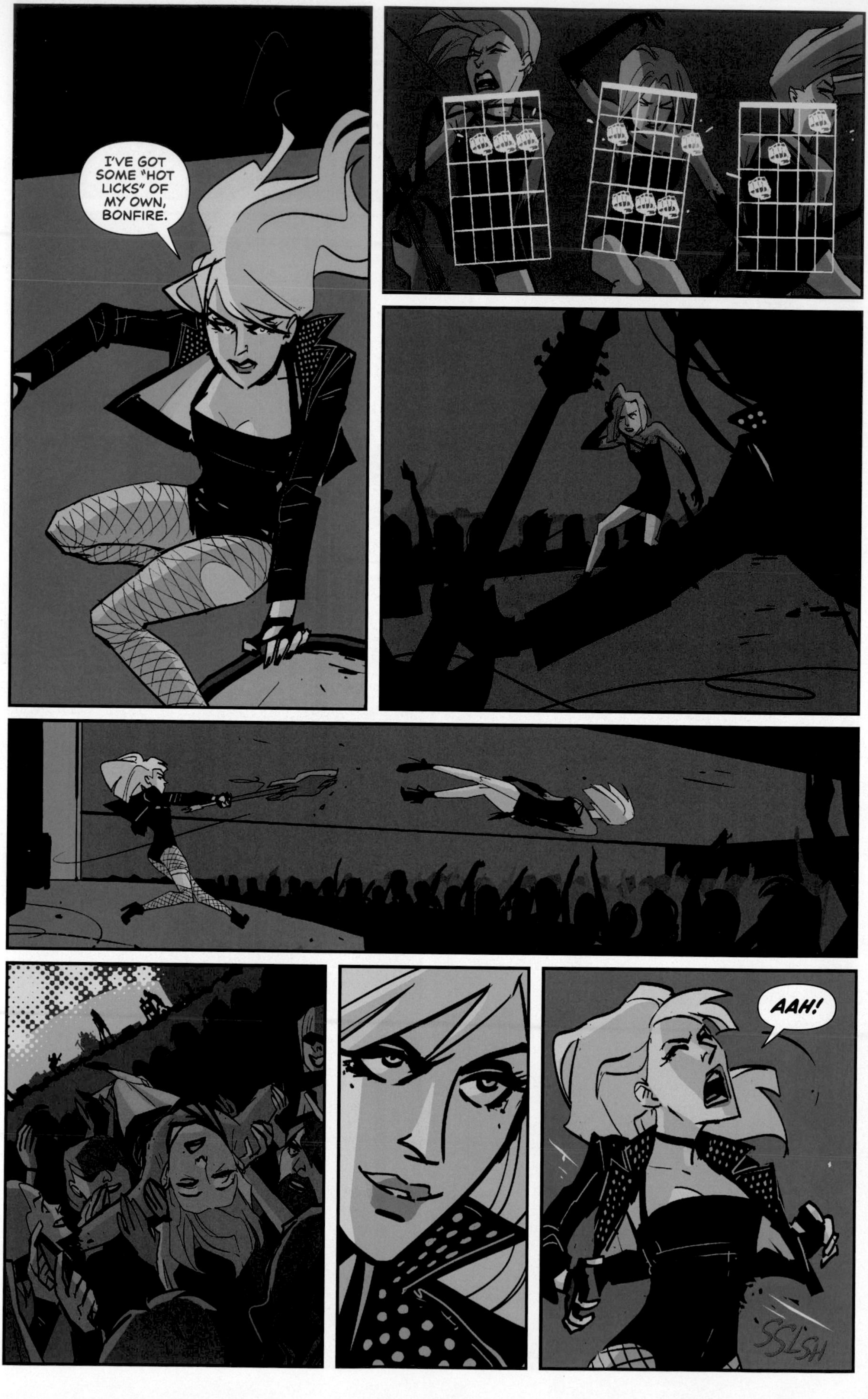
I'VE GOT SOME "HOT LICKS" OF MY OWN, BONFIRE.
AAH!
SSLSH

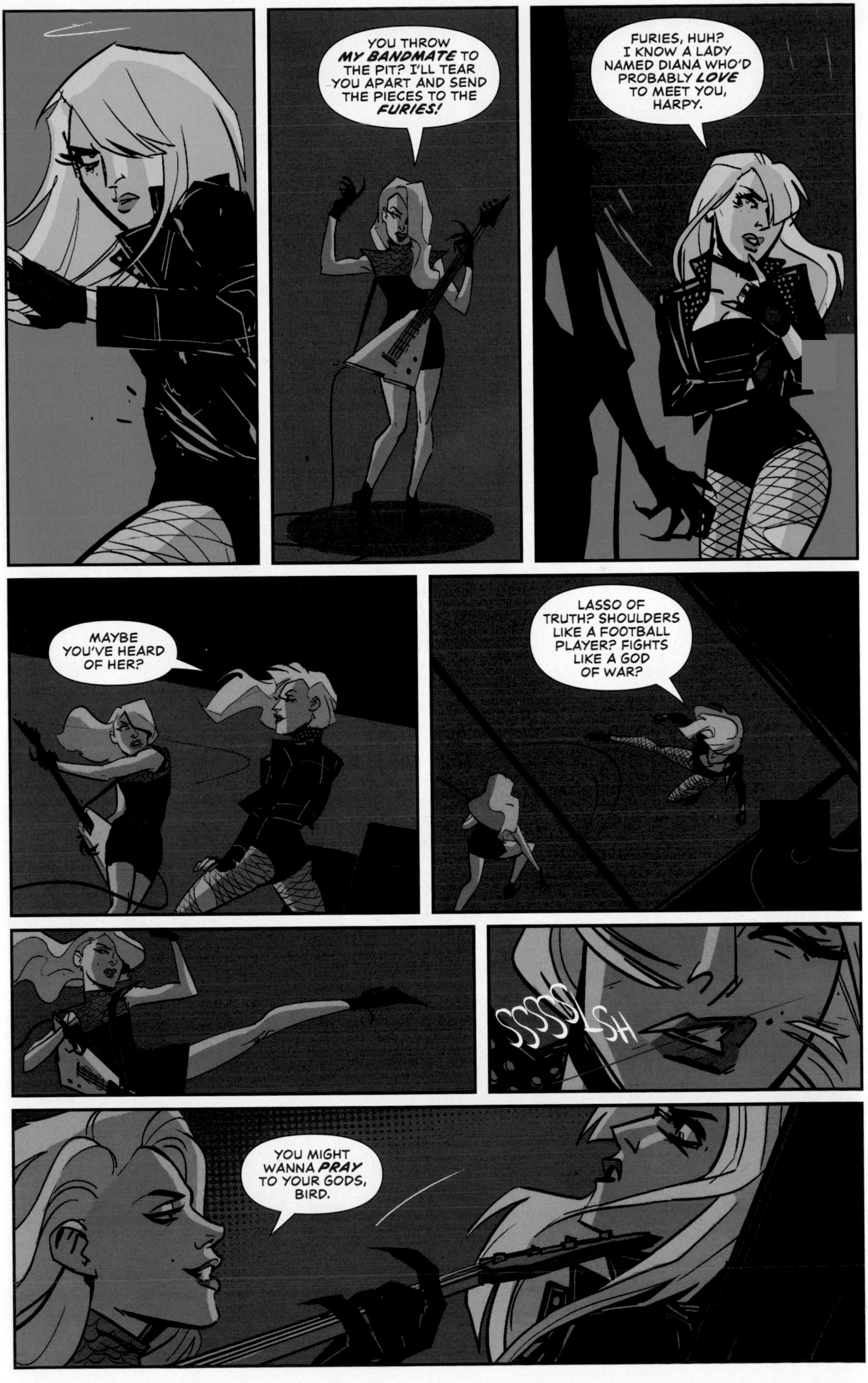
YOU THROW MY BANDMATE TO THE PIT? I'LL TEAR YOU APART AND SEND THE PIECES TO THE FURIES!
FURIES, HUH? I KNOW A LADY NAMED DIANA WHO'D PROBABLY LOVE TO MEET YOU, HARPY.
MAYBE YOU'VE HEARD OF HER?
LASSO OF TRUTH? SHOULDERS LIKE A FOOTBALL PLAYER? FIGHTS LIKE A GOD OF WAR?
SSSSSLSH
YOU MIGHT WANNA PRAY TO YOUR GODS, BIRD.

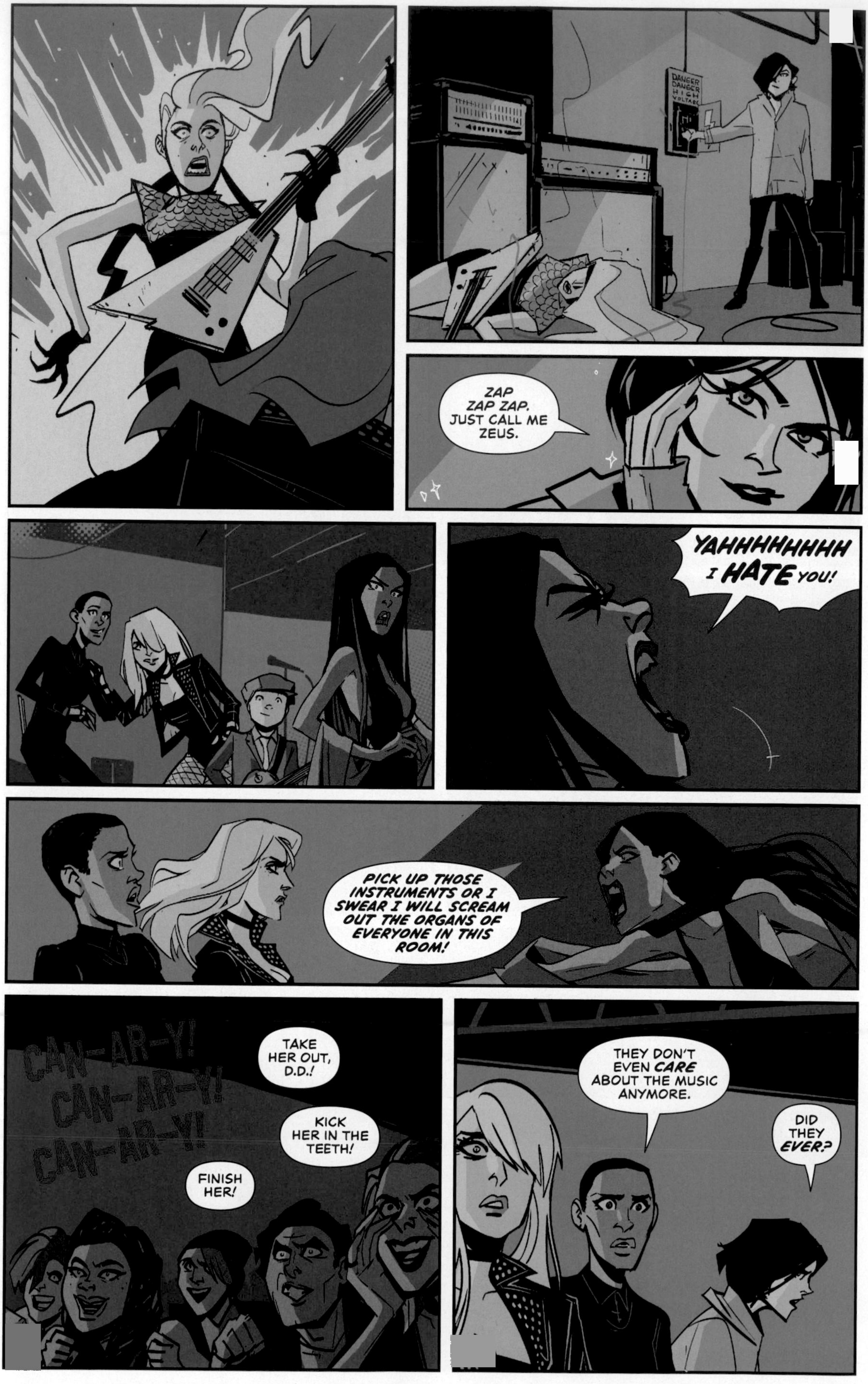
DANGER
DANGER
HIGH
VOLTAGE
ZAP ZAP ZAP. JUST CALL ME ZEUS.
YAHHHHHHHH I HATE YOU!
PICK UP THOSE INSTRUMENTS OR I SWEAR I WILL SCREAM OUT THE ORGANS OF EVERYONE IN THIS ROOM!
CAN-AR-Y! CAN-AR-Y! CAN-AR-Y!
TAKE HER OUT, D.D.!
KICK HER IN THE TEETH!
FINISH HER!
THEY DON'T EVEN CARE ABOUT THE MUSIC ANYMORE.
DID THEY EVER?

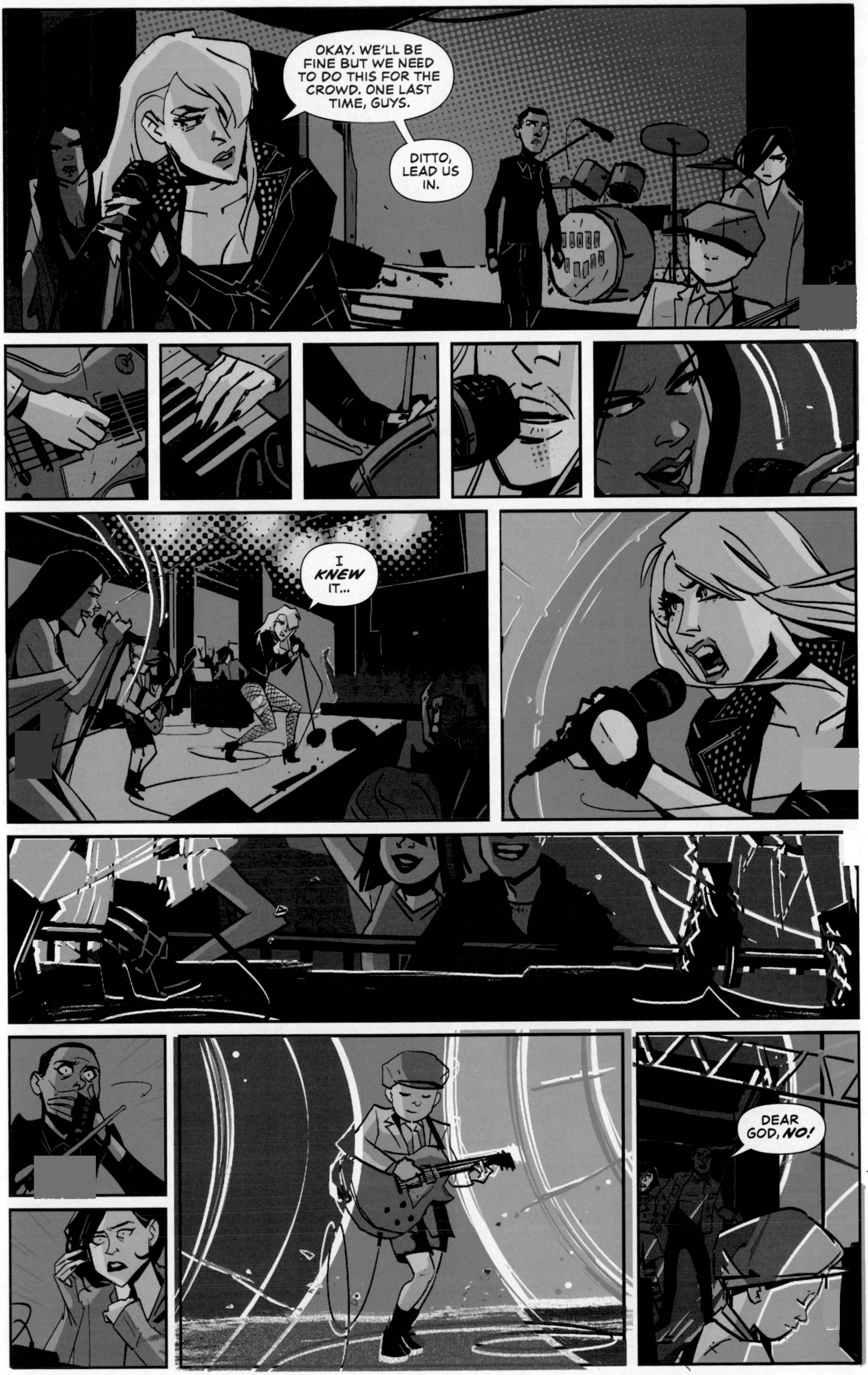
OKAY. WE'LL BE FINE BUT WE NEED TO DO THIS FOR THE CROWD. ONE LAST TIME, GUYS.
DITTO, LEAD US IN.
I *KNEW* IT...
DEAR GOD, *NO!*

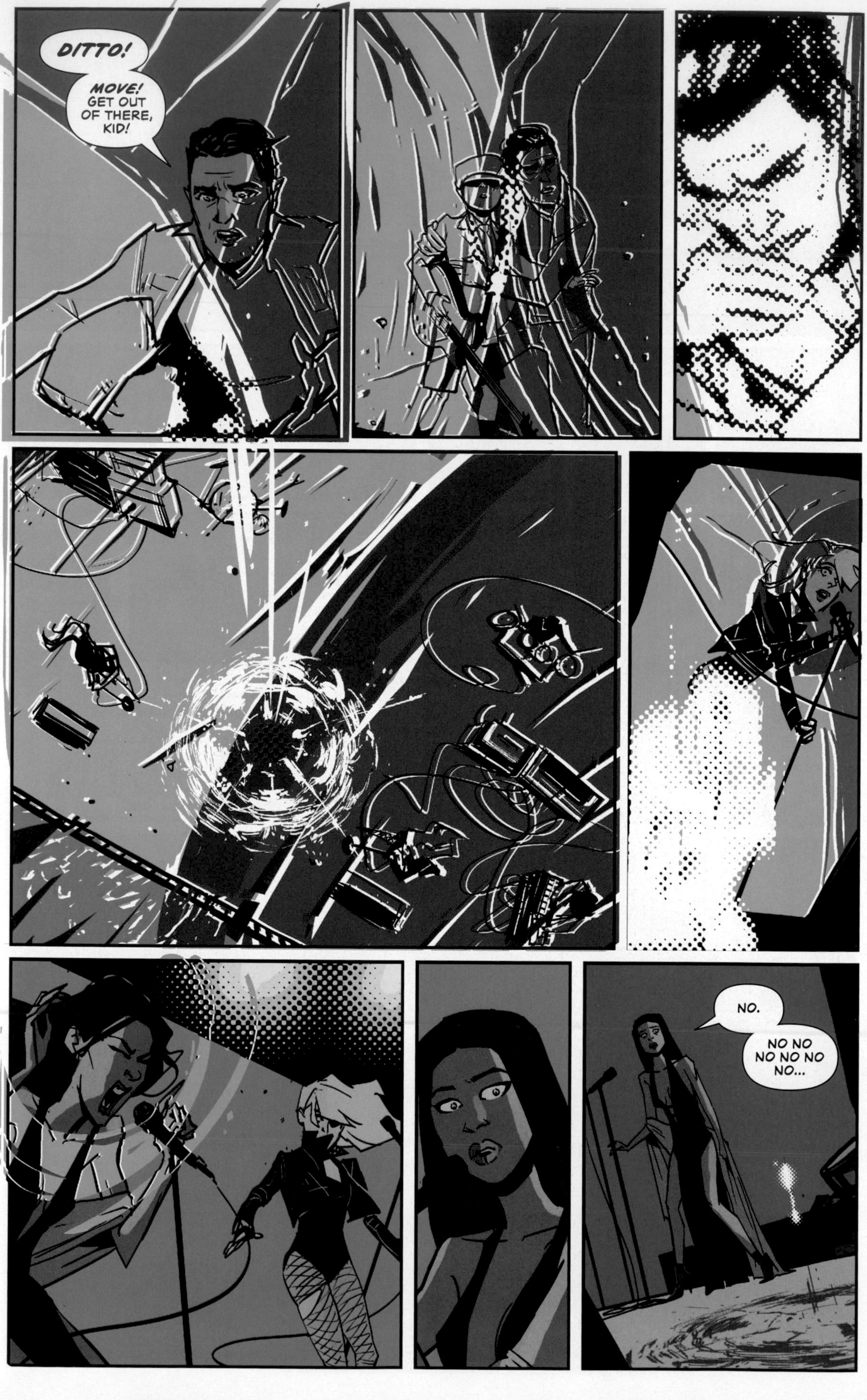
DITTO!
MOVE! GET OUT OF THERE, KID!
NO.
NO NO NO NO NO NO...

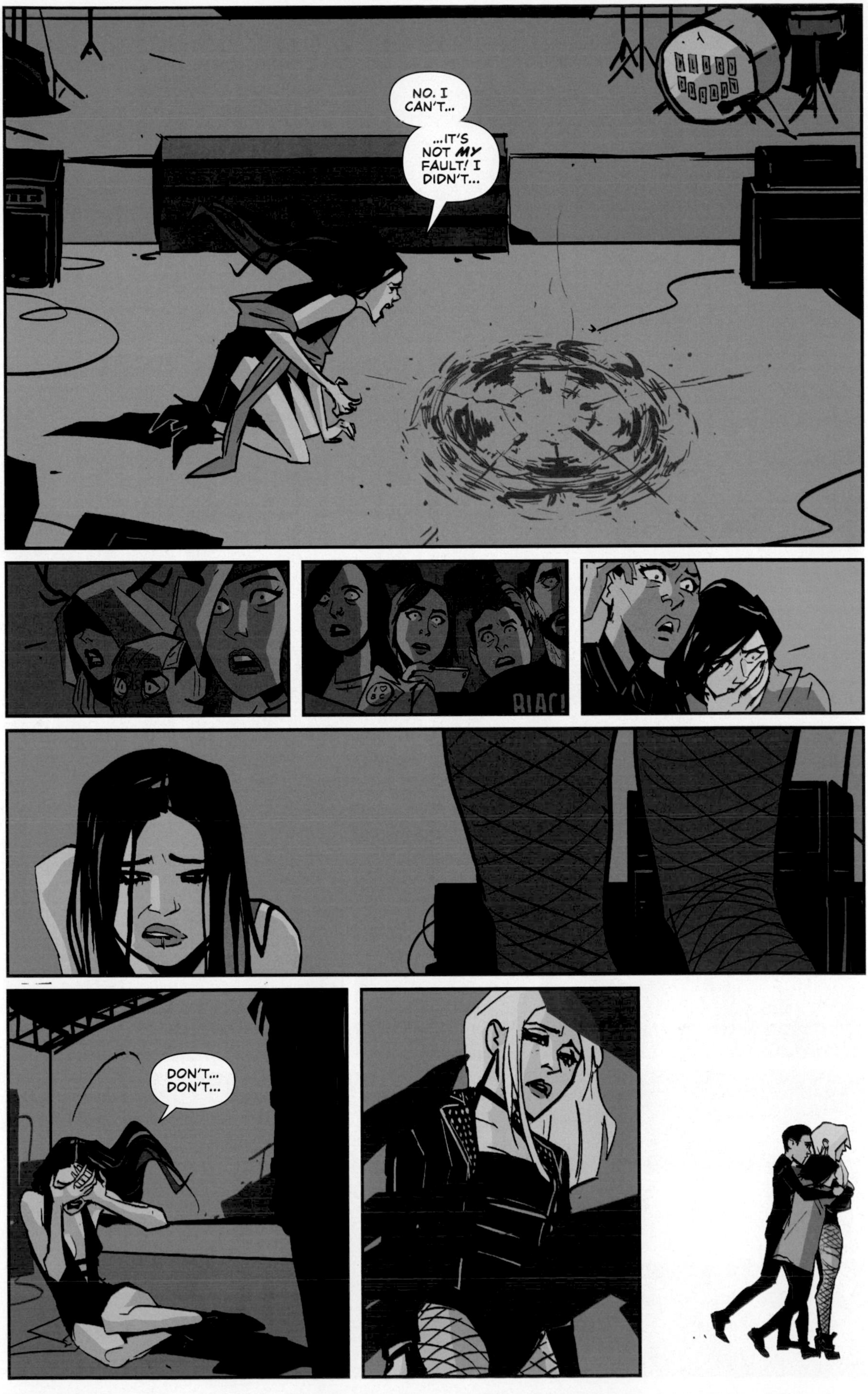
NO. I CAN'T...
...IT'S NOT MY FAULT! I DIDN'T...
DON'T... DON'T...

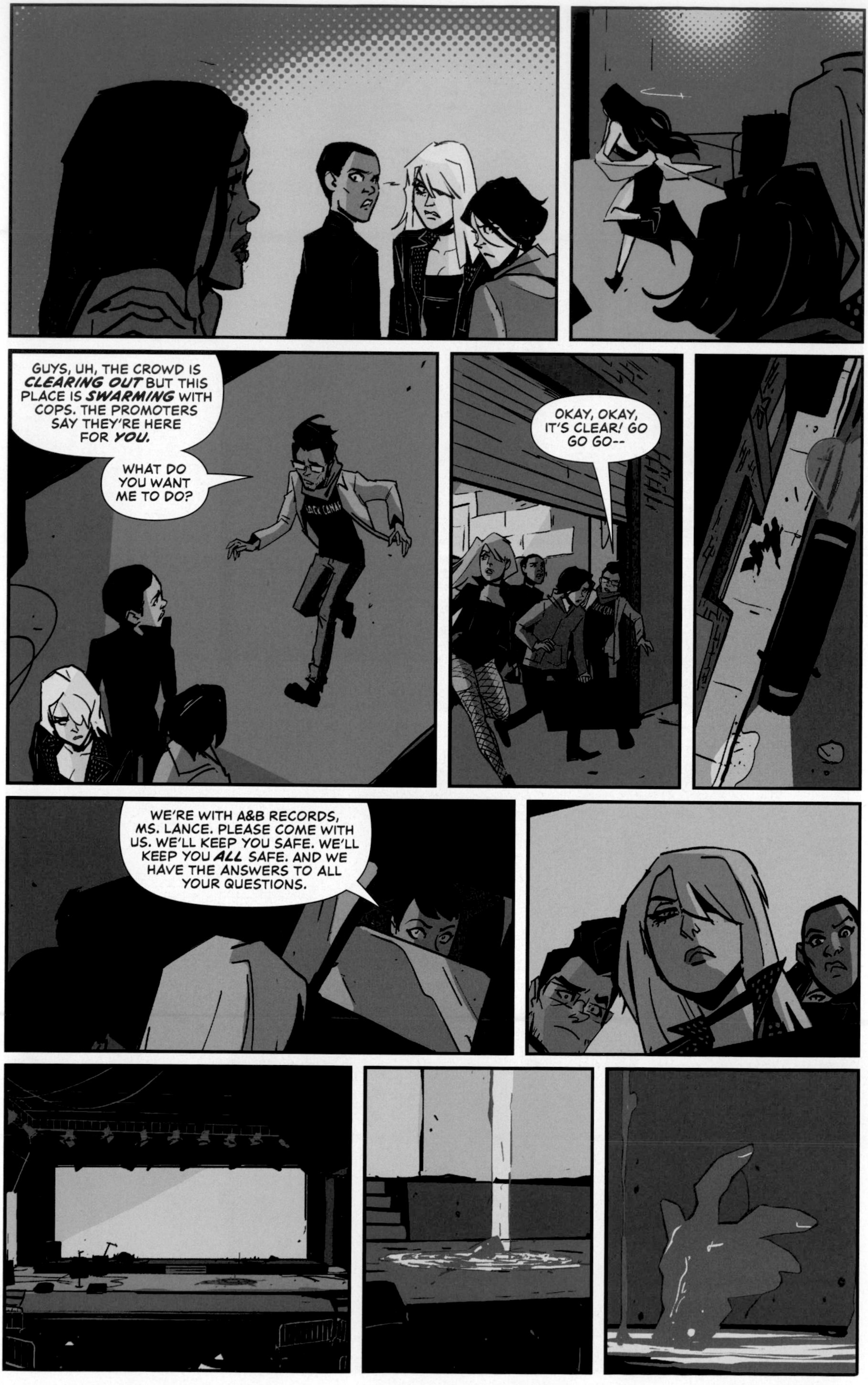
GUYS, UH, THE CROWD IS CLEARING OUT BUT THIS PLACE IS SWARMING WITH COPS. THE PROMOTERS SAY THEY'RE HERE FOR YOU.
WHAT DO YOU WANT ME TO DO?
OKAY, OKAY, IT'S CLEAR! GO GO GO--
WE'RE WITH A&B RECORDS, MS. LANCE. PLEASE COME WITH US. WE'LL KEEP YOU SAFE. WE'LL KEEP YOU ALL SAFE. AND WE HAVE THE ANSWERS TO ALL YOUR QUESTIONS.

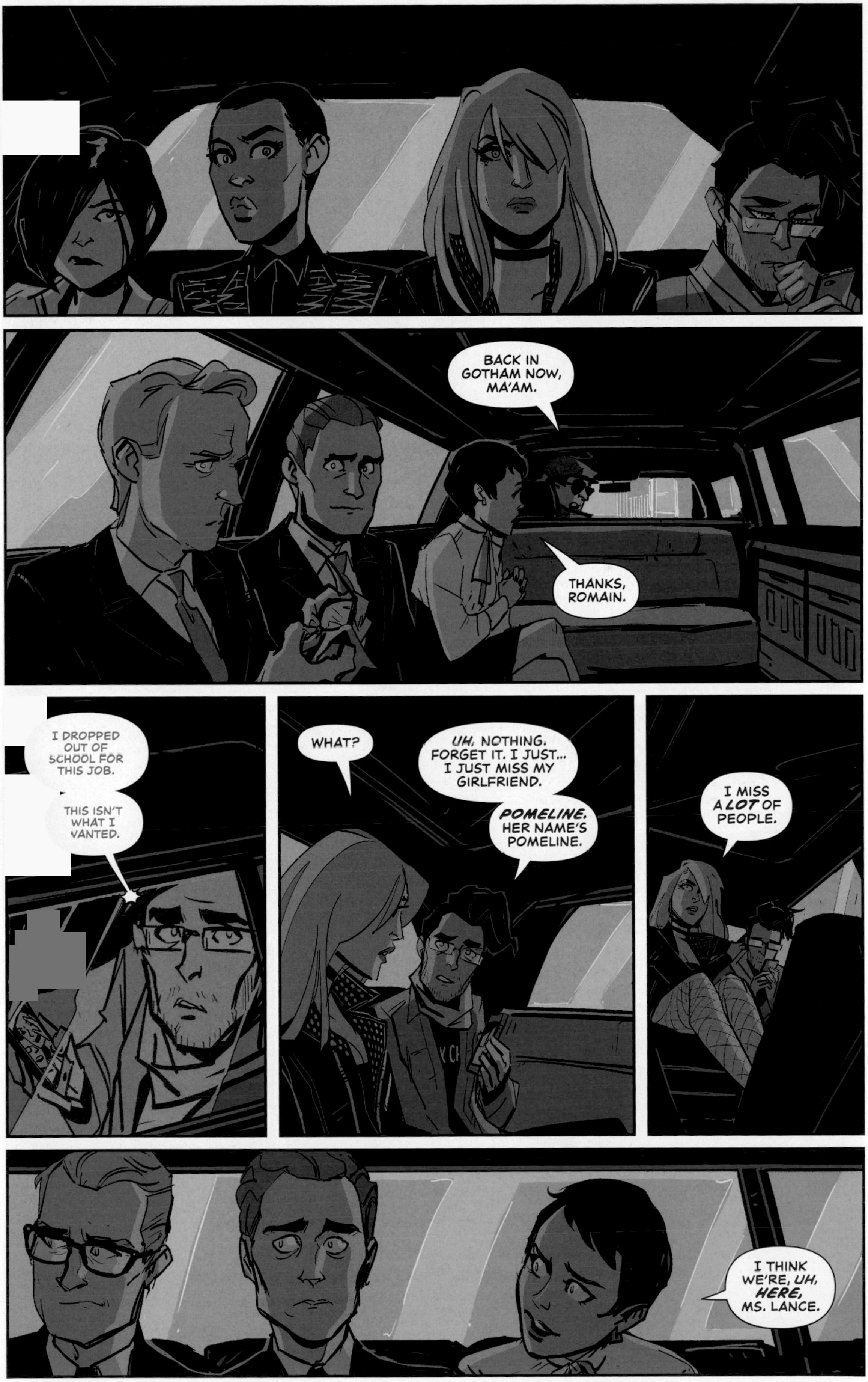
BACK IN GOTHAM NOW, MA'AM.
THANKS, ROMAIN.
I DROPPED OUT OF SCHOOL FOR THIS JOB.
THIS ISN'T WHAT I WANTED.
WHAT?
UH, NOTHING. FORGET IT. I JUST... I JUST MISS MY GIRLFRIEND.
POMELINE. HER NAME'S POMELINE.
I MISS A LOT OF PEOPLE.
I THINK WE'RE, UH, HERE, MS. LANCE.

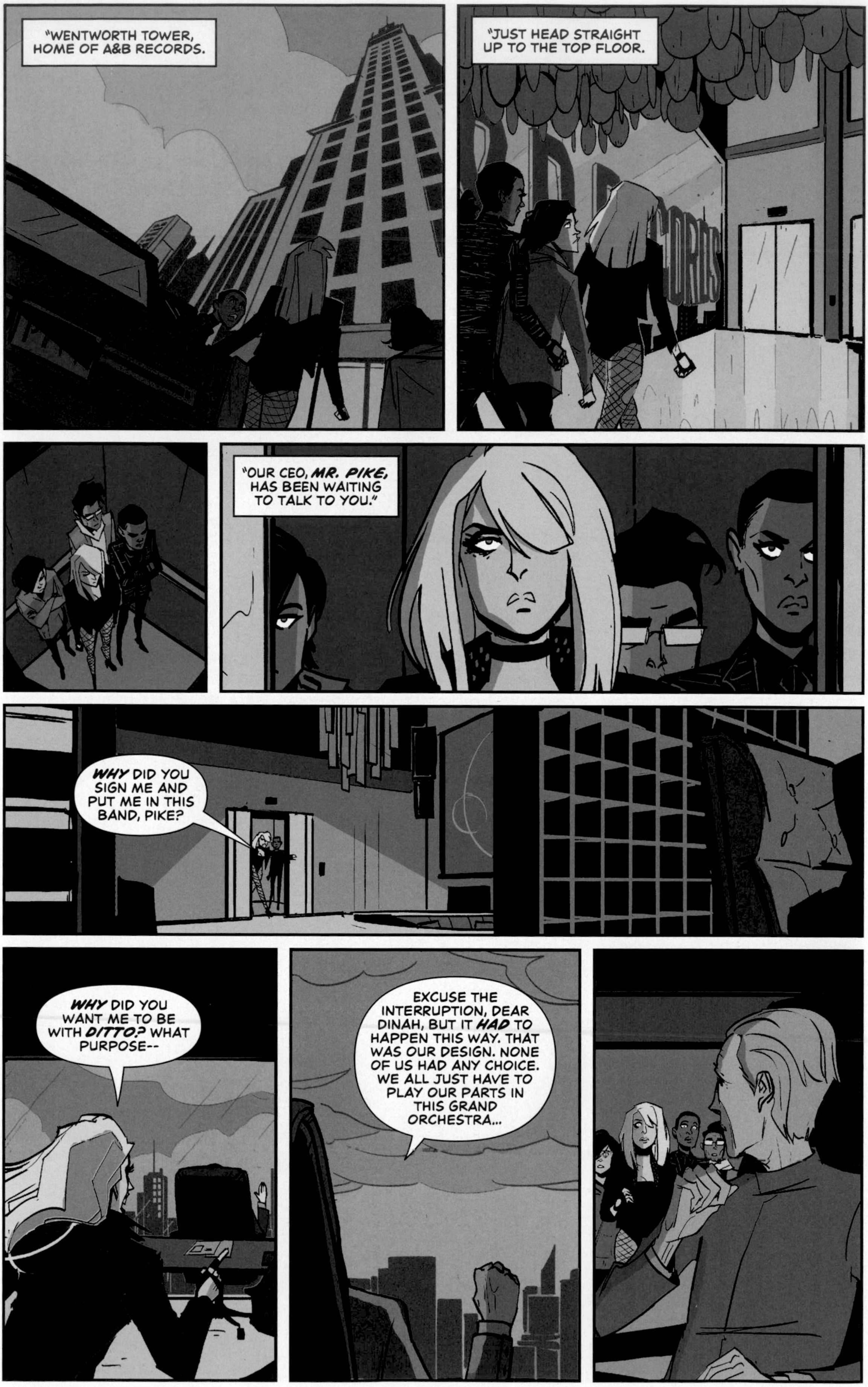
"WENTWORTH TOWER, HOME OF A&B RECORDS.
"JUST HEAD STRAIGHT UP TO THE TOP FLOOR.
"OUR CEO, MR. PIKE, HAS BEEN WAITING TO TALK TO YOU."
WHY DID YOU SIGN ME AND PUT ME IN THIS BAND, PIKE?
WHY DID YOU WANT ME TO BE WITH DITTO? WHAT PURPOSE--
EXCUSE THE INTERRUPTION, DEAR DINAH, BUT IT HAD TO HAPPEN THIS WAY. THAT WAS OUR DESIGN. NONE OF US HAD ANY CHOICE. WE ALL JUST HAVE TO PLAY OUR PARTS IN THIS GRAND ORCHESTRA...

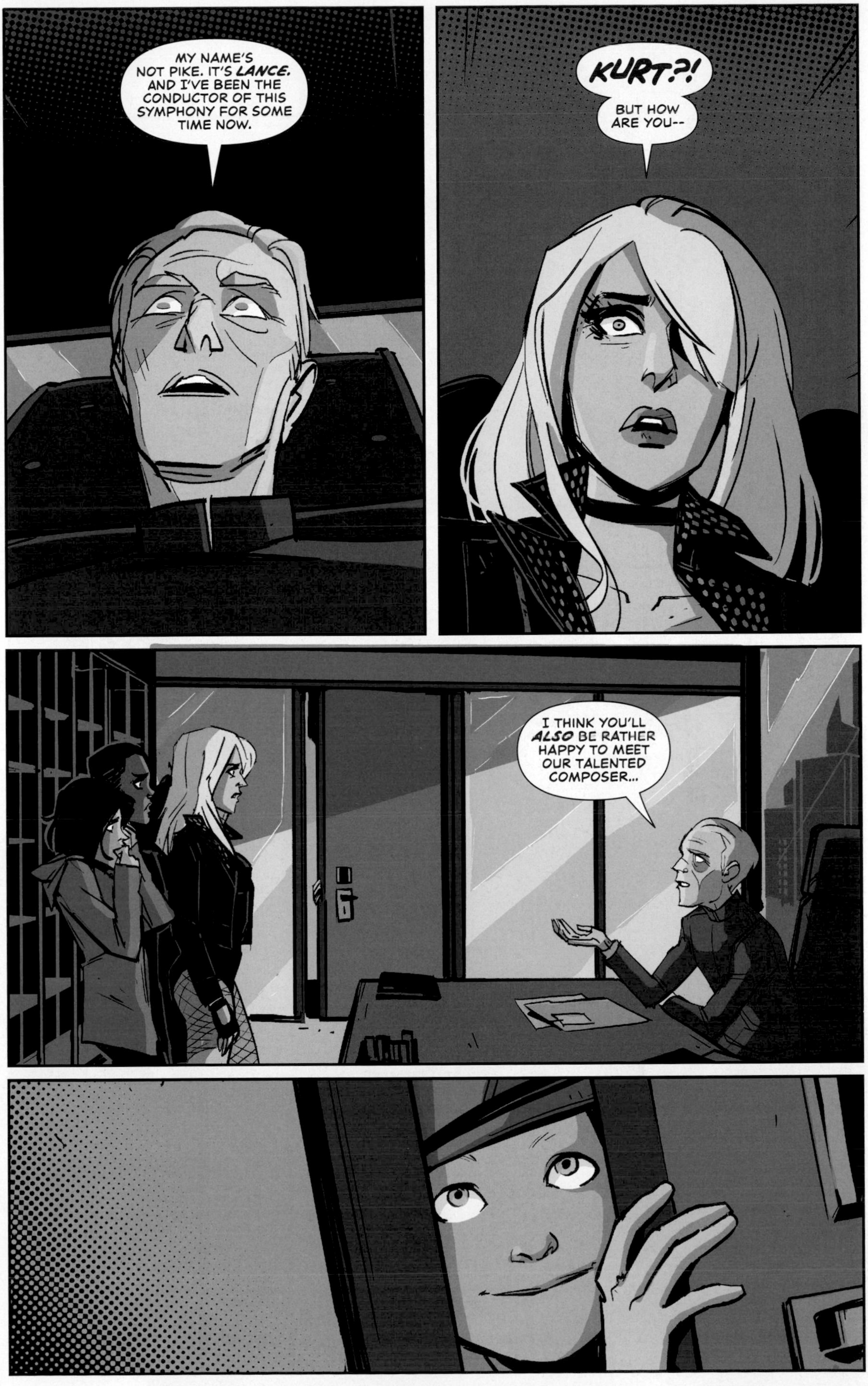
MY NAME'S NOT PIKE. IT'S *LANCE.* AND I'VE BEEN THE CONDUCTOR OF THIS SYMPHONY FOR SOME TIME NOW.
KURT?!
BUT HOW ARE YOU--
I THINK YOU'LL *ALSO* BE RATHER HAPPY TO MEET OUR TALENTED COMPOSER...

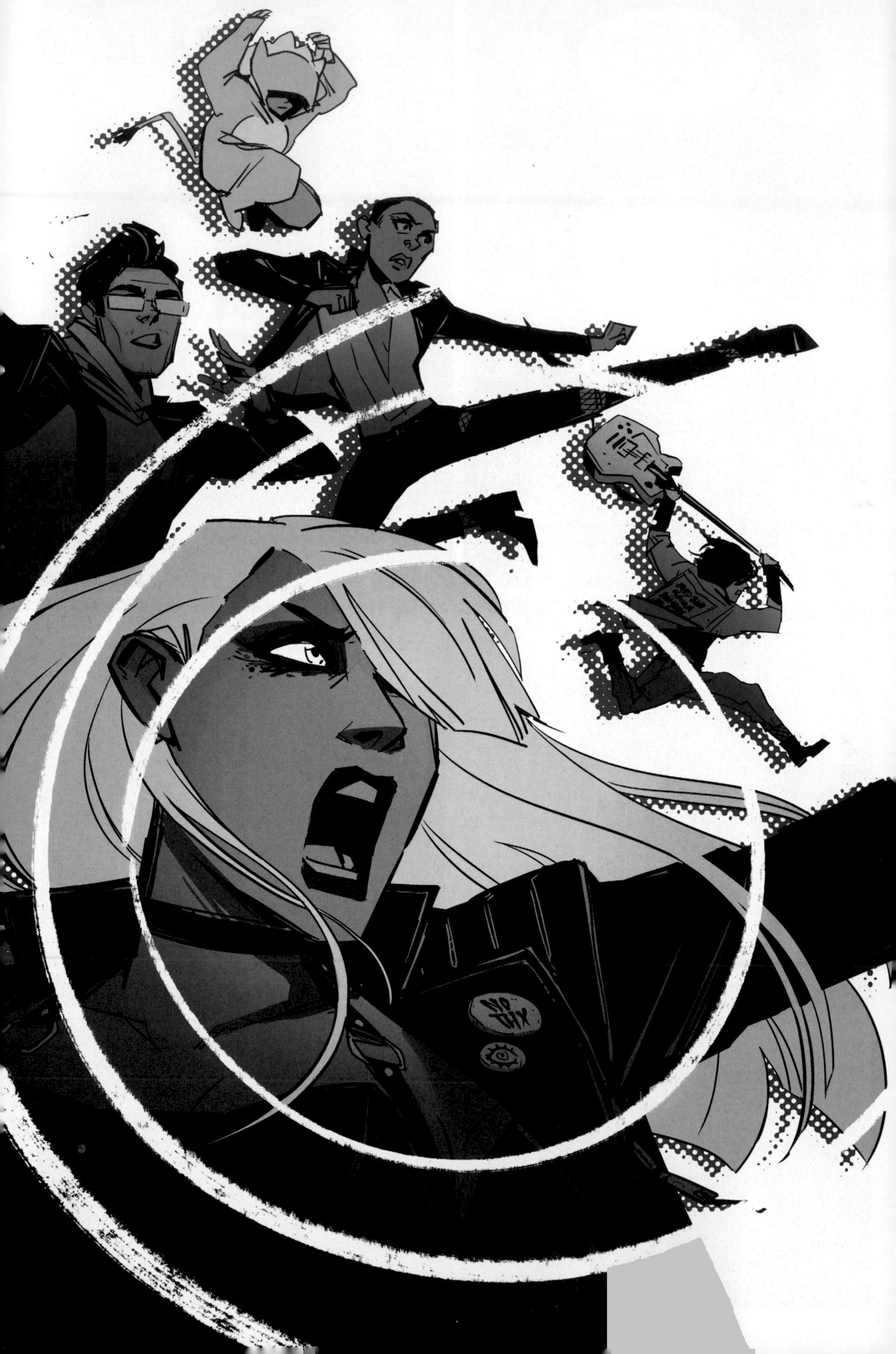
NO THX

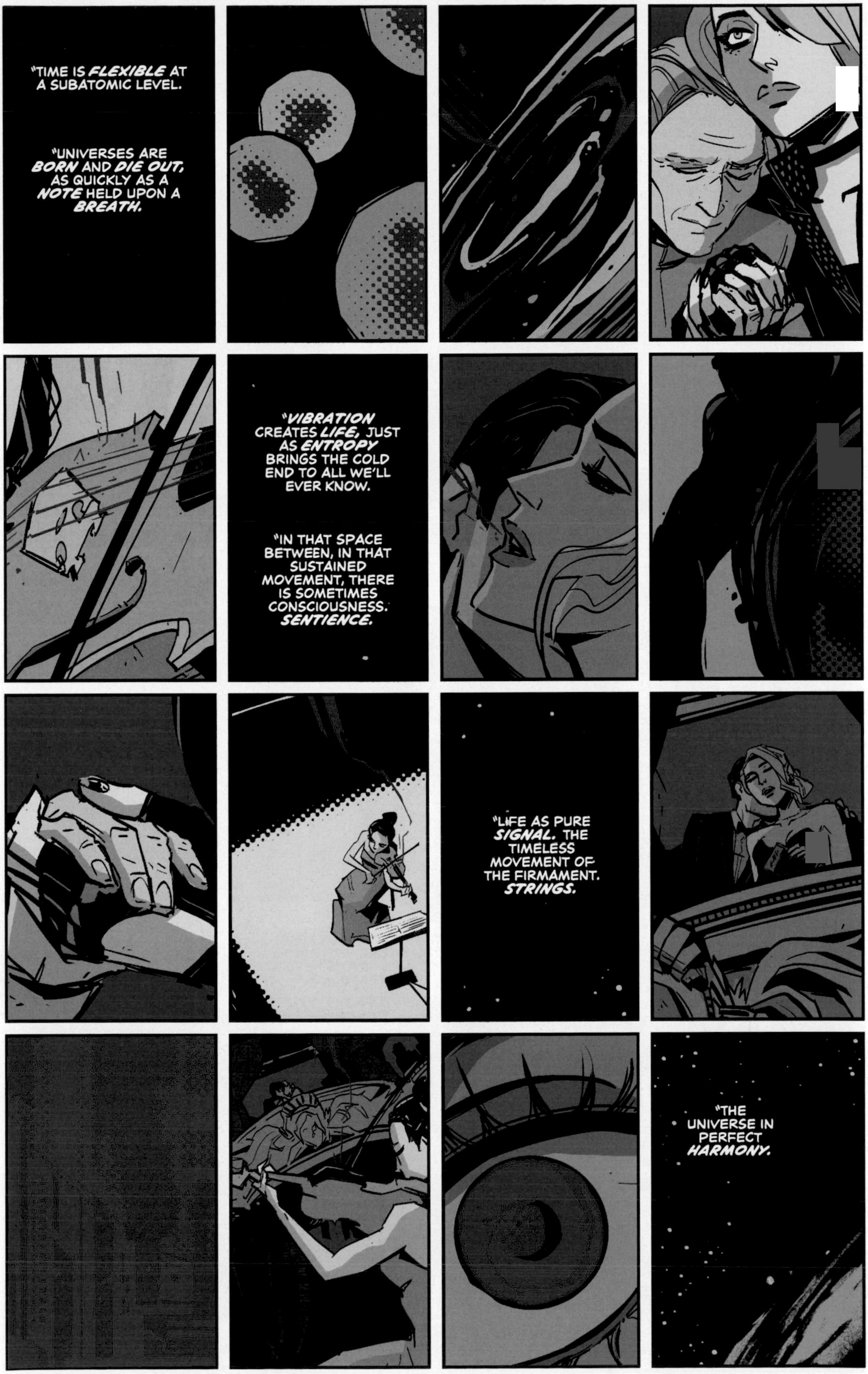
"TIME IS FLEXIBLE AT A SUBATOMIC LEVEL.
"UNIVERSES ARE BORN AND DIE OUT, AS QUICKLY AS A NOTE HELD UPON A BREATH.
"VIBRATION CREATES LIFE, JUST AS ENTROPY BRINGS THE COLD END TO ALL WE'LL EVER KNOW.
"IN THAT SPACE BETWEEN, IN THAT SUSTAINED MOVEMENT, THERE IS SOMETIMES CONSCIOUSNESS. SENTIENCE.
"LIFE AS PURE SIGNAL. THE TIMELESS MOVEMENT OF THE FIRMAMENT. STRINGS.
"THE UNIVERSE IN PERFECT HARMONY.

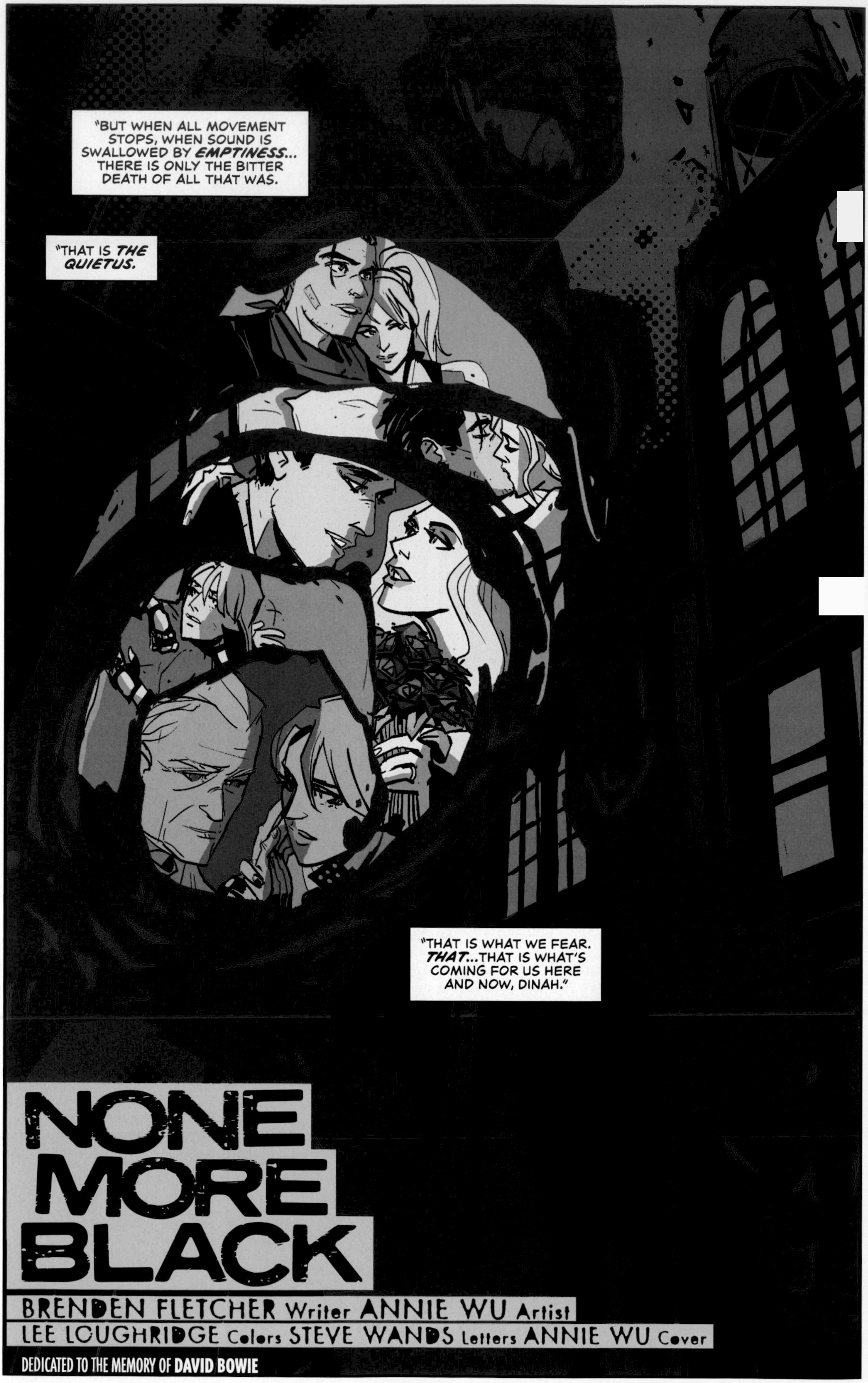
"BUT WHEN ALL MOVEMENT STOPS, WHEN SOUND IS SWALLOWED BY EMPTINESS... THERE IS ONLY THE BITTER DEATH OF ALL THAT WAS.
"THAT IS THE QUIETUS.
"THAT IS WHAT WE FEAR. THAT...THAT IS WHAT'S COMING FOR US HERE AND NOW, DINAH."
NONE MORE BLACK
BRENDEN FLETCHER Writer ANNIE WU Artist
LEE LOUGHRIDGE Colors STEVE WANDS Letters ANNIE WU Cover
DEDICATED TO THE MEMORY OF DAVID BOWIE

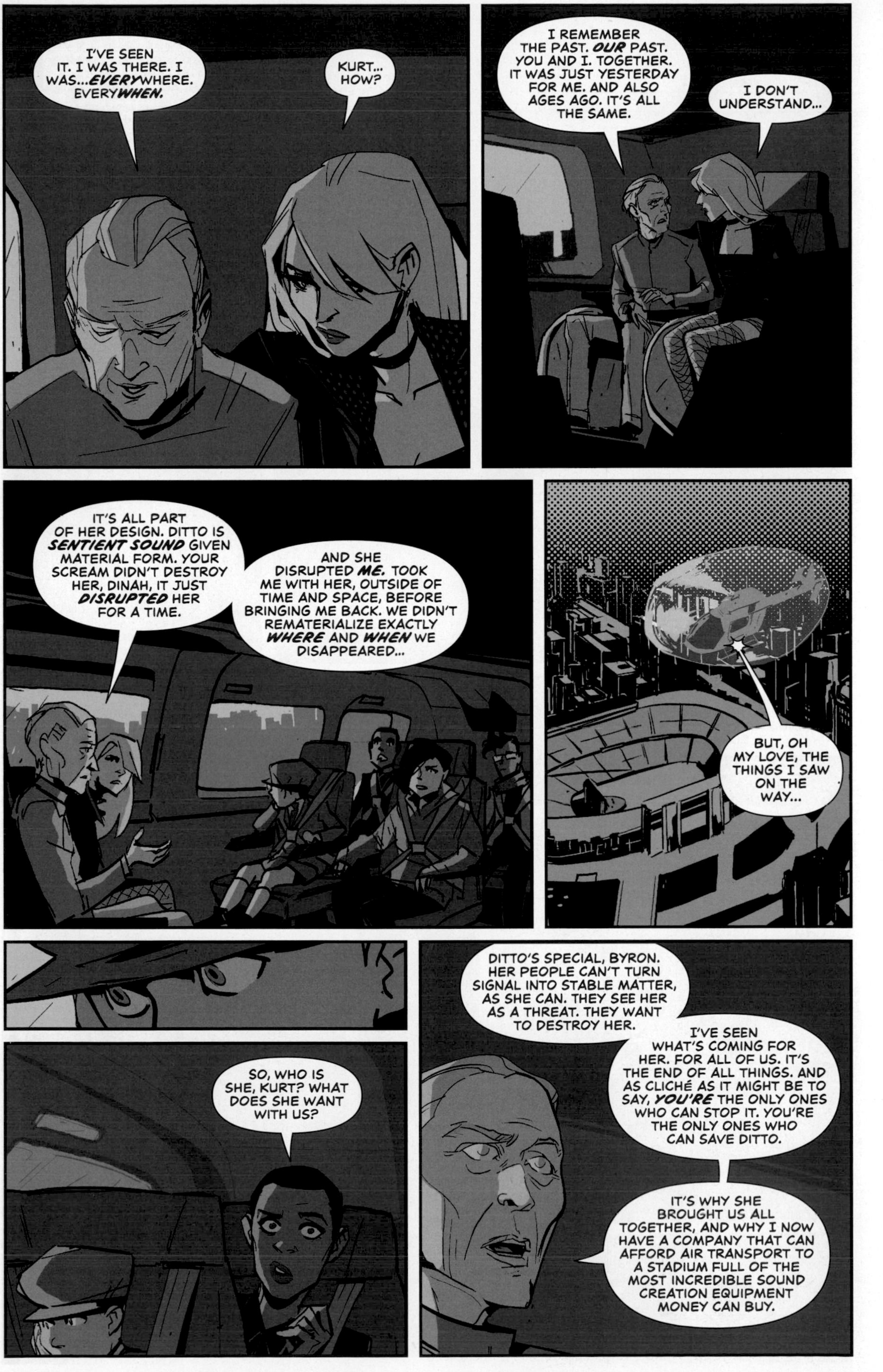
I'VE SEEN IT. I WAS THERE. I WAS...EVERYWHERE. EVERYWHEN.
KURT... HOW?
I REMEMBER THE PAST. OUR PAST. YOU AND I. TOGETHER. IT WAS JUST YESTERDAY FOR ME. AND ALSO AGES AGO. IT'S ALL THE SAME.
I DON'T UNDERSTAND...
IT'S ALL PART OF HER DESIGN. DITTO IS SENTIENT SOUND GIVEN MATERIAL FORM. YOUR SCREAM DIDN'T DESTROY HER, DINAH, IT JUST DISRUPTED HER FOR A TIME.
AND SHE DISRUPTED ME. TOOK ME WITH HER, OUTSIDE OF TIME AND SPACE, BEFORE BRINGING ME BACK. WE DIDN'T REMATERIALIZE EXACTLY WHERE AND WHEN WE DISAPPEARED...
BUT, OH MY LOVE, THE THINGS I SAW ON THE WAY...
SO, WHO IS SHE, KURT? WHAT DOES SHE WANT WITH US?
DITTO'S SPECIAL, BYRON. HER PEOPLE CAN'T TURN SIGNAL INTO STABLE MATTER, AS SHE CAN. THEY SEE HER AS A THREAT. THEY WANT TO DESTROY HER.
I'VE SEEN WHAT'S COMING FOR HER. FOR ALL OF US. IT'S THE END OF ALL THINGS. AND AS CLICHÉ AS IT MIGHT BE TO SAY, YOU'RE THE ONLY ONES WHO CAN STOP IT. YOU'RE THE ONLY ONES WHO CAN SAVE DITTO.
IT'S WHY SHE BROUGHT US ALL TOGETHER, AND WHY I NOW HAVE A COMPANY THAT CAN AFFORD AIR TRANSPORT TO A STADIUM FULL OF THE MOST INCREDIBLE SOUND CREATION EQUIPMENT MONEY CAN BUY.

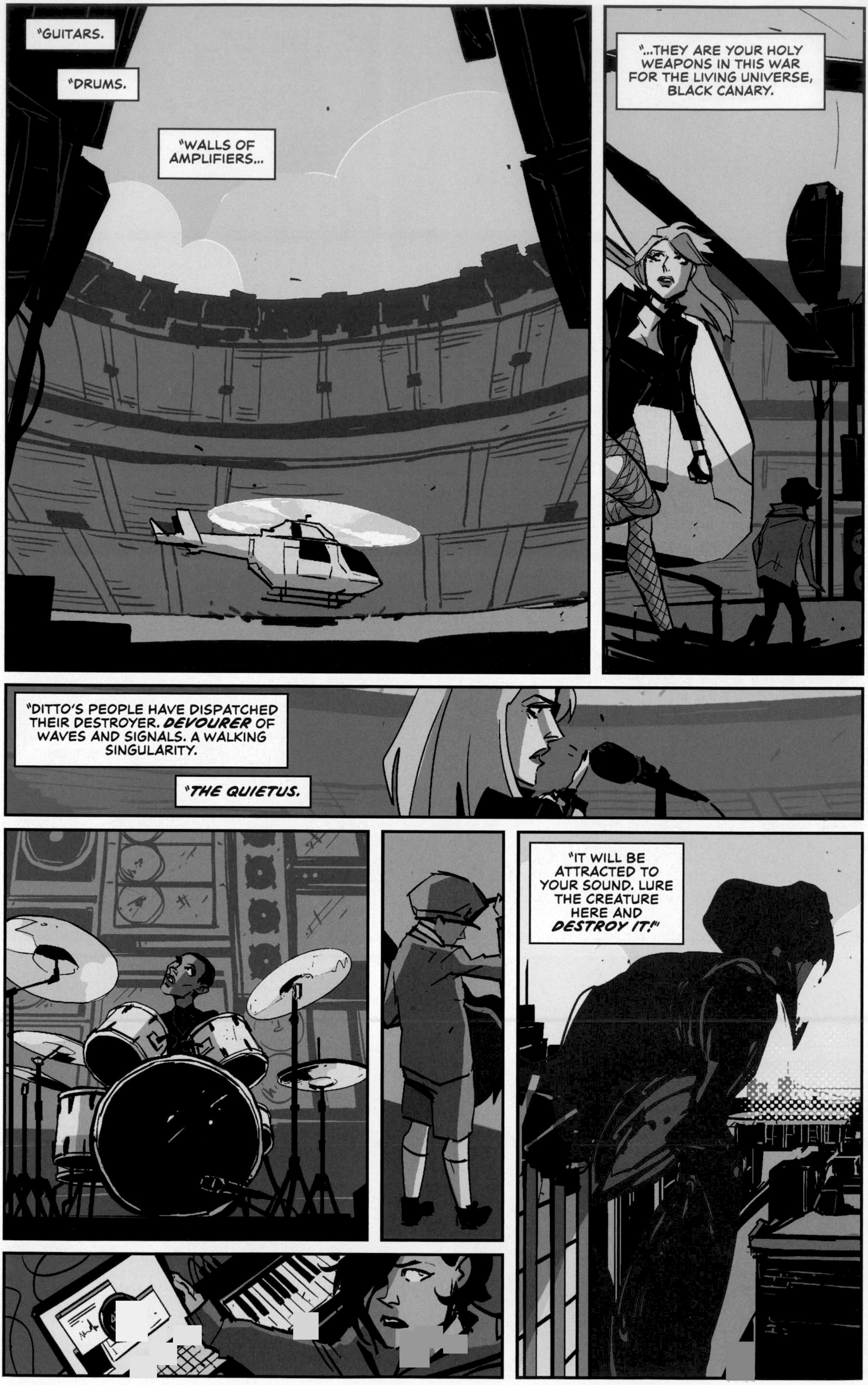
"GUITARS.
"DRUMS.
"WALLS OF AMPLIFIERS...
"...THEY ARE YOUR HOLY WEAPONS IN THIS WAR FOR THE LIVING UNIVERSE, BLACK CANARY.
"DITTO'S PEOPLE HAVE DISPATCHED THEIR DESTROYER. DEVOURER OF WAVES AND SIGNALS. A WALKING SINGULARITY.
"THE QUIETUS.
"IT WILL BE ATTRACTED TO YOUR SOUND. LURE THE CREATURE HERE AND DESTROY IT!"

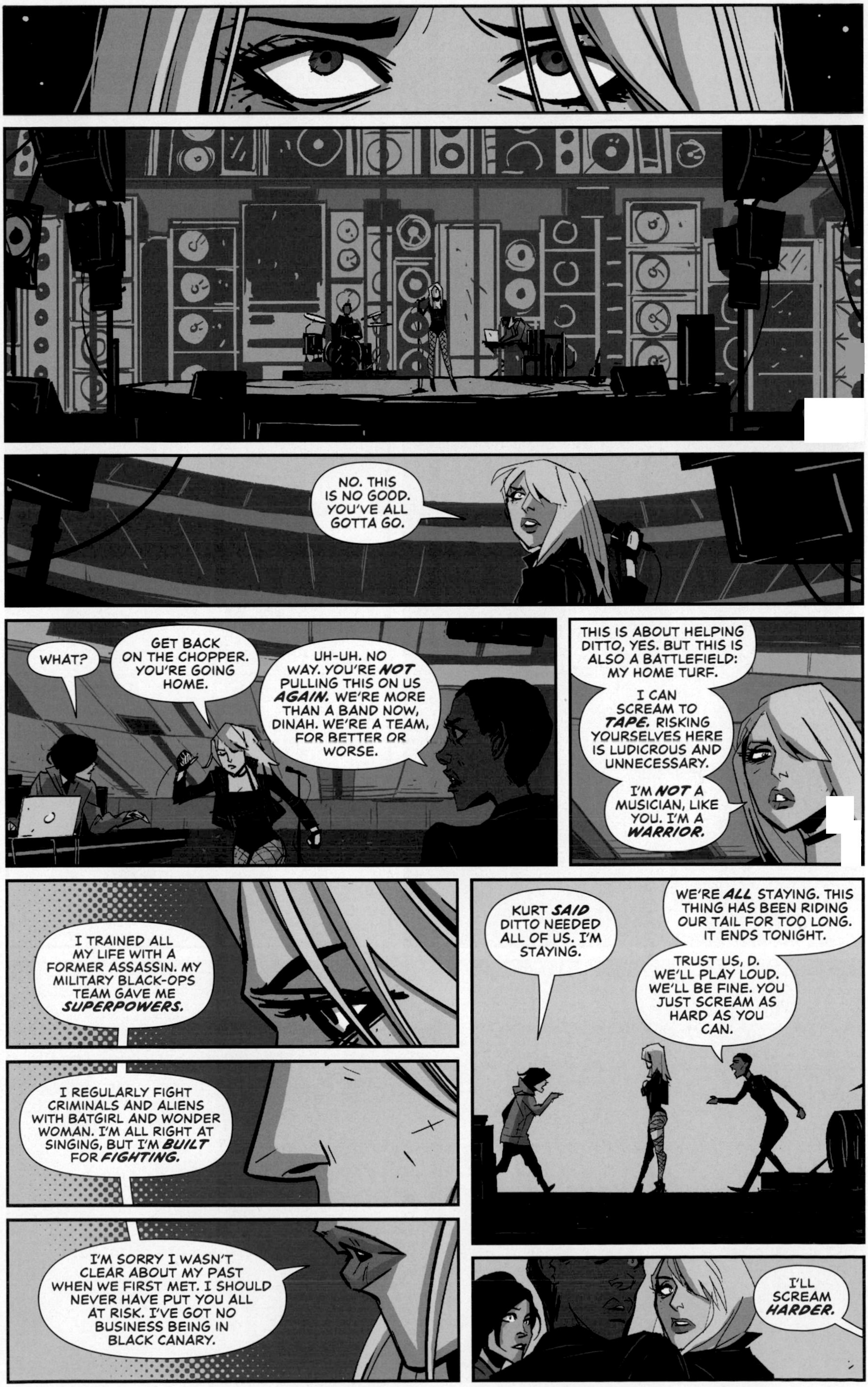
NO. THIS IS NO GOOD. YOU'VE ALL GOTTA GO.
WHAT?
GET BACK ON THE CHOPPER. YOU'RE GOING HOME.
UH-UH. NO WAY. YOU'RE NOT PULLING THIS ON US AGAIN. WE'RE MORE THAN A BAND NOW, DINAH. WE'RE A TEAM, FOR BETTER OR WORSE.
THIS IS ABOUT HELPING DITTO, YES. BUT THIS IS ALSO A BATTLEFIELD: MY HOME TURF.
I CAN SCREAM TO TAPE. RISKING YOURSELVES HERE IS LUDICROUS AND UNNECESSARY.
I'M NOT A MUSICIAN, LIKE YOU. I'M A WARRIOR.
I TRAINED ALL MY LIFE WITH A FORMER ASSASSIN. MY MILITARY BLACK-OPS TEAM GAVE ME SUPERPOWERS.
I REGULARLY FIGHT CRIMINALS AND ALIENS WITH BATGIRL AND WONDER WOMAN. I'M ALL RIGHT AT SINGING, BUT I'M BUILT FOR FIGHTING.
I'M SORRY I WASN'T CLEAR ABOUT MY PAST WHEN WE FIRST MET. I SHOULD NEVER HAVE PUT YOU ALL AT RISK. I'VE GOT NO BUSINESS BEING IN BLACK CANARY.
KURT SAID DITTO NEEDED ALL OF US. I'M STAYING.
WE'RE ALL STAYING. THIS THING HAS BEEN RIDING OUR TAIL FOR TOO LONG. IT ENDS TONIGHT.
TRUST US, D. WE'LL PLAY LOUD. WE'LL BE FINE. YOU JUST SCREAM AS HARD AS YOU CAN.
I'LL SCREAM HARDER.

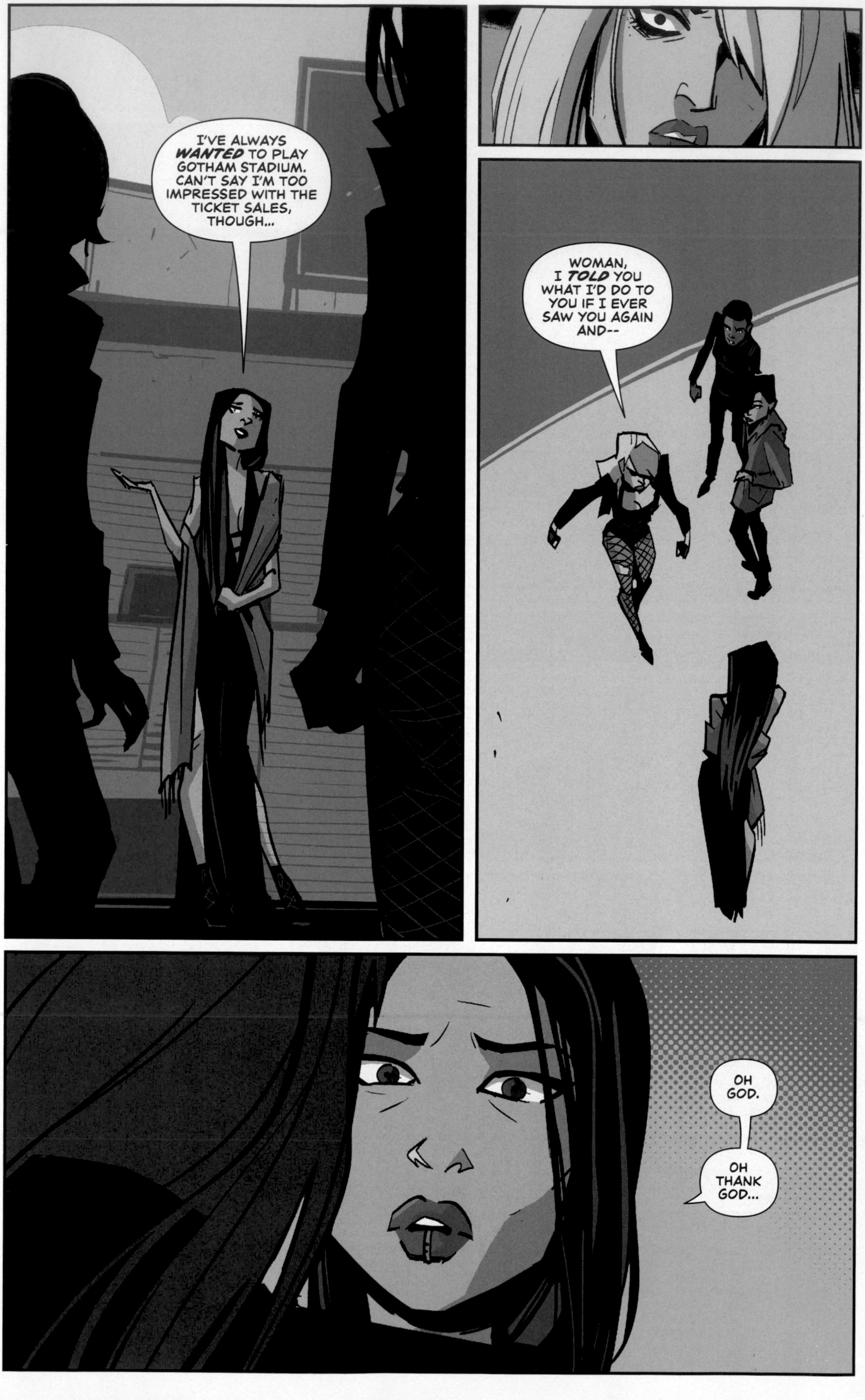
I'VE ALWAYS WANTED TO PLAY GOTHAM STADIUM. CAN'T SAY I'M TOO IMPRESSED WITH THE TICKET SALES, THOUGH...
WOMAN, I TOLD YOU WHAT I'D DO TO YOU IF I EVER SAW YOU AGAIN AND--
OH GOD.
OH THANK GOD...

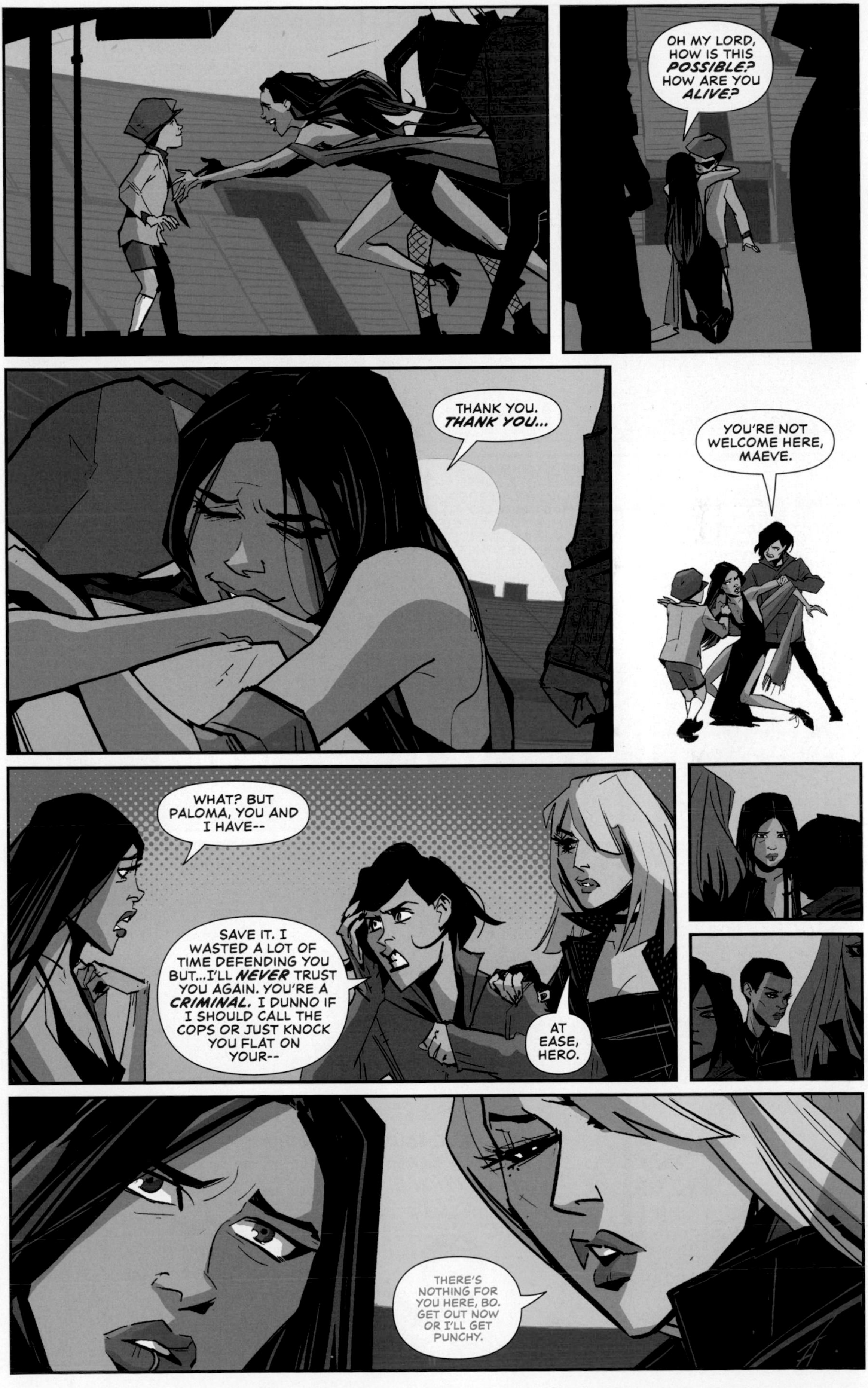
OH MY LORD, HOW IS THIS POSSIBLE? HOW ARE YOU ALIVE?
THANK YOU. THANK YOU...
YOU'RE NOT WELCOME HERE, MAEVE.
WHAT? BUT PALOMA, YOU AND I HAVE--
SAVE IT. I WASTED A LOT OF TIME DEFENDING YOU BUT...I'LL NEVER TRUST YOU AGAIN. YOU'RE A CRIMINAL. I DUNNO IF I SHOULD CALL THE COPS OR JUST KNOCK YOU FLAT ON YOUR--
AT EASE, HERO.
THERE'S NOTHING FOR YOU HERE, BO. GET OUT NOW OR I'LL GET PUNCHY.

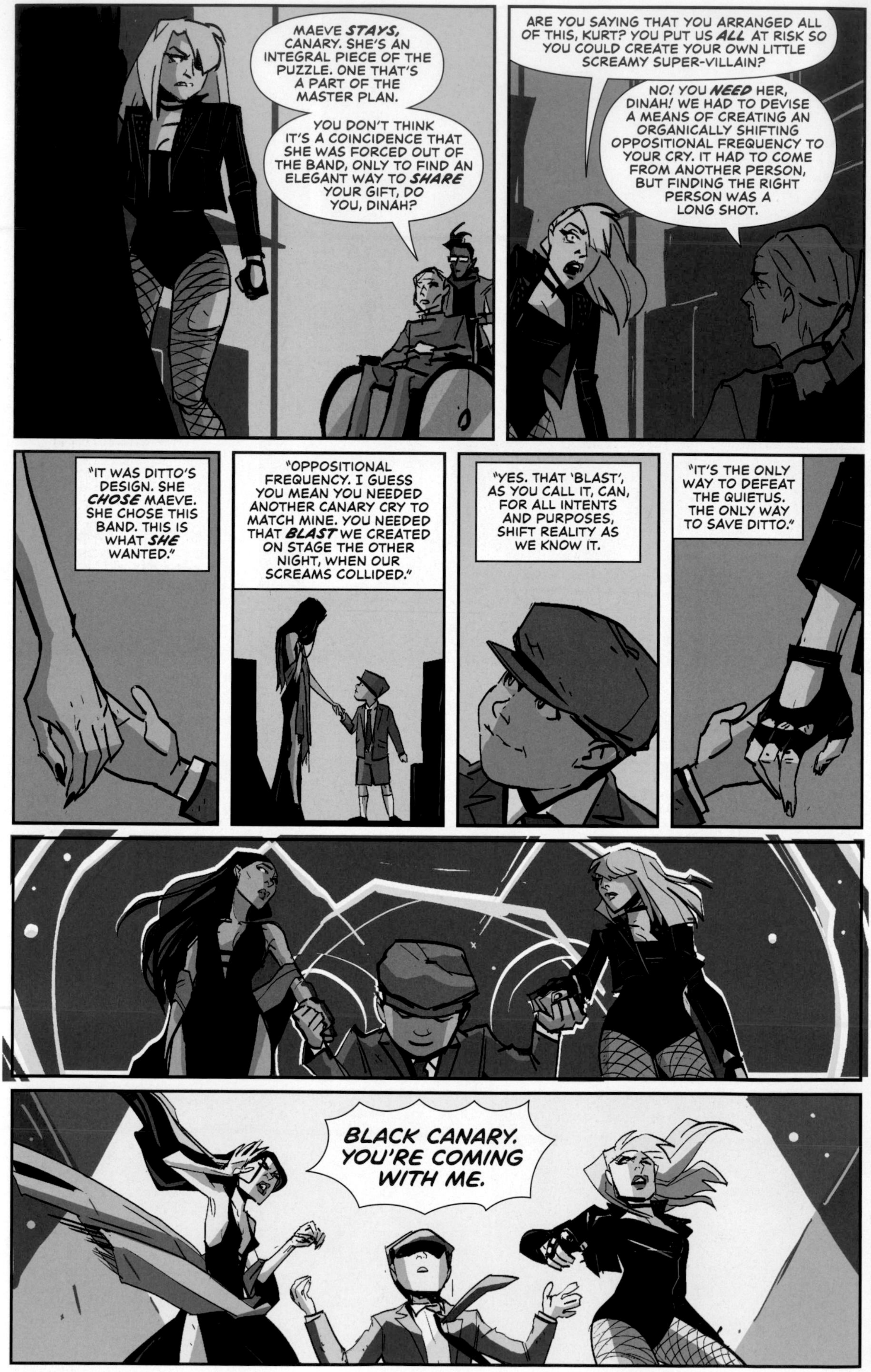
MAEVE STAYS, CANARY. SHE'S AN INTEGRAL PIECE OF THE PUZZLE. ONE THAT'S A PART OF THE MASTER PLAN.
YOU DON'T THINK IT'S A COINCIDENCE THAT SHE WAS FORCED OUT OF THE BAND, ONLY TO FIND AN ELEGANT WAY TO SHARE YOUR GIFT, DO YOU, DINAH?
ARE YOU SAYING THAT YOU ARRANGED ALL OF THIS, KURT? YOU PUT US ALL AT RISK SO YOU COULD CREATE YOUR OWN LITTLE SCREAMY SUPER-VILLAIN?
NO! YOU NEED HER, DINAH! WE HAD TO DEVISE A MEANS OF CREATING AN ORGANICALLY SHIFTING OPPOSITIONAL FREQUENCY TO YOUR CRY. IT HAD TO COME FROM ANOTHER PERSON, BUT FINDING THE RIGHT PERSON WAS A LONG SHOT.
"IT WAS DITTO'S DESIGN. SHE CHOSE MAEVE. SHE CHOSE THIS BAND. THIS IS WHAT SHE WANTED."
"OPPOSITIONAL FREQUENCY. I GUESS YOU MEAN YOU NEEDED ANOTHER CANARY CRY TO MATCH MINE. YOU NEEDED THAT BLAST WE CREATED ON STAGE THE OTHER NIGHT, WHEN OUR SCREAMS COLLIDED."
"YES. THAT 'BLAST', AS YOU CALL IT, CAN, FOR ALL INTENTS AND PURPOSES, SHIFT REALITY AS WE KNOW IT.
"IT'S THE ONLY WAY TO DEFEAT THE QUIETUS. THE ONLY WAY TO SAVE DITTO."
BLACK CANARY. YOU'RE COMING WITH ME.

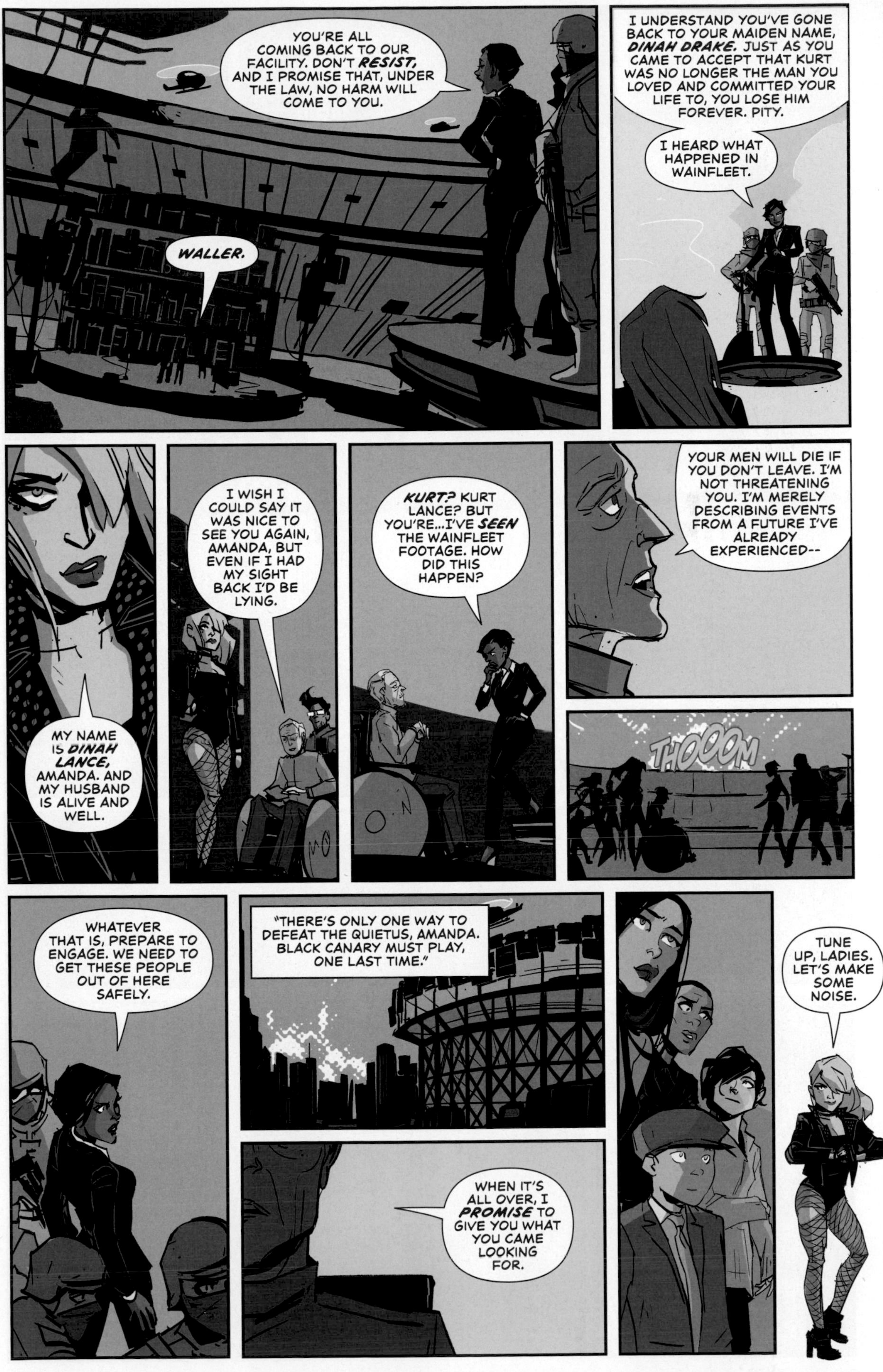
YOU'RE ALL COMING BACK TO OUR FACILITY. DON'T RESIST, AND I PROMISE THAT, UNDER THE LAW, NO HARM WILL COME TO YOU.
WALLER.
I UNDERSTAND YOU'VE GONE BACK TO YOUR MAIDEN NAME, DINAH DRAKE. JUST AS YOU CAME TO ACCEPT THAT KURT WAS NO LONGER THE MAN YOU LOVED AND COMMITTED YOUR LIFE TO, YOU LOSE HIM FOREVER. PITY.
I HEARD WHAT HAPPENED IN WAINFLEET.
MY NAME IS DINAH LANCE, AMANDA. AND MY HUSBAND IS ALIVE AND WELL.
I WISH I COULD SAY IT WAS NICE TO SEE YOU AGAIN, AMANDA, BUT EVEN IF I HAD MY SIGHT BACK I'D BE LYING.
KURT? KURT LANCE? BUT YOU'RE...I'VE SEEN THE WAINFLEET FOOTAGE. HOW DID THIS HAPPEN?
YOUR MEN WILL DIE IF YOU DON'T LEAVE. I'M NOT THREATENING YOU. I'M MERELY DESCRIBING EVENTS FROM A FUTURE I'VE ALREADY EXPERIENCED--
THOOOM
WHATEVER THAT IS, PREPARE TO ENGAGE. WE NEED TO GET THESE PEOPLE OUT OF HERE SAFELY.
"THERE'S ONLY ONE WAY TO DEFEAT THE QUIETUS, AMANDA. BLACK CANARY MUST PLAY, ONE LAST TIME."
WHEN IT'S ALL OVER, I PROMISE TO GIVE YOU WHAT YOU CAME LOOKING FOR.
TUNE UP, LADIES. LET'S MAKE SOME NOISE.

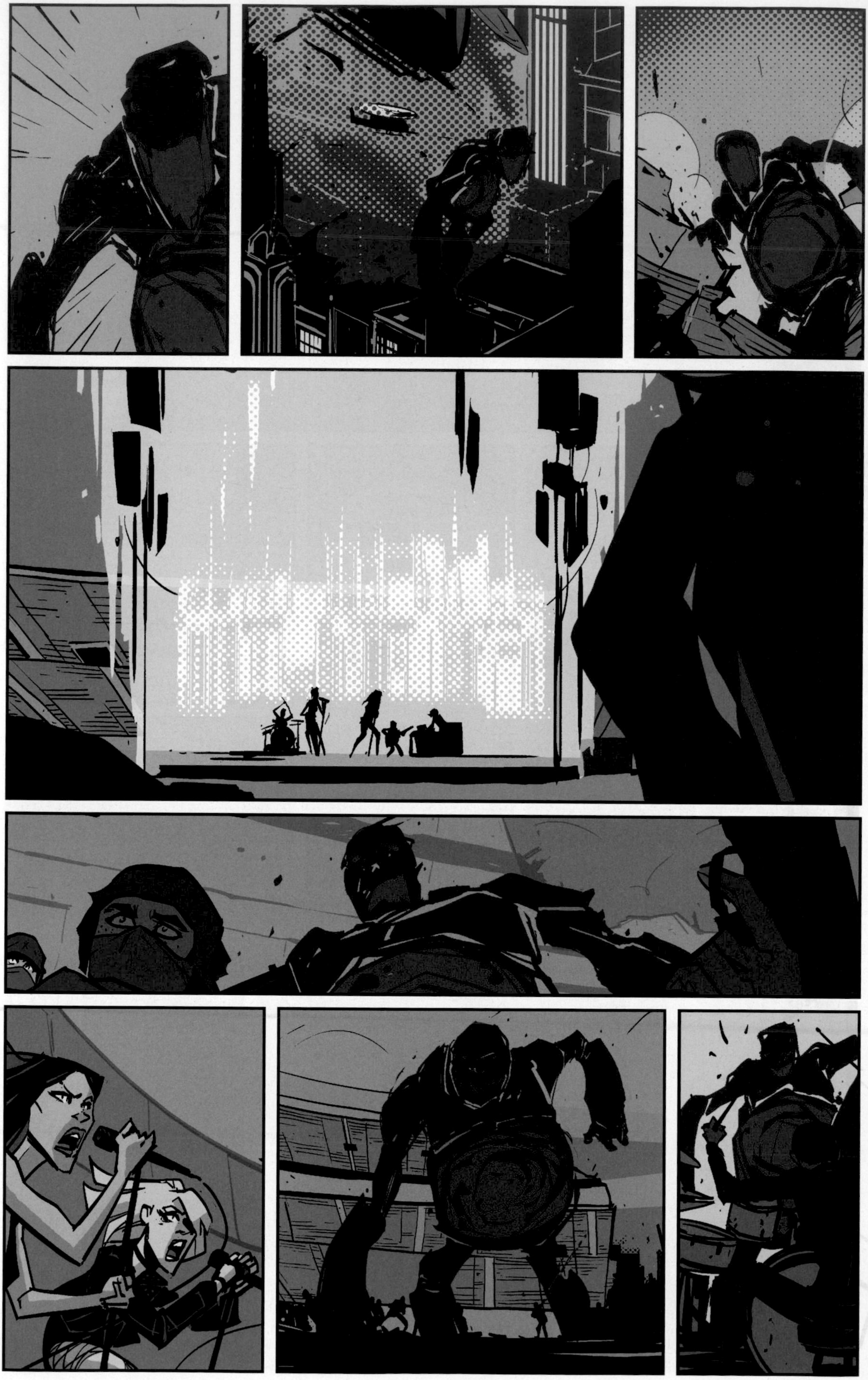

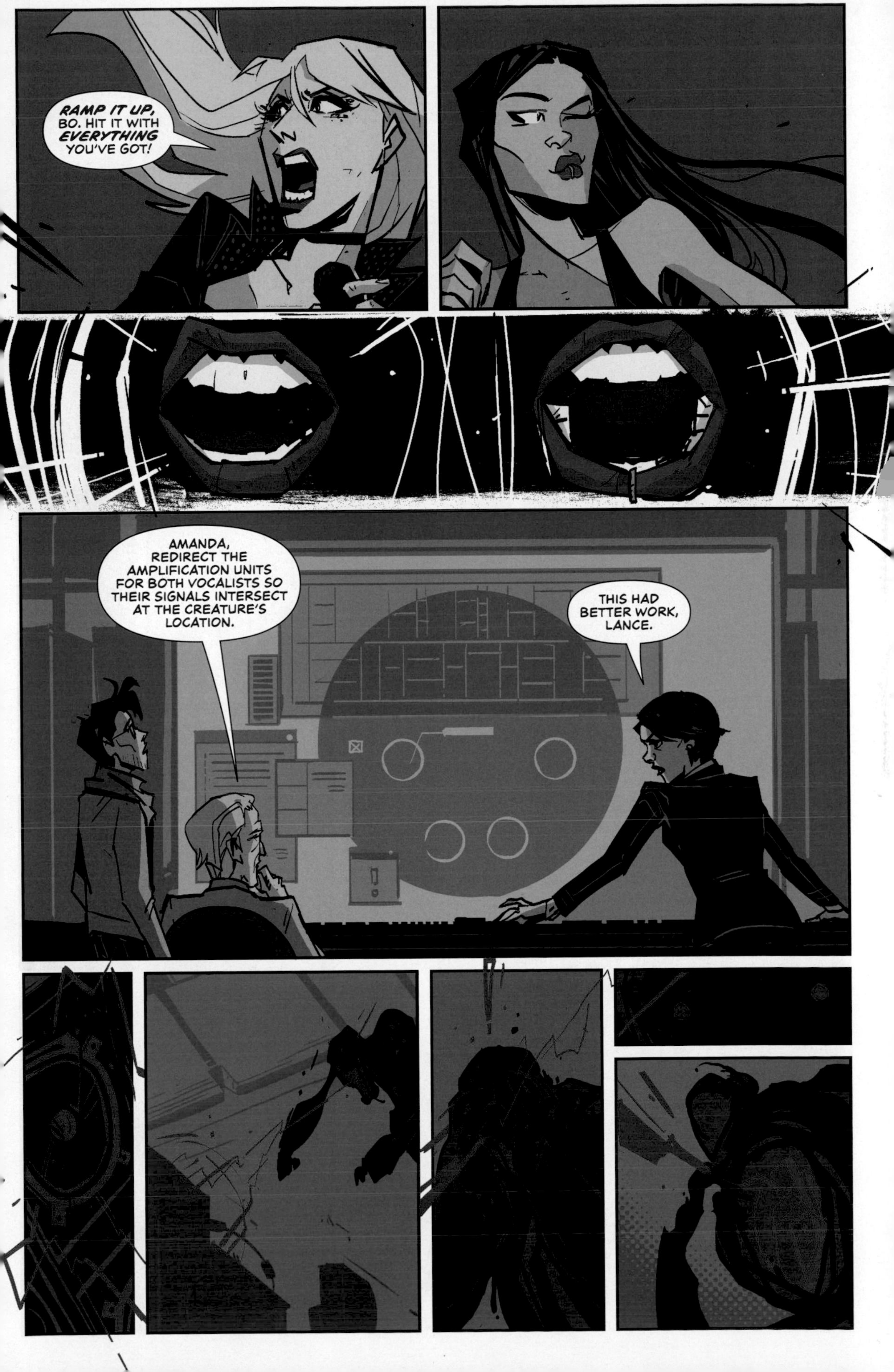
RAMP IT UP, BO. HIT IT WITH EVERYTHING YOU'VE GOT!
AMANDA, REDIRECT THE AMPLIFICATION UNITS FOR BOTH VOCALISTS SO THEIR SIGNALS INTERSECT AT THE CREATURE'S LOCATION.
THIS HAD BETTER WORK, LANCE.

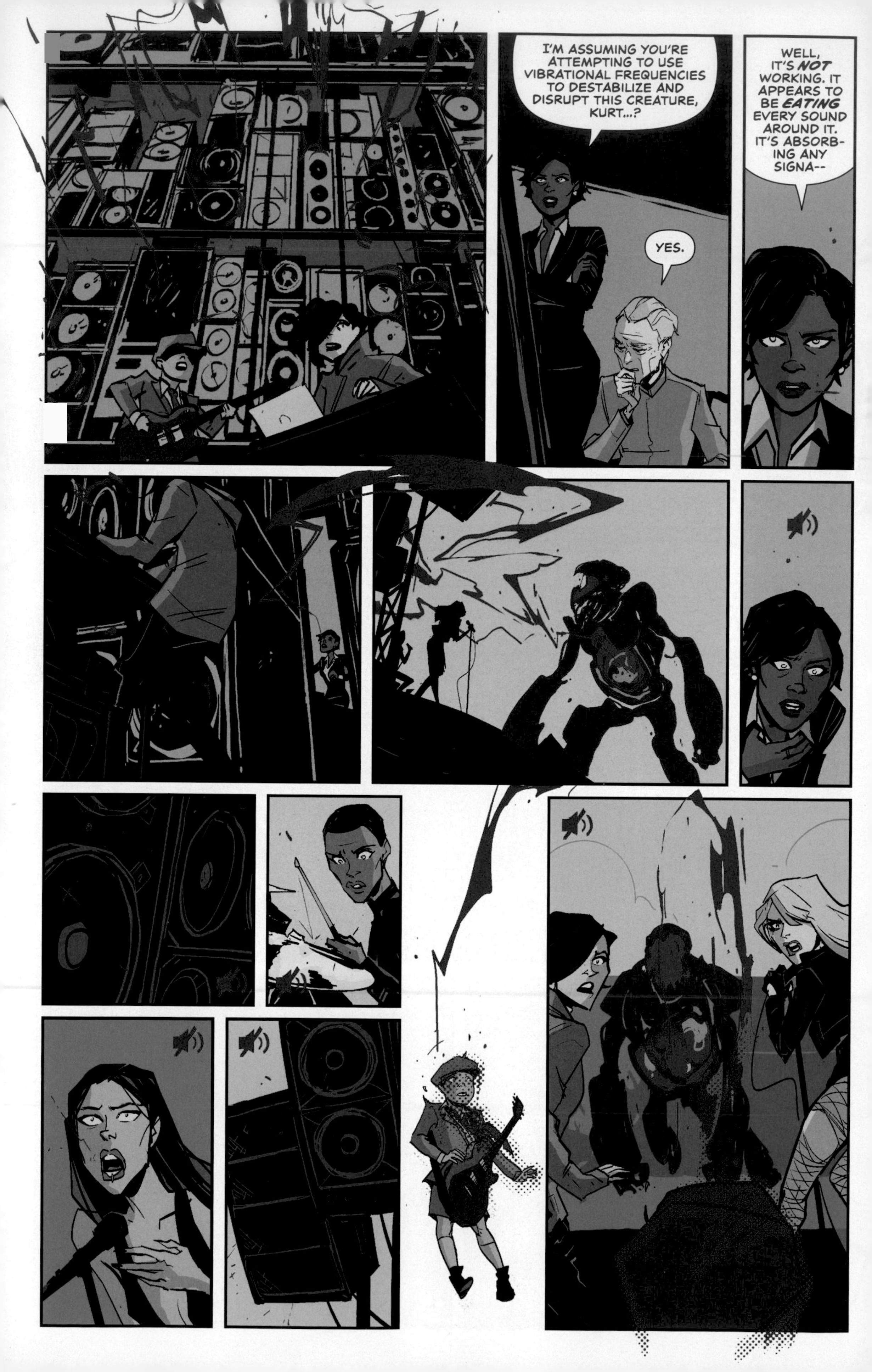

I'M ASSUMING YOU'RE ATTEMPTING TO USE VIBRATIONAL FREQUENCIES TO DESTABILIZE AND DISRUPT THIS CREATURE, KURT...?
YES.
WELL, IT'S NOT WORKING. IT APPEARS TO BE EATING EVERY SOUND AROUND IT. IT'S ABSORBING ANY SIGNA--

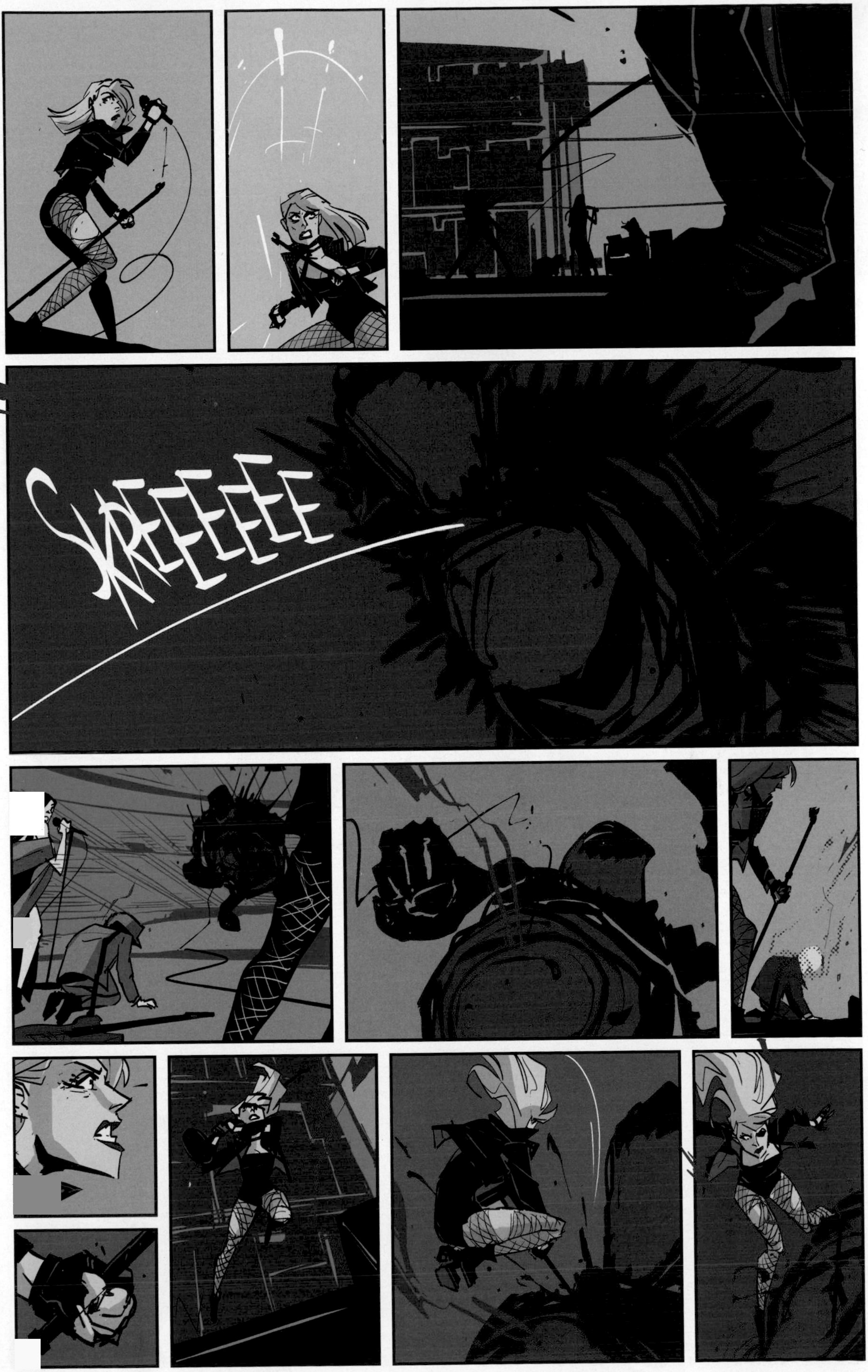
SKREEEEEE

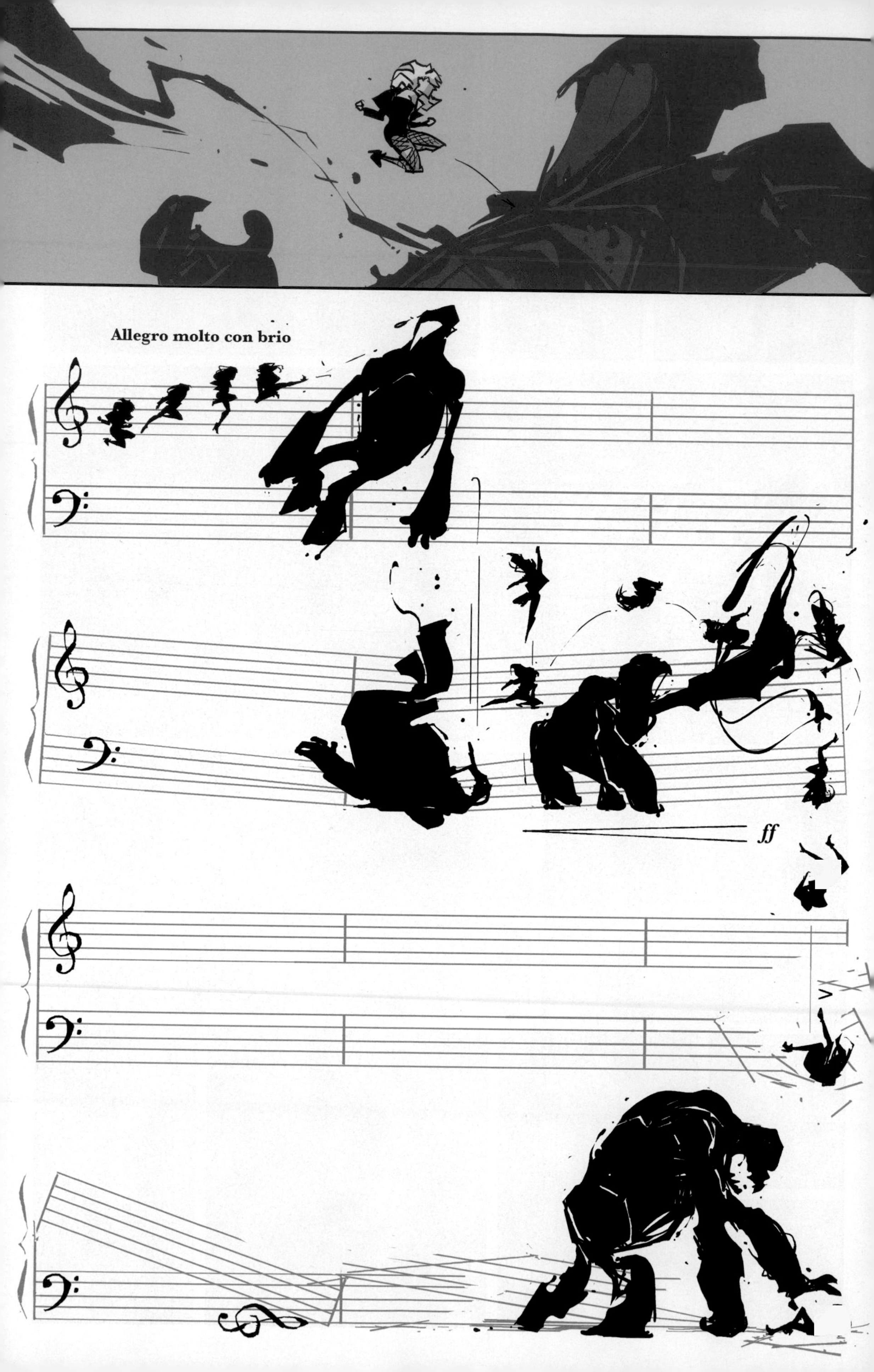
Allegro molto con brio
ff

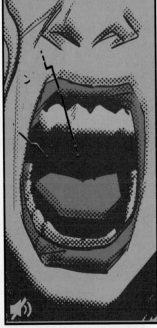

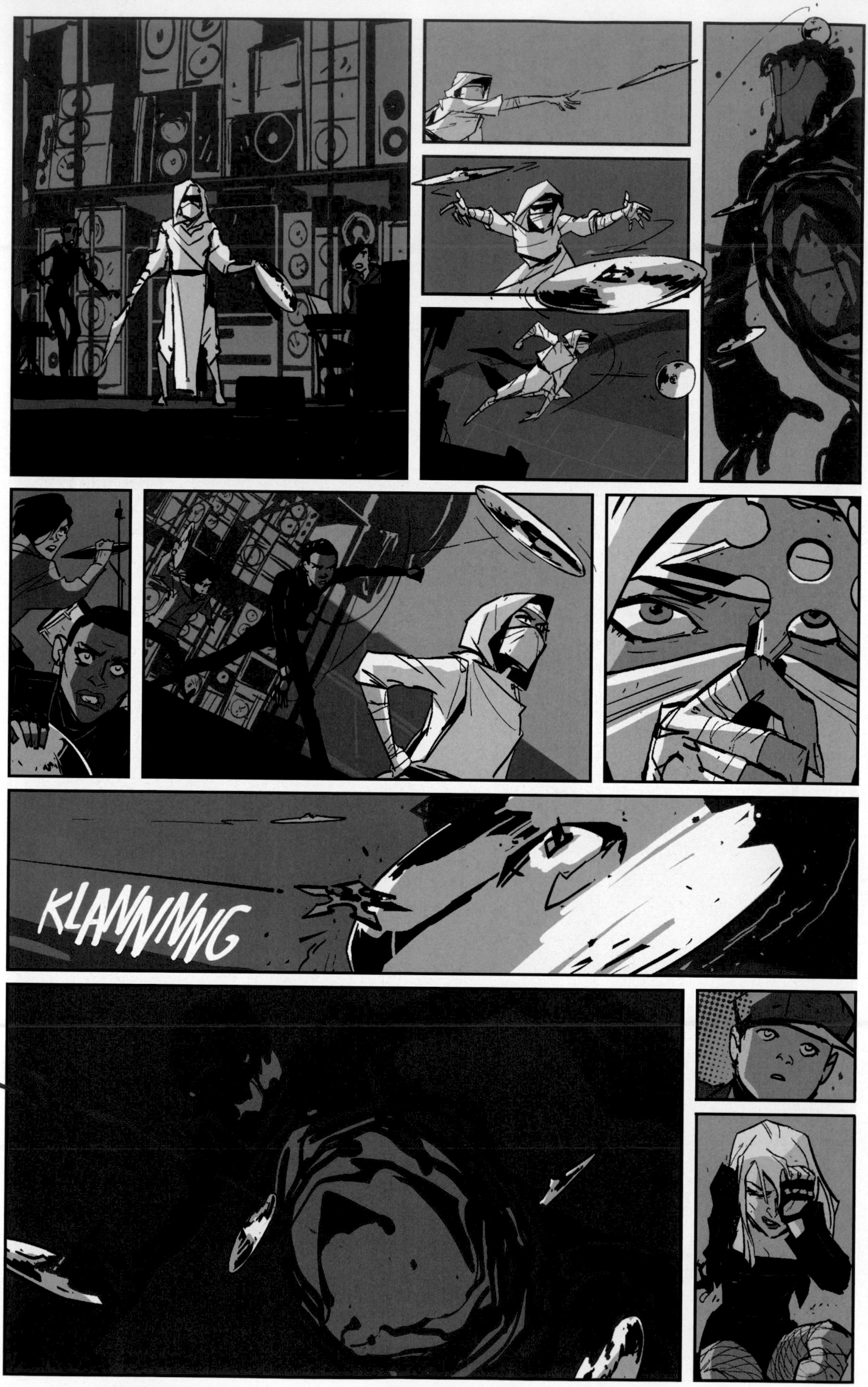
KLANNNNG

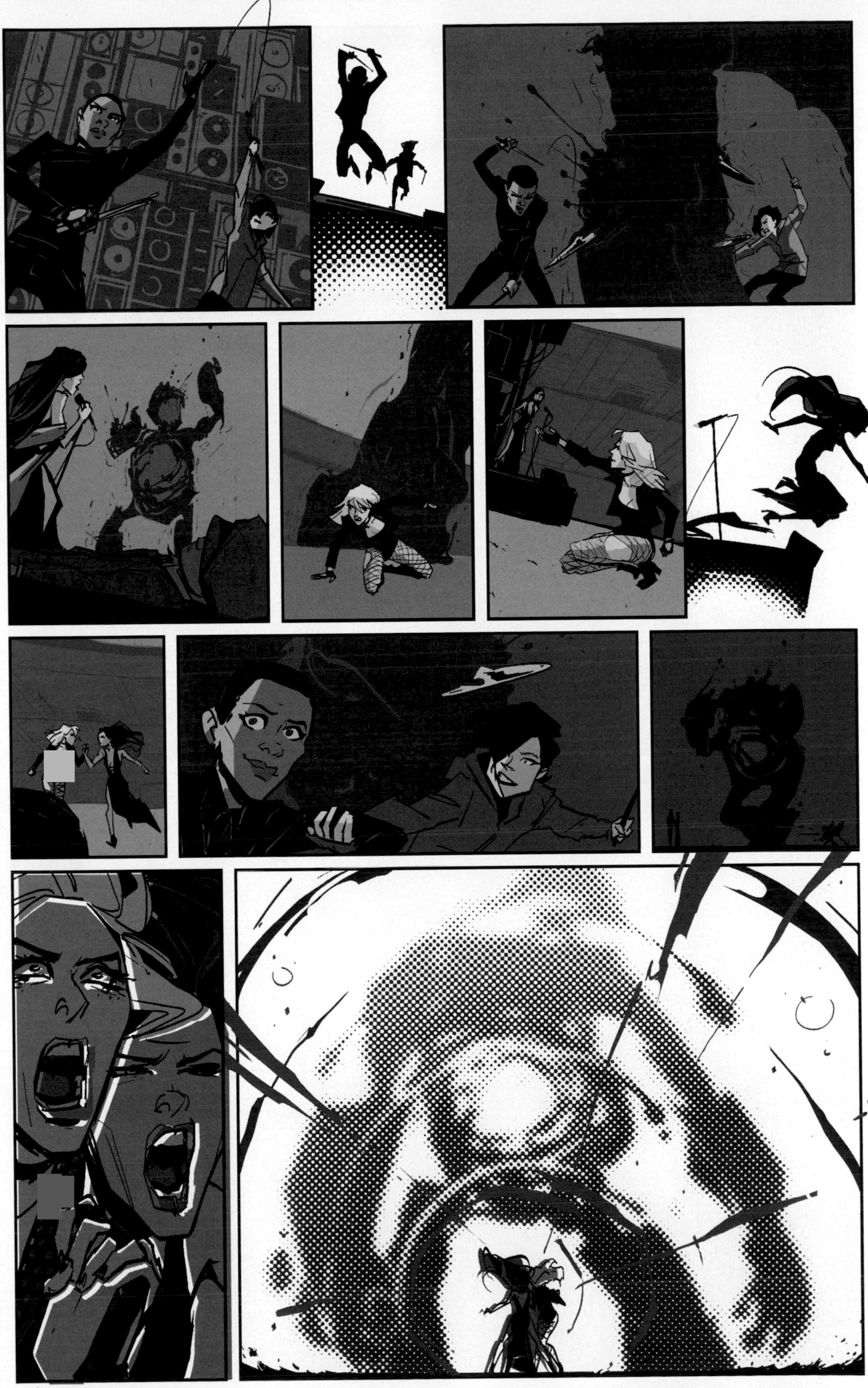

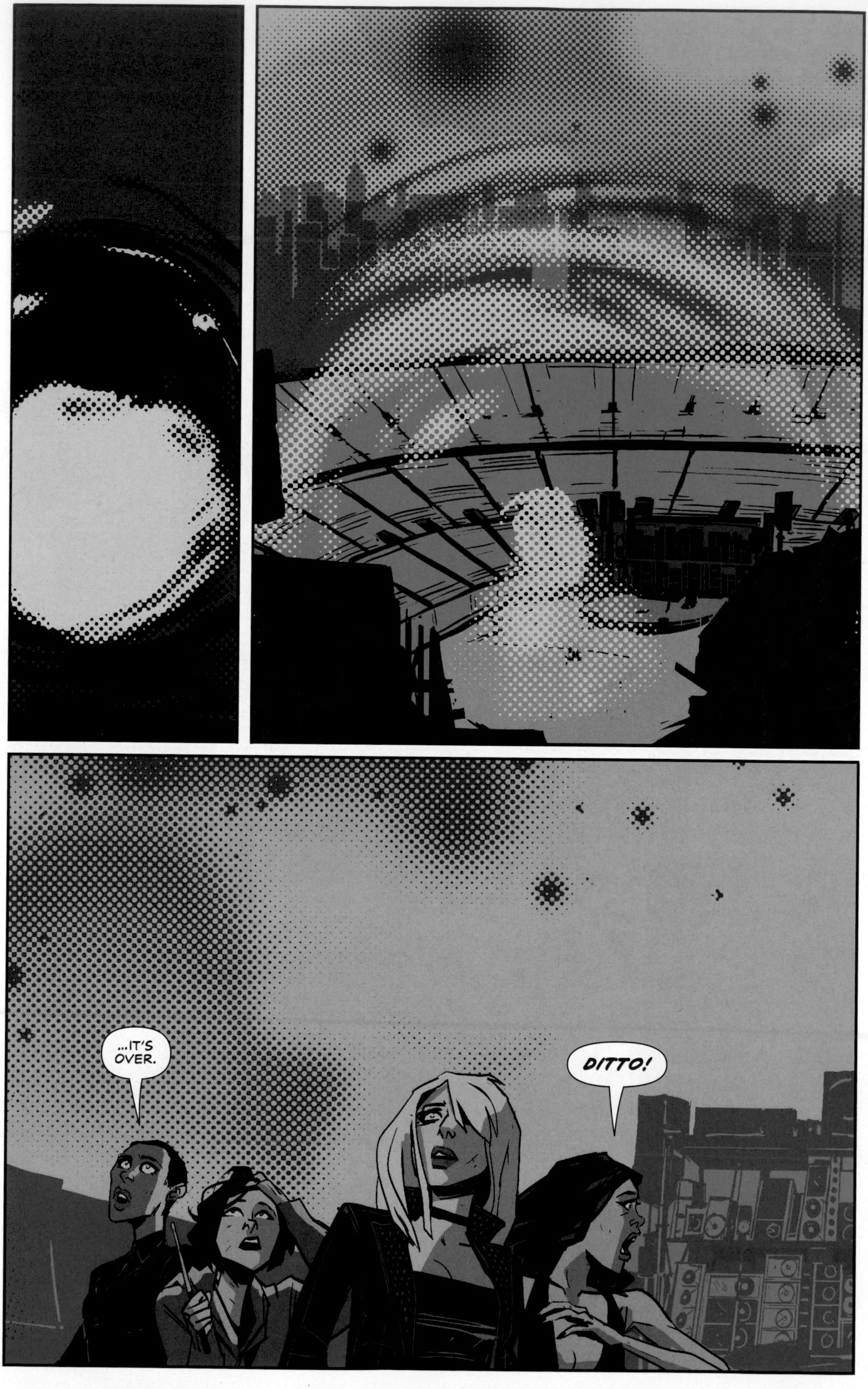
...IT'S OVER.
DITTO!

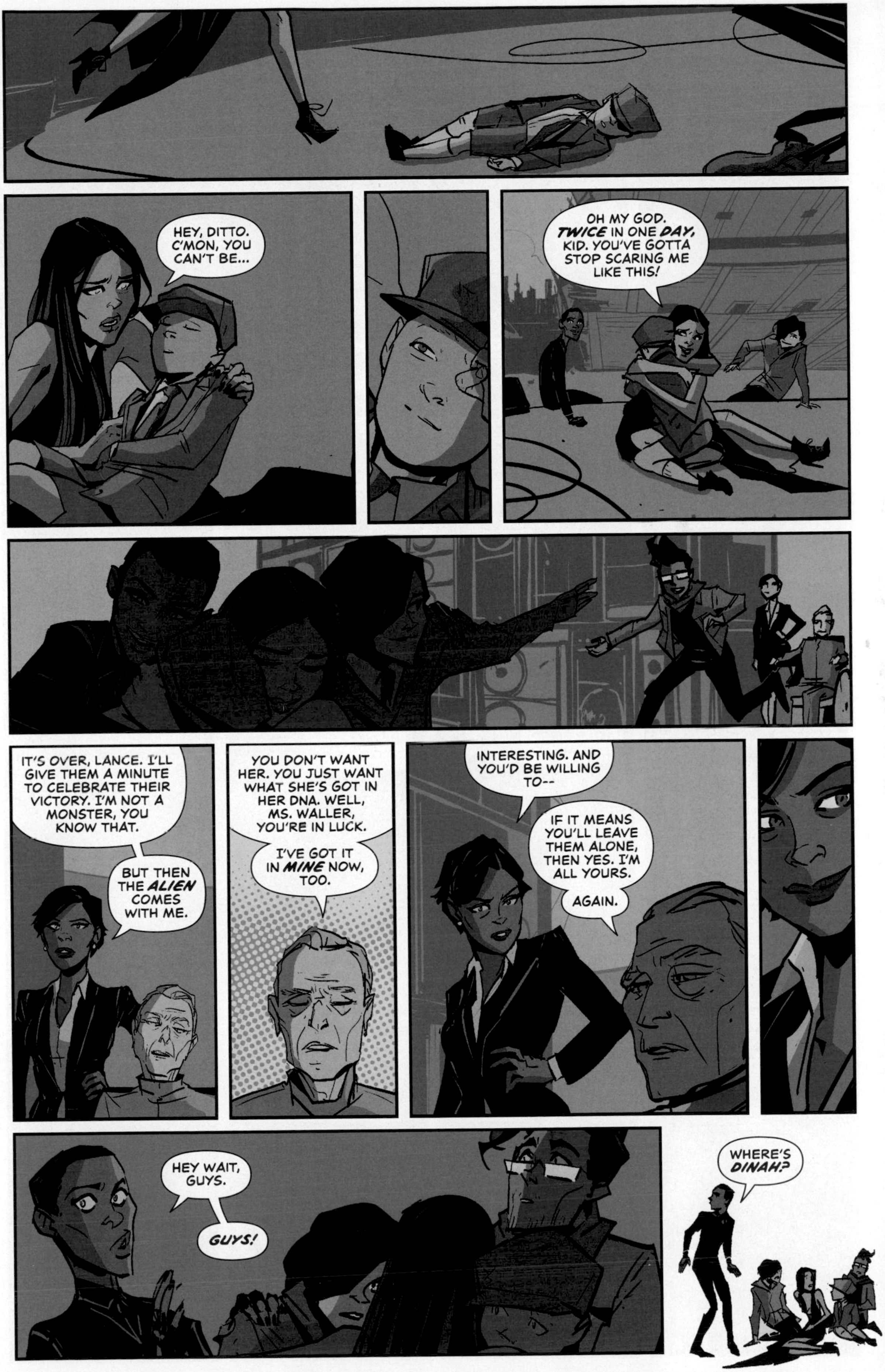
HEY, DITTO. C'MON, YOU CAN'T BE...
OH MY GOD. TWICE IN ONE DAY, KID. YOU'VE GOTTA STOP SCARING ME LIKE THIS!
IT'S OVER, LANCE. I'LL GIVE THEM A MINUTE TO CELEBRATE THEIR VICTORY. I'M NOT A MONSTER, YOU KNOW THAT.
BUT THEN THE ALIEN COMES WITH ME.
YOU DON'T WANT HER. YOU JUST WANT WHAT SHE'S GOT IN HER DNA. WELL, MS. WALLER, YOU'RE IN LUCK.
I'VE GOT IT IN MINE NOW, TOO.
INTERESTING. AND YOU'D BE WILLING TO--
IF IT MEANS YOU'LL LEAVE THEM ALONE, THEN YES. I'M ALL YOURS.
AGAIN.
HEY WAIT, GUYS.
GUYS!
WHERE'S DINAH?

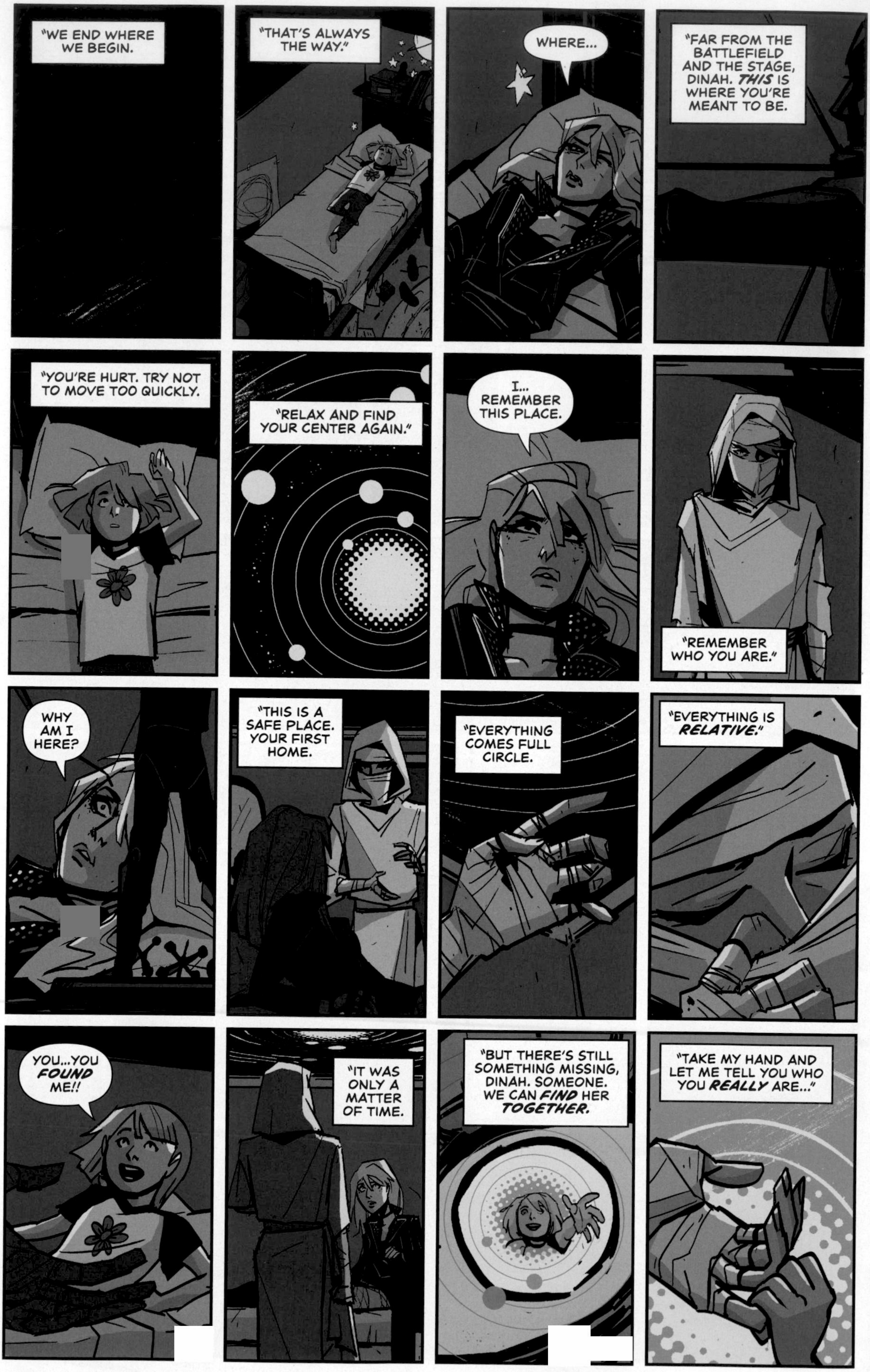
"WE END WHERE WE BEGIN.
"THAT'S ALWAYS THE WAY."
WHERE...
"FAR FROM THE BATTLEFIELD AND THE STAGE, DINAH. *THIS* IS WHERE YOU'RE MEANT TO BE.
"YOU'RE HURT. TRY NOT TO MOVE TOO QUICKLY.
"RELAX AND FIND YOUR CENTER AGAIN."
I... REMEMBER THIS PLACE.
"REMEMBER WHO YOU ARE."
WHY AM I HERE?
"THIS IS A SAFE PLACE. YOUR FIRST HOME.
"EVERYTHING COMES FULL CIRCLE.
"EVERYTHING IS *RELATIVE.*"
YOU...YOU *FOUND* ME!!
"IT WAS ONLY A MATTER OF TIME.
"BUT THERE'S STILL SOMETHING MISSING, DINAH. SOMEONE. WE CAN *FIND* HER *TOGETHER.*
"TAKE MY HAND AND LET ME TELL YOU WHO YOU *REALLY* ARE..."

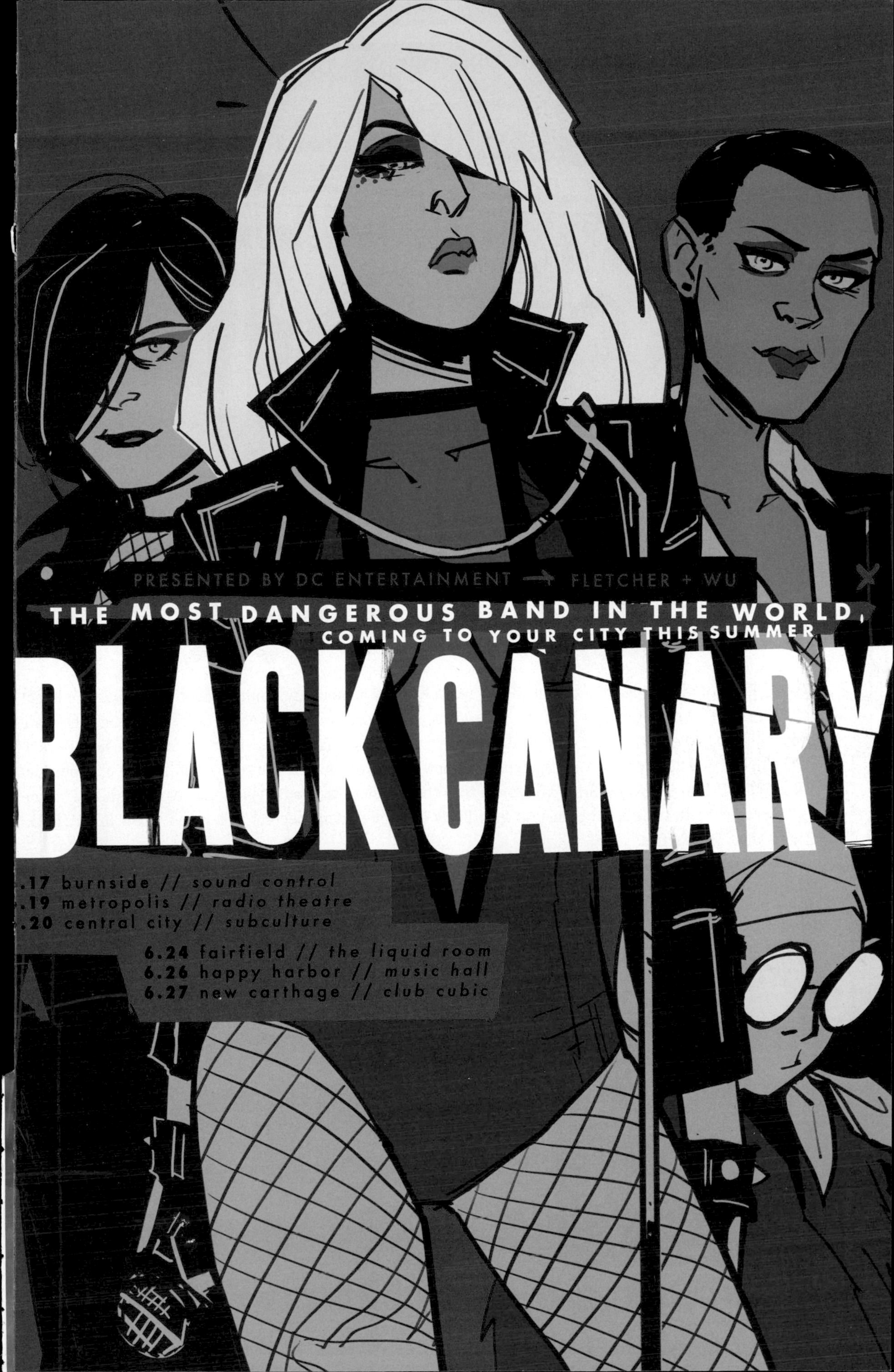
PRESENTED BY DC ENTERTAINMENT → FLETCHER + WU
THE MOST DANGEROUS BAND IN THE WORLD, COMING TO YOUR CITY THIS SUMMER
BLACK CANARY
.17 burnside // sound control
.19 metropolis // radio theatre
.20 central city // subculture
6.24 fairfield // the liquid room
6.26 happy harbor // music hall
6.27 new carthage // club cubic

BURNSIDE TOFU The zine for people with the right kind of taste

WHO IS BLACK CANARY?

BY TANTOO LA BICHE

presents a special PULL-OUT GUIDE!

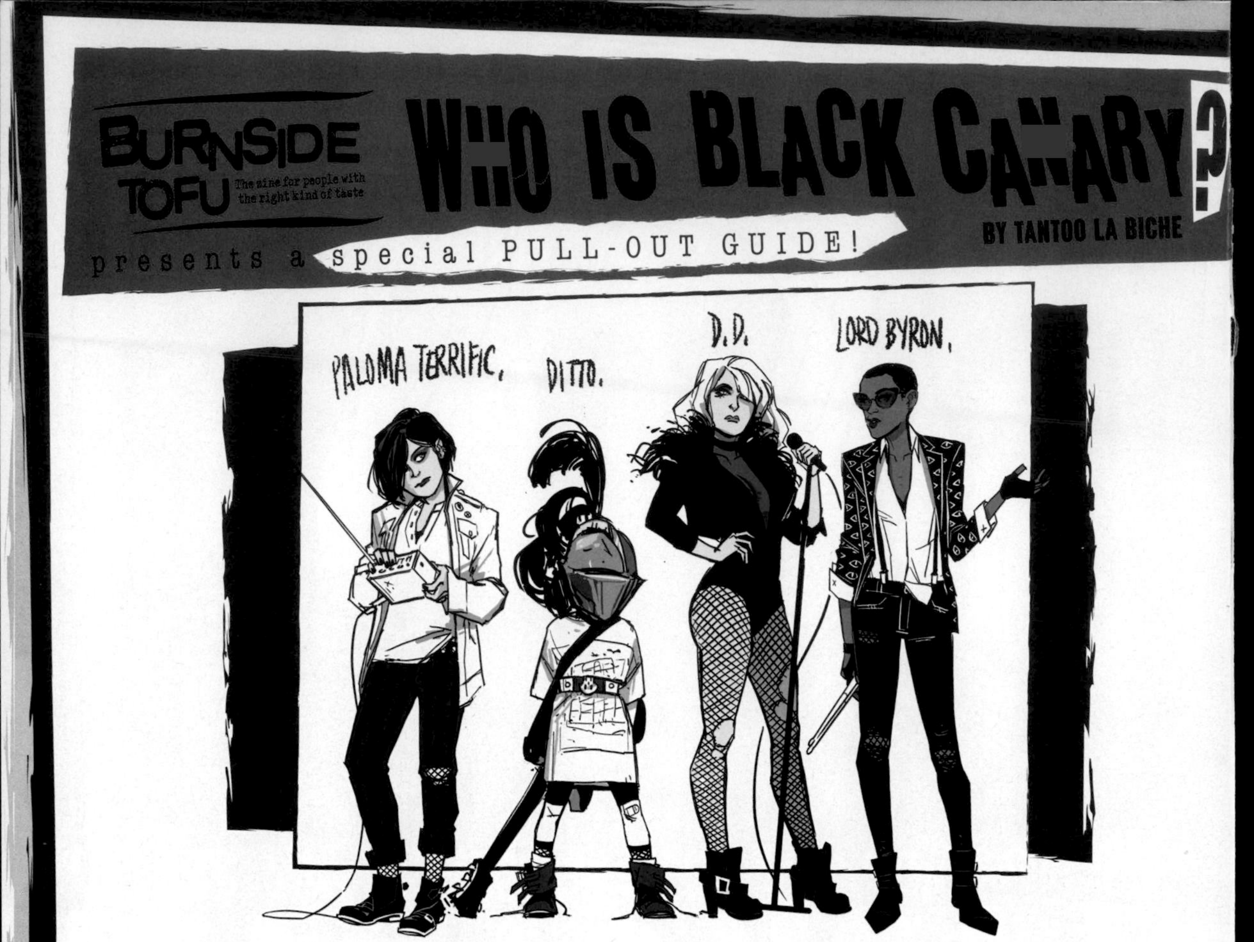

PALOMA TERRIFIC,
DITTO.
D.D.
LORD BYRON.

Who is Black Canary? Good question. If you're an average music fan, you probably know that the band is a four-piece out of Gotham City with a recently released, critically celebrated three-song EP. You probably also know that hitting one of their gigs is a potentially dangerous endeavor for those not trained in the art of self-defense. What you might not know, however—unless you're an avid reader of Burnside Tofu (WHICH YOU TOTALLY SHOULD BE)—is that there's more to the ladies in this band than meets the eye. Burnside Tofu stole a few moments with Black Canary during load-out at a recent show in Fairfield. Here's what we learned:

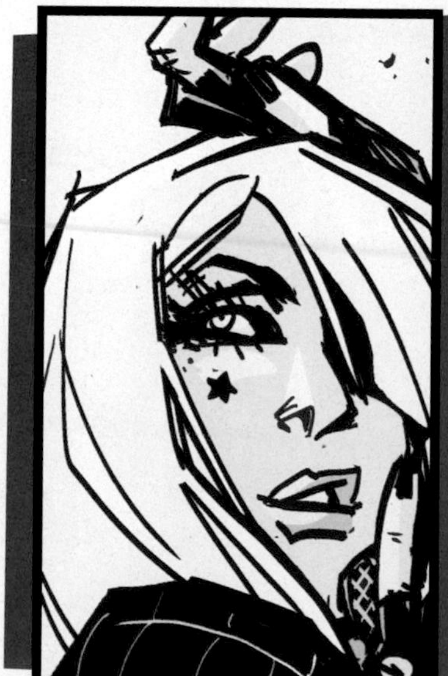

1. DON'T MESS WITH D.D.: Our reporter (ME!) was *maybe* waiting for the band outside the Liquid Room stage door, *maybe* hiding in a shadowy spot just around the corner from the dumpster by the bus. BIG MISTAKE! If you learn anything from this issue of Burnside Tofu let it be that you should never sneak up on D.D. even if it's in the interest of hard-hitting music journalism. You might end up on the painful end of a judo throw.

2. D.D. = "DINAH"???: The former Ashes on Sunday singer was forthcoming with a truly sincere apology for the judo throw, but not with information about her past. As she came to the assistance of this reporter, her bandmate Lord Byron asked "Dinah" if everything was OK. When questioned about her real name, D.D. offered a playful wink and returned to the load-out.

"I go through a pair a day. It accounts for a quarter of the band's budget." - D.D. on her fishnet tights

3. LORD BYRON IS THE BAND:

Byron was kind enough to talk to Burnside Tofu about the origin of the band and her part in it. It turns out that Lord Byron is the mastermind behind Black Canary, pioneering their sound, co-writing every song and even handling some of the lighter aspects of the business. This band has been her life's ambition, and though she seems pleased with how quickly and sharply their star has risen, it's clear that the controversy surrounding Canary is a cause of some concern.

"Bass is my one true love. But this drum kit is my piece on the side." - Lord Byron

4. DITTO IS HOW OLD?:

According to Black Canary tour manager Heathcliff Ray–who, I might add, seems suspiciously young himself–guitar magician "Ditto" is a full 19 years of age (with a gland condition) and legally allowed to play the stage of most, if not all, music venues. Burnside Tofu was born only a short while ago, Heathcliff, but was not born yesterday. Ditto looks no older than 12. BT has reached out to the band's management and label for confirmation.

"..." - Ditto, clearly too in awe of reporter Tantoo La Biche to answer a single question

5. PALOMA IS REALLY TERRIFIC:

The Tofu-mobile broke down outside the Liquid Room. As the Canary tour bus drove away from the venue, it pulled up alongside and offered assistance. Paloma Terrific popped the hood, worked her magic and the Tofu-mobile was right as rain. In fact, the car hasn't required a tune-up since! Super terrific, Paloma!

"Confession: All of my keyboard lines are cribbed from old Franz Waxman film scores. Okay, maybe not all of them." - Paloma Terrific

6. D.D. IS NOT THE ORIGINAL SINGER:

Byron and Paloma started the band in college with a theater student named Maeve. The trio was quickly signed to a record deal and began working on their debut album, even going so far as to shoot a music video for their first single. And then Maeve was bought out, dropped from the contract and replaced by D.D. It was at this point that the band gained the name Black Canary. What happened to Maeve? And why the name Black Canary?

DEBUT TOUR IS THE FINAL TOUR:

There are strong hints that Black Canary might be a one-EP, one-tour band. Say it isn't so! More to come...

BURNSIDE TOFU
The zine for people with the right kind of taste

BUILDING BLACK CANARY

BY TANTOO LA BICHE

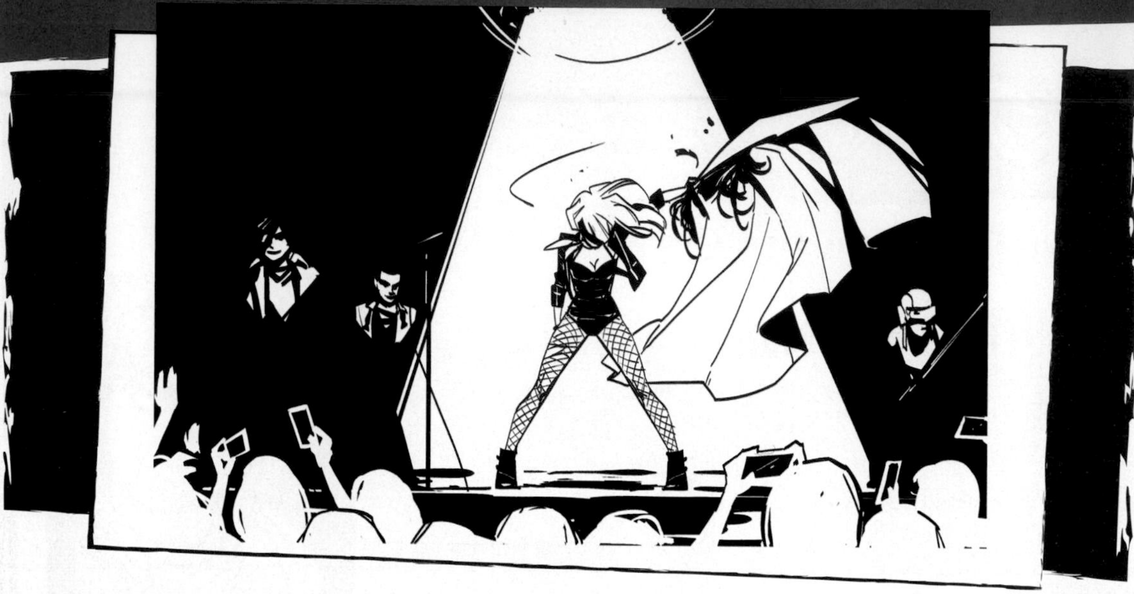

Most bands come together in an organic way. Friends join friends to make music, bond, have a good time. Not so with Black Canary. While the Gotham four-piece hit all the right notes with their debut EP, the shifty manner in which they became a band shows all the signs of being a manipulated third-party mash-up. Whose idea was it to throw them together? Where's the money coming from? Why this challenging, expensive tour? And just who are the people supporting Black Canary on the road?

Ace reporter Tantoo La Biche (YES, yours truly!) tracked down a representative of Canary label A&B Records who agreed to spill the beans (anonymously) about what they know of the band's formation.

The rep claims the order to disband the original group (with singer Bo Maeve) came from the top...as did the mandate to add D.D. to the lineup. With new guitarist Ditto in place, the label upped their financial commitment, putting their full weight behind breaking Black Canary big. That's where the tour came in.

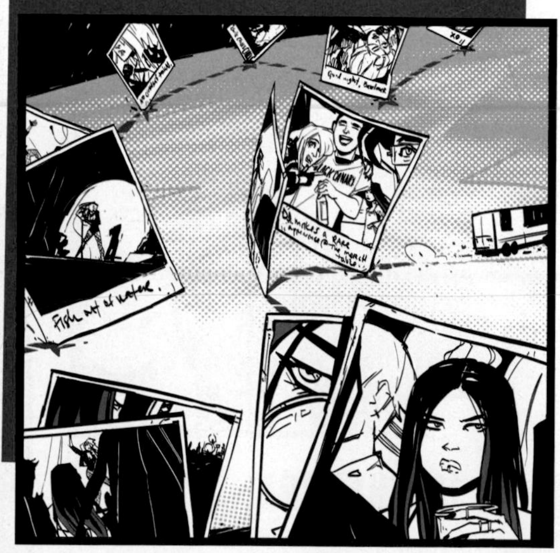
XO!!
BLACK CANARY
DD makes a RARE appearance @ the MERCH table.
Fish out of water.

DREAM TOUR?

A&B Records has apparently never financed a tour this large for a band as green as Black Canary. Just under 30 dates in 30 days is a grueling schedule for even the most seasoned touring acts, but to thrust this on a group as fresh as this was just begging for disaster. Burnside Tofu has tabulated the top three most costly performances of the tour so far:

1. **WIZARD'S WAND** - Detroit: $50,000+ (Caved-in roof, destroyed PA system speaker, damaged flooring, walls, structural supports, etc.)

2. **RADIO THEATRE** - Metropolis: $8,400 (Damaged bar beyond repair, overloaded PA system, giant hole in parking lot [how did they manage that?])

3. **SUBCULTURE** - Central City: $3,800 (Stage floorboards demolished, lighting grid bent, general human suffering)

DREAM (TOUR) MANAGER

The job of keeping the band organized while on the road falls to the tour manager. Black Canary seems lucky that young Heathcliff Ray has agreed to stick it out with them in this capacity, given all he's had to go through to keep them on schedule (and alive) these past few weeks.

"I wasn't expecting the job to be so...action-packed," Ray admitted when we caught him selling shirts at the band's merch table before a recent show. Burnside Tofu wasn't able to find a record of employment for Ray before his job for Canary's management company. His last known position was at Gotham Academy...as a student.

DREAM MACHINE

Florence "Flo" Mandelbaum drives Black Canary from city to city, from gig to gig, in a 2003 MAGISTRATE EX2 ENTERTAINER BUS provided by the label (virtually unheard of for a breaking band like this!). This thing is wild, sleeping six comfortably with front and rear lounges for hangouts and jams. Flo handles the machine with precision and care, but confirms to Burnside Tofu that she was actually hired as the band's traveling sound professional, not their chauffeur. When questioned about a possibly compromising lack of sleep between mixing the band's live shows and driving them around, Flo clutched her large coffee and stared off into the distance.

D.D. REVEALED

Burnside Tofu believes we have uncovered some shocking and definitive answers about Canary's lead singer, "D.D."

Our contact at A&B slipped us heavily redacted documents from the U.S. military showing proof of marriage between a person by the name of Dinah Drake and one Kurt Lance. All other details are illegible, though there's a hint that seems to refer to both being members of something called "Team 7."

It's all starting to come together. If these documents are relevant and true, Black Canary's "D.D." is really ex-military operative Dinah Drake. The fact that she's been hiding her identity from fans and the press—and the redacted nature of the marriage docs—suggest her time in the military was most likely spent in a highly skilled, top-secret group. Has she been keeping secrets to ensure the safety of others—possibly her old teammates—or is she in hiding from the government? And what's her current marital status? Is Dinah still married to Kurt Lance? If so, where is he?

Burnside Tofu won't rest until these burning questions are answered!

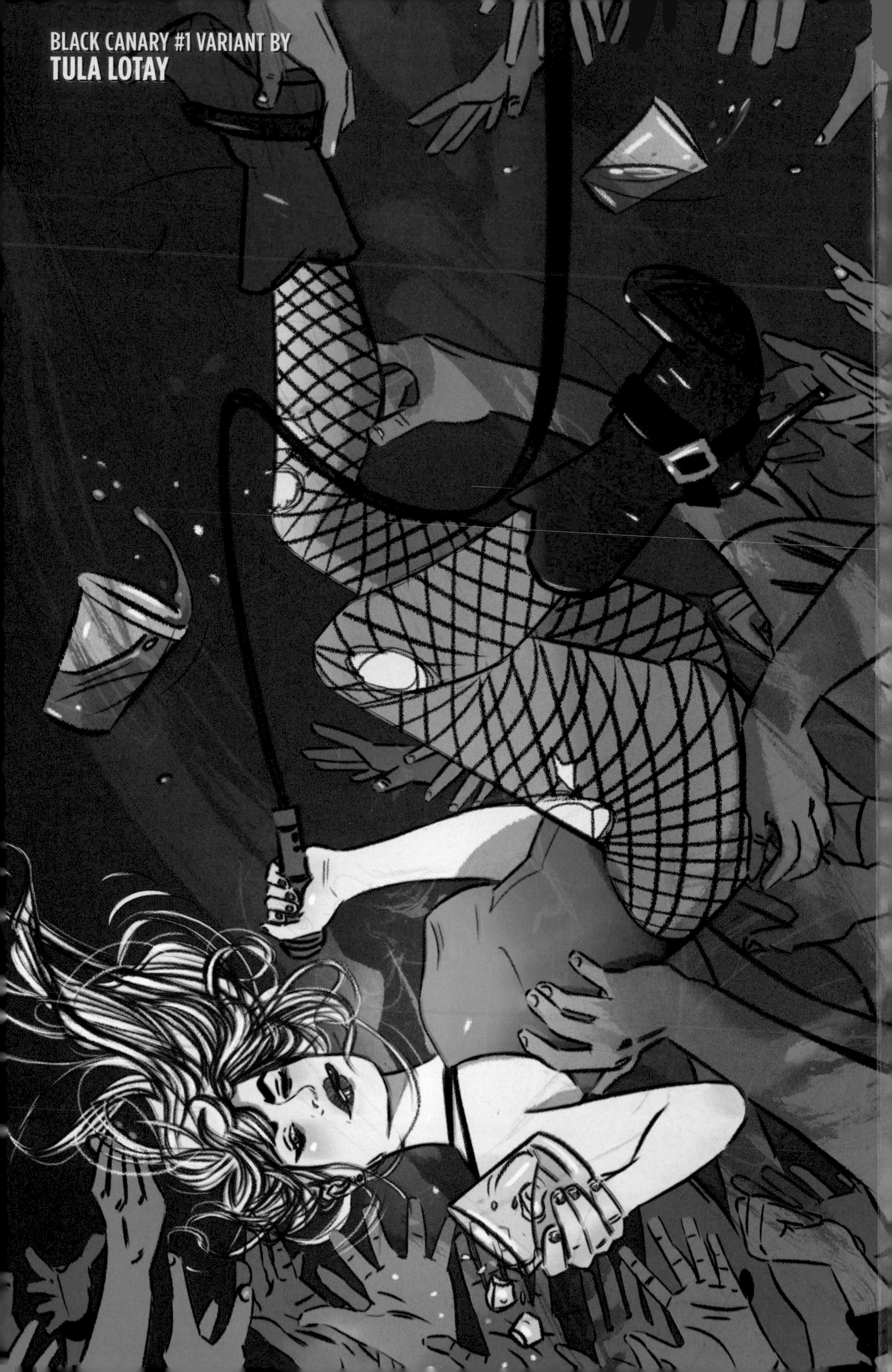

BLACK CANARY #1 VARIANT BY
TULA LOTAY

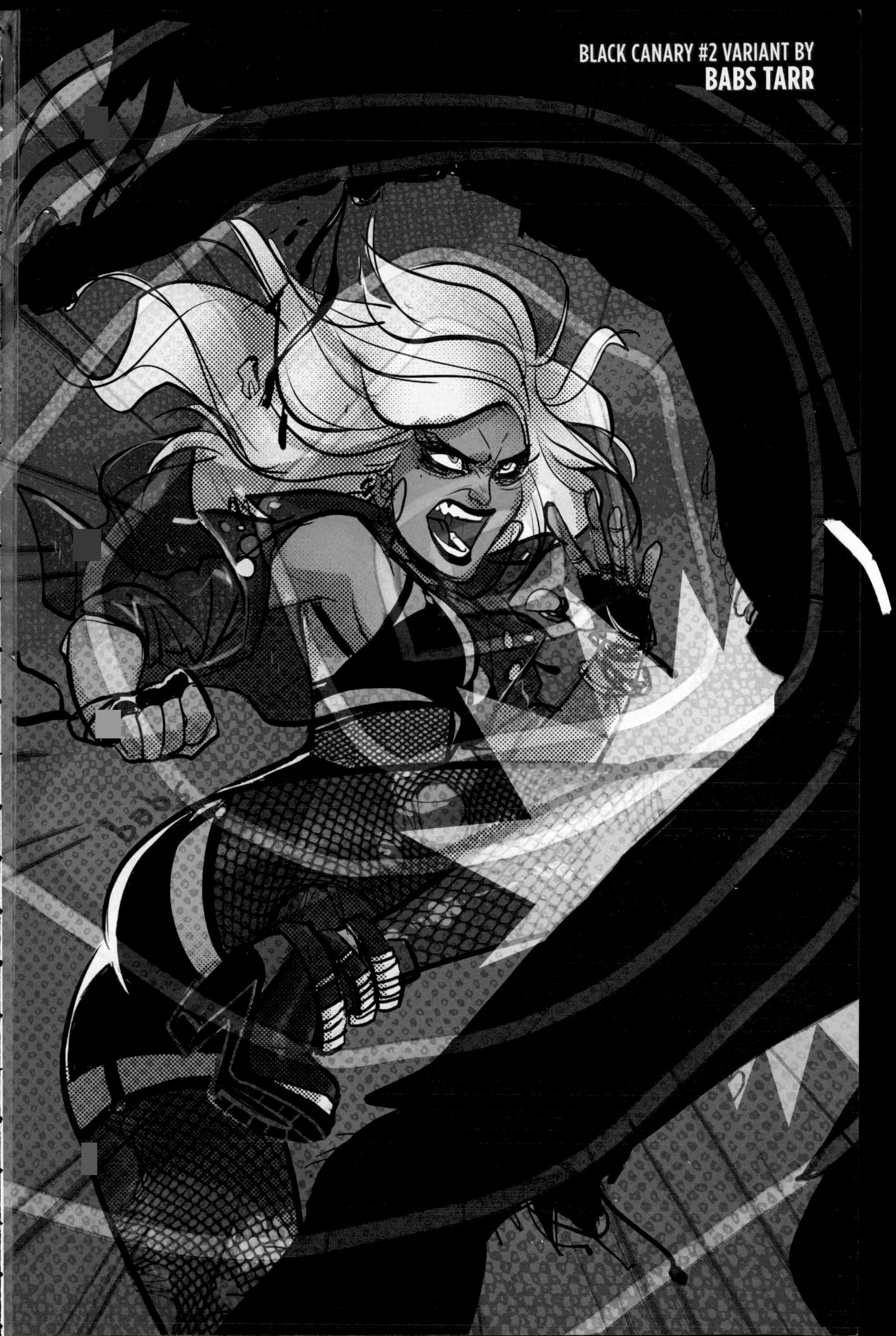

BLACK CANARY #2 VARIANT BY
BABS TARR

BLACK CANARY #3 VARIANT BY
DAVE BULLOCK

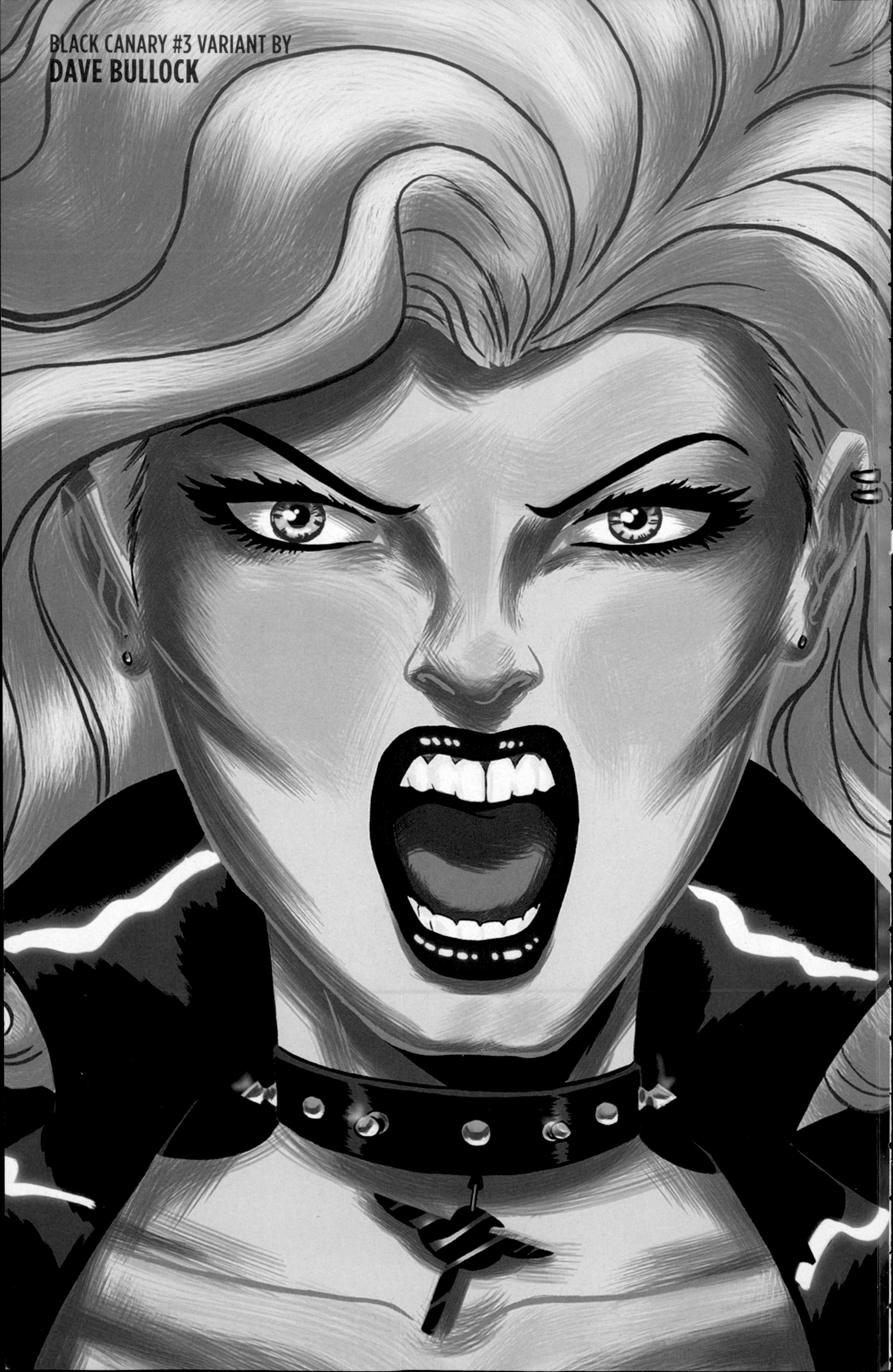

BLACK CANARY #4 GREEN LANTERN
75TH ANNIVERSARY VARIANT BY
EVAN "DOC" SHANER

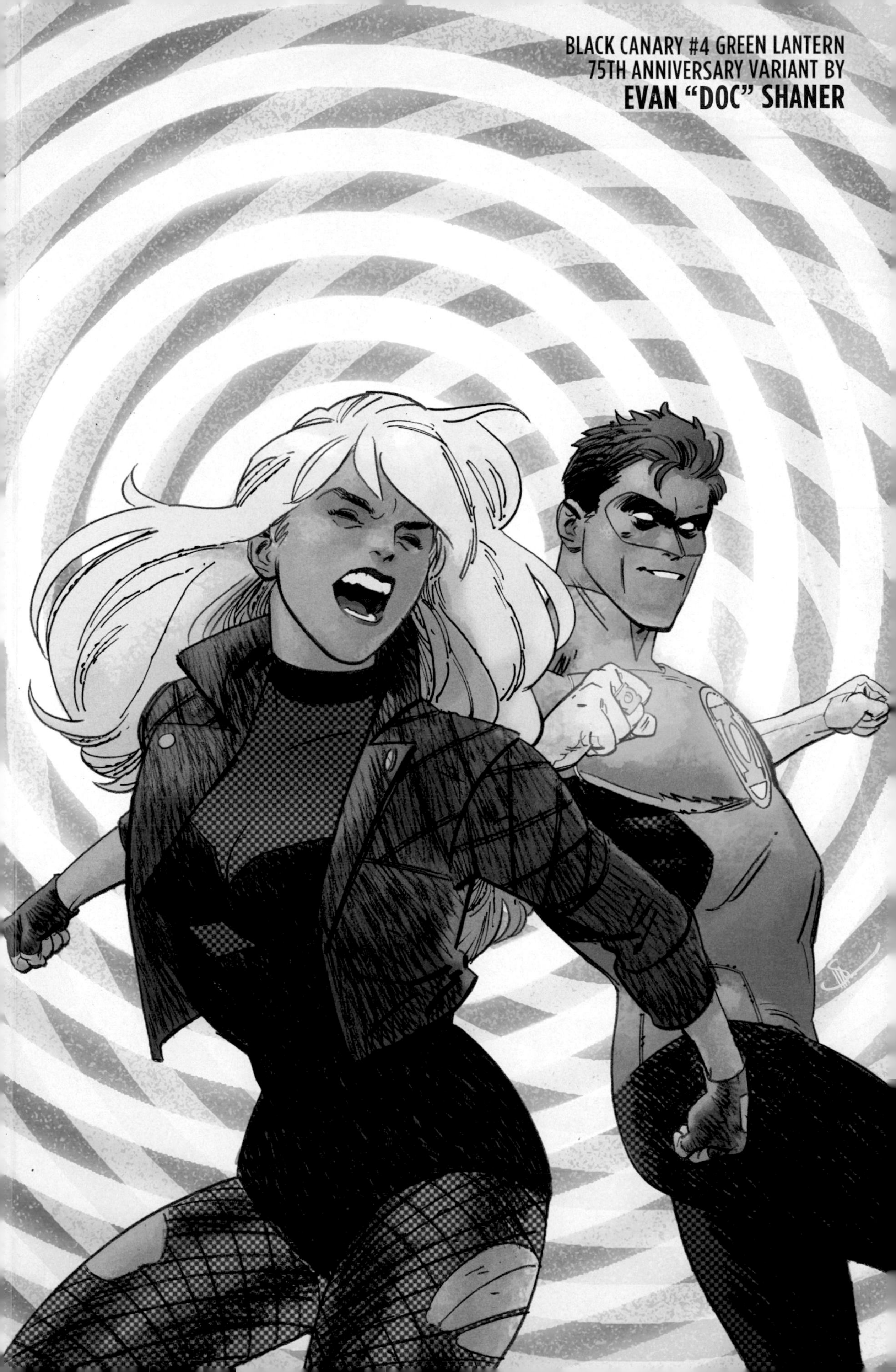

BLACK CANARY #5 MONSTER VARIANT BY
MIKE & LAURA ALLRED

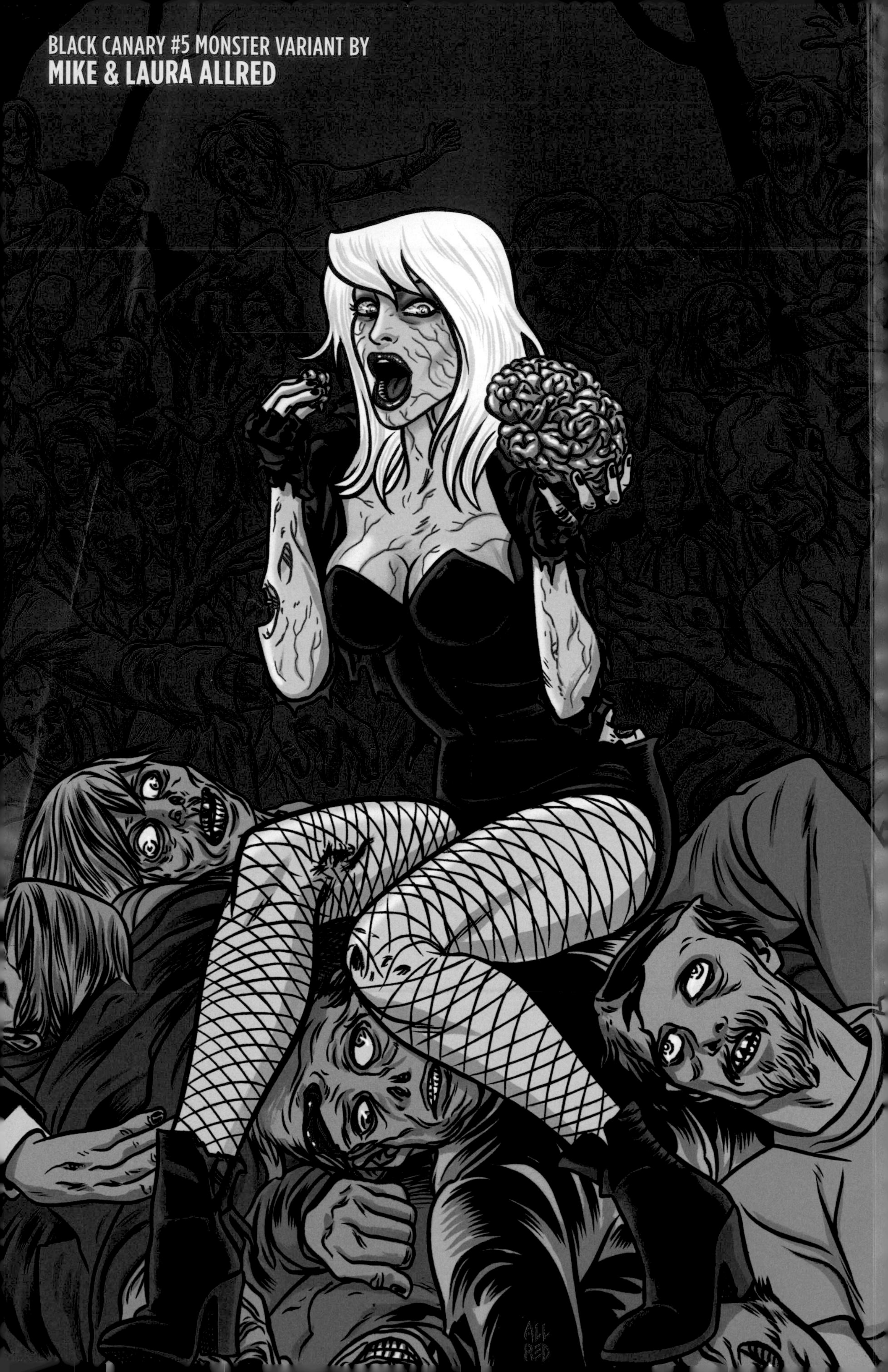

BLACK CANARY #6 *LOONEY TUNES* VARIANT BY
PIA GUERRA & SPIKE BRANDT

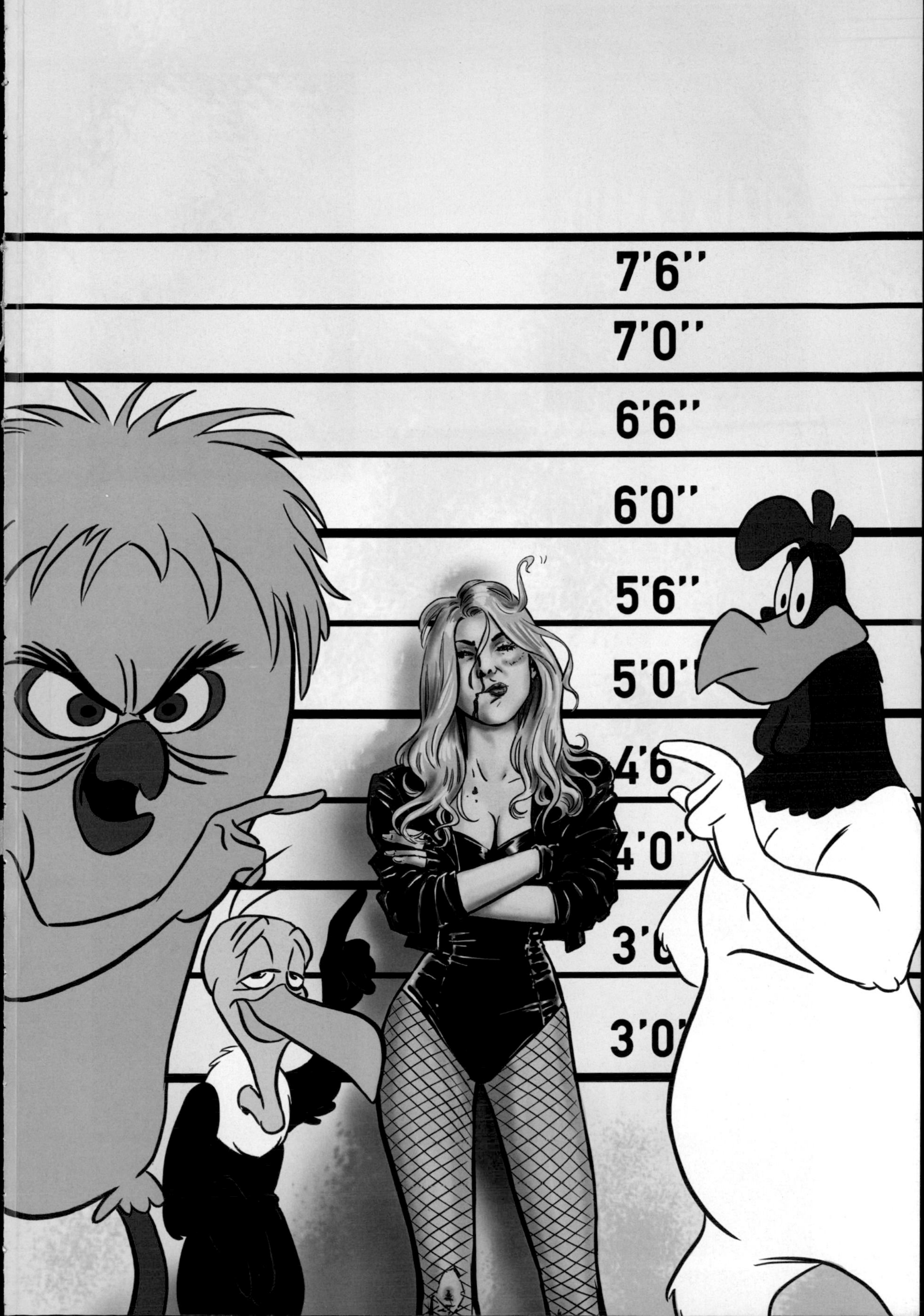
7'6"
7'0"
6'6"
6'0"
5'6"

BLACK CANARY SKETCHBOOK
ART BY **ANNIE WU**

BLACK CANARY
FLETCHER WU

BLACK
CANARY

Black
Canary.
1

BLACK
CANARY

BLACK
CANARY
FLETCHER WU

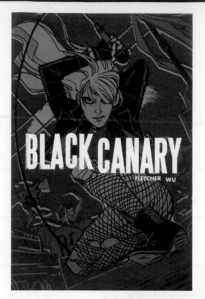

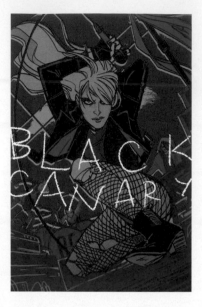

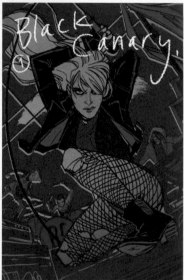

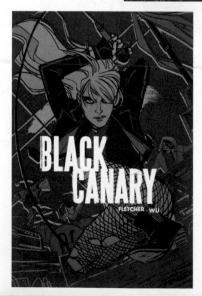

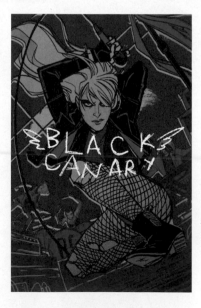

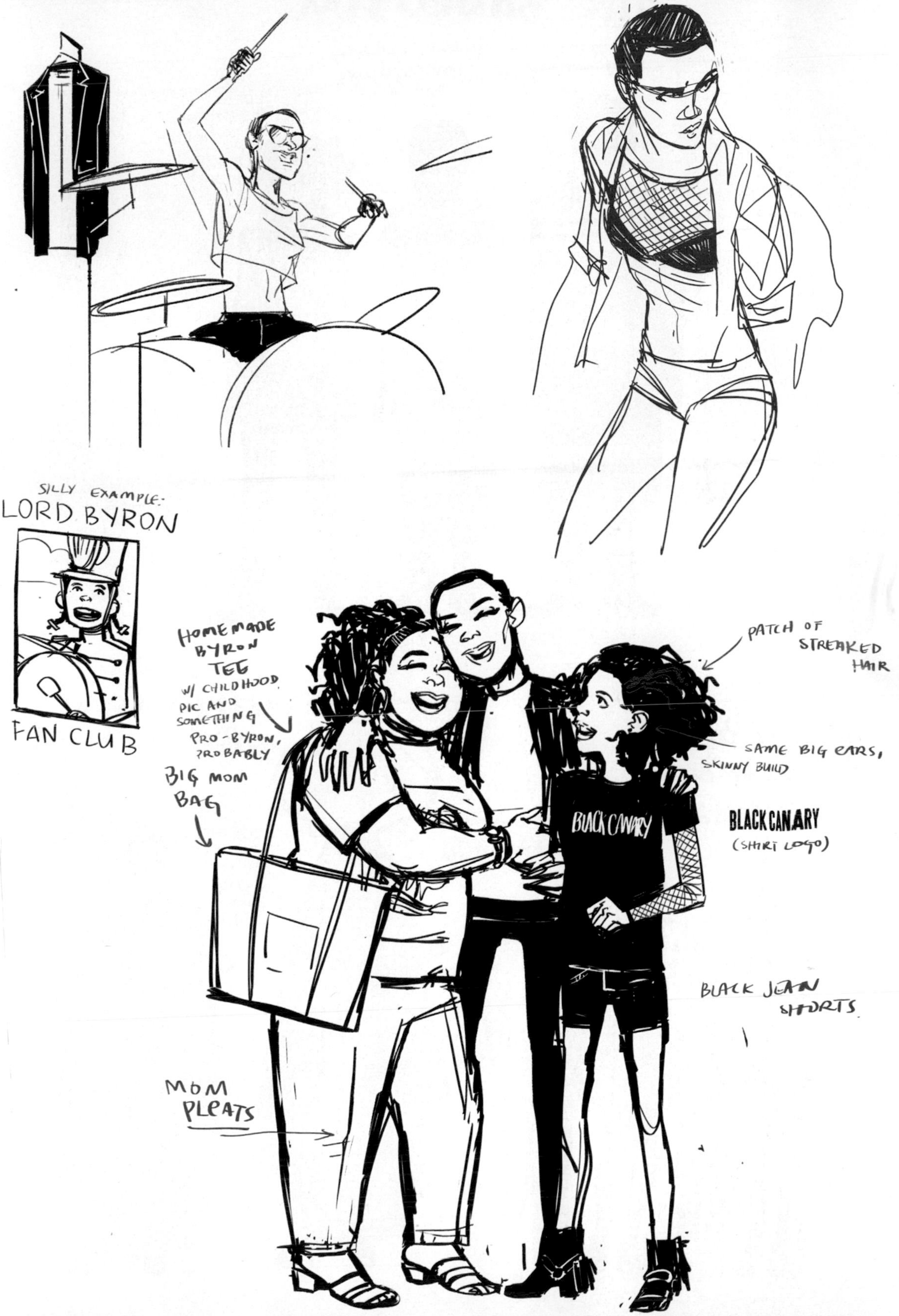
SILLY EXAMPLE:
LORD BYRON
FAN CLUB
HOMEMADE BYRON TEE w/ CHILDHOOD PIC AND SOMETHING PRO-BYRON, PROBABLY
BIG MOM BAG
MOM PLEATS
PATCH OF STREAKED HAIR
SAME BIG EARS, SKINNY BUILD
BLACK CANARY
BLACKCANARY
(SHIRT LOGO)
BLACK JEAN SHORTS

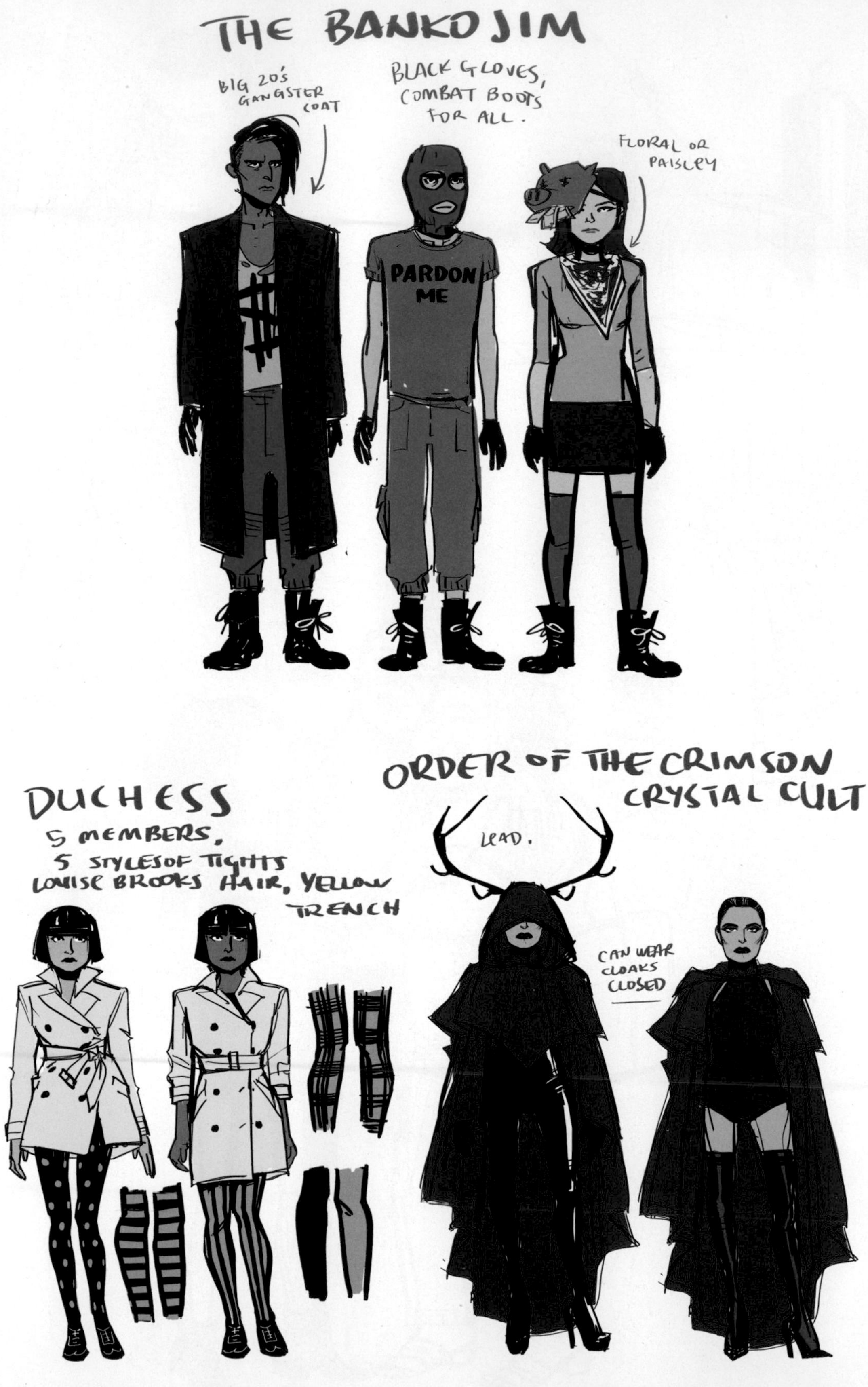

THE BANKOJIM
BIG 20's GANGSTER COAT
BLACK GLOVES, COMBAT BOOTS FOR ALL.
FLORAL OR PAISLEY
PARDON ME
DUCHESS
5 MEMBERS, 5 STYLES OF TIGHTS
LOUISE BROOKS HAIR, YELLOW TRENCH
ORDER OF THE CRIMSON CRYSTAL CULT
LEAD.
CAN WEAR CLOAKS CLOSED

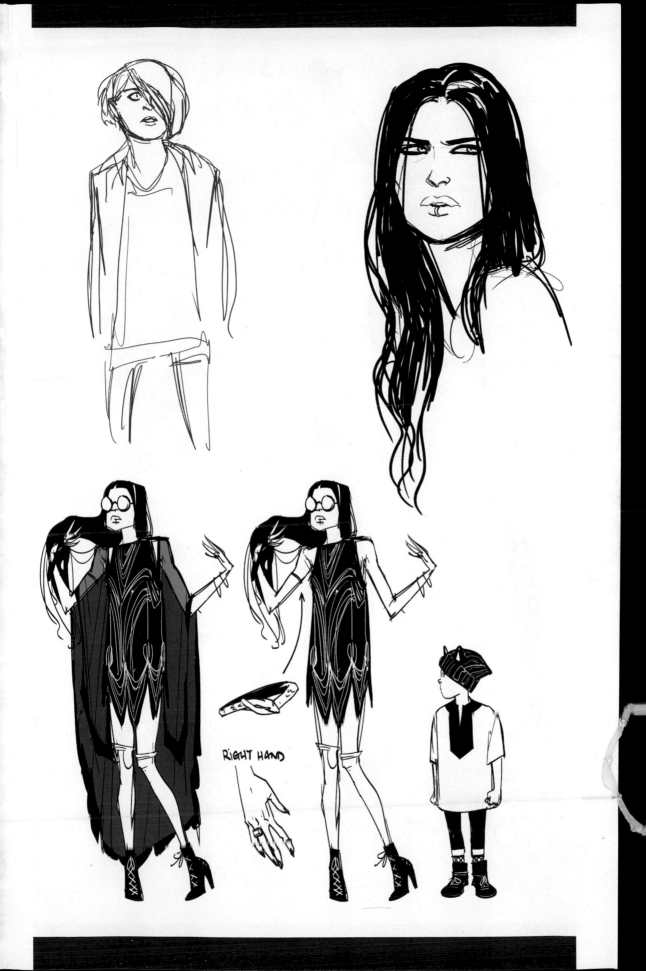

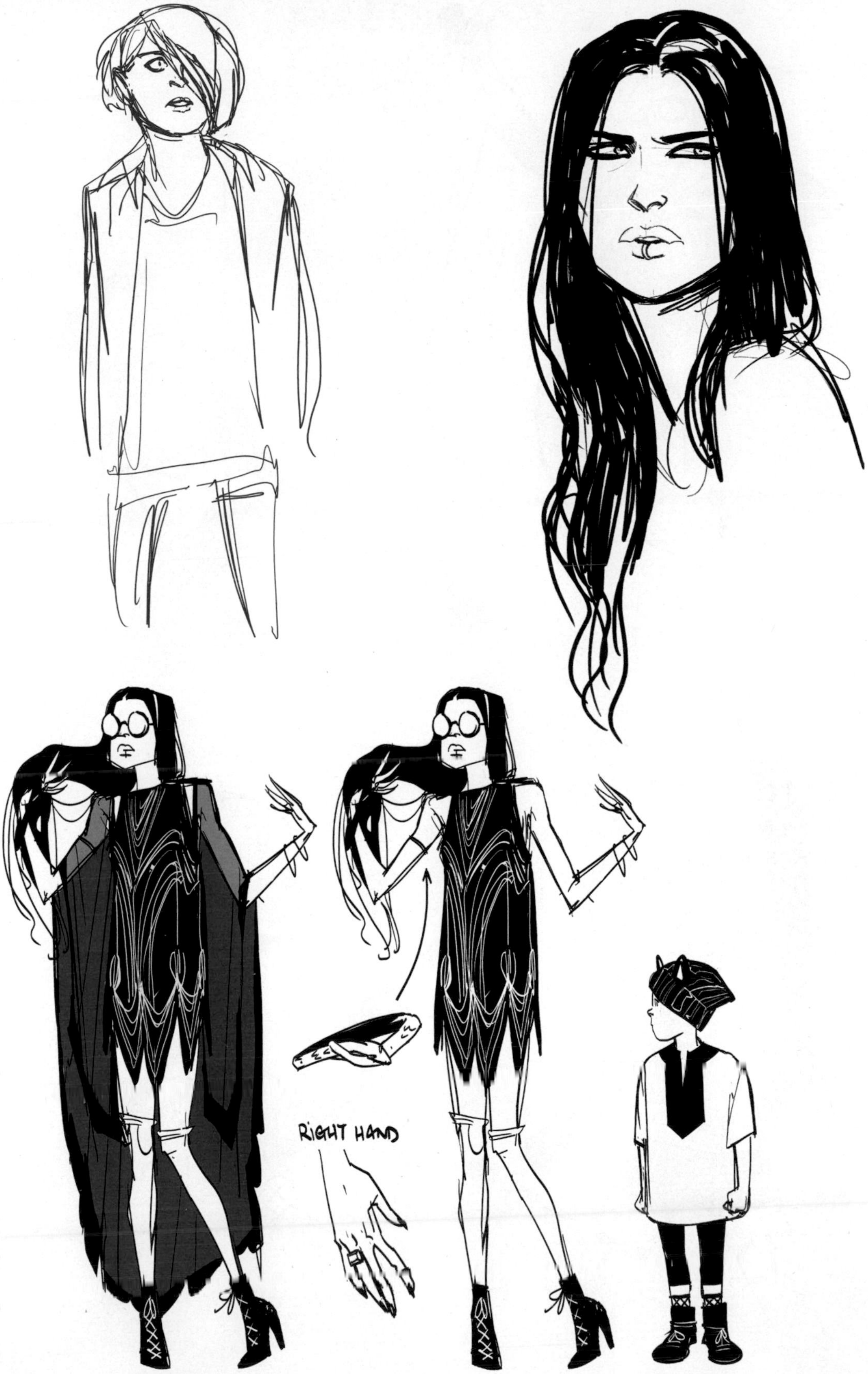
RIGHT HAND

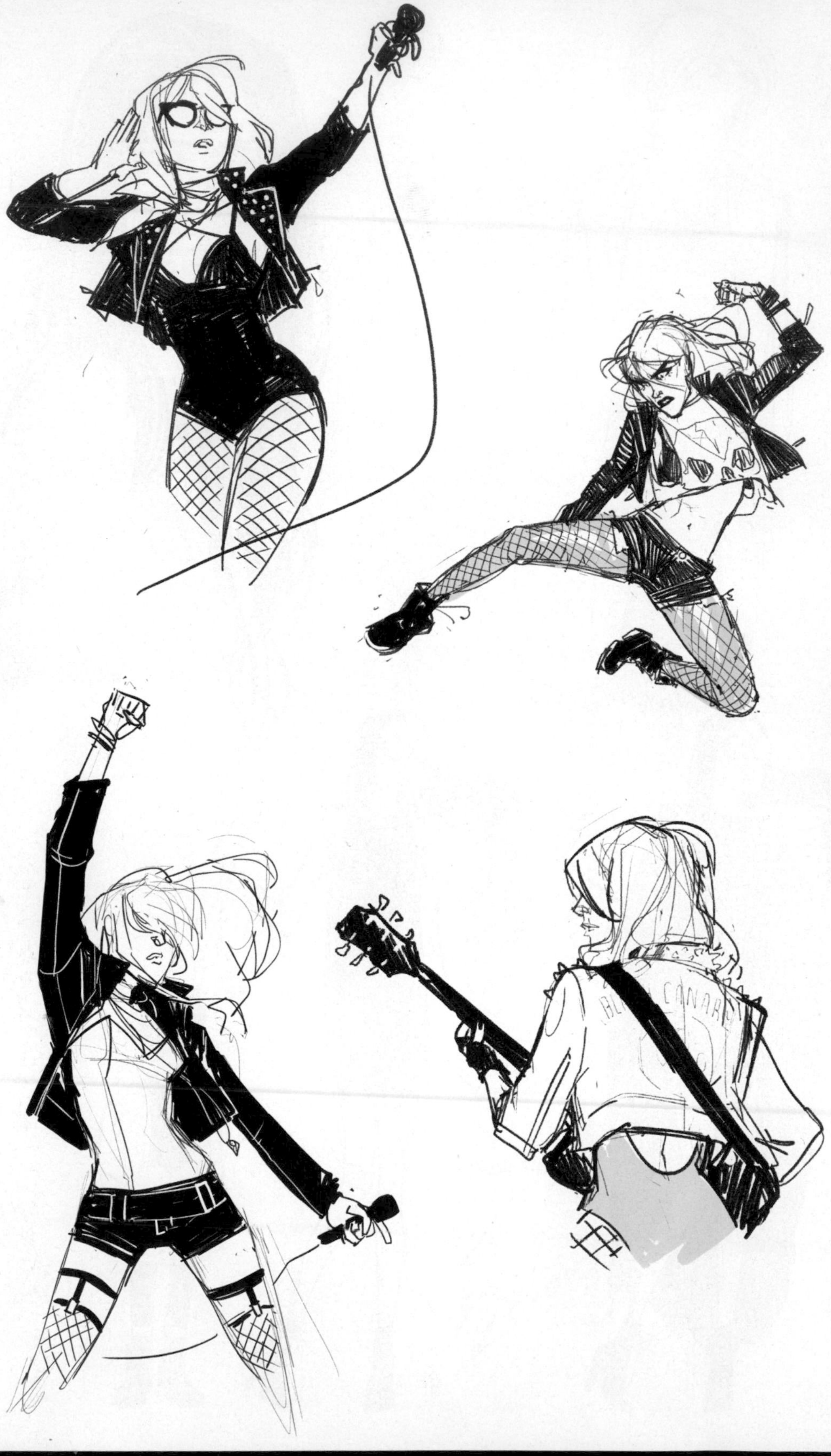

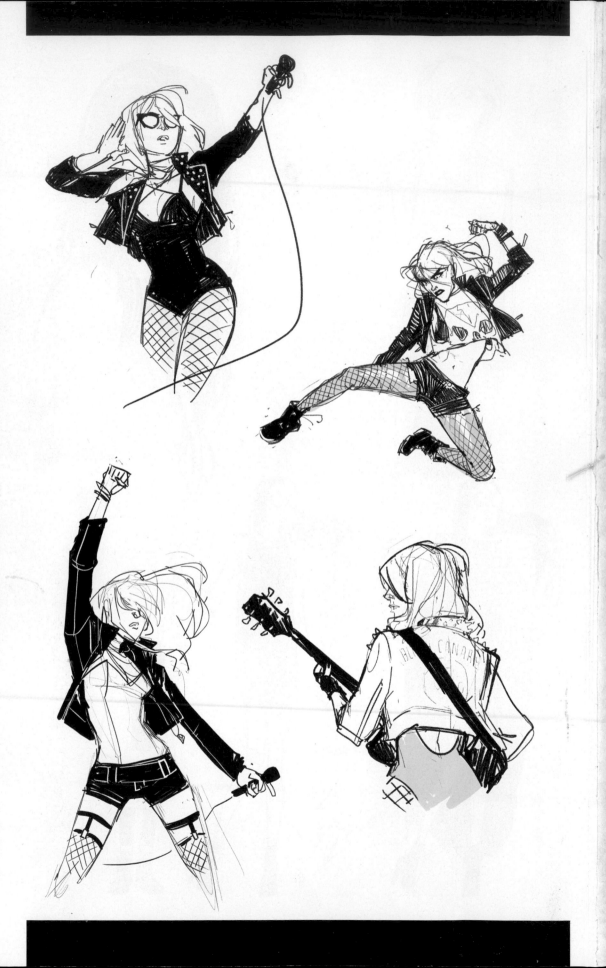